P9-ARD-088

Black Prophets of Justice

Black Prophets of Justice

ACTIVIST CLERGY BEFORE THE CIVIL WAR

David E. Swift

LOUISIANA STATE UNIVERSITY PRESS
Baton Rouge and London

Manufactured in the United States of America
First printing

98 97 96 95 94 93 92 91 90 89 5 4 3 2 1

Designer: Laura Roubique Gleason
Typeface: Bembo
Typesetter: G&S Typesetters, Inc.

Library of Congress Cataloging-in-Publication Data

Swift, David Everett, 1914–
Black prophets of justice : activist clergy before the Civil War / David E. Swift.
p. cm.
Bibliography: p.
Includes index.
ISBN 0-8071-1461-8 (alk. paper)
1. Afro-American clergy—Biography. 2. Afro-American clergy—Political activity. 3. Afro-American Presbyterians—Biography. 4. Afro-American Congregationalists—Biography. 5. Race relations—Religious aspects—Christianity. 6. United States—Race relations.
I. Title.
BR563.N4S97 1989
285'.108996073—dc 19
[B] 88-30327
CIP

The Amos G. Beman Papers are quoted courtesy of the Collection of American Literature, Beinecke Rare Book and Manuscript Library, Yale University. Quotations from the correspondence of Henry H. Garnet to Alexander Crummell, dated May 13, 1837, appear courtesy of the Schomburg Center for Research in Black Culture, the New York Public Library, Astor, Lenox, and Tilden Foundations.

The paper in this book meets the guidelines for permanence and durability of the Committee on Production Guidelines for Book Longevity of the Council on Library Resources. ♾

In memory of Jane Nichols Swift (1917–1987)

Let justice roll down like waters
and righteousness like an ever flowing stream.

—Amos 5:24

CONTENTS

ILLUSTRATIONS

ACKNOWLEDGMENTS

In the completion of this work I have incurred debts to many people. My thanks go to the staff in many libraries and the curators of many manuscript collections who have responded to my needs. I am grateful in particular to Betty Gubert at the New York Public Library's Schomburg Center for Research in Black Culture and to Esme Bhan at the Moorland-Spingarn Research Center at Howard University. I have been assisted again and again by the Presbyterian Historical Association in Philadelphia. Special thanks go to Gerald W. Gillette, manager of research and library services, and to Mary Plummer for making the Association's resources available to me. The staff members of the Olin Library at Wesleyan University have been warmly helpful over the years. I think particularly of Joan Jurale, Edwin Allen, Steven Lebergott, Edmund Rubacha, and Elizabeth Swaim.

It has been a special privilege to talk with Charlotte Mebane and Henriette Edmonds, great-granddaughter and great-great-granddaughter, respectively, of Henry Highland Garnet, one of the major figures in this book. (My thanks to Joel Schor for having told me of them.) I much appreciate Mrs. Mebane's formal permission to use numerous quotations from Garnet's unpublished writings in this work.

James H. Nichols read certain sections of this work dealing with American Presbyterianism at large. I am grateful for his suggestions.

I thank James H. Smylie, who, as editor of the *Journal of Presbyterian History,* encouraged me in the writing of several articles for publication in that periodical. One long article dealt with Samuel Cornish and Theodore Wright, two of the protagonists in this work. And I am grateful to Nancy Smith, editor of the *Wesleyan,* for help in preparing for that magazine a short article on Charles Ray, another of the chief characters in this book.

I am indebted to several members of the Northeastern Seminar on Black Religion: to Randall Burkett for reading an earlier version of this work and giving me useful reminders and cautions, to Richard Newman for painstaking editorial suggestions, and to David Wills for a close reading of the introductory chapters and helpful suggestions thereon.

David White shared with me his original monograph on James W. C. Pennington, a shortened version of which appeared in the *Connecticut Historical Bulletin.* Before I had completed my writing, R. J. M. Blackett generously allowed me to see his excellent chapter on Pennington that was soon to appear in his book *Beating Against the Barriers: Biographical Essays in Nineteenth-Century Afro-American History.* Blackett also read and commented helpfully on an earlier version of this book.

My primary indebtedness is to colleagues on the Wesleyan University faculty. Robert O'Meally invited me to give a lecture on my work at the Center for Afro-American Studies. Janice Willis and I together taught a course on black and white religion in America, and I learned much from her. Eugene Klaaren's fascination with theology and his willingness to respond to my queries have been especially valuable. I thank him also for his careful reading of the introductory and concluding parts of this work at an earlier stage. Franklin Reeve read the whole of the manuscript, found cause for enthusiasm, and offered enticing suggestions for amplifying the discussion. Clarence Walker's concise and vigorous reactions to the work caused me to think more carefully about some basic questions. My most extended and thought-provoking exchanges were with Jerome Long and Edgar Beckham. I am grateful to the latter for sharing his understanding of Pennington after an intensive reading of his autobiography, sermons, and speeches. Jerome Long gave me solid help in setting my story more firmly in the context of wider Afro-American experience. As usual in my discussions with him, his comments on that subject turned my thoughts in fresh directions.

Finally, I owe a special debt to Gayraud Wilmore, for his published work, for personal exchanges over the years, for the encouragement I have been given by his support of this project, and for the challenge of his critical comments upon reading the near-final typescript.

In the final analysis, however, I claim responsibility for all failure to use cogent suggestions fully, as well as for all errors of fact and deficiencies in interpretation.

Without the help of typists I would have been lost. Alice Pomper labored long on the first version. I remember her accuracy, her fortitude in dealing with revisions, and her buoyant good humor withal. Anna Barron went at the final revision with heartening zest. Lauren Cowdrey and Debbie Sierpinski helped out. And Margaret Briggs wrapped up the project with skillful expedition.

In the final preparation of the manuscript I incurred a heavy debt to editor Mary Berry for her crusade for clarity and complete citations, and to John Easterly for his calm and able editorial supervision.

What I owe to Trudy Marth, administrative assistant in Wesleyan's Department of Religion, is beyond telling. Her professional skills and encouragement have made all the difference.

Last and most important is what I have been given by Jane Nichols Swift. The economy and vividness in her use of words were a recurrent joy. Her stylistic suggestions were always on target. And I was immeasurably supported by her long-standing concern with the issues at stake in this book.

Black Prophets of Justice

I. THE CAST OF CHARACTERS

The Afro-American freedom movement of the latter nineteenth and the twentieth centuries has been rooted in the religious life and efforts toward liberation of slaves and free blacks before the Civil War. Albert Raboteau's *Slave Religion: The "Invisible Institution" in the Antebellum South* and Gayraud Wilmore's *Black Religion and Black Radicalism: An Interpretation of the Religious History of Afro-American People* have provided excellent overviews of the interweaving of religion and resistance among Afro-Americans during those antebellum years. The following pages are an intensive examination of a small, but crucially important, part of that pre–Civil War story. The protagonists are six ministers of independent black Presbyterian and Congregational churches: Samuel Cornish, Theodore Wright, Charles Ray, Henry Highland Garnet, Amos Beman, and James W. C. Pennington.[1]

There were two distinct phases in the founding of independent Afro-American churches. The first lasted from the latter decades of the eighteenth century into the second decade of the nineteenth. Earliest to be formed were African Baptist churches in Georgia, South Carolina, and Virginia. Most of the members of these churches were slaves. In the 1790s African Methodist and African Episcopal churches were founded. Richard Allen and Absalom Jones led a walkout of black worshipers from the

1. Albert P. Raboteau, *Slave Religion: The "Invisible Institution" in the Antebellum South* (New York, 1978); Gayraud S. Wilmore, *Black Religion and Black Radicalism: An Interpretation of the Religious History of Afro-American People* (2d ed.; Maryknoll, N.Y., 1983).

largely white Saint George's Methodist Episcopal Church in Philadelphia. Allen became the founding minister of the Bethel African Methodist Episcopal Church and Jones, the first pastor of Saint Thomas' African Episcopal Church. In New York City another black separatist movement led to the founding of the (African Methodist Episcopal) Zion Church under the leadership of James Varick. During the early years of the nineteenth century, Thomas Paul took the lead in forming the Joy Street Baptist Church in Boston and, a few years later, the Abyssinian Baptist Church in New York City. Primary factors in the birth of these independent northern black churches were the vision of founders such as Allen, the increase in the number of Afro-Americans attending white Methodist and Baptist churches in northern cities, and whites' efforts to "keep them in their place" by segregated seating and other restrictions.

The second phase in the development of independent Afro-American churches began in the second decade of the nineteenth century. By 1816 there were enough African Methodist Episcopal (AME) churches to form a denomination. In 1822 AME Zion (AMEZ) churches followed suit. African Baptists, heirs of a strong white denominational tradition of decentralization, did not organize regional associations of black Baptist churches until the 1830s. In 1840 the black American Baptist Missionary Convention, aiming to be a national body, was formed. By 1858 its leaders insisted that all churches in the convention cut their ties with white Baptist associations.[2]

The founding of the first independent black Presbyterian and Congregational churches was roughly contemporary with the formation of African Methodist denominations. The first African Presbyterian church in Philadelphia was gathered in 1807 and in New York City, in 1822. Soon thereafter black Congregational churches were organized in New Haven and Hartford. By 1860 there would be between twenty and thirty black Presbyterian and Congregational ministers. They remained, at least formally, members of primarily white presbyteries and Congregational associations. Six of these pastors stand out as unique in their time for the degree and consistency of their social activism and for the new Afro-American institutions they took the lead in forming.

Samuel Cornish was born free in Delaware and was tutored for the ministry by members of the Philadelphia Presbytery. As missionary to poor blacks in New York City, he drew together the initial members of

2. James M. Washington, *Frustrated Fellowship: The Black Quest for Social Power* (Macon, Ga., 1986), 24–41.

the First Colored Presbyterian Church, later to develop into one of the strongest black organizations of the country. He was the founding editor in 1827 of the first black newspaper, *Freedom's Journal,* and a decade later launched the *Colored American,* the most substantial and longest-lived black journal prior to Frederick Douglass's papers in the late 1840s and the 1850s.

Cornish's successor at the First Colored Presbyterian Church was Theodore Wright, the first Afro-American graduate of a theological seminary (Princeton). During a nineteen-year pastorate, Wright saw a small and struggling institution become a large and influential middle- and upper-class black church. This congregation and its minister were heavily involved in the educational, reform, and protest efforts of New York City's black community.

New England–raised Charles Ray made Cornish's second newspaper, the *Colored American,* into the voice of a significant segment of black people throughout the North. By extensive visitation in local communities, Ray won a widespread body of supporters, not only for the paper but also for the civil rights petition campaigns it promoted during the five years of its publication. Ray's subsequent twenty years of Congregational ministry were devoted to low-income black people in lower Manhattan.

Henry Highland Garnet was born into slavery in Maryland. He escaped with his family when he was almost nine years old. By 1840 he had secured a college degree from Oneida Institute and was Ray's flamboyant colleague in New York State political activism. More than a few blacks and whites viewed him as a dangerous influence, for he defended American slaves' right, if not mission, to violent revolt. After pastorates in Troy and Geneva, New York, and after five years in Great Britain and Jamaica, he became for many years the forceful and controversial pastor of the Presbyterian church in New York City founded by Cornish and consolidated by Wright.

Amos Beman played a role in both the city of New Haven and the entire state of Connecticut similar to Wright's and Ray's in New York State. During his long pastorate at the Temple Street African Congregational Church, Beman became, for many of New Haven's black and white people, the very model of black intelligence, zeal for education, and discipline in the Christian life. He frequently took the risks of harboring fugitive slaves, and he spearheaded Connecticut blacks' efforts to recover the franchise, lost several decades earlier.

Like Garnet, James W. C. Pennington had escaped from slavery, but not until the age of twenty. Helped by the tutoring of interested whites, he made remarkable progress in self-education. At the age of thirty-three, he was endorsed by Hartford's white Congregational clergy for the pastorate of that city's Fifth (African) Congregational Church. His autobiography and several of his sermons were published. Pennington and Garnet both traveled to the British Isles and won acclaim as antislavery lecturers. Pennington was called to the ministry of the First Colored Presbyterian Church in New York City after Wright's death and before Garnet's pastorate.

For all their high visibility and the distinctiveness of their achievements, black Presbyterian and Congregational activist clergy actually built upon the previous decades of expanding African Baptist and Methodist church life. As Wilmore has put it, "The real independence movement among black churches—which adopted the name 'African' to signify its pride of ancestral heritage and solidarity—grew out of the mass appeal that the Baptists and Methodists had in both the free and the slave communities. These churches made the first radical thrust for self-determination."[3]

Samuel Cornish's early life was an example of black Presbyterian pioneering that moved on from the African Baptists' and Methodists' radical thrust. Cornish had been born in Delaware only a few years after Richard Allen founded the Bethel African Methodist Episcopal Church in Philadelphia. Both of Cornish's brothers became pastors in the AME denomination. It was in Allen's church that the first mass meeting of blacks was held in 1817 to protest the founding and promotion of the American Colonization Society (ACS). These black people viewed the ACS as a mammoth plot to send free Afro-Americans back to Africa. Cornish, in Philadelphia at the time studying for the Presbyterian ministry, may well have attended the meeting. At any rate, when he started editing *Freedom's Journal* a decade later, he vigorously espoused the position expressed at that meeting in Allen's AME church.

There were many other intersecting and parallel currents linking the pastoral, educational, and protest efforts of black Presbyterian and Congregational clergy on the one hand and those of AME Zion, AME, and African Baptist clergy on the other. Rev. Morris Brown, later to become an AME bishop, had helped train the leaders in the Charleston, South Carolina, AME church who became active participants in the 1822 Denmark Vesey slave conspiracy. AME Zion pastor Jehiel Beman was the fa-

3. Wilmore, *Black Religion and Black Radicalism*, 91.

ther of Amos Beman, the distinguished New Haven black Congregational minister. And AME Zion pastor Hosea Easton, an activist and educator in Hartford when Amos Beman was teaching school there in the mid-1830s, must have been a persuasive example to the young man about to heed a ministerial call.

Daniel Payne, Garnet's forerunner as minister of the first black church in Troy, New York, was a lifelong, devoted friend of Theodore Wright. Pastor of AME churches in Washington, D.C., and Baltimore, Payne was elected a bishop at the AME General Conference of 1852. He was a zealous historian of his denomination. Payne crusaded for a better-educated AME clergy and established and became president of Wilberforce University, the first black institution of higher learning in the country. It is no wonder that he was especially respected by education-minded black Presbyterian and Congregational clergy.

Certain ministers of African Baptist churches in the North were also important forerunners or contemporaries of the activists whose careers are the focus of this work. Nathaniel Paul, son of an Exeter, New Hampshire, black veteran of the American Revolution, formed the African Baptist Church in Albany the same year that Cornish launched the First Colored Presbyterian Church in New York City. Five years later, on July 5, 1827, Paul delivered a stirring address at a celebration by blacks in New York City of the official termination of slavery in New York State. Cornish printed the full text of the speech in *Freedom's Journal,* founded four months earlier.

Thomas Paul, already referred to as founder of Baptist churches in Boston and New York City, was Nathaniel's older brother. A few months before the launching of *Freedom's Journal,* Thomas Paul had met with others at the home of the fiery Boston black radical David Walker to pledge support for the paper. Both Paul and Walker became agents for Cornish's journal in the Boston area. And it was in Paul's church, a few years later, that William Lloyd Garrison held the founding meeting of the New England Anti-Slavery Society.

Boston's black Baptist ministers as a group were indeed conspicuous during the antebellum decades for their systematic speaking out against slavery and unjust treatment of northern blacks. Most spectacular for his efforts to help fugitive slaves was Leonard Grimes, pastor of the black Twelfth Baptist Church in Boston. Prior to coming to Boston, he had served a two-year prison term in Virginia for helping slaves escape.[4]

4. James Oliver Horton and Lois E. Horton, *Black Bostonians: Family Life and Community Struggle in the Antebellum North* (New York, 1979), 46–50.

Finally, there were two black Episcopal clergymen, with education and powers of self-expression comparable to Cornish's and Wright's, who were close co-workers for a few years with black Presbyterian ministers in New York. Peter Williams, Jr., rector of Saint Philip's (African Episcopal) Church, was chosen, along with Cornish and Wright, to sit on the Executive Committee of the American Anti-Slavery Society (AASS). A few months later, however, after antiabolition and antiblack riots, Williams was ordered by his bishop to withdraw from his AASS post. He did so. Alexander Crummell, schoolmate, in both high school and college, of Henry Garnet, was refused admission to the General Theological Seminary because of his race. Studying privately with Episcopal clergy in Boston and Providence, Crummell gained ordination as a priest and organized a small congregation of poor, laboring blacks in New York City. He was active in black New York state conventions in the 1840s but then left the American scene. He became an effective missionary educator in Africa and an eloquent spokesman for the "redemption of Africa" by Christian Afro-Americans.

The ministries of these clerical activists, whether Presbyterian, Congregational, African Methodist, African Baptist, or Episcopalian, were inextricably intertwined with their protest and reform efforts. The ministries bore witness to the power of a caring and judging God and to the essential oneness and basic worth of all mankind. The activism was agitation that aimed at liberation. It strengthened the movement for the immediate abolition of slavery, broadened free blacks' visions of what they could become, and attacked the white repression—especially in education, employment, and political life—that barred the way to Afro-American progress.

For all these linkages with black clergy in other denominations, there were distinctive elements in the experiences of Cornish, Wright, Ray, Garnet, Beman, and Pennington. In the final analysis, theirs was a unique group achievement. Singular abilities, aspirations, and education, as well as close interaction with one another, brought remarkable results in a creative process that issued in new Afro-American institutions: black Presbyterian and Congregational churches, black newspapers, black vigilance committees (to aid fugitive slaves and prevent kidnappings), large-scale petition campaigns, and politically oriented statewide black conventions.

2. THE LAY OF THE LAND

Cornish, Wright, Ray, Garnet, Beman, and Pennington wrote a new chapter in Afro-American religion in a time of special ferment in the nation. They defined themselves as committed Christians, as unapologetic blacks, and as full-fledged Americans. The three inheritances were at times in conflict with one another, but these men tried to weave a fabric of order and understanding that was faithful to the best in all three legacies.

Being Christian meant for these ministers preaching a biblical message—a liberation theology based on the Exodus, the Old Testament prophets, and Jesus Christ. God, they insisted, was in charge of history; hence those who persisted in oppression, which clearly flouted God's will, would be defeated, crushed, scattered. And the divine promise was as sure as the divine threat. The deprived and brutalized *could* shake loose from their hopelessness and lead lives more free and satisfying. The enslaved *would* go free, yet they must themselves lay hold of that promised freedom.

The church affiliation of these six activists was with white denominations directly descended from Puritanism, a tradition strongly emphasizing education and political involvement. In this affiliation, black Presbyterians and Congregationalists parted company to some extent from African Methodists and Baptists, the great mass of Afro-Americans belonging to black churches.

The differences can easily be overstated. All black ministers accepted the freeing of the oppressed, and heartfelt experience of the living Christ (or Jesus) was central to that liberation for Afro-American Baptists, Methodists, Presbyterians, and Congregationalists. For clergy in all four traditions, preaching was rooted in biblical texts. There were, however, important differences in liturgy and in degrees or types of social activism. The liturgy of Presbyterians and Congregationalists stressed order and predictability. The worship service was centered on a carefully prepared sermon that drew from the preacher's systematic study of theology and the Bible. Christ as the Word, the meaningful expression of the divine intention, was emphasized.

The liturgy of most Baptist and Methodist churches, in contrast, centered on the Holy Spirit. Worship flowed freely from singing to prayer and back again. The preacher's power lay in his openness to the winds of the Spirit and in his ability to draw his congregation into more and more intense participation in that same Spirit.

To generalize about the degree of social radicalism and political activism flowing from each of these denominational streams and from that of notable black Episcopalians such as Peter Williams, Jr., and Alexander Crummell is hazardous. Far more intensive study of the careers of scores of antebellum black ministers is sorely needed. Part of the picture, however, is clear. In the large-scale slave conspiracy of 1822 in Charleston, South Carolina, the large AME church was a training center for lieutenants in the cause. Nine years later in Virginia, Nat Turner, acknowledged as a Baptist exhorter, led the bloodiest slave revolt of the nineteenth century. From the 1840s through the Civil War, Sojourner Truth, an AMEZ itinerant preacher and singer of spirituals, won over camp meeting crowds and conference audiences by the power of her abolitionist, antiracist, and feminist message, the fervor of her singing, the simplicity of her manner, and the sharpness of her wit. And prominent male ministers of the major black denominations, such as Richard Allen (AME), Nathaniel Paul and Samuel H. Davis (African Baptist), and Peter Williams, Jr. (Episcopalian), delivered memorable excoriations of slavery and racism.

Granted the striking witness for freedom by such individuals, the fact was that the earliest black Presbyterian and Congregational ministers were more likely to be systematic workers for radical social reform than were black clergy of the other denominations. This activity on the part of Cornish, Wright, and the others was consonant with nearly two centuries of white Presbyterian and Congregational ministers' political, and even revolutionary, involvement: in the English Puritan ferment of the early 1600s, in the Cromwellian revolution, in the shaping of political institutions and practices in the New England colonies, and in the mustering of popular support for the American Revolution.[1] Antebellum black ministers in these denominations had no monopoly on black clerical activism, but they turned a spotlight, for many blacks and whites, on the social and political goals of the black freedom movement at large. They also initiated the journals, petition campaigns, state conventions, and legislative lobbying that were foundation stones of gradual political empowerment. The systematic study of the Bible and Protestant theology and the careful preparation of sermons had been invaluable training for the writing of cogent editorials and the delivering of powerful addresses attacking slavery and a caste-ridden society.

Americans at large during the early nineteenth century were affected by a widespread religious movement that came to be called the Second Great Awakening. The Awakening resulted in a remarkable intensification of American piety. Individual prayer life and group worship were revitalized. Conversions from indifference to heartfelt acceptance of Christ and his claims were promoted in revival meetings. A spate of new evangelistic, educational, charitable, and reform organizations came into being. Taken together, these developments constituted the Evangelicalism of early nineteenth century America and its "benevolent empire."

Black people and their ministers benefited in some cases from the quickened Christian consciences of whites. In other cases they suffered from whites' paternalism and ill-conceived projects. White Evangelical concern over the ignorance and vices of many lower-class urban blacks issued in substantial white assistance in the founding and later financing of black Presbyterian churches in Philadelphia, New York City, and Troy, New York. The same was true for black Congregational churches founded in New Haven and Hartford, Connecticut, and Portland, Maine. Moreover, Evangelical promotion of foreign and domestic missionary work strengthened black ministers' urge to evangelize unchurched blacks in the United States, the West Indies, and Africa.

Two movements, one an encouragement and the other a threat to American blacks, were energized by white social concern stemming from the Second Great Awakening. The abolition movement was greatly strengthened in the 1830s as a result of the revivalist preaching of such

1. James Hastings Nichols, *Democracy and the Churches* (Philadelphia, 1951); Michael Walzer, *The Revolution of the Saints: A Study in the Origins of Radical Politics* (New York, 1970).

whites as Charles G. Finney. From the 1820s to the Civil War, some white Evangelical abolitionists—both clergy and laity—developed into the black activist clergy's staunch and valued allies.

With very different implications for blacks, the American Colonization Society was founded by whites in 1816. Motivated in part by Evangelical altruism, the ACS aimed to colonize in Africa American free blacks and slaves freed for this purpose. Many black leaders saw the white colonization program as an evasion of the whites' obligation to underwrite racial justice in America. Most activist black clergy consistently and bitterly attacked the ACS.

Cornish, Wright, Ray, Garnet, Beman, and Pennington saw themselves not only as Christians but also as black Christians and black Christian Americans. Samuel Cornish affirmed this in entitling his longest-lasting newspaper the *Colored American*. Whatever the shade of their skin, these men identified fully with Afro-Americans, whether enslaved or free. They also insisted on full participation in the American heritage of self-determination. In so doing they declared war on long-standing Euro-American assumptions of "white over black." This meant challenging established attitudes born of the slave trade, white ownership of slaves, and the confinement of free blacks to the bottom of a caste structure built on race. (As Winthrop D. Jordan has so richly shown, black had come to be associated in many white minds with the savage, the licentious, the enslaved, and the fundamentally inferior.)[2]

Most tragic for Afro-Americans was the inevitable toll that generations of enslavement and insistence on black inferiority by whites took from black people's respect for themselves. Activist black clergy grappled with this pernicious inheritance by themselves becoming persons of striking accomplishment. They also tried to strengthen other blacks' sense of their own worth by highlighting notable black achievers, past and present. In their newspapers, their speeches, and occasionally a book, Cornish, Ray, and the others told about glorious early African empires and about individual Afro-American intellectuals, poets, soldiers, sailors, leaders of slave revolts, shipowners, businessmen, physicians, and outstanding religious leaders. In so doing, these minister-journalists were pioneers in the recording of Afro-American history by Afro-Americans.

Along with affirming themselves and their fellows as people of African descent, these six thought and spoke of themselves as full-fledged

2. Winthrop D. Jordan, *White over Black: American Attitudes Toward the Negro, 1550–1812* (Baltimore, 1969).

Americans. Like other black leaders, they embraced the Declaration of Independence, especially Thomas Jefferson's words as to all men being "created equal, . . . endowed by their creator with inalienable rights; . . . among these . . . life, liberty and the pursuit of happiness." They saw the United States Constitution, in spite of its provisions based on slave-owning, as in essence a democratic document. Free-born Charles Ray and slave-born James Pennington went further. They spoke of the architects of the American republic as "our founding fathers."

The six committed themselves to the American political process. Those in New York State urged blacks with enough property to qualify for the franchise to exercise that right. These ministers led in the organized petitioning of state governments. Some of them lobbied with individual legislators and campaigned for national political parties. They insistently attacked such federal policies as the continuation of slavery in the District of Columbia, the annexation of Texas, and fugitive slave acts facilitating slave owners' recovery of runaways. When the Civil War came, the surviving four all urged blacks to enlist in the Union army.

Between the Revolution and the Civil War, diverse understandings of what it meant to be an American unfolded. Some were encouraging to Afro-Americans and some hostile. The vigorous white abolitionism of the immediate postrevolutionary period had interpreted the Declaration of Independence as outlawing slavery. Drawing on the same Enlightenment stress on universal human characteristics and rights as Jefferson had, these abolitionists endorsed monogenesis and attributed racial differences to variety in environmental influences exerted over long periods of time. Activist black clergy strongly supported this position, setting the biblical account of the Creation in the book of Genesis alongside the Declaration of Independence as complementary authorities.

Other forces during the first half of the nineteenth century were inviting whites to look at the world and America as a hierarchy of peoples and to believe in polygenesis. These influences highlighted the ways in which people differed, not the qualities shared by all. Here, too, a statement by Jefferson was influential. Only a few years after he had written the original text of the Declaration of Independence, Jefferson the slave owner had spoken: "I advance it . . . as a suspicion only, that the blacks, whether originally a distinct race, or made distinct by time and circumstances, are inferior to the whites in the endowments both of body and mind."[3]

3. Thomas Jefferson, *Notes on the State of Virginia,* ed. William Peden (New York, 1972), 143.

These words rankled for decades in the thoughts and feelings of black leaders. Jefferson's supposition, however, was reinforced by shifts in population and conservative responses to black and white reform movements between 1810 and 1850.

During these four decades there was substantial European, and especially Irish, immigration into the United States. Many of the newcomers were Catholic, and most had had little education. Poor and in desperate need of jobs and housing, they tended to settle in the cities. The same decades brought a surge of free blacks into the cities of the North. Many were recently emancipated, coming from the South or the rural areas of the North. They, too, were ill educated, poor, and ready to grasp at menial work, however poorly paid. Bitterly antiblack feelings developed among the white immigrants and were a major ingredient in political reverses suffered by black political activists in the 1840s and 1850s.

Among the longer-resident and mostly Protestant middle- and upper-class whites in the United States, anxiety grew with the upswing of poverty, drunkenness, and crime among the urban poor. Except for mission-minded Evangelicals, these more advantaged whites distanced themselves from both groups struggling for the bottom rung of the economic and social ladder. In the process they dwelt on the rich legacy from their own forebears, especially the contributions of England and Scotland to the common-law tradition and to representative government. The Anglo-Saxons' special embodiment of integrity, love of freedom, and capacity for forceful leadership was given memorable expression in the novels of Sir Walter Scott, which were immensely popular in America, both South and North.[4]

The northern Protestants' response to the expanding presence of Roman Catholics, along with the southern slave owners' reaction to the increasingly aggressive abolition movement, led both groups to stress the inherent, if not eternal, variations in capacity of people from different cultures or races. Scientists aided those who sought social control of the lower classes and the lower race. As Reginald Horsman has put it, "By 1850 there were very few scientists prepared to defend the inherent equality of the different races of the world. . . . In less than fifty years the emphasis in studying human beings had shifted dramatically from the general to the particular, from what was universal to what was unique."[5]

4. Reginald Horsman, *Race and Manifest Destiny: The Origins of American Racial Anglo-Saxonism* (Cambridge, Mass., 1981), 11, 15, 22, 39–41.

5. *Ibid.*, 60, 61.

It is ironic, if hardly surprising, that precisely during those antebellum years when Afro-Americans were making great strides forward in higher education, the professions, journalism, business enterprise, and religious and political organization, most upper-class northern whites, including most abolitionists, were more confidently labeling black people a race inherently inferior to whites in intellect and ability to govern. Blacks' subordination was reinforced by the contention of many white Evangelicals that blacks had something special to offer in their being "natural Christians," possessing humility and gentleness rather than the mind, the drive, and the selfishness necessary for government and for dominating cultural influence. Accordingly, in the 1850s, when northern hostility toward slavery was increasing, the campaign by black leaders for equal participation in the political process was generally rejected by whites, both ardent Evangelicals and others.[6]

In the face of these developments strengthening whites' negative views of black people's capacities, black activist clergy persisted in defying racist categories. They did so as Christians and in the name of what it meant to be Americans. They invoked the pervasive belief of the time in the glorious possibilities to be won by human effort on the continent of North America. This dominant optimism in editorials, sermons, and speeches was never dashed for long by what seem, at this remove, devastating political or personal setbacks. In 1840 Henry Garnet, Theodore Wright, and Charles Ray were spokesmen for a black state convention in Albany seeking reenfranchisement of Afro-Americans. The three men composed an address to the state's black people urging them to get busy and shape their own futures. God has, they declared, destined America to be the home of Afro-Americans. He has also intended that human beings in general, and Americans in particular, "be ever progressive." "The deep foundations of political injustice are now being broken up. . . . Let every [black] man . . . arouse himself." The movement for the franchise is the cause of truth and will prevail, for it has in it the "mightiness of God."[7]

Convinced that the 1830s and 1840s were a time for the shattering of old tyrannies, black activists founded and shaped new Afro-American institutions and programs: politically involved black churches, black journals, action to help fugitive slaves, systematic visitation of scattered black

6. George M. Fredrickson, *The Black Image in the White Mind: The Debate on Afro-American Character and Destiny, 1817–1914* (New York, 1971), chap. 3; Horsman, *Race and Manifest Destiny*, 60f., 264–66, 274f.

7. *Colored American*, November 21, 1840.

communities, and political campaigns seeking legislation to erase institutionalized injustice.

Cornish, Wright, Ray, Garnet, Beman, and Pennington had a major share in these developments. But many other black people, whether prominent or obscure, forwarded them. Conspicuous examples of prominent laypeople include Philip Bell, journalist raised in the AME Zion church; David Ruggles, frontline fighter for fugitives and against kidnappers; and Frederick Douglass. And among influential clergy were Episcopalian Peter Williams, Jr., AMEZ bishop Christopher Rush, and Baptists John T. Raymond and Nathaniel Paul.

As for the more obscure, Carol George has provided a helpful reminder that local ministries by less well known black clergymen made solid contributions to the abolition movement, to the granting of civil rights, and to the heightened self-awareness that is an important theme in this work. Upon occasion the work of the well-known activist clergy and that of the less well known converged in a public event. For instance, Theodore Wright presided over literally dozens of public meetings at the First Colored Presbyterian Church, drawing from New York City's black community at large to raise funds for fugitive slaves, to honor certain white abolitionists, to gather petitions for the black vote in New York State, and to further other causes. Personal friendships and common commitment among black clergy of the various denominations meant that these men often warmly encouraged the involvement of their members in such gatherings. Similarly, the success of Cornish and Ray's *Colored American* depended substantially on the support of fellow clergy in securing subscriptions and in submitting news from far-flung black communities. Some of these clerical supporters were designated agents of *Freedom's Journal*. Many who were not welcomed Ray as itinerant promoter of the paper.[8]

Against the background of general white racial prejudice, in select situations activist black clergy won whites over to a more positive view of blacks' capacities. White Presbyterian and Congregational ministers in Philadelphia, New York City, Princeton, the Albany area, and New Haven assisted in the theological training of Cornish, Wright, Garnet, and Pennington. And white clergy met with them and with Beman and Ray in presbyteries or Congregational association meetings over the

8. Carol V. R. George, "Widening the Circle: The Black Church and the Abolitionist Crusade, 1830–1860," in Lewis Perry and Michael Fellman (eds.), *Antislavery Reconsidered: New Perspectives on the Abolitionists* (Baton Rouge, 1979), 75–95.

years of their pastorates. In some cases these experiences led whites well beyond the usual paternalistic pride or concern.

Another group, white abolitionists by the hundreds in state or regional conclaves, was rocked by Wright's and Ray's attacks on northern prejudice. In scores of more general public gatherings, large numbers of whites concerned about slavery, free black "elevation," temperance, or caste oppression came away shaking their heads in admiration over the intellectual ability, eloquence, and justified indignation of a Wright, a Ray, a Garnet, a Beman, or a Pennington. In a very few cases these associations led to lasting friendships, such as those between Evangelical abolitionist Lewis Tappan and Theodore Wright, or between upstate maverick Christian and notable philanthropist Gerrit Smith and all six of these black pastors.

These activist black ministers were both elite and marginal. They had secured an uncommon level of education, much of it on their own. They were unusually articulate in both the spoken and the written word. And they were notably ambitious, although the degree of this quality, or the way it was expressed, varied greatly among the six. One of the marks of their ambition was the denominational affiliation they had chosen. White Presbyterian and Congregational churches were, or aimed to be, churches of the middle or upper classes. These six ministers were, then, men of aspiration (for themselves and for their people) and of influence to a marked degree, but they were also distinctly vulnerable. Often on the margin between black and white cultures, they experienced a special variety of disappointment, rebuff, rage, and isolation.

Although white Presbyterian and Congregational clergy were often eager to support black ministers' efforts to "uplift" poor and seemingly ignorant and immoral blacks in northern cities, most had no intention of treating these black pastors as their equals. Cornish and his colleagues, however, did intend such equality. In a sense, they thrust themselves upon whites, rejecting the assumption of a fundamental difference between the races that so permeated white consciousness. As a result, they were in a position to be especially hurt by whites. Black men who, by virtue of ability, education, and ambition, were peers of white clergy and other community leaders were just as subject to insults and exclusion by railroad conductors and omnibus drivers as were black people at large. Likewise, the insult of Negro pews in white churches was imposed on these distinguished ministers as it was on all people of color. As black clergy in white denominations, they knew special disappointments and humiliations. Ordained under the same general expectations as white Presbyterian and Congregational clergy and attending the same presbytery and association meetings, they nevertheless could not secure their bright children's admission into the local private schools of quality that were often run by city churches of these denominations. These black ministers themselves also suffered social ostracism when presbytery meetings ran over a day or two, being offered neither the lodging nor the meals generally provided visiting ministers by members of the hosting church.

The pervasive evil of prejudice seemed to these men an extension of the moral enormity of slavery. The depth of the evil was evident in the fact that "good" (that is, churchgoing and seemingly decent) white men and women were so generally implicated. The perception of this general moral blindness meant heavy wrestling for black clergy and anguished queries such as this from Cornish: "Is prejudice in the sight of Deity . . . a secret bosom sin to be connived at? . . . This cannot be, right must eventually reign. . . . It cannot be from the very nature of things, that the coloured population are alone decreed to perpetual degradation and bondage. If I could believe this, I would at once . . . denounce my bible and declare there is no God."[9]

Thus the lives of black activist clergy, seemingly so privileged compared with those of slaves, included descent into the depths of suffering, helplessness, anger, and doubt. As a result, they knew firsthand the experiences of the Old Testament prophets and the authors of the slave songs and, on occasion, spoke their hard-won faith with a power beyond anything uttered by even the most radical white clergy of their day. It was this power, even more than their striking intelligence, that won them widespread respect and support among black people, both in their congregations and further afield.

In addition to the daily burden of white attitudes and practices that "disrecognized" blacks, there was special financial vulnerability for activist black pastors.[10] In instance after instance, the churches they ministered to had been founded with substantial assistance from white churches and well-wishers at large in the white community. Trained to expect a living wage from their churches, as was the case for their white counterparts,

9. *Rights of All,* July 17, 1829. *Rights of All,* founded by Cornish after the collapse of *Freedom's Journal* in the spring of 1829, seems to have been issued only six times, all in 1829.

10. The word *disrecognized* is borrowed from the remarkable black sharecropper whose pseudonym was Nate Shaw. Theodore Rosengarten, *All God's Dangers: The Life of Nate Shaw* (New York, 1974).

these ministers generally did not take other gainful employment, as did most of their African Methodist and Baptist colleagues. White assistance was episodic, however, and black church members' resources were limited. The result was periodic appeals by these clergy to their white associates/patrons and periodic "begging" missions to the surrounding white churches. Because these black clergy were relentless critics of northern Christian collusion with southern slave owning and of northern barriers to black education and employment, they not infrequently offended socially conservative white clergy and church members.

Instances of presbyteries or associations formally seeking to control the radicalism of black pastors were rare, yet individual white clergy were sometimes outspoken in their anger at black clerical criticism of the ecclesiastical hands that fed them. The result for these black activists was sharply limited churchmanship beyond work in the local congregation. This limitation, however, along with the special rebuffs encountered by these men working on the margin between the world of black churches and the world of white churches, freed them and energized them for their vocation of social protest.

These six activist ministers' faith in Afro-Americans' capacities imposed heavy expectations on their people, along with imparting renewed self-respect. They invited their parishioners to be upwardly mobile—to acquire or strengthen middle- and upper-class characteristics. They urged literacy for adults as well as children, acquisition of property, and active participation in social institutions beyond the family. This meant recurrent requests for financial support for the church (and thereby for the minister's salary), for black newspapers, for fugitive slaves, and for a whole range of cultural, relief, and political efforts. The fact that so much of the time these pastors won such broad support was as significant as the steady litany of ministerial disappointment over shortfall in contributions.

To be a black Presbyterian or Congregational minister before the Civil War was a demanding calling. Comparatively few men were suited for it or ready to undertake it. Although the number of black churches in these denominations grew slowly to between twenty and thirty by 1860, when a pastorate was vacated by a black minister, the church would often be served for years by white substitute preachers or by a black aspirant not yet qualified to be accredited by ordination at the hands of white clerical associates.

Many factors promoted close relationships, both as colleagues and as friends, among those who did become black Presbyterian and Congregational clergy: similarities in the quality and even content of education; anger at the continuing atrocity of slavery; frustration over the seemingly impassable barriers thrown up against them and their families by caste restrictions; determination to bring about social change; and commitment to the preaching and worship, educational efforts, and pastoral care promoted by their denominations. In myriad ways these men taught one another, promoted one another, worked shoulder to shoulder, and, in times of bitter personal loss, gave one another lifesaving support.

3. PRESBYTERIAN PASTOR AND PIONEER JOURNALIST: SAMUEL CORNISH IN THE 1820s

We wish to plead our own cause. Too long have others spoken for us. Too long has the publick been deceived by misrepresentations, in things which concern us dearly.

—*Freedom's Journal,* March 16, 1827

Samuel Cornish was a pioneer in three respects. He was the first black man to undergo the normal exacting training and testing procedures required for Presbyterian ordination. He was founder of the first black Presbyterian church in New York City. And he was the first Afro-American journalist. By some criteria, his was not a successful life. His longest pastorate was for six years, and he had wanted to resign after only four. His first two editorships were for only six months each. He moved his family from New York City to the country, back again, and to the country once more, seeking but never finding a wholesome environment and good schools for his four children. His two daughters each died at age twenty-two, one after a long illness. One of his two sons was drowned at the age of ten. During the last years of Cornish's life, from 1840 to 1858, he had no sustained influential role, either as a black leader or as a churchman.[1] However, a careful look at the journals he edited and at his interaction with black leaders, white clergy, and white abolitionists makes clear that he was a force to be reckoned with during the 1820s and 1830s. John Hope Franklin has called him "perhaps the outstanding black journalist before the Civil War."[2] It is impossible to imagine the striking ca-

1. For a judicious summation of Cornish's later life, see Jane H. Pease and William H. Pease, *Bound with Them in Chains: A Biographical History of the Antislavery Movement* (Westport, Conn., 1972), 159–61.

2. John Hope Franklin, *From Slavery to Freedom: A History of American Negroes* (New York, 1952), 249.

reers of Theodore Wright and Henry Highland Garnet except against the background of what their forerunner had accomplished.

Born in a free black family in Delaware in 1795, Cornish came north to Philadelphia in 1815. There he secured more schooling and became settled in his desire to be a Presbyterian minister, an almost unheard-of post for a black man. By then African Methodist Episcopal and African Methodist Episcopal Zion churches were each numerous enough in the cities of the North to be forming denominations, but there was only one black Presbyterian church in the country. The First African Presbyterian Church in Philadelphia had been founded in 1807 with the help of a number of white Presbyterian ministers in that city. Its minister for the first fifteen years was John Gloucester, a former slave from Tennessee. As a slave, and under the tutelage of his missionary owner, Gloucester had preached with power to his fellow slaves. When the two had come to Philadelphia, Gloucester's owner freed him, and he began street-corner preaching and singing in the city's black community. In spite of the opposition of African Methodists, Gloucester had a church with 123 members by 1811, when it was formally accepted into the Philadelphia Presbytery. Cornish, arriving in Philadelphia a few years later, must have been as much struck by the effectiveness of Gloucester's ministerial leadership as by the singularity of this black Presbyterian church. The special quality of the Presbyterian ministry would be aptly defined several decades later by another black minister of this first African Presbyterian church: "The claims of the Gospel as preached by Presbyterian clergymen, are addressed more to the conviction of the conscience and understanding of the people, than to prejudices and passions." Invidious though this implicit comparison with Methodists was, it identified what especially appealed to Samuel Cornish in the Presbyterian ministry.[3]

Some two years after he had come north, Cornish was presented to the Philadelphia Presbytery, a body made up of the minister and a lay elder from each of the area's Presbyterian churches. His sponsor was Ezra Ely, pastor of the large Pine Street Presbyterian Church. Ely's predecessor at Pine Street, Archibald Alexander, had been deeply involved in the founding of John Gloucester's ministry. Ely's own experience as pastor of

3. Howard N. Christian, "Samuel Cornish, Pioneer Negro Journalist" (M.A. thesis, Howard University, 1931), 1f., 5; Andrew E. Murray, *Presbyterians and the Negro—A History* (Philadelphia, 1966), 32f.; William T. Catto, *A Semi-Centenary Discourse, Delivered in the First African Presbyterian Church, Philadelphia, . . . Including a Brief Notice of Rev. John Gloucester, Its First Pastor* (Philadelphia, 1857), 60.

New York City's almshouse and hospital had given him a strong sense of the loneliness and suffering into which the urban poor, and especially poor black people, could easily sink. Black mutual aid societies and churches in Philadelphia, New York, and Baltimore had proved their effectiveness in lessening such distress.[4]

The Philadelphia Presbytery agreed to take Cornish under its care "in the hope that he might be useful to the Africans." Four ministers were designated to oversee his studies, since he "had not received a regular education." They were also charged with arranging board and room for him so as to relieve him of manual labor and allow him a year of full-time study. Over a period of eighteen months, Cornish delivered three written discourses to the presbytery, each on a single verse of Scripture, and he read a sermon on a fourth verse. After intensive study of a textbook on theology, he wrote a summary of the arguments in each of its four parts. He took the same examination on natural theology as three white candidates for the ministry and was questioned on several of the sciences he had studied. In October 1819 the presbytery licensed Cornish to preach as a probationer. In actuality, because illness had struck John Gloucester, Cornish already had been preaching at the First African Presbyterian Church once each Sunday over the year prior to his licensure.[5]

Cornish's association with Gloucester's church gave him a vivid lesson in the financial problems likely to beset a black church. He discovered how excruciatingly difficult keeping afloat was for a church founded and housed with substantial white assistance. The First African Presbyterian Church had had outside help from the start. Benjamin Rush, formerly a Presbyterian layman, had made clear to a friend why he had given money toward this church's initial lot and building. First, Gloucester was an impressive preacher and drew crowds of listeners. Second, said Rush, helping this church was a socially prudent move: "This late great increase [in Philadelphia's black population] is from emigration from the Southern States. It will be much cheaper to build churches for them than jails."[6] Over the years, however, white assistance for any one black church was undependable, in part because several new ones had recently been built,

4. Raymond A. Mohl, *Poverty in New York, 1783–1825* (New York, 1971), 93.

5. Minutes of the Philadelphia Presbytery, October 2, 21, 1817; October 21, 1818; April 20, 1819; October 20, 21, 1819 (MS at Presbyterian Historical Association, Philadelphia).

6. Benjamin Rush to Samuel Bayard, October 23, 1810, cited in Murray, *Presbyterians and the Negro*, 33*n*4. Philadelphia's free black population had increased from 4,210 to 6,352 between 1800 and 1810. Leonard P. Curry, *The Free Black in Urban America, 1800–1850: The Shadow of a Dream* (Chicago, 1981), 247, 250.

and all needed help. In 1815, only four years after the completion of Gloucester's church building, he had reported a financial crisis, and the presbytery had urged its member churches to help. Three years later there was another crisis, because the First African Presbyterian Church had had to construct a gallery to accommodate a growing congregation. The presbytery sent Gloucester out to the white churches in Philadelphia and nearby to preach and preside over special collections for the relief of the black Presbyterian church. Gloucester's assignment must have been an arduous, if not an embarrassing, one, his problems being compounded by his need to raise $1,500 to buy the freedom of his wife and four children. After three months of these engagements, he ruptured a blood vessel. During the remaining four years of his life, he never really recovered his health.[7]

After being licensed to preach, Cornish spent six months as a missionary to slaves on the eastern shore of Maryland. He was then recruited by a New York City society to work in the black ghetto around Bancker Street, an area rife with poverty, grogshops, prostitution, and gambling. A number of evangelists, most of them white, were at work in this and other destitute areas of the city. There was a standard method: obtain quarters for a mission church, hold two or three services there on Sunday, conduct a Sunday school for children, give Bible lectures, hold prayer meetings on weekday evenings, and visit families in their living quarters. Each evangelist tried to develop an ongoing church in the area. Cornish seemed at first to be strikingly successful. About a year after coming to the city, he organized the First Colored Presbyterian Church with twenty-four members. In 1824—his congregation numbering several hundred, of whom eighty were members of the church—Cornish was formally installed as pastor by the presbytery of New York. That same year a new place of worship, a brick building measuring sixty-two by fifty feet, was built at Elm and Canal streets. Cornish raised some of the $13,000 construction expense by approaches to white individuals, such as the wealthy tobacconist Jacob Lorillard. Much of this cost, however, was carried over as a debt that would rapidly become a millstone.[8]

Cornish had been persuaded against his better judgment to approve

7. Minutes of the Philadelphia Presbytery, April, 1815; April 23, October 21, 1818; April 21, 1819; April 20, 1821.

8. Mohl, *Poverty in New York*, 204ff.; Minutes of the New York Presbytery, April 16, 18, July 1, 1822 (MS at Presbyterian Historical Association, Philadelphia); *Colored American*, September 29, 1838.

the uptown construction of his congregation's fine new home. A number of white Presbyterian clergy had promised continued financial support to supplement the church's yearly income, undoubtedly small, from members' contributions, but these promises had proved to be hollow. The church's outstanding debt in 1825 was nearly $10,000. A year later the amount had increased, the church being unable to meet interest charges. Cornish asked the presbytery to accept his resignation because of the church's embarrassments. The presbytery did arrange to have the church building sold at auction but refused to allow Cornish to give up his pastorate. Noting that "it is of great importance to the moral and religious improvement of the coloured population of this City that a suitable place be provided for them in order to secure for them the means of grace," the presbytery searched out rented quarters. It affirmed full confidence in Cornish, instructed him to start visiting white Presbyterian churches in the city, and laid before these churches the critical financial need of the city's black Presbyterians. For eighteen months Cornish remained in this role, so painfully reminiscent of the one Gloucester had played nearly ten years earlier. Finally, in the spring of 1828, at the continued urging of his church and himself, the presbytery allowed Cornish to withdraw. For some time his primary interests had lain elsewhere, but the solid work he had done from 1821 to 1826 had not been in vain. It provided the base on which the First Colored Presbyterian Church would make a remarkable resurgence in the 1830s under the leadership of Theodore Wright.[9]

By 1826 Cornish had become a self-appointed public defender of American blacks in the face of blatant slurs in New York newspapers. The negative statements were of two sorts: crude expressions of Negrophobia and calmly reasoned argument for the colonization of free blacks in Africa, since they had no future in the United States. The most notorious of the Negrophobic journalists was Mordecai Noah, an early Zionist and editor of several New York papers. He relentlessly trumpeted the scandalous doings of blacks and doubted the wisdom of freeing slaves at all: "What do our colored citizens do but fill our almshouses and prisons and congest our streets as beggars?" Noah's tirades capitalized on the miseries of poor blacks, many of them newly arrived from the South, by speaking to the resentments of low-paid whites, many of them also recent immigrants. The Irish, with a long history of oppression in their home country, especially disliked being forced to compete with blacks

9. Minutes of the New York Presbytery, April 16, 18, 1822; April 20, 22, 1824; April 22, October 13, 1825; April 18, 19, 21, July 3, October 10, 12, 1826; April 15, 16, 17, 1828.

for those menial jobs that, in America, were associated with black labor, enslaved or free.[10]

Blacks and immigrant Irish also competed for the cheapest housing. In 1825 over 20 percent of New York City's blacks lived in a notorious center of vice and crime, the Sixth Ward north and east of Five Points, an unhealthy filled-in swamp. The poorest of the Irish were clustered around Five Points itself. Cornish's work in the Bancker Street ghetto in the early 1820s had been only a few blocks from this unsavory location. Although the center of black population would move north and west by the 1830s, the First Colored Presbyterian Church, after the two years in a new church they could not afford, would remain well into the 1840s in the general area of Cornish's first missionary work.[11] Thus the ministers and members of this black Presbyterian church knew well the misery of the poor and the hostility of the Irish. Noah's efforts to exploit that misery and hostility angered Cornish and provoked several letters of rebuttal in New York papers between 1822 and 1827.

Ominous as Irish attitudes were for blacks, Cornish saw a greater threat in the American Colonization Society, for its race prejudice was disguised, and its program had already won substantial support among middle- and upper-class whites during the early 1820s. The case for the colonization of American blacks in some other country had been made as early as 1781 by Thomas Jefferson. He had argued against the continued coexistence of whites and free blacks: "Deep rooted prejudices entertained by the whites; ten thousand recollections, by the blacks, of the injuries they have sustained; . . . [and] the real distinctions which nature has made; will produce convulsions which will probably never end but in the extermination of one or the other race."[12] Black revolt in Haiti in the 1790s and a large-scale slave conspiracy in Virginia in 1800 had increased white Americans' interest in the possible removal of blacks by colonization, but no program was actually launched until the founding of the ACS in 1816.

The founder of the ACS was Robert Finley, a successful Presbyterian minister in New Jersey's Somerset County. Finley had been appalled by the poverty, criminality, and irreligion among the country's growing

10. Ralph D. Carter, "Black American or African: The Response of New York City Blacks to African Colonization, 1817–1841" (Ph.D. dissertation, Clark University, 1964), 121. The quotation from Noah is cited by Carter as having appeared in the New York *Enquirer: For the Country,* August 1, 1826.

11. Robert Ernst, *Immigrant Life in New York City, 1825–1863* (New York, 1949), 39–44.

12. Jefferson, *Notes on Virginia,* 138.

black population. He saw that the established Evangelical societies for home missions and Bible and tract distribution were useless in alleviating these problems. Finley found himself called to a new task, the colonizing of America's free blacks in Africa. Securing the support of Princeton faculty and friends, he proceeded to Washington, D.C., carrying a letter of introduction to President James Madison, a fellow Princeton graduate. Assisted by Francis Scott Key, a wealthy and well-known resident of Georgetown, Finley mustered a blue-ribbon gathering in December 1816 to found the American Society for Colonizing the Free People of Color in the United States.

Over and above this prestigious backing, the odds seemed to be with Finley from the start. Great Britain had already provided a model in its colonizing of poor blacks from London on the Sierra Leone River in northwest Africa. And the enterprising American black ship captain Paul Cuffe built up more than a little interest in African colonization among his people in America. Cuffe had visited Sierra Leone, having piloted his own trading vessel across the Atlantic. Finley had sought advice from Cuffe and gained his support.[13]

White response to the founding of the American Colonization Society was strongly favorable. Southern slave owners and northern investors in the plantation economy supported the program because it gave promise of removing from the South those free blacks whose presence was a constant invitation to slaves to seize the same status, by revolt if not by escape. Northerners opposed to slavery, however, knew that in some southern states laws prohibited manumission unless the freed slave left the state within a prescribed period, and that some slaves would be ready to board a ship for Africa in order to gain their freedom. Many other northern whites saw in the colonization program what Finley had: a solution to the grave problems arising from a rapidly increasing free black population and a way of bringing Christianity to Africa.[14]

13. P. J. Staudenraus, *The African Colonization Movement, 1816–1865* (New York, 1961), 8f., 17–21, 26–31; Henry N. Sherwood, "Paul Cuffee," *Journal of Negro History,* VII (1923), 153–229; Sheldon H. Harris, *Paul Cuffee: Black America and the African Return* (New York, 1972), 24–31, 38–41, 50–54. A recent article by Douglas R. Egerton argues that Virginia legislator Charles Fenton Mercer was the true founder of the ACS. Douglas R. Egerton, "'Its Origin Not a Little Curious': A New Look at the American Colonization Society," *Journal of the Early Republic,* V (1985), 463–80. Egerton's thesis, however, does not negate the importance of Finley in mustering support for the ACS.

14. Curry, *The Free Black in Urban America,* 244f. Although the percentage of blacks in New York City's population, for example, had fallen from 10.5 to 8.8 between 1800 and 1820, the actual number of black people had increased by over 70 percent, from 6,367 to 10,886.

Influenced by a number of these considerations, President Madison had supported the American Colonization Society program from the beginning. His successor, James Monroe, sent two federal agents to help the society scout out a location in West Africa suitable for a colony. By late 1821 a treaty deeding Cape Mesurado, south of Sierra Leone, to the society had been signed by the local king. The land was named Liberia (after the Latin *liber,* "freeman"), and its capital was christened Monrovia in gratitude for President Monroe's support.[15]

To Finley's surprise, however, the free black response to the colonization program was generally hostile. As noted earlier, some three thousand black men gathered early in 1817 at Philadelphia's Bethel African Methodist Episcopal Church to discuss the recently founded movement. James Forten, a well-to-do black sailmaker, reported on the occasion to Paul Cuffe: "Indeed the People of Colour, here was very much fritened at first. They were afrade that all the free people would be compeled to go, particularly in the southern States. . . . There was not one sole that was in favour of going to Africa. They think that the slave holders want to get rid of them so as to make their property more secure." Cuffe held his peace in the face of this surge of opposition.[16] A large meeting of blacks was also held in New York City, and resolutions of protest against the colonization scheme were passed. There, as in Philadelphia, no newspaper was willing to publish word of the black people's opposition to the ACS's projected program.[17]

Undaunted by the nearly unanimous opposition of northern blacks, the American Colonization Society reiterated its double message in its monthly, the *African Repository:* Free blacks were trapped in degradation and uselessness, and the ACS offered a timely and useful outlet for Evangelical benevolence. It urged ministers to preach Independence Day sermons favoring colonization, as well as to take up special collections for the national society. The receipts of over $4,700 in 1823 had more than tripled by 1826. Another factor worked in the colonizationists' favor after 1822. In that year, a conspiracy for a slave revolt organized in Charleston

15. Staudenraus, *African Colonization Movement,* 51–65.

16. William L. Katz's introduction to William Lloyd Garrison, *Thoughts on African Colonization* (1832; rpr. New York, 1968), ix. Cornish was in Philadelphia at the time and may well have attended this meeting.

17. An account of the gathering in New York City and of the resolutions there unanimously adopted was published fifteen years later in Garrison, *Thoughts on African Colonization.*

sent waves of fear through the white population, both southern and northern.[18]

It was Samuel Cornish who broke the deceptive silence in public print regarding black opposition to the American Colonization Society. In so doing he would, over the next fifteen years, provide a perceptive analysis of the attitudes of many Anglo-Americans toward black people and would begin to formulate a countervailing Afro-American position. Cornish's most extended rebuttal of antiblack material in New York City papers in the mid-1820s was provoked by the seemingly calm reasoning of David Hale, the reputable editor of the New York *Journal of Commerce*. Hale had written an editorial supporting colonization in Africa and pointing out why New York City would be better off without its black population. Cornish answered on the basis of over five years of daily association with lower-class blacks and whites. He declared that the behavior of low-class whites in the city was worse than that of blacks. It was true that refined and educated black people deplored the crude conduct of some poor persons of their race, yet in fact it had been slavery, not emancipation, that had coarsened them. The right path to follow, then, was to uplift poor and ignorant free blacks, not to colonize them.[19]

Other black ministers were as disturbed as Cornish over the abusive editorials in white newspapers and over mounting support among public-spirited whites for the American Colonization Society. Early in 1827, a small group gathered to consider countermeasures and decided to launch a newspaper. Those present at the meeting included Nathaniel Paul, founding pastor of Albany's First African Baptist Church; William Hamilton, one of the original trustees of the AME Zion denomination; and Peter Williams, Jr., pastor of Saint Philip's (African Episcopal) Church, a black Episcopal church. Also at the gathering were Samuel Cornish and John Russwurm, a recent graduate of Bowdoin College. The group chose these two to be senior and junior editors, respectively, of the forthcoming weekly. By the time the first issue of *Freedom's Journal* appeared in March, fifteen agents, all black, had agreed to promote the new paper in their communities, scattered from Maine to Maryland.[20]

In important respects, Cornish's acceptance of the post of senior editor

18. Staudenraus, *African Colonization Movement*, 120.

19. Carter, "Black American or African," 192f.; Alice Adams, *The Neglected Period of Anti-Slavery in America, 1808–1831* (Boston, 1908), 92. Cornish's rebuttal of Hale appeared in *Genius of Universal Emancipation* (edited by the Quaker Benjamin Lundy), October 7, 1826, and in several New York City papers.

20. Carter, "Black American or African," 135; *Freedom's Journal*, March 16, 1827.

of this paper was not so much leaving the ministry as continuing it in a new context, and with a far larger congregation. White Congregationalist and Presbyterian minister-editors were a frequent phenomenon, but the journals they edited were explicitly, if not narrowly, religious periodicals. *Freedom's Journal* was sui generis. Its coverage was comprehensive; its editorials were political, moral, practical in tone, and rarely identifiable as written by a minister, except that Cornish drew upon biblical language when he was confronting entrenched evil. Cornish was fully aware that he managed the paper and wrote its editorials not as an individual but as a spokesman for his people. Black leaders who had chosen him for the post had done so not just because he was a well-educated minister but because he had already manned the barricades; he had already spoken out acceptably in letters to the white press. Ten years later, in another time of crisis and opportunity for black people, New York City would again turn to Cornish, choosing him for the editorship of the *Colored American*. That they did so proves that he had been generally faithful to the convictions and interests of large segments of black people in his earlier editorial tasks.[21]

Cornish's ambition as editor was to change the attitudes of both blacks and whites. The prospectus for *Freedom's Journal* was suffused with his sense of mission: "We deem it . . . expedient to establish a paper . . . for the moral, religious, civil and literary improvement of our injured race." The paper made clear that it hoped also to reach the minds of whites: "Daily slandered, we think there ought to be some channel of communication between us and the public; through which a single voice may be heard, in defence of *five hundred thousand free people of colour.*"[22]

An overview of the content of *Freedom's Journal* during the six months of Cornish's editorship reveals four kinds of material of primary importance: (1) coverage of activities in the black community (for example, accounts of meetings of mutual relief, literary, temperance, and fraternal societies; announcements of marriages and funerals; advertisements for schools, boardinghouses, and merchandising firms run by and appealing to blacks); (2) biographies, history, or current events highlighting black accomplishments and building up black pride; (3) editorials exhorting

21. What Benjamin Quarles has said of the *Colored American*, edited primarily by Cornish and Charles Ray, was true of Cornish's earlier journal: "[It] generally furnished an accurate barometer of Negro thought." Benjamin Quarles, *Black Abolitionists* (London, 1969), 184.

22. *Freedom's Journal*, March 16, 1827.

black people to be up and doing to improve, to elevate, their lives; and (4) a varied literature of protest against whites' attitudes toward, and treatment of, black people. These categories of material, of course, often overlapped. Reporting on the specific activities of organizations in the black community in New York City or elsewhere highlighted both black achievement and black aspiration. It gave readers a sense of pride in their local leaders, their local communities, and the black community in the North. Moreover, such reporting was an invitation to readers to participate in some of the many agencies of improvement. Finally, and not least important, the fact that black people now had their own paper, edited by one of them, was itself a fresh reason for pride and a weekly refutation of white generalizations regarding the inferiority of blacks.

To evoke its readers' pride in being black, *Freedom's Journal* gave considerable space to persons and places that were striking examples of black achievement, present and past. The first five issues of the newspaper carried installments of a life of Paul Cuffe, whose colonization efforts have been noted.[23] Cuffe was a model of intrepid enterprise, economic success, and practical efforts to improve the lot of his fellow blacks. His father, a Massachusetts slave, had bought his own freedom and had become a successful farmer; he and his Wampanoag wife had ten children. Paul, born in 1759, had decided that oceangoing trade would be more lucrative than farming. He became a skilled boat builder and mariner. Before he was twenty-five, he was master of his own twelve-ton covered vessel and had made many profitable trips along the New England shoreline. Cuffe had contacts with the commercial elite of southeastern Massachusetts and Rhode Island, many of whom were Quakers.

Not only Cuffe's success as a navigator and a trader but also his early insistence on his political rights as an American made him exemplary to Cornish. During the American Revolution, when he was about twenty years old, he had been forced off the seas to start a two-year interlude at farming. The state tax collector in his area called on Paul and his brother John, reminding them of the "personal tax" each was required to pay. The brothers protested and petitioned the state legislature for the right to vote, since they were being taxed. After considerable debate, a new law was passed providing for equal treatment of blacks and whites in taxation and in voting rights. The political struggle of Cuffe and his brother was important to Cornish, who lived in a state where only blacks with a $250

23. "Memoirs of Capt. Paul Cuffee," *Freedom's Journal,* March 16, 23, 30, April 6, 13, 1827, reprinted from the Liverpool *Mercury,* where it had appeared in October 1812.

freehold and evidence of being taxpayers could vote. He looked toward the day when the property requirement would be abolished for blacks as it had been for whites earlier in the 1820s. Also dear to Cornish's heart was the way Cuffe had secured public schooling for his children. He had donated land and a new schoolhouse to his hometown in Massachusetts, making the gift contingent on the education's being available to all the town's children.[24]

Another source of pride for Cornish was the newly established nation of Haiti and the heroic figure of Toussaint L'Ouverture, who had led the island's black revolt against the French government in the early 1790s. Eleven articles on Haiti appeared in *Freedom's Journal* during the first six months when Cornish was editor. There had been considerable recent promotion of the emigration of free blacks from the United States to Haiti. Strongly supported by Richard Allen and James Forten in Philadelphia, the black Haytian Emigration Society had persuaded several thousand to go to the island in 1824 and 1825. By 1826, however, many of these new settlers had returned to the United States, dissatisfied with the Haitian climate, as well as with linguistic, religious, and legal barriers against their assimilation into the culture. Accordingly, the Haitian story was used in *Freedom's Journal* not to promote emigration but as a clear illustration of black people's capacities, if left on their own.[25]

Cornish, the primary author of editorials in the early issues of the paper, knew, however, that far more was needed to energize discouraged or indolent black people than accounts of other men's great deeds, whether Paul Cuffe's or the Haitians'. He used two other approaches. First, he urged his fellows to raise the level of their own living and to open doors of greater opportunity for their children. Second, he protested, often angrily, against the roadblocks that whites were constantly putting in the way of black people. There was frequent reference in these editorials to the virtues of industry, temperance, prudence, and prosperity. In emphasizing them Cornish was affirming the self-discipline and the achievements of the leaders of the black community. He was also reminding white readers that many blacks lived by the same principles as did upstanding whites, and that generalizations about the degraded way of life

24. *Freedom's Journal,* March 16, 1827.

25. Installments of an article on Toussaint L'Ouverture appeared in *Freedom's Journal,* May 4, 11, 18, 1827. (Associate editor Russwurm also had a special interest in Haiti, having been born a slave in nearby Jamaica.) Floyd J. Miller, *The Search for a Black Nationality: Black Emigration and Colonization, 1787–1863* (Urbana, Ill., 1975), 74–82.

of blacks were, in large measure, untrue. Finally, Cornish was seeking to convince improvident blacks that there really were dividends to be earned by effort and a more ordered life. A change in habits not only would benefit the individual but would help the whole race. Such exhortation was standard language among white reformers and educators of the time, but Cornish's message was both more realistic and more compassionate, for he joined it with fervent attacks on those whites who were making life so hard for blacks of whatever station in life: "None have suffered so much [as we] from the hands of people professing the Christian name."[26]

Cornish had a deep commitment to sobriety and hard work as avenues to a better life, but his central hope lay in education. His own experience in preparing for Presbyterian ordination had painfully taught him the disadvantages facing even a bright and ambitious young person who had not had sound elementary and secondary schooling. And by 1827 Cornish had children of his own. Over three years earlier he had fallen in love with and married Jane Livingston, a wealthy young black woman living in New York City. At the time Cornish became editor of *Freedom's Journal,* the couple had a daughter and a son, aged about three and one, and another son either just born or shortly to arrive. Accordingly, when Cornish spoke or wrote about the quality of education available to black people, his concern was both general and personal.[27]

In seeing education as pivotal for black advancement, Cornish was endorsing the long-standing American assumption that education was essential for moral training, for economic success, and for community welfare. Black leaders in particular, in light of the depressed status of their people, saw education as the sine qua non of progress. Over against this conviction, however, stood facts that promoted apathy. Prevailing patterns of employment excluded almost all black people from nonmenial labor. Social custom and legal barriers prevented most from casting a vote, let alone standing for election. And the intellectual pursuits of upper-class whites seemed either inaccessible or irrelevant to most black people. Taken together, these factors eliminated, in the eyes of most

26. Frederick Cooper, "Elevating the Race: The Social Thought of Black Leaders, 1827–50," *American Quarterly,* XXIV (1972), 604–25. Cooper used 1827 as the beginning date of his analysis, confirming the importance of *Freedom's Journal. Freedom's Journal,* March 16, 23, 1827.

27. The Cornishes lived at 276 East Fourth Street. Jane Livingston Cornish was to die in 1844, but Cornish kept the property until 1855, only three years before his own death. Christian, "Samuel Cornish," 13. In the *Colored American,* October 7, 1837, Cornish gives the ages of his children as thirteen, eleven, ten, and two. (The youngest was a daughter.)

whites and many blacks, the chief reasons for anything more than an elementary education for blacks. Moreover, the antiblack prejudice that barred Afro-Americans from skilled employment and from the vote also fostered laws requiring that publicly funded schools (that is, schools for the poor) be segregated. In smaller communities the result was often no public schooling at all for blacks. Where no laws existed mandating segregation (in Boston, Providence, and Philadelphia, for example), intense harassment of black children often effectively prevented them from attending public schools. Even in private schools, the earlier practice of occasionally including black pupils was being abandoned.[28]

Often the only schooling available to black children in the North, through the first third of the nineteenth century, was in Sunday schools run by white or black churches. Teachers there taught children how to read and how to behave. The pupils memorized Bible verses and began the cultivation of their minds. The ambience of a Sunday school for black children differed markedly in a school connected with a black church from one sponsored by a white church. Teachers in the latter often supported African colonization and, at least tacitly, accepted slavery in the South. Those in the former might be active abolitionists.

In the larger cities there were private weekday schools for blacks. These were frequently charity schools run by nondenominational boards of directors composed of whites of wealth and social eminence who were committed to educating the poor. The focus was on elementary education. Teachers aimed to impart, along with the rudiments, a realization of the value of work and of moral self-discipline, as well as religious knowledge. The best white-run schools for blacks, in terms of social outlook and interest in carrying bright children into higher levels of learning, were the schools organized by whites firmly opposed to slavery. In Philadelphia, Quakers, with a long-standing witness for emancipation, had taken the lead. In New York City it was the New York Manumission Society, which in 1787 had founded the first African Free School for free black and slave children.[29]

The New York African Free School program, which received substantial financial help from the state and the municipality, had two buildings able to accommodate close to one thousand students when Cornish came to the city in the early 1820s. The original basic curriculum had included

28. Curry, *The Free Black in Urban America,* 147–50.

29. Carleton Mabee, *Black Education in New York State: From Colonial to Modern Times* (Syracuse, 1979), 25f., 35–39, 43f.

reading, penmanship, arithmetic, grammar, geography, and for the girls, needlework. By the 1820s the boys' school also offered astronomy, navigation, and natural philosophy (that is, science). Faithful to the typical agenda of white benefactors, these schools tried to inculcate piety, thrift, and industry. The quality of the teaching and the ambition of the white teachers for their black pupils exceeded anything available elsewhere, according to the testimony of such gifted graduates of the school as James McCune Smith, physician; Ira Aldridge, Shakespearean actor; Peter Williams, Jr., Alexander Crummell, and Henry Highland Garnet.[30]

Items on black education appeared almost weekly in *Freedom's Journal* during the six months of Cornish's editorship. Most were contributed by people other than the editors, yet these writings echoed themes that Cornish and Russwurm endorsed. The exhortations in three articles by "Philanthropos" were typical. The expenditure of eight to twenty-four dollars a year on a child's education can confer an invaluable blessing. If this much cannot be afforded, use the free schools. The hundreds of children who "parade the streets" each day, rather than attend school, do so "to the disgrace of their parents and the mortification of our reflecting brethren." The evils accruing to the black community from the "loose and depraved habits" of many of these young are incalculable. The benefits of education, as sketched by Philanthropos, were escape from the "groveling and selfish habits" of the uneducated; "noble sentiments," fortitude, and perseverance gained from reading, reflecting, and conversing with the like-minded; and finally, the likelihood of rising to a respectable station in life, if not genuine wealth. With astonishing optimism another author concluded that educated blacks would gain "vantage ground in every profession and department of life. . . . Then how much longer will the monster Prejudice be seen stalking abroad?"[31]

Cornish saw his commitment to better education for his people as a religious mission: "Without [education], man is little superior to the brute creation—with it, he is a companion for the angels." The senior editor lashed out at whites, and especially Presbyterians, for excluding blacks from quality education in academies connected with their churches.

30. Rhoda G. Freeman, "The Free Negro in New York City in the Era Before the Civil War" (Ph.D. dissertation, Columbia University, 1966), 320–24; Charles C. Andrews, *The History of the New-York African Free-Schools . . .* (1830; rpr. New York, 1969).

31. Donald M. Jacobs (ed.), *Antebellum Black Newspapers: Indices to New York "Freedom's Journal" (1827–1829), "The Rights of All" (1829), "The Weekly Advocate (1837), and "The Colored American" (1837–1841)* (Westport, Conn., 1976), 48f.; *Freedom's Journal,* March 30, April 6, 13, 1827; "Amicus," *Freedom's Journal,* June 8, 1827.

And he blamed his fellow blacks for joining whites in accepting a gross double standard for educating the young of the two races. Among blacks there was a miasma of underexpectation, and most free schools for blacks reflected it: "A little smattering, and a few words recommendatory from his teacher, are all they look for from a boy of colour." Reflecting this underexpectation, and equally destructive, was the poor quality of the teaching staff in most of these free schools. Black schoolchildren, declared Cornish, grew dull under dull teachers. Black parents, however, were not supposed to object, because almost any white was considered by the general community good enough to teach blacks. Cornish challenged the trustees of these schools to visit more often and to examine students more thoroughly.[32]

The root cause of American whites' and blacks' underexpectation of free blacks was, of course, the slave system. Although Cornish himself had never been a slave, he well knew, as did all other black activists of the time, that enslavement was the primary evil for American blacks—the essence of white oppression. *Freedom's Journal* did not advocate slave revolt, as its Boston agent, David Walker, would do in 1829 in his fiery *Appeal . . . to the Coloured Citizens of the World.* Instead, Cornish and Russwurm pressed for immediate emancipation by law, a bold position for the time. They called for federal action to end this national disgrace, declaring that slavery represented such a threat to the nation's health and future unity that slaveholders' convictions about their property rights had to be overridden. Emancipation by purchase (the path Great Britain would soon follow in the West Indies) would be outrageous. "There is," declared *Freedom's Journal,* "no reason in the world why the slave-holder should be hired to be just." If emancipation can be effected under the Constitution, fine; if not, amend the Constitution. Urging President John Quincy Adams to put the welfare of two million slaves as high on his agenda as that of a hundred thousand Indians (Cherokees, presumably), the paper declared of emancipation, "Whether we choose it or not, the thing will be done. . . . It can neither be divided nor shunned. It is just one simple thing, and is to be taken so, as much as a declaration of war."[33]

32. *Freedom's Journal,* May 18, June 1, 1827.

33. *Ibid.,* March 30, April 6, 13, 1827. Bella Gross, in an early article on *Freedom's Journal,* reminded readers that in this defense of immediate emancipation in 1827, the editors were taking a more radical position than that of any of the well-known white antislavery crusaders of the time. Even William Lloyd Garrison would not shift from support of African colonization to public avowal of immediatism until 1830. Bella Gross, "*Freedom's Journal* and *The Rights of All,*" *Journal of Negro History,* XVII (1932), 243. According to the biog-

The decision to end slavery had been made by 1818 in all northern states, although in a number of states, including New York, a process of gradual abolition had been mandated. The day specified by the New York legislature for the freeing of all slaves was July 4, 1827. It was a day of jubilant celebration by black people throughout the state. *Freedom's Journal* gave extensive coverage of local community programs and parades. Many New York whites, however, were far from happy over these developments. The antiblack editor Mordecai Noah profoundly regretted "the grand coloured Jubilee with which we are threatened." Noting that the Africans intended to celebrate July 4 with a grand parade, he hoped that no disruption of the city's "order and well being" would result, but saw a great chance of "excess, extravagance, and riot of every sort." And Noah predicted that New York City's black criminal and pauper population would rise dramatically as a result of the migration of freed blacks into the city. Cornish, himself inclined to preach propriety and sobriety to his fellow blacks, acknowledged that he had long been opposed to public parades. But he accused Noah of trying to foment hostility between lower-class whites and black people.[34] Another unsavory piece by Noah after July 4 also drew fire from Cornish. Reminding Noah that his fellow Jews had often been persecuted in Europe, Cornish again took him to task for trying to stir up trouble: "The mob want [that is, lack] no leader. Blackguards among the whites, are sufficiently ready to insult decent people of colour."[35]

The ending of slavery in rural New York and the inflow of freed or escaped slaves from the South increased the struggle for jobs in New York City. In spite of his own comparatively advantaged financial situation, Cornish was as concerned over employment possibilities for blacks as he was over educational matters. Indeed, the two areas overlapped. Many former slaves had become skilled in some craft while still in the South. Often they had practiced their trades with no limitation other than paying an annual sum to their masters. Northern whites resented the competition of such skilled blacks and the stigma of association with them. Frederick Douglass, a skilled caulker, was prevented from follow-

raphy of Garrison by his children, he was persuaded to abandon colonization privately by a Baltimore black man in 1827. One wonders whether he did not also read Cornish's *Freedom's Journal*.

34. Editorial in the *Morning Chronicle* quoted in *Freedom's Journal*, June 29, 1827. Cornish had made clear to blacks that drunkenness on the part of black participants in parades was the primary reason for his opposition. *Freedom's Journal*, March 30, 1827.

35. *Freedom's Journal*, August 24, 1827.

ing his trade in the North. Accordingly, many skilled former slaves, like other blacks and immigrant whites, sought work as common laborers or seamen. They also served the black community as its shopkeepers, barbers, or bootmakers. Cornish, remarkable among black ministers of this decade for his economic emphases, was especially distressed by skilled whites' refusal to accept blacks as apprentices. "To suppress genius and industry," he declared, "is impolitic and cruel." He was unwilling to accept the excuse given by those in the skilled trades that their white apprentices would not work with "coloured boys." This pattern could be changed, he insisted, if employers would stop letting their hiring policies be governed by white apprentices and journeymen. Rather, let employers take a firm stand and "discountenance the evil."[36]

If the passivity of employers in the face of racially prejudiced workers was culpable, even more so were the distortion of facts and the active pessimism of colonizationists. Cornish quoted from a sermon by a white minister urging contributions by the congregation to the American Colonization Society. The preacher estimated that at least three-quarters of blacks living in northern towns and cities were "idle, ignorant and depraved." "Visit our jails and penitentiaries," the preacher continued, "and you will find them crowded with coloured convicts. Beyond a doubt their moral character is far more debased than any part of the white population." Cornish declared that less than 25 percent of free blacks belonged in the colonizationists's grim description. To prove his point, he noted the substantially larger percentage of New York City's whites in the almshouse than of the city's blacks. And even if the proportion of blacks in prison exceeded that of whites, it did not prove that their characters were more debased: "The coloured man's offence, three times out of four, grows out of the circumstances of his condition, while the white man's, most generally, is premeditated and vicious."[37]

Worst of all, in Cornish's view, was this white minister's and the American Colonization Society's fatalism about the condition of American blacks. The colonizationist preacher had concluded with the prediction that "until human nature is radically changed, they will never attain

36. Leon F. Litwack, *North of Slavery: The Negro in the Free States, 1790–1860* (Chicago, 1965), chap. 5; *Freedom's Journal,* April 13, 1827; Charles H. Wesley, "The Negroes of New York in the Emancipation Movement," *Journal of Negro History,* XXIV (1939), 71f.

37. *Freedom's Journal,* March 30, 1827. For statistics on the proportion of blacks and whites in the almshouse and in prison in New York City, see Curry, *The Free Black in Urban America,* 113f., 119, 124.

or participate in the privileges of American freemen. . . . Remaining here they must continue ignorant, degraded and depraved." Responding, as black preacher to white preacher, Cornish made a powerful theological/ethical statement: "*To concede so much to prejudice is to deify it.* There is a just God who reigns. . . . However inveterate prejudice may be, it is still an evil. . . . The sentiments advanced by the reverend speaker . . . *are the very strongholds of slavery and oppression.*"[38]

Two months later, a white editor took Cornish to task for attempting to set other blacks against the ACS "by rendering them distrustful of its object, and suspicious of the motives of these wise and philanthropic men." "It is evident," that editor continued, "that Nature never intended a black and white population to reside among one another to any extent." Cornish restated his position carefully. Yes, many friends of the blacks with pure motives did support the society. They saw it as promoting emancipation, evangelizing Africa, and suppressing the slave trade. But many others, equally trustworthy, opposed the society. Cornish considered them the realists. He saw colonization as a retarding emancipation. (Why else would large slave owners like Henry Clay support the society?) He believed that one true missionary family, like that of Lott Cary, a former slave and early Baptist missionary from Virginia to Liberia, could accomplish more in ten years toward converting Africans to Christianity than the whole colony of Liberia could in twenty years. As to the slave trade, Cornish declared that it had not been suppressed but merely shifted to another strip of African coast by Liberia's presence. He reiterated the black demand for equal privileges in America. And as for nature's intentions, he asked, "Does the Editor attempt to fathom the purposes of Deity? . . . or has he prescribed the conduct of the Almighty, and dictated the future course of his Providence?" Again, as with the colonizationist preacher, Cornish insisted that God's ways are not tailored to what men may consider practicable.[39]

If a white journalist was disturbed by Cornish's poisoning the minds of black readers regarding the American Colonization Society, influential Presbyterian clergy were pained and angry. Those most outspoken in print were two members of the faculty of Princeton Theological Seminary, Archibald Alexander and Samuel Miller. Alexander had been a prominent

38. *Freedom's Journal,* March 30, 1827.

39. Georgetown *Columbian and District Advertiser,* May 29, 1827; *Freedom's Journal,* June 8, 1827; Wilmore, *Black Religion and Black Radicalism,* 105f.

Presbyterian minister in Philadelphia and had had a special concern for the black community in that city. He had also been one of the early supporters of Finley's vision of an Afro-American colony in Africa. Alexander could only view Cornish's radical criticism of the American Colonization Society with dismay. Certain that he knew what would be best for American blacks, he wrote, "It behooves those who industriously sow prejudices against Colonization in the minds of the free people of colour, to consider what injury they may be inflicting on them and their posterity. . . . If I were a coloured man, I would not hesitate a moment to relinquish a country where a black skin and the lowest degree of degradation are so identified, that scarcely any manifestation of talent, scarcely any course of good conduct can entirely overcome the contempt which exists."[40]

Samuel Miller, former minister of the First Presbyterian Church in New York City and professor of ecclesiastical history at Princeton, went further than Alexander: He publicly attacked Cornish's journal and warned the black editor to soften his criticism of the ACS or, he said, the paper would lose its white subscribers. Getting only a rebuke in response, Miller announced in the New York *Observer* that he was cutting off his subscription to *Freedom's Journal,* being "entirely dissatisfied with the spirit and apparent tendency of that paper." Students and other faculty at Princeton—with the conspicuous exception of Theodore Wright, student agent for the *Journal* at the seminary—followed Miller's lead.[41]

To understand the anger of Miller and other white clergy who warmly supported the American Colonization Society, one needs to keep two points in mind. First, from its founding, the society had struggled with the problem of too few black volunteers for emigration. A high mortality rate in Liberia and word of armed warfare with the African population and of difficult living conditions tended to discourage potential colonists. For ten years the white press had, as has been discussed, cooperated with the society by refusing to print resolutions passed by gatherings of American blacks rejecting the program of the society. But now, through frequent, well-argued pieces, the editors of *Freedom's Journal* were consolidating black resistance to emigration. The ongoing problem of too few volunteers gave promise of growing more serious.

Second, whites such as Alexander and Miller, who were conscious of

40. James W. Alexander, *The Life of Archibald Alexander, D.D., L.L.D.* (Philadelphia, 1857), 395–97.

41. *Freedom's Journal,* September 7, 21, 1827; *Colored American,* October 14, 1837.

their church's having done much to assist free black people, undoubtedly reacted emotionally to the flat rejection, by most black leaders, of this most recent effort by white altruists. It was as though immature children were willfully disobeying their benevolent parents. Cornish, who owed much to white Presbyterian clergy in Philadelphia and New York for his ministerial training and for support in his efforts as pastor of the First Colored Presbyterian Church in New York, was himself in a most awkward position. Not only were 1826 and 1827 the years of his first outspoken public opposition to the American Colonization Society; these were also the years during which, by instruction of the Presbytery of New York, he was supposed to be visiting white Presbyterian churches in the greater New York area to solicit funds to help the First Colored Presbyterian Church get out of debt. It is little wonder that Cornish could not put his heart into this begging program, as he called it. In 1828 he renewed his request to the presbytery and was allowed to resign from his ministerial post. It seems likely that his subsequent efforts to secure pastorates or to be used as a substitute in white pulpits were hampered by a measure of distrust and resentment among white Presbyterian clergy.

In mid-September 1827, having completed the six months to which he had originally agreed, Cornish resigned the editorship of *Freedom's Journal,* in part for health reasons. He planned to move to the country and there resume the work of the ministry, perhaps as a rural missionary. What had been the overall impact of Cornish's work on white readers and on black? The circulation of the paper probably reached its peak in the summer of 1827 with perhaps 1,250 to 1,350 subscriptions. White readers were a small minority. One commented in a letter to the paper, "The Editors of our [white] Papers are so narrow contracted, that they never mentioned the *Freedom's Journal.*" This man had run across the twenty-second issue just by chance. He was delighted with its contents and wrote asking for all the back issues.[42]

A very different reaction, already mentioned, came from some whites deeply involved in the American Colonization Society. Like the Princeton professors, the perennial philanthropist Gerrit Smith, who would later become a radical abolitionist and close friend of Cornish, had been antagonized. In October 1827 Smith wrote to the ACS: "The turn that *negro-learning* takes in this country is not always favorable. It is certainly

42. Carter, "Black American or African," 163*n*60; *Colored American,* September 19, 1837; Letter from S—B— in *Freedom's Journal,* September 14, 1827; for another white's favorable reaction, see *Freedom's Journal,* July 13, 1827.

not so with the editors of Freedom's Journal, a paper I was at first disposed to patronize [that is, make a donation beyond the subscription price] and which I still take. . . . My heart is fully set on discharging the patriotic duty of contributing to relieve our country of its black population."[43]

What was the impact of Cornish's *Journal* on American blacks? The founding of the paper and its circulation reflected a corporate, not an individual, achievement. If there were roughly 1,300 black subscribers by the summer of 1827, it can be concluded that several thousand black people read at least parts of a weekly issue. The most eloquent statement of what the *Journal*'s anticolonization message had meant to black Americans was made by Theodore Wright a decade later. In September 1837, addressing a gathering of white abolitionists in the New York State Anti-Slavery Society, Wright recalled how widespread the colonization spirit had been among whites, both slaveholders and those opposed to slavery. He also remembered the unanimous opposition of hundreds of thousands of free blacks, who could not get their views before the public: "Then we despaired . . . [but] Freedom's Journal, edited by Rev. Sam'l E. Cornish, announced the facts in the case, our entire opposition. It came like a clap of thunder, . . . and the nation awoke as from slumber."[44]

Educating black people had been central in Cornish's work as a journalist. Within a few months of his moving his wife and three small children to the country, he had accepted a position as agent of the New York Manumission Society's African Free Schools in New York City. Charles C. Andrews, veteran white teacher in these schools, described Cornish as he saw him, soon after the latter became an agent: "a man of . . . piety, education, and gentlemanly manners," well qualified to give practical guidance to parents.[45]

Attendance at the African Free Schools in 1827 had dropped from that of the preceding decade and a half. Less than one-fourth of black school-age children attended at all, and many of these irregularly. Cornish went at his new assignment with energy. His chief task was visiting the families of pupils and of potential enrollees, many of whom he must have known during his earlier missionary work in the Bancker Street area.[46] By late January 1828 the African Dorcas Association had been set up to provide clothes, caps, and shoes for children wanting to attend school

43. Gerrit Smith to the ACS, October 10, 1827, cited by Early Lee Fox, *The American Colonization Society, 1817–1840* (Baltimore, 1919), 32.

44. Carter G. Woodson (ed.), *Negro Orators and Their Orations* (New York, 1925), 87f.

45. Andrews, *African Free-Schools*, 69f.

46. *Ibid*.

but unable to do so for lack of suitable clothing. The ministerial advisory committee for this project included Baptist Benjamin Paul, Episcopalian Peter Williams, Jr., AME Zion bishop Christopher Rush, and Cornish. By the 1830s school attendance had doubled, and four more schools opened in 1831 and 1832.[47]

Some fifteen months after Cornish had resigned his editorship of *Freedom's Journal,* John Russwurm, who had succeeded him as senior editor, made a decision that shocked Cornish and many of the paper's subscribers: He accepted a position as administrator of Liberia's school system. *Freedom's Journal* ceased publication in March 1829. Cornish and other black leaders in New York City tried to recover the paper's original momentum by founding a new paper, the *Rights of All.* Intended as a weekly, it actually appeared only monthly, with Cornish evidently doing most of the writing. Carrying no advertisements and never able to build up a body of subscribers comparable to the first paper, the *Rights of All* died after six months. However, those six issues provided an important bridge between black activism of the 1820s and that of the 1830s.

The *Rights of All* dealt with most of the same themes that Cornish had pursued in 1827, but his economic concerns were even more prominent. With a convention gathering in July 1829 to amend the charter of New York City, the black editor urged that in the new charter, "the pursuit of an honest living, will be secured to all our citizens." For instance, blacks seeking licenses as cartmen (porters and peddlers) should be guaranteed fair consideration. Cartage was in demand in urban centers in all seasons. It was comparatively unskilled work and required little outlay of capital. Hard work and long hours brought proportionally higher income. Here was a chance for the ambitious poor man to get ahead. In most northern cities, however, blacks were largely blocked from securing licenses, and New York City had one of the worst records. The usual excuse given by the authorities was "the delicacy of the matter." Presumably this was a reference to potential hostility on the part of the Irish and other recent immigrants, who would resent the competition. Yet these immigrants, declared Cornish, are often "hardly civilized" when they are granted licenses. Delicacy indeed! Did not the delicacy rather attach itself to denying licenses to all blacks, many of them born and raised in the city, of good character, and in some instances taxpayers?[48]

Licenses for peddlers and porters were only one part of Cornish's pro-

47. *Freedom's Journal,* February 1, March 7, June 13, September 12, 1828; Andrews, *African Free-Schools,* 69f.; Curry, *The Free Black in Urban America,* 153.

48. Curry, *The Free Black in Urban America,* 18f.; *Rights of All,* July 17, 1829.

gram for the economic betterment of free blacks. Just as whites had their dream of bettering the situation for blacks and solving America's problem by colonizing them in Africa, Cornish had his own dreams for elevating the race by persuading urban blacks to become farmers. Having lived most of his first twenty years in the country, he saw the agricultural life as conducive to virtue and freer of the costly consequences of racism than life in the city. The productivity of the soil was color-blind, as were markets for agricultural goods. For those with no farming experience, Cornish blithely insisted that only a year was needed to acquire the requisite skills and knowledge.[49]

Cornish knew perfectly well that most urban blacks had neither the resources nor the desire to become farmers. For those who would stay in the city, he urged a wiser use of money by the lower classes and a reordering of values by those with more means. Money and time should go toward education in all its forms. Black academies and a black college should be founded to provide training in the mechanical arts as well as a sound classical education. These ambitious proposals issued in a shining vision of what could well be called bourgeois success. Knowledge is power, will lead to wealth as well as refinement, and will dispel prejudice: "But raise up sons learned and enterprising, with assets of 20 or 30 thousand dollars—but rear daughters intelligent and polished heiresses to their tens and hundreds of thousands, and the fair sons and daughters of Columbia will forget the laws of lights and shades."[50]

The reverse side of Cornish's faith in education was his sense of shame over the ignorance and seeming boorishness of so many of his fellow blacks. These feelings caused him to oscillate between a demand for equal rights for blacks and an admission that blacks were not yet ready for (or perhaps even did not yet deserve) that equality. The glaring political inequality in the New York State of 1829 was, as already shown, that a black man's eligibility to vote depended on his owning $250 worth of real estate, whereas no such requirement obtained for whites. By 1837, Cornish would be one of the leaders in a vigorous black petition campaign to persuade the state legislature to eliminate this differential in voting qualification. In 1829, though, he had a more modest goal. He urged those who did own enough property (and who paid taxes, which was also required) to exercise their right to vote, and he made the exaggerated

49. *Rights of All,* May 29, June 12, 1829.
50. *Ibid.*, September 18, 1829.

claim that there were a thousand black men in the city who fell in this category.[51]

During the summer and fall of 1829, Cornish's *Rights of All* devoted much space to a far grosser violation by whites of blacks' civil rights than a differential in voting requirements. Mob violence broke out against blacks in Cincinnati. This was to be the forerunner of many brutal and terrifying episodes in both the North and South during the 1830s.[52] The trouble in Cincinnati stemmed from the surge of migration into the city by blacks from the South in the latter 1820s. Most of the states newly formed after the Revolution had passed laws either forbidding black immigration or allowing entrance only after the blacks showed proof of freedom and posted a sizable bond guaranteeing good behavior. Ohio's restrictive statutes had included the demand of a $500 bond, but there had been no systematic enforcement. By 1829, however, whites had become alarmed. Between 1826 and 1829 Cincinnati's black population had increased from 4 percent of the total population to 10 percent. The number of local white colonization societies in Ohio had jumped from one in 1825 to forty-five by 1830. In July 1829 Cincinnati announced that after thirty days it would start enforcing the $500 bond requirement. Anticipating a black exodus, whites almost immediately started raiding the black ghetto. The violence reached a climax late in August, when about three hundred whites attacked the homes of a large number of blacks. In self-defense, blacks fired into the mob and killed at least one white and wounded others. Although the mob was dispersed, the threat of further mob action and of arrest for failure to post the $500 bond drove a substantial percentage of the black community out of Cincinnati. Many of these exiles went to Upper Canada, where, they had heard, land was available for settlement.[53]

The summer issues of the *Rights of All* gave extensive news coverage to, and editorial comment on, the events in Ohio. It was clear to Cornish

51. *Ibid.*, July 17, 1829. In 1826 only 60 of 12,499 blacks in New York County were listed as paying taxes. Of these 60, only 16 had sought and been given authorization to vote. By 1835 over four times as many would be qualified to vote, indicating a growth in property owners, taxpayers, and the will to exercise the right to vote. Yet the numbers remained far less than Cornish's estimate. Freeman, "The Free Negro in New York City," 119, 122.

52. Leonard L. Richards, *"Gentlemen of Property and Standing": Anti-Abolition Mobs in Jacksonian America* (London, 1971), *passim*.

53. Litwack, *North of Slavery*, 70–73; Richards, *Gentlemen of Property*, 34f.; Curry, *The Free Black in Urban America*, 104f. Litwack estimated that 1,100 to 2,200 blacks had left Cincinnati. Curry's estimate was lower.

that recent white immigrants into the United States had been prominent in the rioting: "Who does not wish to live in the goodly city of Cincinnati; we recommend all the outlaws of foreign countries to go there. The authorities have driven away all the virtuous and respectable people of color, to make room for the dregs of other countries. 'Hail, Columbia, happy land.'" This crisis in Ohio induced blacks there and elsewhere to take another look at possibilities for emigration out of the United States, and it led Cornish to remind his readers of Haiti. It was not that he wanted blacks to leave the United States; "it is but just and right that they should be amply provided for here." But for those who have decided to go, "why not emigrate either to Canada or the beautiful island of Hayti, where the people are civilized, the laws good and well-administered?"[54]

This new openness on Cornish's part to black emigration did not, however, mean any lessening of his opposition to the Liberia project. Indeed, from the initial issue of his new journal, he had resumed his steady fire at the American Colonization Society. When the final issue of the *Rights of All* appeared in October 1829, Cornish had recently attended a meeting in New York City at which distinguished speakers had warmly endorsed the work of the ACS. His subsequent remarks were as bitter as any he had ever published. The first speaker was Thomas H. Gaullaudet, the innovative and renowned principal of the Hartford Deaf and Dumb Asylum. Cornish had come in too late to hear most of the speech but wrote, "As the gentleman has Rev. to his name, I judge that it consisted in the slander of the colored population of the north, and the asserting of the impossibility of their ever becoming anything in this country." Next had come Francis Scott Key, the well-to-do Maryland lawyer who had helped found the ACS. Cornish had found him boring, but also infuriating: "[He] asserted the impossibility in the very nature of things, while prejudice dwelt in his little heart, which cannot be bigger than a cherry; of [black people's] ever having any privileges in this country—*they must always be degraded and oppressed . . . Satan is stronger than the Deity. . . .* Is it not hypocrisy for such men to profess a belief in the bible? Is not F. S. Key a Pagan, and his God a bat or a mole? . . . How dare such a man speak of the triumphs of the Cross, or the Progress of light?"[55]

Basic to Cornish's beliefs was a God who intends justice. Fatalistic acceptance of prejudice or injustice in American society was blasphemy in

54. *Rights of All*, September 18, 1829.

55. *Ibid.*, May 29, July 17, September 18, October 9, 1829.

his eyes. But the continuing virulence of antiblack feelings and the entrenchment of these feelings in social policy meant that Cornish asked himself the same theological questions he addressed to colonizationists—for example, "Can it be that prejudice will always be too strong for the influence of the grace of God?"[56]

The *Rights of All* died after its October issue. It seems never to have had a chance financially, in part because of its not selling space to advertisers. After four issues Cornish was already out of pocket over $170. Of the eight hundred copies distributed, many were complimentary. Cornish's message, however, was being reaffirmed and would be widely circulated that same year by another medium. As noted earlier, David Walker, son of a slave father and free mother and Boston agent for both of Cornish's papers, published his searing piece *Appeal . . . to the Coloured Citizens of the World* late in 1829. The work's four chapters attacked slavery, the ignorance of blacks, "the [white] Preachers of the Religion of Jesus Christ," and the program of the American Colonization Society. Walker's message went two steps beyond Cornish, which frightened white readers. He urged slaves to throw off their chains—with violence where necessary—and he thunderously proclaimed that God would soon smash the American nation if it did not change its ways: "Can the Americans escape God Almighty? If they do, can he be to us a God of Justice? God is just, and I know it. . . . I tell you Americans! that unless you speedily alter your course, *you* and your Country are gone!" In the course of his angry pages, Walker had special praise for two men, AME bishop Richard Allen and Cornish. Quoting an anti-ACS paragraph from the *Rights of All,* Walker praised Cornish as one who had "the welfare of his brethren truly at heart," and he urged his readers to see the absolute necessity of giving the *Rights of All* the support it needed for survival. That Walker, a militant radical, should have so endorsed Cornish and his paper is clear indication of the radicalism of Cornish's own position on many of the issues confronting his race in the 1820s.[57]

Cornish, in spite of the high voltage of some of his scathing attacks on whites, would remain committed to social change via persuasion and legislation. He would be an influential older co-worker with Theodore

56. *Ibid.,* July 17, 1829.

57. David Walker, *Appeal . . . to the Coloured Citizens of the World, But in Particular . . . Those of the United States of America . . . 1829.* 1830; rpr. in Herbert Aptheker (ed.), *"One Continual Cry": David Walker's Appeal . . . Its Setting and Its Meaning* (New York, 1965), 85, 104, 122–26, 130f., 134.

Wright and Charles Ray as they emerged into leadership in the 1830s. He also would be senior editor of the impressive *Colored American* for three years in the latter 1830s. He had, however, already made crucial contributions in the 1820s. He had proved himself as a candidate for the intellectually demanding Presbyterian ministry. He had gathered what would later develop into a large and strong black church in lower Manhattan. And he had been the forceful and courageous editor of the first two black newspapers published in the United States. In those posts he had spoken out in criticism of the American Colonization Society, whose program was such a favorite of Anglo-Saxon Evangelicals, especially white Presbyterian clergy. In this policy, so calculated to alienate whites important to Cornish's own future ministerial career, the radical David Walker had found encouragement, as did other black leaders in the 1820s and succeeding decades.

4. EDUCATION, ABOLITION, AND BLACK-WHITE INTERACTION: THEODORE WRIGHT AND SAMUEL CORNISH, 1830 TO 1836

They keep us down, drive us out of their schools, mob and break down our schools and then point at us in scorn as an inferior race of men. "Can't learn anything." Why don't they let us try?

—Theodore Wright, 1836

Samuel Cornish's protégé Theodore Wright was actually only two years younger than Cornish, but he did not enter his career as a pastor (in the church Cornish had founded) until 1828, nine years after Cornish had been licensed to preach. Whereas Cornish was the trailblazer for the subsequent network of Afro-American Presbyterian and Congregational churches, Wright was its founding father. By becoming a conspicuously successful minister, as Cornish never was, Wright had a more solid influence on younger colleagues. Deeply satisfied by his work as pastor, Wright remained at the First Colored Presbyterian Church for the whole nineteen years of his ministerial career. The membership grew from 75 to 413 during those years, and there were good reasons for the growth.

Making the most of his seminary education, Wright delivered thoughtful, well-expressed, and fervently biblical sermons. His worship services included music from a fine choir and active congregational participation in prayer and hymns. The Sunday school program (for adults as well as children) was strong. Wright's nature, his upbringing, and his seminary experience enabled him to engage white reformers with both assurance and honesty. Firmly based in his pastorate, he spoke out in anger against race prejudice, especially in educational institutions. A perceptive and forceful minister and protester, Wright identified, won over, and nurtured able young black men, who became his colleagues in activist ministry.

Cornish had established himself as a hard-hitting black journalist and

Wright was emerging as a remarkable young black minister just as the white movement for the immediate abolition of slavery was being born. Cornish and Wright's most basic concern for reform had always been and would be to end slavery, which was evil in itself and the very basis of the American caste structure. For both of them, ignorance among blacks in the North was the parallel of southern enslavement. They fought with passion to end the barriers preventing black education beyond the most elementary level. These two black ministers joined forces with whites in the American Anti-Slavery Society at its founding in 1833. White Evangelical leaders in that society learned from their outspoken black associates and were persuaded for a time to take on Cornish and Wright's antisegregation agenda. As a result the 1830s brought an unprecedented close association between these black pastors and a few deeply committed white reformers. But both the outspokenness of black leaders and their association with leading white abolitionists increased resentment among such antiblack and antiabolition elements as recent immigrants from Europe. The 1830s proved to be a violent decade in which both conspicuous black reformers and white radicals were at risk.

More is known of Wright's family background than of Cornish's. The former was born in 1797 in New Jersey, but his family soon moved to Providence, Rhode Island, and then to Schenectady, New York.[1] His father, R. P. G. Wright, had been a native of Madagascar. Theodore's parents' political leanings show in their having named their son Theodore Sedgwick, after the distinguished Massachusetts jurist and legislator by that name. Sedgwick had been a Federalist member of the United States Congress or Senate from 1788 to 1801. Fourteen years before Theodore Wright's birth, Sedgwick had defended a Massachusetts slave woman against her master, from whom she had fled. He had won the case, arguing that the Massachusetts Bill of Rights of 1780, in affirming all men to have been born free and equal, had effectively abolished slavery.[2]

Evidently R. P. G. Wright and his wife had done their best to secure good schooling for their son from early on, but often their efforts had been blocked. Theodore later warmly remembered three white Methodist teachers who had opened their school to blacks. They had treated black children just as children: "They did not lacerate our young and

1. Wright's comments on his early life, in *Proceedings of New England Anti-Slavery Society, May 24–26, 1836* (Boston, 1836), 21.

2. Amos G. Beman, "Thoughts for the Times" (Clipping from an unidentified newspaper in Amos Beman Scrap Book [Amos G. Beman Papers, James Weldon Johnson Collection, Collection of American Literature, Beinecke Rare Book and Manuscript Library, Yale University, New Haven], II, 50); *Dictionary of American Biography,* VIII, 449–51.

tender minds by those cruel and unusual proscriptions which . . . repress the ardor of the colored youth" and drive them out of schools. The Methodist effort collapsed, and formal schooling was again impossible. For several years the Wrights taught their children at home.[3]

An important part of young Wright's education came from the example of his activist father. When Theodore was nineteen years old, his father traveled to Philadelphia and participated in the meeting at the Bethel AME Church that unanimously rejected the program of the newly founded American Colonization Society. Some three years later Theodore enrolled in New York City's African Free Boys' School. There, under the guidance of Cornish, he made real progress in his studies and also, in the words of an early biographer, "learned the tactics of struggle." Although he graduated from this school, his applications for admission to a number of colleges were unsuccessful. In later years he would refer bitterly to these rejections. In 1825, however, he did secure admission into Princeton Theological Seminary and was one of a class of fifteen who graduated three years later.

Wright was treated well by his white fellow students at Princeton Theological Seminary. In the fall of 1836, eight years after his graduation, he returned to the seminary at commencement. Although he had been back to his alma mater without incident a number of previous times, this year he was humiliated at the close of an alumni meeting by being called "nigger" and kicked several times by a Princeton alumnus. Wright wrote to his former professor Archibald Alexander and described the assault. He was anxious that word of this episode might damage his reputation, but he also feared blame's being placed on the seminary, for which he had deep respect. During his seminary years and thereafter, he had "enjoyed the immediate counsel and support of the beloved Professors, and a delightful intercourse with the students." Wright continued, "I always feel, when at Princeton, that I am in the midst of fathers and brethren in the holy and responsible work to which we are devoted."[4]

3. Sermon by Wright on October 26, 1837, at the dedication of the First Free Church (for black people) in Schenectady. Reprint from Schenectady *Freedom's Sentinel* in the *Emancipator,* December 28, 1837; George E. Carter and C. Peter Ripley (eds.), *Black Abolitionist Papers, 1830–1865,* Microfilm, hereinafter cited as *BAP* (Sanford, N.C., 1981), reel 2, item 398; Mabee, *Black Education in New York State,* 39.

4. Sources for both of the preceding paragraphs are "Address of the Rev. Theodore S. Wright Before the Convention of the New York State Anti-Slavery Society, on the Acceptance of the Annual Report, Held at Utica, September 20, 1837," in Carter G. Woodson (ed.), *Negro Orators and Their Orations* (New York, 1969), 87; Bella Gross, "Life and Times of Theodore S. Wright, 1797–1847," *Negro History Bulletin,* III (1939–40), 134; and *Emancipator,* October 26, 1836.

There was, however, another side to this picture. As has been noted, Wright had been the agent for *Freedom's Journal* at Princeton Theological Seminary. Within a few weeks of the paper's founding, he had persuaded many students and faculty to subscribe. But most had canceled their subscriptions when Samuel Miller, professor of ecclesiastical history, had publicly condemned the paper for its vigorous criticism of the American Colonization Society. It is noteworthy that in spite of Wright's great appreciation of the Princeton faculty on most counts, he remained throughout his life as consistent and outspoken an enemy of the American Colonization Society as did Cornish.[5]

In December 1828, only a few weeks after Wright's graduation from the seminary, he was engaged by the presbytery of New York to serve for a year as stated supply of the First Colored Presbyterian Church. He was to be paid $500 for the year, provided this amount could be secured through donations from white churches in the presbytery. A sizeable schoolroom was rented and used for worship. By October 1829 Wright had breathed new life into New York's First Colored Presbyterian Church. To the delight of all, the membership had risen to 120 and the worshipping congregation to 200.[6]

In 1830 Wright was installed as pastor, and the presbytery, seeing evidence of continued health at the black Presbyterian church, chose a committee to raise funds to secure a new church and designated six men, presumably whites, to "hold the same as trustees of said congregation in trust for the Presbytery of New York." By October 1831 this committee reported that $9,000 had been raised toward the $12,500 needed to purchase from the German Lutherans a hundred-year-old church close to the Bancker Street ghetto. The committee members had themselves underwritten the remaining $3,500. By April 1832 the black church had 217 members, almost twice as many as it had two and a half years earlier. Weekly prayer meetings being held in the most commodious private dwellings had been so crowded that many had had to be turned away. And pastor Wright reported that, to his knowledge, there had not been a single case of drunkenness or flagrant crime in the whole congregation over the previous year. Presbytery records for 1830, 1831, and 1832 make

5. "Address . . . Before the Convention of the New York State Anti-Slavery Society," in Woodson (ed.), *Negro Orators*, 87.

6. Minutes of the Presbytery of New York, April 17, 1828, April 21, October 14, 15, 1829. Wright had been ordained by the Presbytery of Albany early in 1829, his home church still being at that date in Schenectady.

it clear that this was a time of general quickening of heartfelt Christianity in member churches, yet something especially striking was occurring in Wright's church. Members won during Cornish's early ministry who had fallen away during the later 1820s had been drawn back, and a steady flow of brand-new members, begun in 1829, would continue for a decade. In 1840 the membership would number four hundred, making this the largest black church in New York City after the eight hundred–member mother church of the AME Zion denomination.[7]

Wright himself had done much to secure the $9,000 toward a new building for his membership. During 1831 he had visited the congregations in the New York Presbytery "to present the claim of our enterprise." By the late winter or early spring of 1832, however, he was prostrated by a severe and lingering malady, and in June he was still ill enough to wonder whether he would survive. It seems probable that exhaustion from overwork had been a major factor. This is reminiscent of John Gloucester's having been stricken over a decade earlier in the course of his visiting white Presbyterian churches in the greater Philadelphia area to seek financial help for his own First African Presbyterian Church.

Wright's slow convalescence prompted him to write a revealing pastoral letter sent to his membership in June 1832 from his parents' home in Schenectady. Wright's letter shows his theology at work. Struggling with discouragement, he identified with his members' restiveness. He reminded them and himself that God's ways are mysterious; even when "storms of adversity beat upon us, . . . still may we unreservedly commit ourselves to him." Warning his people that Satan is always ready to tempt believers into bitterness against God because of setbacks in their lives, Wright invoked Christ's suffering on the cross and his words "Let not your heart be troubled." The pastor then reminded his church members how fortunate they were, in fact, as compared with their fellows in slavery, "without a bible, . . . without a spiritual guide, . . . and crushed to the earth in . . . this land of boasted liberty." Remember, he wrote, how far the church had come in three years. Wright finished his review of recent history by comparing his church to the disciples of Jesus, after his crucifixion. Walking to Emmaus and joined by a stranger, the disciples had told him of the tragic outcome of Jesus' life and then, in a blaze of recognition, realized that the stranger was the risen Christ himself. Likewise, Christ had become vividly present for members of the First Col-

7. *Ibid.*, April 22, 1830; October 11, 1831; April 17, 1832; *Colored American*, March 28, 1840.

ored Presbyterian Church. As a final spur toward gratitude, Wright reminded the church members of how much worse it would now be if he had died of his illness, or if he had been stricken a year earlier when he had been in the midst of visiting white churches to seek financial help.[8]

A full half of Wright's pastoral letter was devoted to reasons for gratitude. Considering how poor his health still was, this was remarkable evidence of a fundamentally positive makeup. Equally remarkable was the energy with which, in the last quarter of his letter, he drove home the need to be up and doing for the cause of the church, as well as the need to save individuals from a desolating end. The message was true to revivalistic Presbyterian theology: "As you know, He lived, groaned and expired, and now lives, to save sinners. O! then, brethren, importunately pray, and exert all your powers to rescue from the agonies of a second death, the souls for whom He died. . . . Your companions, your children, your neighbors, your parents, while unreconciled to God, however orderly, or amiable their natural or acquired qualities may be, . . . yet they are in danger of eternal death, for they yet lack the one thing needful—a new heart." Wright's final awful reminder was that the cholera epidemic that had killed millions in Europe and Asia and had now hit southern Canada would soon be taking its toll in New York City.[9] (Indeed, thousands did die of cholera in New York City in just a few days in 1833.)

The New York Presbytery's minutes show that once Wright recovered his health, he had a solid attendance record at that body's meetings. (He was usually present for three or four of the six to eight meetings a year, a record as good as that of many other members.) Evidently in good repute with the denomination, and having a church that was growing year by year, he would seem to have had a promising future as a churchman. There were, however, three persisting problems in his life in the presbytery in the later 1830s: his church's inability to pay off its debt, his own periodic personal humiliation when he was treated like a pariah in some parts of presbytery meetings, and profound disagreement between Wright and the presbytery over the appropriate response of the church to the continuation of American slavery. As to finances, the continuing indebtedness of Wright's church necessitated his again visiting the churches

8. *A Pastoral Letter, Addressed to the Colored Presbyterian Church, in the City of New-York, June 20th, 1832* (New York, 1832). A foreword by the elders who arranged publication, dated October 1, 1832, speaks of Wright as still absent on account of his health. His leave from the pulpit must have been for over six months.

9. *Ibid.*

making up the presbytery to present the needs of his church. However, the financial situation for the First Colored Presbyterian Church continued to be precarious, with members' contributions all needed for current expenses, including Wright's salary.[10]

Paralleling the embarrassment of resuming these begging visits to white churches were Wright's and Cornish's mortifying experiences in attending meetings of the presbytery. Cornish later recalled, "I have seen a minister of Jesus Christ sitting in Presbytery, with his white brethren in the ministry, who, though it had been announced that full provision was made among the church members for every brother . . . yet [was] left by himself in the church for three successive days, without dinner or tea, because no christian family could be found in the congregation, who would admit him to their table, on account of his color."[11] Wright's and Cornish's treatment in the presbytery meetings was of a piece with the insults and inconvenience that they and other blacks suffered regularly if they tried to worship in a white church, eat in a white restaurant, or use public transportation on land or water. But to meet such denigration among fellow clergy and even fellow abolitionists was especially painful. As the next chapter will show, during the latter 1830s Wright, Cornish, and their younger colleague Charles Ray would deliver many frontal attacks on these expressions of prejudice as part of a many-sided crusade for blacks' civil rights.

In 1834 and 1835 what seemed to the presbytery of New York a far more grievous problem than the finances of a black church or the public humiliation of an individual black minister was troubling this body of churchmen. What appeared to be grave doctrinal errors were being advanced within the denomination at large and specifically by some Presbyterian clergy in New York City. Those who were especially perturbed by what seemed to be heretical beliefs and dangerous practices became consolidated in the Old School party. The innovators had become known as the New School men. New School Presbyterians included more itinerant preachers than did the Old School. Such itinerants believed in engineering revivals and in the use of "new measures," which included protracted meetings (sometimes for several days) and the use of "anxious seats" in the front. There the unconverted would become the subjects

10. Lewis Tappan Notebook, March 3, 1836 (MS in Lewis Tappan Papers, Department of Manuscripts, Library of Congress).

11. *Colored American,* March 11, 1837.

and objects of intense prayer by the converted. New measures also included encouraging women to share in public prayer.

New School ministers were accused of emphasizing a person's ability, through an act of will, to have a significant share in his own conversion. They also were said to believe that moral effort and achievement after conversion were an indispensable part of the process of salvation. Some, such as the spectacularly successful revivalist Charles G. Finney in his later career, asserted the possibility of a kind of moral perfection in this life. Old School Presbyterians made much of maintaining earlier Calvinist and Presbyterian emphases on divine sovereignty, human depravity, and the total dependance of man upon divine grace for salvation. In 1830 a number of New York Presbyterian clergy who would be labeled New School, with Samuel Cox of Quaker ancestry prominent among them, had requested and received permission to set up a new group, the Third Presbytery. These same ministers would play a major role in the founding in 1836 of Union Theological Seminary, more liberal in doctrine than Princeton and desirous of continued close cooperation with the Congregationalists.[12] By 1834 the minute book of the Presbytery of New York, which during the early 1830s had shown exuberance over revitalized religion in its churches and over the spread of the temperance movement, now bemoaned the spread of heretical doctrines. The next year this presbytery joined others in formal condemnation of such errors. This led to schism in the denomination.

By the mid-1830s a substantial number of New School Presbyterians had become radical abolitionists. Chillicothe Presbytery, in southern Ohio, had been especially aggressive on the slavery question. Year after year it had sent antislavery resolutions to the General Assembly and had seen them tabled. In 1835 it sent to all presbyteries a general letter recommending the barring of slaveholders from communion, and it asked for reactions. When the Presbytery of New York considered the Chillicothe Presbytery manifesto on slavery, it referred it to a committee and then tabled it. A resolution was drawn up: "While we deplore the evils of slavery, it is highly inexpedient, in the judgment of this Presbytery, for the next General Assembly of the Presbyterian Church to adopt any measures whatsoever, touching the question of slavery in the United States." Twelve ministers and nine lay elders voted for the resolution. Only two

12. Robert Hastings Nichols, *Presbyterianism in New York State: A History of the Synod and Its Predecessors,* edited and completed by James Hastings Nichols (Philadelphia, 1963), 116, 120, 129.

ministers, Cornish and Wright, voted against it. The white vote reflected ecclesiastical, theological, and economic fears. There was the fear that debate on the slavery question would split a church with a heavy southern contingent. And there was the fear that northern theological conservatives would be outvoted by liberals except where ties with the South, in the main conservative, were maintained. The economic fear was expressed in the denominational journal the *Presbyterian:* "Interference with the prosperity of the whole south was more to be deplored by an evangelical spirit than the present existence of slavery."[13]

There was, indeed, an economic interest in southern slavery for the General Assembly itself. In 1835 about $96,000 had been transferred by the assembly's trustees from northern stockholdings to southwestern banks, where a lively domestic slave trade was enabling the payment of high interest rates. The assembly's annual income for that year was increased by $2,660. In 1836 more holdings were transferred and in 1837, more again.[14]

Some three and a half years later Wright notified the Presbytery of New York of his withdrawal in order to join the Third Presbytery. It can only be assumed that the Third Presbytery's being more favorable to revivalism and to active abolitionism made that body seem a more congenial association than the one Wright was leaving. And, as will be noted, Samuel Cox, one of the architects of the Third Presbytery, had become a close friend and special admirer of both Cornish and Wright during the mid-1830s. The surprising fact, then, is not that Wright shifted presbyteries, but that Cornish did not. Perhaps the fact that Cornish had no church of his own at this time would have made the move more problematic for him.

Although the differences between the outlook of the Presbytery of New York and that of the Third Presbytery were significant, neither group could muster enough concern for slaves or oppressed free blacks to be an adequate instrument for Cornish and Wright's drive toward radical reform. Two new organizations founded in the early 1830s, the national black conventions and the American Anti-Slavery Society, gave more promise. It was the need of Cincinnati's black people for a new home and

13. Murray, *Presbyterians and the Negro,* 92f.; Minutes of the Presbytery of New York, April 20, 21, 1836; *Presbyterian,* April 30, 1836, cited by Victor B. Howard, "The Anti-Slavery Movement in the Presbyterian Church" (Ph.D. dissertation, Ohio State University, 1961), 33f.

14. Howard, "Anti-Slavery Movement," 34.

the threat of violence in other cities similar to that in Cincinnati that provided the impetus for the first of the national conventions. In July 1830 several representatives of the Ohio blacks, doubtless encouraged by Cornish's supportive editorials of the previous fall in the *Rights of All,* had come to New York City seeking help. A public meeting at the Abyssinian Baptist Church had formed the Wilberforce Colonization Society to effect land purchases in Canada and to help organize a colony thereon. A committee of five chosen to work out specific next steps included Theodore Wright, who had been at the First Colored Presbyterian Church only eighteen months. One immediate consequence of this committee's work was that AME bishop Richard Allen summoned a few black leaders to a conference in Philadelphia in September 1830, and this group initiated the annual black conventions of 1831 through 1835. Although neither Cornish nor Wright was active in these gatherings, what the conventions did and did not accomplish was important for subsequent black activism.[15]

It is difficult to pinpoint the accomplishments of these five black conventions. They considered and issued statements on many of the matters that Cornish had dealt with in his journals in 1827 and 1829: the American Colonization Society, black education, temperance, the persecution of free blacks, and colonization in Canada.[16] However, these assemblies rarely moved from speeches, committee reports, and annual addresses to other, more direct means of empowering blacks or influencing whites. Perhaps the greatest long-term achievement of the gatherings was to give as many as thirty-five able and articulate blacks—mostly laymen from places as far apart as Maine and Washington, D.C.—a chance to get to know one another and a forum in which they could share strongly held convictions on race matters or could thrash out differences. One significance of the conventions was that they built a network of associations on which Cornish, his fellow proprietor, Philip Bell, and his junior editor, Charles Ray, could capitalize when they launched another journal, the *Colored American,* in the spring of 1837. If H. N. Christian, Cornish's biographer, was right in saying that the founding of black newspapers led directly to the black national conventions of the early 1830s, it was

15. Cornish remained on the periphery of the annual gatherings, perhaps because of the early movement's anticlerical bias after Bishop Allen's death in the spring of 1831. As for Wright, he was probably too new in the New York City community in 1830 to 1831 to be a natural choice as a delegate. Moreover, he was being stretched to the limit in trying to raise funds for a church building, and during much of 1832 he was desperately ill.

16. See Howard H. Bell (ed.), *Minutes of the Proceedings of the National Negro Conventions, 1830–1864* (New York, 1969).

equally true that the black press of the late 1830s was a less parochially New York City enterprise than it might have been, thanks to the preceding conventions.

By 1835 Cornish was fundamentally at odds with the point of view of the Pennsylvania laymen who tended to dominate the conventions, especially the wealthy William Whipper, James Forten, and Robert Purvis. The 1835 convention, 40 percent of whose delegates were Pennsylvanians, created the American Moral Reform Society to implement its concerns. When Cornish began editing the *Colored American* in 1837, he made clear his judgment that this society was a futile organization. Although the general goals of these "moral reformers" were unexceptionable, these liberals, declared Cornish, lacked both "definite objects of benevolence and definite measures of action." Equally important, these Philadelphians were too closely tied to William Lloyd Garrison and his stress on moral suasion to the exclusion of political activism. Finally, the Reform Society's leaders were too anxious to play down their blackness in the interest of full integration of blacks and whites.[17]

Cornish did become involved, heart and soul, in one national convention project for a few months. When delegates gathered in Philadelphia in 1831, several white men with a special interest in the black situation proposed the founding of a black college. One of these whites, Rev. S. S. (often referred to as Simeon) Jocelyn, had been born and brought up in New Haven and he had studied with Nathaniel Taylor, whose theology was a Congregational parallel to that of some New School Presbyterians. Licensed to preach in 1822, Jocelyn had begun to serve a small congregation drawn from the New Haven black community. By 1827 he had identified himself with black opposition to the American Colonization Society.[18] In 1829, when Jocelyn's congregation had been formally organized into a church and he had been ordained, Theodore Wright had been present, along with a large percentage of the New Haven black community.[19] By 1831 Jocelyn was convinced that New Haven would be the ideal location for the first black college.

The white men other than Jocelyn who were welcomed to the 1831 national black convention included Arthur Tappan, New York silk merchant, ardent Evangelical, and philanthropist, and William Lloyd Gar-

17. *Colored American,* August 26, 1837.

18. *Freedom's Journal,* August 1, 1827.

19. Handwritten account (probably by Simeon [or S. S.] Jocelyn) in Amos Beman Scrap Book (Amos G. Beman Papers), III.

rison, whose hard-hitting abolitionist paper, the *Liberator,* was entering its sixth month of publication. Jocelyn, Tappan, and Garrison, upon invitation, presented to the convention a plan for founding a college "for the liberal education of young men of Colour, on the Manual Labor System." The curriculum was to have a strong scientific component and also give practical training in agriculture and mechanical trades. The trio endorsed New Haven as the site and $20,000 as the sum needed to launch the institution. An anonymous donor (Arthur Tappan) had already pledged $1,000 if the other $19,000 could be raised. Convention delegates asked about New Haven as the location and were assured that its citizens were "friendly, generous, pious, and humane," its laws just, its contacts with wealthy blacks in the West Indies promising, and the presence of Yale College an advantage for a new institution of learning. The convention unanimously adopted this plan for a college, but with the stipulation that the majority of its trustees should be black. Samuel Cornish, who had proposed such a college some two years earlier, was unanimously chosen general agent for the institution and was charged with the collection of funds. Arthur Tappan was appointed treasurer. Cornish began soliciting contributions for the college in Philadelphia, where he was well-known from a decade or more earlier. He was greatly encouraged by the liberality of donations.[20]

By early September New Haven whites proved to be far less hospitable than Jocelyn had portrayed them at the convention. In part they had been shocked by recent violence in Virginia. In late August Nat Turner had led at least seventy slaves in a bloody revolt. Fifty-seven whites had been killed, and over a hundred slaves had died—some lynched, some tried and executed. The white reactions over the country were often hysterical. Many in the North, as well as in the South, found confirmation for their suspicion that educated blacks were a threat to white society. Furthermore, prominent abolitionists such as Arthur Tappan and William Lloyd Garrison were wrongly blamed for the Turner revolt.

In New Haven many citizens reacted with horror to word of the plans to locate a black college there. Tappan's brother Lewis later recalled, "The people seemed to fear that the city would be overrun with negroes from all parts of the world . . . 'A negro college by the side of Yale College!' 'The City of Elms disgraced forever!' 'It must not and shall not be!' Even persons of calm judgment and philanthropic views on most sub-

20. "Minutes and Proceedings of the First Annual Convention of the People of Colour . . . 1831," in Bell (ed.), *Minutes of the National Negro Conventions,* 5–9.

jects, were carried away by the clamor."[21] The mayor of New Haven called a public meeting. Resolutions were presented: (1) The combined enterprises of immediate emancipation of slaves and educating free blacks represented "an unwarrantable and dangerous interference" with the interests of whites, and (2) founding a college for blacks in New Haven would damage Yale College and several schools for girls also located there; (3) hence the officials and citizenry of New Haven planned to use all lawful means to prevent such a development. Some seven hundred voted for these resolutions. Jocelyn, Roger Baldwin (later governor of Connecticut and United States senator), and two others opposed them.[22] The black college project had been dealt a mortal blow. Summoned to the 1832 national black convention, Cornish announced pledges of between $2,000 and $3,000, but there is no indication that he ever renewed fund-raising for a college.[23]

At the time he was fund-raising in Philadelphia, Cornish had been serving as temporary pastor for Philadelphia's First African Presbyterian Church. In the summer of 1832 he returned to New York City. The Philadelphia church, which had tried unsuccessfully in 1824 to woo him back from the First Colored Presbyterian Church in New York, undoubtedly had tried to keep him. But New York City had been Cornish's wife's lifelong community; the two owned a home there in an attractive location on Fourth Street, and he hoped for better education for his children there than in Philadelphia. Equally important, after ten years in New York and the last five much in the public eye, Cornish must have felt that the community offered him more scope. Also, and this was no small consideration, Theodore Wright, his close friend and co-worker, was firmly located in New York City. The two were soon heavily involved in trying to improve educational opportunities for blacks closer to home than the proposed black college in New Haven.

Early in 1833 Cornish and Wright led the way in founding the Phoenix Society, a practical and visionary effort at elevation through a variety of cultural and economic assistance programs in New York City. AME bishop Christopher Rush was named president. Cornish was employed as general agent, money for his salary being donated by Arthur Tappan, treasurer of the organization. The aims of the society were basic educa-

21. Lewis Tappan, *The Life of Arthur Tappan* (New Haven, 1870), 148f.

22. "Negro College," New Haven *Palladium,* reprinted in Niles *Register,* October 1, 1831; Tappan, *Life of Arthur Tappan,* 150.

23. "Minutes and Proceedings of the Second Annual Convention . . . of the Free People of Color . . . 1832," in Bell (ed.), *Minutes of the National Negro Conventions,* 24, 28.

tion for children, vocational advancement for young men, and cultural stimulation for adults. The Dorcas societies, which Cornish had used in 1828 to increase black children's school going, were revived, and women who loaned destitute children the needed clothes were encouraged to reclaim them if such children failed to attend school. Centers were to be set up to assist young men toward apprenticeships as mechanics and toward longer-term employment. A host of cultural opportunities for adults also were planned: a lecture series, a number of circulating libraries, and "mental feasts" at which black men and women read and discussed essays or poems written by some of their number. The Phoenix Society organized branches in several of the city's wards, and homes were visited to encourage blacks to participate. Although there is no hard evidence as to the scope of programs actually carried out, and although Cornish was the only staff member charged with follow-through, much seems to have been accomplished. At the national convention in June 1833 in Philadelphia, it was unanimously recommended that Phoenix Society branches be formed in every state on the model of those in New York City. In December 1833, at the founding of the American Anti-Slavery Society, whites and blacks cited the work of the Phoenix Society as one of the foremost antislavery forces in the country.[24]

Closest to the hearts of Cornish and Wright of all the spin-offs from the Phoenix Society was the founding of a high school for blacks that would equip them for teaching, preaching, or college admission more adequately than anything available in New York City. As noted earlier, the closest approach to a good grammar school, with elements of a high school, available to New York City youth had been the African Free Boys School taught by the longtime white principal Charles C. Andrews. But black leaders in the early 1830s were pressing the New York Manumission Society to employ more blacks as teachers in its schools. Andrews, under fire for blatant remarks about race and caste differences and for showing too much approval of the American Colonization Society, had resigned. In spite of his social conservatism, Andrews had been uniquely able to carry some of his students into advanced secondary education. On his leaving, there was all the more crying need for schooling at a higher level than any available. Wright and Cornish, joined by the black Episcopal priest Peter Williams, Jr., took the lead in trying to meet that need.

24. American Anti-Slavery Society, *First Annual Report* (New York, 1834), 46. By 1836 Wright had succeeded Rush as president of the Phoenix Society.

Williams's own education, like Cornish's and Wright's, had been extensive, though much of it in the form of individual tutoring. Born about 1780, Williams was Cornish's senior by ten to fifteen years. His father had been a slave until 1796, when he had bought his own freedom, and had eventually owned his own home and other property. He had also been one of the founders of the parent AME Zion church. Young Peter, like his father, was a person of marked ambition. Having graduated from the African Free School, he had become an Episcopalian and studied for the Episcopal priesthood with a local rector. Having worshiped for many years with a black congregation at Trinity Church, in 1818 Williams had organized this group as a separate black church, later named Saint Philip's Episcopal Church.[25]

In 1833 Wright, Cornish, and Williams opened a private high school for blacks headed by a white principal who had studied at Yale and Amherst. The Phoenix High School had "ten or twelve promising youths" by the end of the year.[26] By 1836, with Theodore Wright as president of its board of trustees and Cornish on its finance committee, the school was advertising itself in a number of white-edited newspapers as designed "to give colored youth of good talent and morals, a more extended education than they can procure . . . in the public school or otherwise."[27] The school noted that many of its students were deserving of scholarship aid, having the character and intellect entitling them to the education, yet being unable to pay the tuition. To keep the school afloat, $1,500 to $1,800 a year was needed. Cornish and David Ruggles (who was by this time executive secretary of the New York Vigilance Committee, which aided fugitive slaves) had been designated fund-raisers for the school. Sometime in 1836 or early 1837 a female division of the high school was opened in a room under the Broadway Tabernacle, a church recently built to replace the Chatham Street Chapel as a larger New York base for Charles Finney's revival preaching. This girls' high school soon had thirty-five or more students. Both schools were closed down from time to time for lack of money and disappeared for good by 1838.

During the early years of the Phoenix High School, three institutions

25. Mabee, *Black Education in New York State*, 22; Rayford W. Logan and Michael Winston (eds.), *Dictionary of American Negro Biography* (New York, 1982), 660; *Colored American*, March 28, 1840.

26. Mabee, *Black Education in New York State*, 58.

27. Examples of newspapers include the *New York Evangelist*, September 24, 1836, and the *Emancipator*, September 29, 1836.

headed by whites and providing good secondary education for blacks emerged. Wright and Cornish watched their progress with deep interest. The Quaker Prudence Crandall's girls' school in Canterbury, Connecticut, had met with angry resistance when, in 1832, Crandall had admitted the daughter of a worthy local black farmer. White parents withdrew their children, and Crandall proceeded to recruit black girls through the *Liberator.* In April 1833 a new school opened, bringing girls from Philadelphia, New York, Providence, and Boston. A state law was passed banning any school's admission of blacks not living in Connecticut. Canterbury residents tried to burn the school and threw manure into its well. Grocers refused to sell Crandall food, and she was forced to close the school down in 1834. A few months before this school closed, Gerrit Smith, inveterate white philanthropist and Evangelical radical, had opened a manual labor school for sixteen-year-old black males at his home near Syracuse. He had appealed to Cornish, Wright, and Williams to refer able black students to him, which they did, acutely aware of how much rode on their endorsements. Anxious over the Canterbury debacle, which had come so soon after that provoked by the proposed black college in New Haven, Wright wrote Smith, "I presume that before this you have heard that the unprincapalled people of Canterbury have at length persecuted Miss Crandall's School out of existence. An event the most disgraceful and humbling, to the land of intelligence and reputed liberal moral sentiment. . . . Thanks to our Great Protector that hitherto He hath thrown around you and your much loved school, his preserving care."[28] Smith closed down his school after a couple of years, but evidently not because of local opposition.

A more successful radical white effort at black education occurred at the Oneida Institute, also in upper New York State, where Henry Garnet would spend four years and Amos Beman, one. Becoming president of this four-year college in 1833, the Evangelical Congregational minister Beriah Green continued its classical education in a manual labor setting but also committed it to radical abolitionism and to the admission of students irrespective of race. Green seems never to have had the kind of ongoing relationship with black leaders cultivated by Gerrit Smith, yet

28. Ralph V. Harlow, *Gerrit Smith, Philanthropist and Reformer* (New York, 1939), 61; Peter Williams to Gerrit Smith, with postscript on Samuel Cornish's and Theodore Wright's evaluations differing from Williams', August 19, 1834, Theodore Wright to Gerrit Smith, September 29, 1834, both in Gerrit Smith Papers, George Arents Research Library for Special Collections, Syracuse University, Syracuse, New York.

he and his college, which survived for eleven years and admitted at least fourteen Afro-Americans, surely were well known to Wright and Cornish. Indeed, Wright, young Henry Garnet's pastor, may have been instrumental in his application for admission to Oneida in 1835.[29]

Wright and Cornish were as much involved in organized abolition activities in the 1830s as in the promotion of black education. The American Anti-Slavery Society, the most important national abolition institution, was founded in 1833. Many people and events had set the stage. Runaway slaves had opened the eyes of many northern whites to the bitter realities of life in slavery. The slave conspiracies of Gabriel Prosser in Virginia in 1800 and of Denmark Vesey in South Carolina in 1822, as well as the revolt of Nat Turner in 1831, had further eroded the myth of the slave system as a benevolent patriarchy. The Free African Society, organized by Richard Allen and Absalom Jones in Philadelphia in 1787, though originally defined as a mutual assistance society, had soon expanded into antislavery agitation, prevention of the kidnapping of free blacks into slavery, and cooperation with white groups committed to emancipation. By the early 1830s there were approximately fifty black antislavery organizations in the United States. Among whites, the chief credit for early crusading against slavery must go to individual Quakers such as John Woolman and Anthony Benezet, to the Society of Friends as a whole for having rid its membership of slave owning by 1800, and to state and local manumission societies.

For all the gradual preparation, there were brand-new elements in the antislavery picture by 1833. These would bring a degree of white immediatism and of systematic organization never before seen. First, as has been shown, the free black presence in the United States and the group's intense convictions about the moral atrocity of slavery were making themselves felt in a more public way. The black newspapers published from 1827 through 1829, as well as the annual national black conventions, which had an unmistakable abolitionist witness, were the most conspicuous examples of this increasingly audible free black voice. Second, white Evangelicalism, with its revivalistic dynamic and its stress on implementing a person's conversion through morally right behavior, was producing some Christians ardently committed to social justice, as well as to disciplined personal conduct. Arthur and Lewis Tappan, S. S. Jocelyn, and as will be shown, Theodore Weld, came out of this background. And

29. Milton Sernett, *Abolition's Axe: Beriah Green, Oneida Institute and the Black Freedom Struggle* (Syracuse, 1986), chap. 4.

William Lloyd Garrison, though early disillusioned with the church, was committed to social, perfectionist goals consistent with those of radical Evangelicalism.

Finally, the new antislavery momentum had fresh organizing techniques to draw upon in the 1830s. Some of these had been developed in the British abolition movement, which had reached a climax in parliamentary legislation in the very year of the founding of the American Anti-Slavery Society. But closer to home, the American benevolent empire of missionary, education, and moral reform societies had developed its own techniques. These groups, including the American Colonization Society, had complex and effective organizations for winning new members and for raising money. Here then was the context within which a number of remarkable individuals, white and black, fashioned an antislavery network more extensive and more radical than hitherto.[30]

Sixty black and white delegates met in Philadelphia in early December 1833 to found the American Anti-Slavery Society. The Declaration of Sentiments of the new body had been composed by Garrison. Harking back to the Declaration of Independence, also signed in Philadelphia, Garrison's document declared that the aim of this society was to complete the work of the Founding Fathers. To enjoy liberty is an inalienable right. To deny it is to usurp God's role. All those laws that sanction slavery are thus presumptuous violations of God's intention and contrary to the law of nature—hence null and void. The delegates pledged themselves to rely on persuasion to bring an end to the monstrous evil of slavery. Persuasion was to be exerted on the government of each state by its citizens, and all United States citizens could press the national government to end slavery in the Federal District and in the territories.

Among the score or more black men who eventually signed the constitution of the new antislavery society, fully half were or would become ministers—the majority Presbyterian or Congregational. Samuel Cornish, Theodore Wright, his father, R. P. G. Wright, and Peter Williams, Jr., were chosen to sit on the board of managers. By the following spring Cornish, the younger Wright, and Williams were members of the much smaller executive committee, made up exclusively of New Yorkers. Events were soon to prove that being on the central committee of this first national abolition society was no safe, honorific position.

In retrospect, it is clear that one of the most radical aspects of the

30. Donald G. Mathews, "The Second Great Awakening as an Organizing Process, 1780–1830: An Hypothesis," *American Quarterly,* XXI (1969), 23–43.

founding of this new reform society was that the original signatories were both white and black, as well as that, through much of the next seven years, Cornish and Wright sat on its seven-man executive committee. They thus joined in signing the addresses to the public that this body issued from time to time, to lay false rumors to rest or to clarify the real goals of the society. These working associations between whites and blacks (few though the blacks were) and the joint speech making at annual meetings of national and regional antislavery societies meant, for many whites, a dramatic expansion of awareness. The society brought a new realization of the intellectual abilities of black leaders and of the intensity of their outrage over the continuation of slavery in the South and the repression of free blacks in the North. For blacks such as Cornish, Wright, and Williams, having whites publicly join forces with them in an unqualified condemnation of slave owning was surely encouraging. However, the public association of black leaders with white abolitionists could also be dangerous. Negrophobia was raised to a new pitch when the theoretical equalitarianism of white abolitionists was expressed in the appointment of some black leaders to positions of responsibility in the new national society.

A historian of mob violence in Jacksonian America has counted forty-eight antiabolition and racial incidents in the 1830s and 1840s. Of these, nearly three-fourths occurred between 1833 and 1838. It has been noted that European immigrant hostility against blacks had grown with the substantial influx into the major northern cities of free blacks and fugitive slaves during the 1820s. That influx continued during the 1830s. Hard evidence also shows that the growth of wealth among some blacks, the appearance of handsome black-owned homes and substantial black-owned churches, and the presence of a cultivated and well-dressed coterie of black men and women in cities such as Philadelphia and New York all provoked lower-class, and perhaps upper-class, white resentment.[31]

The most destructive of the race riots in New York City before the Civil War occurred only seven months after the founding of the American Anti-Slavery Society and was as much a procolonization and antiabolitionist mob action as it was antiblack. Events in 1832 and 1833 had convinced colonizationists that they had to strike back, or their movement would decline into irrelevance. Local antislavery societies, usually

31. Richards, *Gentlemen of Property,* 14; Emma J. Lapsansky, "'Since They Got Those Separate Churches': Afro-Americans and Racism in Jacksonian Philadelphia," *American Quarterly,* XXXII (1980), 54f., 61, 64.

also anticolonizationist, were on the rise. The ACS's Fourth of July collections had fallen from $12,000 in 1832 to $4,000 in 1833, and the society was facing a $46,000 deficit. The campaign of public criticism of African colonization launched by Cornish in 1827 seemed close to victory. It gained an influential new recruit in the spring of 1834, when Samuel Cox, a popular white Presbyterian preacher, published in the *New York Evangelist* a lengthy recantation of his former strong support for the American Colonization Society. Moreover, he made clear that the one single reason for that shift had been his belated realization that thoughtful free blacks were, almost to a man, opposed to the ACS. Cox cited Cornish, Wright, and Williams as having labored with him patiently and persuasively.[32]

Confidently aggressive methods had characterized white abolitionism from the publication of the first issue of Garrison's *Liberator* in 1831 to the founding of the American Anti-Slavery Society in 1833. Arthur Tappan had long since become notorious for frontal attacks on social behavior, such as prostitution, which he considered blatantly sinful. He and his less well-to-do brother Lewis brought the same vehement moralism to bear on the colonization and slavery questions, thereby winning many followers among serious Christians, both ministers and laity. These aggressive methods, however, in no small part because they were proving effective, were an important element in the buildup of tensions that issued in the New York City riots of July 1834.

During June, New York City papers boiled with slanderous accusations against abolitionists, often made by those same papers and editors that Cornish had tried to call to account in 1826 for their Negrophobia. Now those primarily under fire were radical white Evangelicals, and the accusations often played on widespread white anxiety about racial amalgamation. At this juncture something happened in Cox's church that raised the temperature still further. Arthur Tappan, a pewholder in the Laight Street Presbyterian Church, arrived one Sunday morning to find Samuel Cornish waiting on the steps. For Cornish, who lived on West Fourth Street, Cox's church was far more conveniently located than was Wright's church, over two miles downtown, where he often worshiped. Tappan invited Cornish in and helped him and his children find a seat along the side of the church. In the words of Lewis Tappan, "No little excitement was the result. The devotions of the congregation were much disturbed. The services being over, one or more of the elders or trustees

32. Richards, *Gentlemen of Property,* 23–26. Cox's statement was republished in the *Liberator,* May 3, 1834.

called upon the offending member and requested him in terms very like threatening not to repeat the offense." Cox, seeking to calm the troubled waters, used his customary midweek lecture to warn his congregation against inhuman prejudice. He wondered aloud how white the inhabitants of the Middle East had been or how white Jesus himself would seem to Cox's church members. The *Courier and Enquirer* then attacked Cox for telling his congregation that Jesus was a colored man.[33]

As popular feeling mounted against Cox and Tappan, other white radicals also became the victims of angry rumor. Henry G. Ludlow, minister of the Spring Street Presbyterian Church (Third Presbytery), was accused of having performed the marriage of a white woman and a black man. William Green, an abolitionist merchant, had, it was said, entertained black men at his home to introduce them to his unmarried daughters.[34]

On July 4 blacks and whites gathered in the Chatham Street Chapel to celebrate the ending of slavery in New York State exactly seven years earlier. Crowds of unruly whites, responding to clear invitations in the *Courier and Enquirer* and the *Commercial Advertiser,* filled the galleries and tried to break up the meeting by hooting and stamping. On July 9 a large crowd collected outside the Chatham Street Chapel to protest an integrated antislavery meeting they believed was taking place. When the meeting failed to materialize, the crowd surged uptown to the Bowery Theatre, then back down to Lewis Tappan's home on Rose Street. They broke into the house (Tappan had removed his family earlier) and threw into the street and burned five hundred dollars' worth of furniture. During the next two days the violence escalated. Eventually up to twenty thousand whites were involved. Some took control of the Sixth Ward, north and east of City Hall, the chief center of the black population. Others gravitated further north and west to the churches and homes of notorious white abolitionist clergy.

Influential whites in the city, including Mayor Cornelius W. Lawrence, did little to stop the rioting until, after a number of days of destruction, it seemed likely that the homes and stores of the "respectable" members of the community would soon be under attack. The mayor finally called

33 Tappan, *Life of Arthur Tappan,* 194f.; *Colored American,* October 28, 1837. Lewis Tappan's recollection, thirty-five years after the event, was that Arthur Tappan had invited Cornish into Tappan's own pew. Cornish, three years after the episode, recalled being helped to an inconspicuous spot in the church. This book has followed Cornish's account.

34. Bertram Wyatt-Brown, *Lewis Tappan and the Evangelical War Against Slavery* (Cleveland, 1969), 109–16.

up the city militia and, with reinforcements from Albany, eventually quelled the violence. The rampage had been costly. Three churches had been heavily damaged or destroyed—those of Peter Williams, Jr., and of the white abolitionists Samuel Cox and Henry G. Ludlow. Williams's rectory had been demolished and heavy damage done to the homes of Cox, Ludlow, and Lewis Tappan. An African free school and at least a dozen black homes had been gutted. A mob had roamed the heavily black, low-income Five Points area, unchecked. Whites had been told to put lighted candles in their windows, and homes with darkened windows were assumed to be appropriate targets for demolition. The night sky was lit up by burning buildings.[35] The accurate report that Arthur Tappan had armed and stationed three dozen of his clerks and friends within his store was all that had prevented a crowd from breaking in and ransacking it.[36]

Soon after the rioting had ended, Cornish joined six white members of the executive committee of the American Anti-Slavery Society in a letter to Mayor Lawrence. They made clear that the members of the society had never done or planned "anything inconsistent with their duty as patriots, as Christians, as friends of the Union, and of . . . this city." Reiterating the society's commitment to immediate emancipation without expatriation, they quoted from the body's constitution to prove its disavowal of resorting to violence to achieve its ends. They again declared the AASS's opposition to the American Colonization Society, and in a hard-hitting conclusion Cornish and the others identified the sources of the violence: "We believe some of the daily newspapers (by publishing that there would be meetings when there were to be none, and misrepresenting our principles and actions) excited the populace, and are the authors of all the disorders; and we affirm that the stories in circulation about individuals adopting colored children, ministers uniting white and colored people in marriage, abolitionists encouraging intermarriages, exciting the people of color to assume airs, &c. &c. &c. are wholly unfounded."[37]

Of all black leaders, it was Peter Williams, Jr., who paid the heaviest price during and after the July 1834 riot. His church and rectory had been destroyed. His bishop wrote him advising (that is, instructing) him to

35. Richards, *Gentlemen of Property,* 120.

36. Tappan, *Life of Arthur Tappan,* 203–16; Joel T. Headley, *The Great Riots of New York, 1712–1873* (1873; rpr. Indianapolis, 1970), 79–95; Wyatt-Brown, *Lewis Tappan,* 117–21; Richards, *Gentlemen of Property,* 115–22; Curry, *The Free Black in Urban America,* 101f.

37. Lewis Tappan, Arthur Tappan, John Rankin, Elizur Wright, Jr., Joshua Leavitt, William Goodell, and Samuel Cornish, "To the Honorable Cornelius W. Lawrence," *Emancipator,* July 22, 1834 (Microfilm copy in Carter and Ripley [eds.], *BAP,* reel 1, item 398).

resign from every aspect of the work of the American Anti-Slavery Society and to publicize his resignation as widely as possible. Williams, himself uneasy about pressing too fast for black peoples' rights, followed his superior's instructions.[38]

Theodore Wright's story, during 1834 and thereafter, provides a striking contrast to Williams's. It could be strongly argued that Wright's home and church were as vulnerable to attack in the riots of July 5 to 12, 1834, as those of Williams. Wright had been appointed to the board of managers of the American Anti-Slavery Society in December 1833 and to its executive committee in May 1834, as had Williams. There is, moreover, no evidence to indicate that Wright had absented himself from board or committee meetings. Wright's First Colored Presbyterian Church must have had a church building and congregation of roughly the same size as Saint Philip's, Williams' church, and many of its members were also middle- and upper-class blacks. Moreover, Wright's church, at Frankfort and William streets, could not have been more than two or three blocks from Lewis Tappan's home on Rose Street, which had been an early target of the mob. Two facts, however, were to Wright's advantage. He had only held his pastorate for five years, whereas Williams had ministered to the people in the Saint Philip's building for fifteen years. And rank-and-file rioters may not have associated the formerly Lutheran "swamp church" with a black minister and congregation who had been in possession less than three years. Whatever the reason, Wright was profoundly grateful to have been spared. He wrote to the white radical Gerrit Smith six weeks after the riot: "I feel that myself & dear People are called upon for the exercise of the liveliest gratitude to God for the special preservation which saved us from the fury of the lawless Mob. While the sanctuaries of our brethren were wantonly assailed, ours was saved from injure."[39]

Wright continued publicly to identify himself with aggressive abolitionism, black and white. He was one of five black men on the committee to arrange a large black gathering on August 1, 1834, celebrating passage of the act of Parliament ending slavery in the British West Indies. These same five affixed their names to a printed address, "To Our Colored Brethren," which aimed to broadcast the themes and the spirit of the speeches given at the August 1 jubilee. The document crackled with

38. Carter G. Woodson (ed.), *The Mind of the Negro as Reflected in Letters Written During the Crisis, 1800–1860* (1926; rpr. New York, 1969), 629–34.

39. Theodore Wright to Gerrit Smith, September 29, 1834, in Gerrit Smith Papers.

moral outrage over the continued exploitation of slaves: "*What shall be done for* THEM? What shall WE do?—DO? . . . We will fill every continent and island with the story of the WRONGS done to our brethren, by the Christian, church-going, psalm-singing, long-prayer-making, lynching, tar and feathering, man-roasting, human-flesh-dealers of America! —DO? We will *preach* the Declaration of Independence, till it begins to be put in PRACTICE."[40]

The identification of the document's authors with white abolitionists was total. Blacks should help them in two basic ways. First, blacks should develop good character among themselves: "Let us rear our sons honest, industrious, intelligent—and above all, give them GOOD TRADES, and teach them never to be ashamed of their work or their people. . . . Let us live down prejudice and calumny." Second, blacks can help by contributing money to the cause: "The abolitionists have stood so many mobbings, lynchings, tar-and-featherings and brick-battings in behalf of human rights that we can trust them with our money, while they continue to give as good an account of it as for three years past."[41]

Striking as was Wright's share in this militant document issued so soon after the rioting, the address only partially expressed his own view of how the future was going to work out for black people. In a letter written in late September to Gerrit Smith, Wright responded, from the depths of his biblical faith, to the mob violence that had closed Prudence Crandall's school for black girls, had destroyed Peter Williams's church and home, and had recently ravaged the chief black section in Philadelphia: "O how vane, how utterly futil are the attempts of poor, short sighted narrow hearted men to keep down those whom Jehovah designs to raise from ignorance & oppression."[42] It seems fair to assume that the long-range, God-dependent assurance expressed by Wright in this letter was an integral part of his preaching to his own congregation during those turbulent times. Presumably this tempering of radical reformism with the affirmation that the destinies of races and nations are in God's hands also characterized Wright's conversations with white Presbyterian clergy. If so, it may explain why, remarkably, Wright's fellow ministers in the presbytery never minuted any disapproval of his energetic involvement in the inflammatory abolitionist cause.

40. Quotations used by permission of the Houghton Library, Harvard University (Microfilm copy in Carter and Ripley [eds.], *BAP,* reel 1, item 498).

41. *Ibid.*

42. Theodore Wright to Gerrit Smith, September 29, 1834, in Gerrit Smith Papers; Lapsansky, "'Since They Got Those Separate Churches,'" 63f.

In one respect, violent whites were accurately reading the situation. The 1830s was indeed a decade of unusually close association—closer than before or after—between a few black leaders and a few white abolitionists. This being the case, how did Theodore Wright and Samuel Cornish view such men as Garrison, the Tappans, Samuel Cox, and Gerrit Smith? And how did these whites view their black co-workers?[43]

A first glance reveals an extensive and deep respect felt for Garrison among blacks. Indeed, the *Liberator* would never have survived but for early black support. About 90 percent of the 450 subscribers gained during 1831 were black, and even in 1834 nearly 75 percent of the 2,300 subscribers were black. Theodore Wright, in an address delivered at the 1837 annual convention of the New York State Anti-Slavery Society, would give Garrison his due in a stirring review of the previous twenty years of efforts to liberate blacks in America. He accorded first place, as pioneers, to the three thousand blacks massed in the Bethel AME Church in 1817 to protest the American Colonization Society's program. Second came Samuel Cornish, whose *Freedom's Journal* had first given black people a printed voice. And next, declared Wright, came the *Liberator,* "the voice of Garrison speaking in trumpet tones! It was like the voice of an angel of mercy! Hope, hope then cheered our faith."[44]

As to Garrison's estimation of Wright, the surviving evidence is slight. The white editor's letters to his wife occasionally made reference to attending Sunday service at Wright's church. Garrison and Wright seem to have remained on amicable terms, even through the difficulties of 1839 and 1840, when Wright and most other black leaders in New York City adhered to the large splinter group in the AASS that rejected Garrisonian policies. When Wright died in 1847, the *Liberator* ran a lengthy obituary tribute and a description of the mammoth turnout of blacks for the extended funeral march through the streets of New York City.[45]

Garrison had as little to say about Cornish in his correspondence as about Wright, though he did once report on having heard an excellent sermon by Cornish. In the late 1830s Cornish and Garrison became vig-

43. As the next chapter will show, a great many white abolitionists were skittish about personal association with blacks, even in abolition society meetings.

44. Herbert Aptheker (ed.), *A Documentary History of the Negro People in the United States* (New York, 1965), I, 108f; *Colored American,* October 14, 1837. Wright's speech, "The Program of the Anti-Slavery Cause," was reprinted in Woodson (ed.), *Negro Orators,* 86–92.

45. William Lloyd Garrison to Helen E. Garrison, from New York City, March 16, 1835, in Walter M. Merrill (ed.), *The Letters of William Lloyd Garrison* (6 vols.; Cambridge, Mass., 1971–81), I, 466; *Liberator,* April 2, 1847.

orous spokesmen for opposing views on principle and strategy in fighting slavery and seeking justice for free blacks. Cornish, himself a minister, objected strenuously to Garrison's progressively more vehement anticlericalism. The black editor was equally critical of Garrison's repudiation of political abolitionism and his favoring moral suasion only. Long before these differences of principle emerged, however, there was evidence of tension, perhaps arising from the two editors' feelings of rivalry as spokesmen for black Americans. As mentioned earlier, in 1832 Garrison had published an account of the succession of black meetings and black resolutions protesting the colonization movement. This retrospect ran from 1817 to 1832, yet it contained no description of the anticolonization role of *Freedom's Journal* under Cornish's editorship in 1827. Early in 1837, in his newly founded *Colored American,* Cornish tried to set the record straight. Reprinting an 1827 editorial against colonization, he wrote, "Our object in republishing the article at this time is, to show that intelligent colored people never had but one view of Colonization. . . . We have for ages been unwavering in the opinion that we should someday possess in our native land, *a perfect equality,* in all respects, with our white brethren. This doctrine is neither Tappan nor Garrison. It is *Bibleism,* and we claim some instrumentality in teaching it to both of these good men."[46] It seems possible that Garrison had been reluctant to give Cornish his due because he did not want to dilute the reputation of the *Liberator* as the sole journal in defense of blacks. Garrison's silence was surely a major reason why almost all historians of abolitionism have labeled Garrison its first militant editor and have not acknowledged Cornish's pioneering role.[47]

That there was bound to be some sense of competition between successful black papers and Garrison's journal was indicated by the comments made by black Garrisonians in 1837 at the launching of the *Colored American:* "If the Liberator is to be injured by it, let it [the *Colored American*] go down. . . . May God rebuke those who would put down the Liberator and its editor." Abolitionist papers, white or black, had a limited clientele in the 1830s. The *Colored American* would eventually secure

46. William Lloyd Garrison to Helen Garrison, April 27, 1834, in Merrill (ed.), *Letters of William Lloyd Garrison,* I, 335; Garrison, *Thoughts on African Colonization,* II, 52–57; *Colored American,* May 13, 1837. This editorial had originally appeared in *Freedom's Journal,* June 8, 1827.

47. An early writer on the work of Samuel Cornish, Bella Gross, was puzzled by this same matter. Bella Gross, "*Freedom's Journal* and *The Rights of All,*" *Journal of Negro History,* XVII (1932), 244*n*11.

around two thousand subscribers, at an unknown cost to the *Liberator.* Financial pressures on both papers may well have intensified the cleavages over principle that began to emerge by the fall of 1837.[48]

Cornish's and Wright's relations with leading New York City white abolitionists during the 1830s were both closer and steadier than those with Garrison. This was in part a matter of geographical proximity, but two other factors were more decisive. First, the black community in New York City was far larger than that in Boston, and the achievements of some of its leaders as businessmen, ministers, and journalists guaranteed a measure of real parity between black leaders and influential white radicals. To put it another way, even if there had been a Garrison living in New York City, he would not have become as dominant a figure as was the Garrison who lived in Boston. Second, and perhaps more important, leading white abolitionists in New York City, such as Arthur and Lewis Tappan and Samuel Cox, were all ardent Evangelical Christians, either laymen or clergy. This meant a congruity of religious commitment between these men and black ministers such as Cornish and Wright. Such congruity, as has been shown, was missing between these two black clergy and Garrison.

In 1834, prior to the riot in New York City, Cox publicly acknowledged the roles of Cornish, Wright, and Williams in opening his eyes on the colonization question. Cox paid tribute to the Christian spirit of these three and their "sagacity in the matter of their own interests." He wrote: "Thousands can give a hearty testimony to their prudence, forbearance, calmness, and correctness of procedure in all things. They have no wild schemes or reckless views: and while my heart has bled at their recitals, it has secretly glorified God in them, in view of the excellent spirit they evince under privations and trials of a sort that few of their white brethren could endure for a moment."[49]

Wright's and Cornish's closest relations with white abolitionists were with Arthur and Lewis Tappan and Gerrit Smith. The association of these black ministers and Smith in connection with his school for black sixteen-year-olds has been noted. Letters from Wright and Cornish to Smith bespoke genuine friendship. Smith had, like Garrison, shown

48. Henry Wright to William Lloyd Garrison, March 1, 1837, in *Liberator,* March 18, 1837. Cornish tried to cooperate with the *Liberator.* In late May he ran a warm notice in his journal of Garrison's paper's having been officially adopted by the Massachusetts Anti-Slavery Society. *Colored American,* May 27, 1837.

49. *New York Evangelist,* excerpted in *Liberator,* May 3, 1834.

unflinching fidelity to principle in the face of turbulent hostility. Ray, Garnet, Beman, and Pennington would also become Smith's correspondents and colleagues. Not infrequently, in times of crisis, they would be beneficiaries of his far-flung financial assistance to causes and people he deemed worthy. Yet Smith was, for them too, far more than an occasional source of desperately needed funds.

Cornish and Wright saw the Tappan brothers frequently and served, in some sense, as their fellow soldiers in frontline combat; through much of the 1830s, all four were members of the executive committee of the American Anti-Slavery Society. And all four would stay together, in the large splinter group opposed to the Garrisonians, when the society split apart in 1840. Arthur and Lewis Tappan had been brought up in Northampton, Massachusetts, in a family committed to orthodox Evangelical Christianity. Their mother had taught them to follow their consciences no matter what others thought of them. They became vivid examples of the Puritan contribution to business and to philanthropic enterprise in the United States. Arthur, elected president of the American Anti-Slavery Society year after year, was the wealthier and more socially conservative of the two. After the furor attendant on his inviting Cornish into his church pew, he avoided any public association with black people except on abolitionist occasions.[50]

Even Lewis Tappan, however, who was less cautious than his brother and had less at stake in business, found it very difficult to distinguish between what was foolhardy and what was right in the social mixing of blacks and whites. Nearly two years after the New York City riots, this Tappan unburdened himself to the young white abolitionist Theodore Weld. He recalled his role as chairman of the planning committee for the first anniversary meetings of the AASS. The committee had arranged to have three choirs, two black and one white. The choirs of Theodore Wright's First Colored Presbyterian Church and of Peter Williams's Saint Philip's (African Episcopal) Church had sat on one side of the Chatham Street Chapel. The white choir of the chapel was on the other side. At the time, this blend of cooperation and segregation had seemed just right. After the July riots, however, said Tappan, "many abolitionists . . . talked about efforts at amalgamation etc. . . . The battle is to be fought right here. Prejudice is to be put down. Christ went among the Publicans

50. As will be spelled out in Chapter 5, Arthur Tappan would be especially criticized, by black leaders and by more radical white abolitionists, for doing so little in employing black people in his business.

and samaratans. (He *ate* with them. Oh, horrible!)—they were the *colored people* of that day—and by so doing made himself of no reputation. Let us follow our Leader!"[51] Lewis Tappan tried hard to challenge the customs of caste where it seemed practicable. On one occasion, he invited the executive committee of the AASS to have a meal at his home, and two of those who came were black (probably Cornish and Wright). In 1835 and 1836 Tappan attempted to persuade the committee on arrangements for the May anniversary meetings of the society to approve Theodore Wright as one of the main speakers. Undoubtedly still nervous from the rioting of 1834, the committee voted the proposal down.[52]

It was natural that black and white abolitionists, who had sat together and listened to one another pray and speak at antislavery society anniversaries, should consider attending one another's churches of a Sunday or founding a new specifically interracial church. Of note is Arthur Tappan's hospitable move in escorting Samuel Cornish into the Laight Street Presbyterian Church in the summer of 1834. Lewis Tappan, embarrassed over segregated seating in the Broadway Tabernacle and frustrated in efforts to desegregate Charles Finney's Chatham Street Chapel, weighed the possibility of joining Wright's church. He talked the matter over with S. S. Jocelyn, who advised against it. There was still a heavy debt to be paid off on the First Colored Presbyterian Church. If Tappan became a member, Jocelyn warned him, "some persons now friendly might excuse themselves from giving." Tappan followed Jocelyn's advice, but he not infrequently attended worship services at Wright's church, sometimes taking a fellow white abolitionist with him. On one occasion, he made an address at the First Colored Presbyterian Church in Wright's absence. Early in 1837 a distinguished New Orleans lawyer and slave owner, who was also a Presbyterian elder, was in New York City and looked up Tappan. He wanted to talk with a member of the executive committee of the American Anti-Slavery Society, being somewhat troubled over owning slaves. Tappan had long conversations with him and took him to Wright's church. The abolitionist later recalled, "On witnessing for the first time a commodious and well-lighted church belonging to colored people, a congregation of well-dressed and respectable persons, an organ and a choir of excellent singers and an educated preacher, [he] exclaimed 'This

51. Lewis Tappan to Theodore Weld, March 15, 1836, in Gilbert H. Barnes and Dwight L. Dumond (eds.), *Letters of Theodore Dwight Weld, Angelina Grimké, and Sarah Grimké*, hereinafter cited as *Weld-Grimké Letters* (2 vols; Gloucester, Mass., 1965), I, 275f.

52. *Ibid.*, 276f.

is a new and interesting scene to me and I shall never forget it. . . . How feelingly the minister prayed for slaveholders! How well they sung! How respectable did the church and congregation appear.'"[53]

The board members of the American Anti-Slavery Society very much wanted Theodore Wright to work for them as a full-time agent. In 1837 the society made him an offer for the third time, this one for $1,000 plus travel expenses (a good salary for the time). His work would have been that of a traveling agent in New England. As Weld put it, pressing for the employment of Wright and other blacks, "Surely twenty-five colored men of such talents, characters, and address . . . would do more in three months to kill prejudice (and our cause moves only as fast as that dies) than all our operations up to now."[54] Wright turned down this offer, as he had the others, deciding to continue his ministry at the First Colored Presbyterian Church. It is difficult to overestimate the benefits that accrued—for Wright, for his church, for the black community in New York City, and for the abolition and civil rights movements—from Wright's staying with his pastorate until his death in 1847. He found personal nourishment and had a secure base of religious leadership, social status, and political power among black people by being the effective minister of one of the largest black churches in the country.

The combination in Wright of disciplined intellect, tireless effort toward ending the oppression of slaves and free blacks, and fervent religious faith made him especially influential with able and angry young Afro-Americans. This influence particularly affected Charles Ray and Henry Highland Garnet, but also touched Amos Beman. Wright, Ray, and Garnet would work closely with one another toward social and political reform. In no small measure because of Wright's influence, each of these younger men would, in the long run, consider his ministry his central mission, and his efforts toward social justice a natural expression of that central calling.

53. Wyatt-Brown, *Lewis Tappan,* 177; Lewis Tappan Notebook, February 26, May 22, July 24, 1836; February 2, 1840 (MS in Lewis Tappan Papers); Tappan, *Life of Arthur Tappan,* 197f. Note the recurrence of the word *respectable.*

54. Barnes and Dumond (eds.), *Weld-Grimké Letters,* II, 811.

5. BLACK ENTERPRISE, WHITE PREJUDICE, AND THE BIRTH OF A POLITICAL MOVEMENT: CHARLES RAY, SAMUEL CORNISH, AND THEODORE WRIGHT, 1836 TO 1840

A colored man may be blessed with the highest and most cultivated intellect, may be clothed with all the Christian graces, yet as long as he is debarred from an equal participation in political privilege, he will be despised and trampled on by the majority in power.

—*Colored American,* February 23, 1839

The 1820s and early 1830s had seen the birth of black journalism and the beginnings of black Presbyterianism in New York City. In the latter 1830s and early 1840s, vigorous black organizations came into being to foil "slavecatchers" in the North and to secure the black franchise. Although these action programs were especially strong in New York City and New York State, there were parallel developments in other northern cities and states.

The national black conventions that met annually from 1831 to 1835 had spelled out the many forms of racial oppression in the North but had not been able to shape a program to effect change. In the mid-1830s the American Anti-Slavery Society had committed funds and staff to assisting black communities in their efforts to improve schooling and job opportunities, but this white abolitionist concern for free blacks soon faded. Just as black leaders in 1827 had seen the necessity of creating an independent journal to speak for their people, it was evident a decade later that an independent black action program was needed. This program emerged in three forms in New York City and New York State: the New York Vigilance Committee to aid fugitives and foil those who kidnapped blacks into slavery, a succession of petition campaigns to secure the passage of certain state laws, and the launching of another major black newspaper. All three of these institutions were built on the assumption that blacks themselves had to be the primary agents in bringing racial justice to pass. The new newspaper, launched in January 1837 as the *Weekly Advocate,* changed its name in March to the *Colored American* to make this assumption clear.

Theodore Wright would be a major figure in the planning and financing of the work of the New York Vigilance Committee. Samuel Cornish, again drafted for editorial management, would publicize the work of the vigilance committee and the political action campaigns in the pages of the *Colored American.* But the vigilance committee, the political efforts focused on the New York legislature, and the *Colored American* would also owe much to a third black man, Charles Ray, a young would-be minister raised in Massachusetts. Ray was about twenty-five years old when he first came to New York City and met Wright and Cornish. Although he had finished all the formal schooling he would get, most of his education in journalism, black community leadership, and the art of ministry would come through these two men. His work as a roving reporter for Cornish's paper from 1837 to 1839 would aim at something new for Afro-Americans—the systematic spreading of knowledge among blacks across the North as to what was going on in a score of black communities, small and large. Ray had an insatiable interest in people of all sorts and the ability to secure their confidence. His contagious belief in the possibility of their enlarging their lives and his publicizing of local situations in the paper helped individuals and communities take positive steps. Through his itinerancy he built a broad network of acquaintances and friends that would keep the *Colored American* afloat for nearly five years and would be a significant factor, in the early 1840s, in the staging of successful black state conventions.

Born in 1807, the eldest of seven children, Ray had been raised in Falmouth, Massachusetts. It was said that he was proud to be descended from Indians, English settlers, and the first blacks to be brought to New England. His father was a mail-carrier to the island of Martha's Vineyard and his mother a person of inquiring mind and deep religious interests. Having been given access to a New Bedford minister's library, she was said to have read her way through most of his books. After some schooling in Falmouth, Ray went to work for five years on his grandfather's farm in Rhode Island. He then settled on Martha's Vineyard to learn the trade of a bootmaker.[1]

1. Richard Bardolph, *The Negro Vanguard* (New York, 1961), 68; F. T. Ray and H. C. Ray, *Sketch of the Life of Rev. Charles B. Ray* (New York, 1887). The only other published work on Ray is Monroe N. Work, "The Life of Charles B. Ray," *Journal of Negro History,* IV (1919), 361–71. Most of Work's material is taken from the Rays' book and from I. Garland Penn, *The Afro-American Press and Its Editors* (1891; rpr. New York, 1969).

At about the age of twenty-three, Ray experienced a profound Christian conversion, and he resolved to become a Methodist minister. Encouraged by the offer of financial help from some white abolitionist friends, he secured entrance into the Wesleyan Academy in Wilbraham, Massachusetts, near Springfield. There were no other blacks in the school, but the climate was friendly. Three of the trustees, who were influential in the local community, were committed antislavery men. The principal of the school was Willbur Fisk, a broad-minded, Vermont-born Methodist minister who would become the most widely respected Methodist educator in the country. Soon after Ray's arrival at the academy, Fisk was chosen president of Wesleyan University, to be opened the following year in Middletown, Connecticut, under the auspices of the New York and New England conferences of the Methodist church. The academy in Massachusetts and the college in Connecticut were viewed by Methodists in the region as training grounds for future teachers and preachers in the church.[2]

Ray spent two years in Wilbraham, applied for admission to Wesleyan University, and was accepted by Fisk, who had ample information about him. This admission was a bold move, as Fisk must have realized, since the explosive protest in New Haven against opening a college for blacks in that city had occurred only a year prior to Ray's arrival in Middletown. Three Congregational colleges, Middlebury, Amherst, and Bowdoin, had, to be sure, each admitted and graduated an Afro-American in the 1820s. (Bowdoin's black graduate was John Russwurm, associate editor and then editor of *Freedom's Journal.*) However, the Congregational denomination in general, and these colleges in particular, had a primarily northern constituency. Moreover, the Congregationalists were far more decentralized than the Methodists. They had a substantial number of colleges, and no one of them was looked to as the one national training place for its future ministers. Methodists, in contrast, made up a young denomination in America, with a large constituency in the South and without a tradition of higher education for either its clergy or laity. What seemed to be clearly needed, when the Connecticut college opened, was a truly national institution—one drawing from, and sending graduates back to, both the North and the South.[3]

Fisk's associations with southerners were numerous and influential.

2. David Sherman, *History of the Wesleyan Academy, at Wilbraham, Massachusetts, 1817–1890* (Boston, 1893), 195–97.

3. Harold Wade, Jr., *Black Men of Amherst* (Amherst, Mass., 1976), 5–9.

These were primarily with the parents, usually Methodist, of prospective or current Wesleyan undergraduates or with prominent southern Methodists who were seeking Fisk's advice as to staff for schools or colleges in which they had a special interest. Wesleyan University's first entering class included the sons of at least three southerners of considerable means. One of these fathers was Josiah Flournoy, the owner of several plantations and about 140 slaves in Georgia. In sending his second son to Middletown, Flournoy made clear the opportunity and the challenge: "Should your institution do well and the students prove valuable men to the Church and State and not just coxcombs, foplings and spendthrifts as too many of our young graduates do you will meet with much encouragement from the South among our people [that is, Methodists]."[4]

Fisk had sought advice from his Georgia friend before admitting Ray. The counsel, which arrived too late to be helpful, was cautiously approving: "I can see no objection Educating the Colored young man of whom you spoke in your letter more especially if he be really humble and pious and have something of the Missionary Spirit." Fisk had been a strong supporter of the American Colonization Society for a number of years and surely knew of John Russwurm's having gone to an educational post in Liberia only two years before Wesleyan University opened its doors. It seems likely that both he and Flournoy envisaged some comparable mission post in Africa as Ray's appropriate destination.[5]

When Ray arrived at Wesleyan University, his presence quickly roused antagonism among some of the southern students and a few New Englanders. Some of the most excited of his classmates told Fisk that if Ray were not removed, they would go home. Fisk tried, according to a student's report, to show the angry students "the inconsistency and illiberality of their views," but to no effect. He then said he would lay the matter before his trustees and be guided by their decision. The disaffected students passed a resolution requesting the trustees to remove Ray, but by this time Ray had decided that for him to leave the university at once would be better for others and for himself. Evidently the faculty and the majority of the students were sympathetic with him. Indeed, his classmates raised funds to pay his expenses incurred in coming to college and

4. Josiah Flournoy to Willbur Fisk, March 30, 1831, in Willbur Fisk Papers, Wesleyan University Archives, Middletown, Conn. Methodist connections between the South and New England were reinforced by commercial links between southern planters and New England cotton mill owners.

5. Josiah Flournoy to Willbur Fisk, October 10, 1832, in Willbur Fisk Papers.

returning home. The student reporter praised Fisk for having shown his customary "discretion, manliness, wisdom and firmness" in telling Ray that if he chose to stay, he would be protected.[6]

Presumably to prevent another such episode, Wesleyan's board of trustees passed a resolution "that none but male white persons shall be admitted as students at this institution." Although this action was rescinded less than three years later, it and the episode that provoked it decisively tarnished the reputation of Wesleyan University and its president among black activists in the 1830s and 1840s. For Ray it was, so far as is known, his first bitter experience of persecution for being black. For many years he harbored a deep sense of personal outrage over what had been done to him. Although what roads would have been opened for him if he had been allowed to earn a college degree cannot be known, it is known that the brutal shattering of his educational hopes and his subsequent experience living in New York City transformed his understanding of what it meant to be a black American.[7]

After leaving Middletown, Ray evidently applied to other colleges without success and then went to New York City to visit his sister. Soon after arrival he met Amos Freeman, later to be minister of the Siloam (African) Presbyterian Church in Brooklyn; it was Freeman who introduced him to Theodore Wright. The older man immediately took a special interest in Ray. It was to be a distinctive relationship—like that between David and Jonathan in the Old Testament, Ray later told his daughters. Ray set up his trade as a boot maker in the black district in lower Manhattan, and by 1836 he and Cornish were in the business together. Their shop was only a few blocks from Theodore Wright's home and his church. Ray's experiences in New York City over the next few years were a liberal education in the economic, religious, and cultural life of a hugely diverse black population, as well as in its community roles. He came to know the miserably poor, the strikingly successful, and those of modest means. Ray would live in the city for over fifty years and would work with many people in each of these categories. By the end of his long life, he may well have had a fuller exposure to the desperate

6. Report from O[scar] L. S[chafter] to Samuel Dole, a teacher at the academy in Wilbraham, who sent it to William Lloyd Garrison, December 19, 1832 (*Liberator,* January 12, 1833).

7. Actions taken October 10, 1832, and August 5, 1835, reported in Minutes of the Joint Board of Trustees and Visitors, 1830–68 (MS at Wesleyan University Archives, Middletown, Conn.), 17, 34.

needs, the deep grievances, the talents, and the aspirations of the black people of New York City than any other human being of that time.[8]

The latter 1830s was a time of special ferment and creativity among Afro-Americans in New York City. In the spring of 1837 Ray was offered the position of assistant editor of the *Colored American*. As a result of accepting it, he became a major figure in the agitation and accomplishments of this period. The paper, founded by Philip Bell and Samuel Cornish in January 1837 as the *Weekly Advocate,* had been renamed the *Colored American* within a few weeks. The new name was important; it meant recognition that Afro-Americans were distinctive, had their own agenda, and intended to rely on themselves to get ahead with it.

A number of other black-edited papers had appeared, and after a few issues had disappeared, between the demise of Cornish's *Rights of All* in October 1829 and the appearance of the *Weekly Advocate* in January 1837. Over a score more had appeared by the beginning of the Civil War. None, however, except for Frederick Douglass's journals, begun in 1847, had anywhere near the length of life and the impact of the *Colored American*. Moreover, Douglass's papers were never a comparable voice of black America, for they were always largely subsidized by whites.

In a general way, the *Colored American* was carrying on the work of Cornish's journals of the 1820s and also the work of the annual national black conventions from 1831 through 1835. The familiar themes reappeared: the crucial need for better and more widespread black education; the importance of diligence, thrift, and temperance for black self-elevation; the urgency of the abolitionist enterprise; the general persecution and repression of free blacks by whites; the benefits to be gained by urban blacks' moving to the country to take up farming; and the pernicious motives and program of the American Colonization Society. For all the familiarity, however, the *Colored American* reflected a new mood and new methods of agitation. This journal publicized, more thoroughly than ever before, successful contemporary black enterprise—educational, religious, and especially economic. More intensely and extensively than before, it attacked white prejudice and its destructive results in education, in employment, in public transportation, and especially in the white church. And with better organization than before, it fought for the basic civil rights of black people: the right not to be kidnapped into slavery, the right to be fairly tried if accused of being a fugitive slave, and the right to vote on the same basis as whites.

8. Ray and Ray, *Sketch of Charles B. Ray,* 62.

Some elements in the northern black experience in the 1830s help account for the birth of this remarkable journal in 1837. First was the program of the New York Vigilance Committee, founded in 1835 and led by the fearless and angry New England black David Ruggles, who publicized desperate situations: runaway slaves' being searched out by slave catchers and the terrifying threat of being kidnapped into slavery even if one had been born free. As essential as the physical refuge and sustenance for runaways that Ruggles and his associates could provide was the protection of a jury trial before fugitives or the kidnapped could be whisked away (or back) into slavery. Only state legislation won by black agitation could secure this protection.[9]

Second, with the proved inability of the national black conventions of 1831 to 1835 and their offshoot, the American Moral Reform Society, to carry through a practical program of agitation and reform, black leaders were looking for a new and more effective agency. Abolitionist petition campaigns in Great Britain had played a major role in bringing about Parliament's vote in 1833 providing for the eventual abolition of slavery in the British West Indies. Closer to home the American Anti-Slavery Society, with Cornish and Wright on its executive committee, was orchestrating widespread petitioning of Congress to end the gag rule on (automatic tabling of) abolition petitions. By late 1836 black leaders in New York City had decided to launch their own statewide petition campaign to guarantee alleged fugitives a jury trial and to secure the vote for all adult black males. The founding of the *Weekly Advocate* (soon the *Colored American*) was in part aimed at publicizing this petition campaign.

The third factor in the founding of the *Colored American* was the availability of key personnel to finance and edit the new paper. Philip Bell, who provided initial funding, was the owner and was named co-editor. Bell had grown up in the AME Zion church and continued to have warm feelings for it in his mature years. His natural affinities, however, seemed to be with clergy such as Wright, Cornish, and Ray and with intellectuals such as the physician and Episcopalian layman James McCune Smith. Samuel Cornish, with no ongoing pastorate, became senior editor. In April 1837 Charles Ray, by now widely known in New York State and New England through his attendance, with Wright, at regional abolition

9. Organizations similar to the New York Vigilance Committee were developed a few years later in Philadelphia, Pittsburgh, Detroit, Boston, and Albany. Although whites were on these committees, the groups were primarily black and led by blacks. Jane H. Pease and William H. Pease, *They Who Would Be Free: Blacks' Search for Freedom, 1830–1861* (New York, 1974), 207–12.

meetings, was appointed reporter from the field and promoter of circulation. For all three of these men, work for the *Colored American* would be a labor of love, not a way of supporting a family. In spite of a circulation of 1,250 in New York City by May 1837 and nearly 2,000 subscribers by June 1838, Cornish had been paid a total of only $100 for the first year and in 1839 would ruefully comment, "For sixteen years we have sacrificed all that we made and *half our family income* besides to the sacred cause, and we can do it for sixteen years more." The fact was that only by virtue of an independent income, presumably derived from his wife's assets, had Cornish been able to edit journals in the late 1820s and late 1830s. Ray, too, might well not have been financially in a position to accept the appointment as junior editor in 1837 if his wife of two years had not died in childbirth the previous fall, along with her baby.[10]

There is danger in defining so specifically the factors responsible for the birth of the *Colored American*. There was another element that is harder to describe—the presence in the nation, in the judgment of Cornish, Bell, Ray, and many others, of a powerful tide moving toward change, a potential for radical reform as never before, and a potential for black peoples' throwing off their passivity. Despite all their criticism of white abolitionists for indifference to free blacks, black leaders knew of, and repeatedly bore witness to, the fact that white immediatism had been a major factor in the new spirit. And even more fundamental than black enterprise or white radicalism, as Cornish and Ray saw it, was the energizing will of God himself: "Ten years ago this nation was asleep in their sins; while in that state, there was no hope for the poor slave; . . . but now God hath troubled the waters. The mind of the nation is awake and excited. . . . Righteousness shall prevail."[11]

Cornish called prejudice "more wicked and fatal than slavery itself." In fighting both evils, he saw the black press as "an appropriate engine." "Colored men must speak out in THUNDER TONES, until the nation repent and render to every man that which is just and equal." Free blacks that were scattered in small clusters in approximately five thousand towns could not be reached by any other means. Cornish again resorted to a

10. *Colored American,* May 6, 1837, January 13, 1838, October 5, 1839.

11. *Colored American,* March 4, May 6, 1837; January 13, 1838; October 5, 1839. The image of God troubling the waters drew from the Gospel of John in the New Testament (John 5:2–9). Jesus came upon a crowd of the lame and paralyzed lying near a certain pool in Jerusalem. They were hoping to be placed in the pool by some helper "when the water is troubled" (that is, when the healing angel of the Lord came down into the pool).

biblical image: "A public journal must therefore be sent down, at least weekly, to rouse them up. . . . and where they have been down-trodden, paralyzed and worn out, to create new energies for them, that such dry bones may live."[12]

Cornish and his associates chose Charles Ray to be the living link between the affirmations and exhortations of newsprint and the individual black people in far-flung local communities for whom the paper tried to speak. Ray, in order to play a pastoral role as part of his new work, secured ordination in the Methodist Episcopal Church, the denomination in which he had been brought up. It can be surmised that he was ordained by white Methodist clergy who had known him in eastern Massachusetts or at the academy in Wilbraham. Thus prepared, Ray became a traveling Christian exhorter, an apostle of community development, and a crusader for civil rights.

Ray's specific responsibilities, as he took the boat for New England in June 1837, were to secure subscriptions for the *Colored American* and, when he reached New York State, to get as many signatures as possible on petitions to the state legislature. His first goal upon reaching a given community was to find out what was going on among black people. In informal conversation, often over a meal, and in sermons and lectures, he urged his fellow blacks to make more of an effort to better their own lot and that of their children. Work and save, he would say. Buy property (a house, a farm, a boat, a manufacturing business); found a new school, or support the one you have; attend church; help secure or maintain a decent church building; contribute toward the salary of the minister. In all these ways blacks could hold up to the slave owners and colonizationists the fact that blacks can take care of themselves if given a chance. As Ray left each community, he wrote for the *Colored American* a detailed account of what he had found, especially what was encouraging. In the issues of his and Cornish's paper from 1837 through 1841, these reports provided readers, black or white, with invaluable factual information about black achievement in communities large and small. Here were living models for black emulation.

Ray's first community visits were in his home state of Massachusetts.

12. *Ibid.*, March 4, 1837. The dry bones image drew from Ezek. 37, in which the Lord brought the prophet Ezekiel to a valley filled with dry bones and ordered him to prophesy to them. Ezekiel did as he was commanded, and the bones of individual bodies came together; sinews and flesh came on them, but there was no breath in them. Ordered to prophesy again, Ezekiel did, "and the breath came into them, and they lived, and stood upon their feet, an exceedingly great host."

From New Bedford he wrote of black enterprise and prosperity. The whaler Brig Rising States, owned and operated by black men, had just returned from a long cruise. It had captured every whale but one that had been sighted. When it had set sail, doubters predicted that there would be mutiny or that the ship would never be seen again. According to Ray's report, however, "all say they have the best order and harmony on board: thus showing that colored men respect each other."[13] In visiting Lynn, it was a city school for black children that especially caught Ray's attention. He exulted over the enthusiastic interest of the pupils, the parents' concern for the intellectual improvement of their children, and the caliber of the teacher, a skilled veteran and "an abolitionist of the right stamp."[14]

What Ray held up for imitation, above all, was the spirit of enterprise pervading a whole black community. Three places were especially encouraging: Troy, Buffalo, and Cincinnati. The whites in Troy had the reputation of being both violently antiabolitionist and genuinely supportive of black efforts at self-advancement. When Theodore Weld had barnstormed through upstate New York preaching abolition, riotous mobs had forced him to cut short his lectures. But in Troy there were also efforts by the white town government to assist the black community in strengthening its church and schools. City records for November 1834 noted that a building had recently been put up "for the use of the people of color," that it had been "dedicated to the service and worship of the Almighty God," that Theodore Wright had come up from New York City to preach the dedication sermon, and that a day school for children and an evening school for adults had been begun in the church basement.[15] The black community in Troy, numbering about 300, had given vigorous support to the new church. By late 1836, 30 to 125 attended worship, an average of 53 came to Sunday school, and about 30 children attended weekday school, paying a shilling a week for tuition. Moreover, during the previous year, some $400 had been paid in by the low-income black community to provide fuel and light and to pay preachers and sextons. Several young white men had taken turns preaching until, just be-

13. Ray quoted in *Colored American,* July 22, 1837.

14. Charles Ray to Samuel Cornish, July 16, 1838, from Falmouth , in *Colored American,* July 28, 1838.

15. Handwritten account of the origins of the church that would become in 1840 the Liberty Street Presbyterian Church with Henry Highland Garnet, just out of college, as its pastor, in Liberty Street Presbyterian Church, Session Minutes, 1840–1921 (MS at Presbyterian Historical Association, Philadelphia). Wright, having lived for years in nearby Schenectady, was undoubtedly known to many in Troy.

fore Ray's visit, the church had secured its first full-time black preacher, Daniel Payne.[16]

Payne and other blacks in Troy made the most of Ray's visit in August 1837. On his first Sunday he preached three times—in the Seamen's Bethel Church, in the all-black Liberty Street Presbyterian Church, and in that of the Zion Methodists. Monday night he spoke to a black gathering at Liberty Street on the convictions and purposes of the *Colored American*. He was pleased with the response, thirty paid-up subscriptions and a strong resolution in support of the paper. Tuesday evening he spoke for over an hour to a white audience "on the condition of the colored people and their demands upon the white community to assist them . . . by correcting a corrupt public sentiment,—by rescinding those laws which oppress." Here, too, Ray spoke of the *Colored American* and secured more subscriptions.[17]

The black people of Buffalo held a special place in Ray's affections. In a community of somewhat more than five hundred, about one hundred of the men had steady work with the canal or lake boat traffic and were seldom home. Their incomes, however, were undoubtedly a factor in Ray's securing thirty-two new paid subscriptions to the *Colored American* from a group who had already contributed substantially to the journal. During his nine-day visit he attended meetings of two religious societies, a benevolent organization, and three literary clubs (one for women, one for boys, and one for men). These literary societies devoted winter evenings to debating moral and political issues. Ray found a keen interest in the education of the children—so keen that when the black school was for a time closed for lack of a teacher, children attended white private schools. Back in Buffalo a year later, Ray was moved to rhapsody: "It is among the dearest pleasures of life to meet, after a year's absence, . . . those for whom we have the highest esteem and warmest regard; ESPECIALLY when such emotions are on all sides MUTUAL."[18]

Highlighting Ray's associations with blacks in Troy and Buffalo should not obscure the fact that in 1837 and 1838 he visited dozens of other communities in New England and upstate New York. There was concrete evidence of his effectiveness: new or renewed subscriptions to the *Colored American,* which helped it survive, and frequent commendations of his

16. Report by William Yates, *Emancipator,* December 1, 1836. Yates was a white lawyer and lay preacher who had led some of the services at Liberty Street.

17. *Colored American,* September 2, 1837.

18. *Ibid.,* November 4, 1837; November 3, 1838.

work in the form of letters to the paper from organizations or individuals in the communities he visited. Occasionally whites put in writing their reactions to his sermons or lectures. Shortly before Ray's return to New York City in 1838, the *Colored American* published comments by a white editor who had heard him speak in Union Springs, in upper New York State. Ray had given an address in the Baptist church on the condition of American blacks. He was, reported the editor, "listened to with much satisfaction by a VERY numerous and highly attentive audience," and he had undoubtedly dispelled much of the prejudice against blacks with which many who listened had entered the church.[19]

In the fall of 1839, shortly after he became senior editor and owner of the *Colored American,* Ray visited Ohio for the first time. When he stepped off the Ohio River boat in Cincinnati, it was with special anticipation. The state was distinctive in a number of respects. The black population had grown rapidly. By 1829 whites had grown anxious over black inmigration from the South (some of the ugly expressions of this anxiety have been discussed). When Ray planned his trip to Ohio, he knew that black people there had been as conspicuous for their accomplishments as for their victimization. The majority of black adults among the roughly ten thousand in the state had come out of slavery, in many cases having purchased their own freedom and then that of relatives. What Theodore Hershberg has documented as true of black people in antebellum Philadelphia seems also to have been true of those in Cincinnati. Former slaves were more likely than freeborn blacks to send their children to school and to own property. To judge from the Cincinnati riots of 1829, former slaves were especially resistant to white violence. When about three hundred whites attacked the homes of perhaps three dozen black people, the blacks vigorously defended themselves by firing at the mob. One white was killed and ten blacks were arrested, but the mayor of the city later discharged them all, declaring that they had acted in self-defense.[20]

Ohio in general and Cincinnati in particular were also distinctive for their energetic white abolitionist presence during the mid-1830s. This presence was, as in New York City, both an encouragement to the black community and a provocation to anger among whites. The movement in Cincinnati started in 1834 at the newly opened Lane Theological Semi-

19. *Ibid.*, November 4, 1837; October 27, November 3, 1838.

20. Theodore Hershberg, "Free Blacks in Antebellum Philadelphia: A Study of Exslaves, Freeborn, and Socioeconomic Decline," *Journal of Social History,* V (1971–72), 183–209; Curry, *The Free Black in Urban America,* 105.

nary. Theodore Weld was at the center, playing a major part in the antislavery debate that went on for eighteen successive evenings and led to a virtually unanimous student endorsement of abolition, as well as a condemnation of the American Colonization Society. When further abolition activity was vetoed by the seminary's trustees, most of the students withdrew. A number, with Weld in the forefront, tried to put their racial convictions into practice by teaching in Cincinnati's black community.[21]

Black political activism developed momentum as early in Ohio as in New York City. In January 1837 the *Weekly Advocate,* forerunner of the *Colored American,* received word of a lively recent meeting of blacks in Cleveland. They had proposed sending petitions to the Ohio legislature to seek the repeal of the black code with its denials to blacks of schooling, the vote, and other civil rights. This Ohio gathering endorsed sending out a black agent to secure signatures for these petitions, as well as to gather data on black schools and black-owned farms and businesses. Over the next two years the Ohio story was followed closely in the columns of the *Colored American.* When Ray took over both editorship and ownership of the newspaper in the summer of 1839, he had good reason to feel that it was time to visit this important Ohio constituency.[22]

Arriving in Cincinnati on a Sunday morning, Ray found that he was due to preach at both an 11:00 A.M. and a 3:00 P.M. service. On Monday he looked in on the black schools, talked with blacks in the streets, visited them in their homes, and took meals with them. He concluded that as to "their mind and principles . . . they are the best population of our people I have ever seen or heard of." They were a united people, who were confident of one another's integrity and free of jealousy. They were interested in developing their minds. An unusually high percentage were property holders. Many were engaged in business, and many others were making money from the river trade over and above their regular wages. The wealthiest black in Cincinnati, a man forty years old, had property worth about $20,000, all accumulated by himself, along with a family to raise and educate. One black trading company employed twenty-five men and was constructing three spacious brick buildings. Ray had an explanation for the energy and purposefulness of Cincinnati blacks: "Many of them have been slaves, and have become free, by the

21. Barnes and Dumond (eds.), *Weld-Grimké Letters,* I, 133–35, 184f., 189–94; Mabee, *Black Freedom,* 154.

22. *Weekly Advocate,* February 25, 1837; *Colored American,* July 22, 1837; February 17, March 15, 22, 29, April 5, 12, 1838.

purchase of themselves. Men who will purchase themselves from slavery, or run away from it, have the proper material in their character, to become industrious, economical and reputable citizens."[23]

Cornish and Ray were not only eager to identify and encourage achievement by others; they were themselves driven by a strong urge to accomplish.[24] Any ambitious black person, however, had to deal with the fact of white prejudice in the same breath with which he spoke of goals and the efforts to reach them. Prejudice constantly prevented self-realization, yet self-improvement seemed essential to disprove the negative assumptions of this prejudice. Cornish, as has been shown, had struggled with this double bind as editor of *Freedom's Journal*. The passage of years had only increased the seeming enormity of the situation. During the latter 1830s Wright, Cornish, and Ray led the public assault on white prejudice. There was good reason why these elite black clergy were central figures in this campaign. In spite of the obstacles that they had had to overcome, they had become distinguished and cultivated men with firm Christian commitment, including the urge to spend themselves in the service of their fellows.

Again and again, however, these men were treated, in restaurants, on boats, and even in church gatherings, as though they were members of some contemptible, or at least embarrassing, subspecies. How could anger not have built up? They rejected physical violence as a futile way of expressing this anger, but the rage could at least be put into words. By words black people could share their anger with one another. Through words they could present the ugly truth to whites, and some of their abolitionist audiences were receptive enough really to listen. And by words they could invoke the wrath of God against deaf agents of injustice. Being at once believers in a righteous God and convinced of their mission as spokesmen for that God, Wright, Cornish, and Ray found release, as the Old Testament prophets had, in bearing witness to God's anger against cruelty and injustice, and to God's power, which would eventually destroy human enterprises built on exploitation.

Between 1834 and 1839 Theodore Wright attended many gatherings of white abolitionists in New England and New York. He and Charles Ray, whom he introduced to these groups, became well known. The evils of

23. *Colored American*, October 12, 5, 1839.

24. There were at least fifty pieces devoted to some aspect of black self-improvement in the *Colored American* in 1837 and 1838, quite apart from Ray's travel reports.

slavery were, of course, first on the agenda. Then these white liberals would turn to the elevation (moral, educational, and religious) of free black people. However, Wright and Ray saw to it that race prejudice was also addressed—prejudice among whites at large, but also prejudice among those present. The bluntness of these black ministers was invited by the friendliness and genuine commitment of many of their white listeners. And as they spoke, Wright and Ray could be sure that much of what they said would reach an audience far greater than those present. There was extensive verbatim reporting of major speeches in the pages of the *Emancipator,* the official organ of the American Anti-Slavery Society. Extensively subsidized by the national society, the *Emancipator* had a considerably wider circulation than did the *Colored American,* and its readership was primarily white. Here was an unprecedented opportunity for black leaders to express their sense of moral outrage to hundreds of whites who might well be sympathetic and presumably had more political clout than did blacks.

Wright took Ray with him in 1834 back to Ray's home territory for the founding of the Massachusetts Anti-Slavery Society. Two years later the older man was a central figure at the annual meeting of the New England Anti-Slavery Society, which had been founded in 1832. He was on the standing committee guiding the agenda, along with the Unitarian preacher Samuel May, the poet John Greenleaf Whittier, and William Lloyd Garrison. Wright spoke again and again. One time it was in support of those immediatist resolutions from the Presbytery of Chillicothe (Ohio) that the Presbytery of New York had permanently tabled only a month before, despite the opposition of Cornish and Wright. These resolutions had endorsed emancipation without remuneration and with no requirement of emigration, and they had condemned helping capture a runaway or excluding blacks from one's church (recommending that the church discipline those who did this).

The black minister from New York had a special message for abolitionists themselves that was a blend of admiration, sadness, and rebuke. It commanded the attention of his white listeners in New England in 1836, at the meetings of the New York Anti-Slavery Society later that same year, and at the New York gathering in 1837. First Wright would review the story of the American liberation movement, referring to the authors of the Declaration of Independence, to the Quakers, to the rise of black protest against the American Colonization Society, and to the birth and growth of radical white abolitionism. By comparing this last movement with early Christian faithfulness under persecution (the stoning of Stephen and the tribulations of Paul), Wright would make clear how deeply religious the grounding of the movement was—or should be: "Talent, power, wealth, the Government and the Church have all been raised against you. But, though you be persecuted even unto death, God is on your side, and he is stronger than them all." Then, with a fine sense of drama, Wright would deflate the self-congratulation among his listeners by making clear how little progress had been made against northern racist attitudes: "Prejudice is slavery. No man can really understand this prejudice unless he feels it crushing him to the dust. It has bolts, scourges and bars, wherever the colored man goes. . . . It excludes us from all stations of profit, usefulness and honor; takes away from us all motive for pressing forward." Reporters bore witness to the impact of Wright's words: "A profound silence and attention commenced with his speaking, and continued to the close. Some of the time the eyes of the whole audience were suffused with tears."[25]

By the fall of 1837 Wright became more explicit in accusing the abolition movement itself of being corrupted by racism. He compared the present movement with that three years earlier, when a black person could count on a white abolitionist's commitment to the basic equality of all human beings. Now, he declared, it is becoming almost as stylish to be an abolitionist as a colonizationist. He said, "It is an easy thing to talk about the vileness of slavery at the South, but . . . to treat the man of color in all circumstances as a man and brother—that is the test." Again and again Wright insisted that as long as caste barriers demeaning blacks were maintained in the North, southerners were strengthened in their convictions that maintaining the slave caste in the South was both appropriate and moral: "Let every man . . . burn out this prejudice, live it down, talk it down, everywhere consider the colored man as a man, in the church, the stage, the steamboat, the public house, in all places, and the death-blow to slavery will be struck."[26]

The facts bore out Wright's accusations. In 1836 a strong conviction had surfaced in the Massachusetts Anti-Slavery Society that admitting black members would frighten away whites who might otherwise join up. And in 1837 the newly formed Junior Anti-Slavery Society in Phila-

25. *Liberator,* June 25, 1836; *Emancipator,* November 2, 1836; *Liberator,* July 2, 1837.

26. "Speech of a Colored Brother, Delivered at the Late Meeting of the N.Y. State Anti-Slavery Society at Utica [on September 20, 1837]," reprinted from the *Friend of Man* in *Colored American,* October 13, 1837; Woodson, *Negro Orators,* 91f.

delphia spent five sessions debating the question, "Is it expedient for colored persons to join our Anti-Slavery Societies?" In New York a women's antislavery society had developed a standard policy denying admission to blacks. Even more troubling was the conclusion in 1838 of the central abolition organization, the American Anti-Slavery Society, that it could no longer afford the program begun in 1834, the deputing of agents to move among black communities to help them in their efforts at economic and educational improvement. Finally, white antislavery societies and abolitionist merchants continued to be resistant to hiring blacks for nonmenial jobs, even though the applicants were equipped with the requisite skills.[27]

The evidence is clear that by the latter 1830s black leaders were growing more impatient with the social bias of white abolitionists, as well as with the sharply limited nature of their commitment to free black advancement. However, that was only part of the picture. Wright, Cornish, and Ray often testified to the immense difference the founders and leaders of the white abolition movement had made in the prospects and attitudes of black people. In response to accusations that abolitionists had worsened relations between the races, Cornish wrote, "Now the SCALE IS TURNED. Abolitionists have thrown off the veil. They have shown that God created all men EQUAL, and of the same blood. . . . Of this the colored man is fully convinced; hence he stands ERECT and acknowledges NO SUPERIOR but God." Ray used a different image to make the same point. Abolitionists had, he wrote, brought about, among black people, "a new creation . . . calling forth energies and powers they were not aware of possessing." He likened this transformation to "the influence of our Declaration of Independence upon the mind and energies of our oppressed nation in 76."[28]

The prevailing sentiments of white America at large were a far cry from those of white abolitionism. Cornish, Wright, and Ray drew up a devastating bill of particulars on the prejudicial treatment of black people. First and foremost among the villains on Cornish's list were clergy and members of Christian churches: "The American Church . . . is the STRONG HOLD of an unholy prejudice against color, more *oppressive* and *fatal* in its

27. Litwack, *North of Slavery,* 216–22; *Colored American,* October 27, 1838.

28. *Colored American,* September 9, 1837; "What Have They Done?" *Colored American,* July 13, 1839. Although this editorial appeared in the issue of the paper that came out just as Ray was leaving Philadelphia for Ohio, the style (especially the smooth reference to biblical themes) suggests that it was he, not Philip Bell, the editor in his absence, who had written it.

results than any other sin. It is not only a generator of . . . darkness, but it is an extinguisher of *the light.*" The extinguishing of the light, in Cornish's view, was the abandonment of all religion by many blacks who had been humiliated in white churches.[29]

The black editor dealt at most length with the church he knew best, the Presbyterian, and especially with the treatment of black clergy by white clergy. He compared the relations between the two groups with those of Jews and outcast Samaritans in Israel. Even a "pious and talented . . . colored minister" had no access to a white pulpit. Presbytery committees responsible for finding substitutes when a white pulpit was vacant passed over the black minister "as though he were an infidel." This nonrecognition was especially humiliating in Cornish's case, for he had been a member of the New York Presbytery longer than all but two of the other clergy. Moreover, since he did not have a church of his own, he was usually available.[30]

During the 1830s Cornish was listed by the New York Presbytery as "without charge." It is quite possible that he was viewed as theologically unsound by those white Presbyterian clergy in New York who had remained in the New York Presbytery (the Old School) when the Third Presbytery (the New School) was formed in the mid-1830s. When Cornish visited Philadelphia late in 1837, he attended worship in the church of the New School minister Albert Barnes, noting, "He is America's unparalleled preacher, though by many of his brethren considered unsound in theology." Cornish also went to a service in a Methodist church and praised the sermon: "The abstruse reasoners of some of our Presbyterian churches, who freeze up their congregations in religious dogmas, would do well to learn of these [Methodist] brethren, that in the simplicity of the gospel, they might win souls to Christ."[31]

Even more humiliating than the bypassing of black ministers when substitutes were needed was their treatment by whites when they attended the presbytery or synod. Having been publicly recognized as a member of the presbytery at an opening meeting, the black minister would enter the sanctuary for a time of worship and take a seat. Time after time, a white person would come to sit in the same pew and then

29. *Colored American,* March 11, 1837. Over a dozen more pieces on prejudice in the church appeared in Cornish's journal before the year was out.

30. *Colored American,* March 11, April 1, 1837. According to Cornish, this bypassing of black Presbyterian clergy went on in Philadelphia much as in New York City.

31. *Colored American,* November 25, December 16, 1837.

suddenly, on discovering that he was near a black person, would hastily shift seats as though the black person had the plague. Equally embarrassing, and more humiliating, was the callous absence, referred to earlier, of hospitality for black ministers at presbytery meetings at mealtime.

The rituals of debasement forced on rank-and-file black members of primarily white churches were equally shameful. In speeches and editorials again and again, Wright, Cornish, and Ray inveighed against the Negro pew. Cornish urged blacks to attend their own churches. If they did go to white churches for convenience or excellent preaching, they should not use the pews set aside for blacks: "Stand in the aisles and rather worship God upon your feet than become a party to your own degradation. You must shame your oppressors, and wear out prejudice, by this holy policy."[32]

When Cornish asked his white fellow ministers whether they did not consider this segregation of worshipers sinful, they admitted that it was. Why, then, he asked, do you not preach against it? Their excuse was that public attitudes were so fixed as to make such preaching futile. Cornish wondered how much "bending to public sentiment" could be reconciled with being an "ambassador" of Christ, "who strove against sin, to blood and to death."[33]

Cornish, his wife, and his four children suffered from "this unholy prejudice" close to home. They lived on Fourth Street, about two miles uptown from Theodore Wright's church, the one they normally attended. Because blacks could not depend on being allowed to board the horsecars (streetcars drawn by horses), in cold weather the Cornishes had only two choices of a Sunday, both undesirable: to stay home or to attend one of the four or five primarily white Presbyterian churches within a quarter mile of home. If the family took the second option, they had to occupy a Negro pew, which Cornish would not do, or stand through the service. His sons, aged eleven and ten, learned the facts of life in race-conscious New York City only gradually. One cold winter Sunday, one of them, "fair and his hair rather straight," was sent to one of these nearby white churches. "He was handed to a pew near the altar and comfortably seated." A week or two later he decided to return to this church with his brother, "whose color and hair, betray[ed] his origin." One white worshiper after another who took seats in the same pew and then saw them "fled . . . as though the leprosy was upon them." Upset by the

32. *Ibid.*, August 19, 1837.
33. *Ibid.*, March 11, 1837.

experience, one of the boys, on returning home, asked, "Mother, why do the white people hate *us* so?"[34]

Wright had his own vicissitudes when he worshiped in a church other than his own. Visiting relatives in New Rochelle, he attended Sunday morning services in a white Presbyterian church. Although he discreetly took a seat in the gallery, he was asked to move to another location. He refused to do so, thinking it wrong to "sanction my own degradation." Protestants were the worst offenders among white Christians, Wright declared. At Tammany Hall or in a Catholic church a black person was treated as whites were. However, among "those who profess to be the most orthodox, nearest the Bible," he found, with few exceptions, the most prejudice.[35]

Wright viewed Quakers, for all their record of opposition to slavery, as having been infected by the same virus. Blacks had recently been encouraged by a strong statement issued by the New York Yearly Meeting of Friends pressing for immediate emancipation. However, the very clerk of the yearly meeting who had signed this document showed another face when a black Presbyterian minister called on him at his home: He "gave him his meals alone in the kitchen and did not introduce him to his family. . . . What can the friends of emancipation effect while the spirit of slavery is so fearfully prevalent?"[36]

Although Wright, Ray, and Cornish stood side by side in protesting the "arranged degradation" of black people in white churches, only Cornish let his anger go in personal attacks on individual churchmen who opposed the abolition movement and supported the American Colonization Society. One of those he assaulted most vigorously was Willbur Fisk, who had been president of Wesleyan University during Charles Ray's brief sojourn there. During the five years before his death in 1839, Fisk had become one of the most prominent Methodists in the country. Not only was he recognized as a devoted and successful educator but he also had done his best to contain and discredit abolitionism within his denomination and so prevent a North-South split among Methodists. He had given continuing and eloquent support to the colonization movement as a solution to American racial problems. His ability and contri-

34. *Ibid.*, March 18, 1837.

35. Speech given by Wright to the New York Anti-Slavery Society on September 27, 1837, in Utica, New York, reported in *New York Evangelist,* November 4, 1837 (Microfilm copy in Carter and Ripley [eds.], *BAP,* reel 2, item 263).

36. Woodson, *Negro Orators,* 91f.

butions had been recognized by the offer of a bishopric, which he had refused, and by the award of an honorary doctor of divinity degree, which he had accepted.

The way Fisk used his power and the rewards he reaped drove Cornish into a fury similar to that which had boiled up a decade earlier against the colonizationist Francis Scott Key. After the 1838 annual meetings of the American Colonization Society, Cornish meditated for readers of the *Colored American* on the four types of men who kept the society going: "the interested slave-holder, the haters of the colored man, the popularity hunting clergy (such as Messrs. Fisk and Bethune [a prominent Dutch Reformed minister]), and the money making editors." All Fisk needed to quench his colonization fervor, declared Cornish, was "a more fruitful field for . . . [his] ambition." Three months later Cornish again attacked Fisk and George Washington Bethune, this time for conspicuous collusion with slaveholding. Cornish labeled them "mountebanks and buffoons to auction into repute colonization and to ridicule the sacred acts of emancipation."[37]

White schools had been infected by the same disease of racism as white churches. Already noted were Cornish's early efforts to offset the results of race prejudice in the New York City school system by improving the African Free Schools. Wright and Peter Williams's founding of the short-lived Phoenix High School for blacks also has been described. In Wright's and Ray's speeches to antislavery conventions in 1836 and 1837 and in Cornish's editorials in the *Colored American,* the deadly impact of racial prejudice on educational possibilities for blacks was driven home again and again. Cornish publicized the price paid by his own children, and Ray described the crushing blow for him in being driven out of college.

Cornish had moved his family back to New York City in 1833, when his older children, both boys, were nine and seven years old. Knowing that Presbyterians valued sound education and assuming that his own record as a student under Presbyterian supervision and as an ordained minister would operate in his favor, he had applied for the admission of these two to a number of Presbyterian schools. Four years later he bitterly recalled what had happened. The boys had been rejected in every case "on account of their complexion, they being mixed blood, a few

37. *Colored American,* June 2, September 8, 1838.

shades below the pure white." In 1837, tormented by the fact that his older children, now aged thirteen, eleven, and ten, had already outgrown the public schools for black children, Cornish renewed his plea in his newspaper "for the admission of our little ones." He guaranteed "the decency of their appearance and the purity of their morals" and promised to pay bills promptly.[38]

Cornish did not confine his search for schooling for his children to printed appeals. He called on the minister of one of the largest white Presbyterian churches in New York City, "*a minister beloved,* and with whom we have sat in Presbytery for ten years." Prominent members of this man's church had just opened a school exactly suited to the ages and preparation of the Cornish boys. The white minister urged Cornish and other blacks to start a school of their own "where your colored children can be taught the higher branches, and not come in contact with the prejudices of the whites." Cornish, knowing that the Phoenix High School was near financial collapse, was goaded into his strongest condemnation of separate schools and even separate churches. Such institutions tended to reinforce prejudice against color and to strengthen "Christian caste," he said. They "shackled the intellect of colored youth." A case can be made for Cornish's being something of a snob. (Indeed Theodore Weld and his fiancée, Angelina Grimké, thought that he tended to "despise the poor as much as their pale brethren.") Cornish was very conscious of his and his family's light skin, and this heightened his urge to get his children into white schools. Yet there was a sound element in his opposition to racially separate institutions. However beneficial for blacks, the existence of these schools did confirm white assumptions about the fundamental differences and inferiority of blacks.[39]

As a result of both the withering effect that Cornish felt racial prejudice was having on his children and the financial pressures because the *Colored American* was bringing in hardly any pay for its editor, he moved his family to Belleville, New Jersey, eight miles from New York, in the spring of 1838. For a few months it seemed an ideal situation, but happiness was short lived. Cornish's second son slipped off a wharf and drowned, and the older boy had to be willing to accept segregated arrangements if he attended the district school.[40]

38. "Appeal to Presbyterians," *Colored American,* October 7, 1837.

39. *Colored American,* April 22, 1837; Barnes and Dumond (eds.), *Weld-Grimké Letters,* I, 496, 498.

40. *Colored American,* June 2, 1838; May 18, 1839.

Ray would be as much concerned as Cornish over the education of the children born to his second wife, whom he would marry in 1840. But in the latter 1830s the educational deprivation on Ray's mind was his own loss of the opportunity to get a college education. In 1836, at a meeting of the New York City Anti-Slavery Society, he publicly denounced "that cruel, unnatural and awfully wicked proscription, which turns us away from the useful arts, and from places of profit and responsibility. . . . O! this heartless prejudice!" He wondered out loud what he might have become over the preceding four years if he had been allowed to complete his Wesleyan University course and thereby develop the mind "that the great Author of my being had intrusted to me." Being driven out by his "Christian brethren" had been a devastating shock that words could not describe.[41]

College opportunities for blacks had somewhat improved between Ray's ouster from Wesleyan and the delivery of this speech to white abolitionists. The Oneida Institute had started accepting Afro-Americans in 1834. In 1835 the great body of students who had withdrawn from Lane Theological Seminary in protest over the ban on abolitionist agitation entered the newly opened Oberlin College. Black students were admitted to the college's preparatory division that first year. By 1839 the total student body of 404 at Oberlin included 12 black men and 3 black women. However, college admission for blacks opened only very slowly.

To understand how deeply grieved Cornish, Wright, and Ray were over the general exclusion of blacks from a college education, their overriding desire for an educated ministry among their people must be remembered. As Cornish saw it, black people were especially in need of well-trained ministers, both to raise the educational slights of their congregations and to give black churches "character and standing" in the church at large. Of the many black clergy Cornish knew who had entered the ministry during the previous twenty years, only two had been given a classical education, whereas over 90 percent of white candidates had been thoroughly trained, often largely at the expense of the church. Cornish exhorted black church members to raise money to assist in the needed education of clergy. However, he also, as he had in the 1820s, continued to criticize whites, especially Presbyterians, for giving stingy scholarship allotments to black aspirants for the ministry, as well as for assuming a double standard as to the necessary qualifications for the

41. *Emancipator,* December 5, 1836.

black ministry versus the white. The refusal of most white theological seminaries to accept black applicants, as in the case of the General Theological Seminary (Episcopal) and Alexander Crummell, was the logical expression, at the highest level, of the attitudes shared by most white clergy and church members.[42]

For rank-and-file Afro-Americans, a major reason for securing a sound elementary and secondary education was to enhance their chances of securing nonmenial employment. However, as Wright told New York abolitionists, even young blacks who had been well schooled in reading, writing, and arithmetic met a stone wall when they tried to find employment as clerks or accountants in stores or business offices. Even radical abolitionists seemed usually to be captives of stereotypes about black inability to handle work as clerks, or they feared other employees' objections to working alongside a black clerk. A correspondent to the *Colored American* took the New York Anti-Slavery Society to task in the summer of 1838 for not employing a single black person in its office. And Arthur Tappan was criticized for never using a black person in his importing establishment except at the most menial level. Private correspondence confirmed that the Tappans viewed blacks as basically unreliable in handling accounts.[43]

Black people could avoid humiliation and rejection by white churches, schools, and colleges by not trying to attend them. They could and did, in many cases, accept the fact that apprenticeship as mechanics, work as artisans or clerks, and licenses as cartmen were closed to them. But a great percentage of the black population of all income levels did have to use public transportation, either occasionally or regularly, and here, too, there were often indignities and hardships to be suffered by way of "special arrangements" for black people. As usual, Samuel Cornish was at hand to record the inhumanity and to berate the perpetrators. He reprinted from the New York *Times* the account of an episode on a horsecar that must have been far from unique. A black man had hailed an omnibus going up Broadway and tried to get in. The driver threatened to whip the would-be passenger, who paused uncertainly, torn between fear

42. *Colored American,* August 12, September 2, 16, 1837. Also see the letters from "A Colored Baltimorean" and Charles Ray's endorsement of their sentiments in *ibid.,* June 17, 24, July 22, 1837.

43. Wright's speech of September 27, 1837, in *New York Evangelist,* November 4, 1837; *Colored American,* July 28, 1838; L. Litwack, "The Emancipation of the Negro Abolitionist," in Martin Duberman (ed.), *The Antislavery Vanguard* (Princeton, 1965), 141f.; Wyatt-Brown, *Lewis Tappan,* 177f.; Pease and Pease, *They Who Would Be Free,* 84f.

of the whip and the need for a ride. White bystanders were convulsed with laughter as the bus drove away without the black man. Cornish furiously attacked this making merry over another's sufferings. He pointed out that if, as may well have been the case, the driver were an Irishman, his own suffering in Ireland and the United States should have made him sympathize with oppressed blacks.[44]

Theodore Wright knew from bitter experience the toll that discriminatory treatment on shipboard sometimes took from black passengers. He told white abolitionists of three cases where death had resulted from the exposure forced on black people who had been refused cabins and had had to stay on deck through a cold and stormy night. One of the casualties had been his wife. The Wrights had been returning from Princeton to Schenectady in 1828, the year of Theodore's graduation from seminary. They had been denied shelter on the boat from Brunswick to New York during a cold and windy rainstorm. Mrs. Wright had caught a bad cold. After several days' layover, they took passage up the Hudson. Again, though it was late fall and the weather was cold, they had been forced to sit on deck. At night Mrs. Wright considered herself lucky to be allowed to sleep in the cook's dirty apartment near the machinery, but she died a few months later from complications brought on by this exposure.[45] Theodore Wright's successor at the First Colored Presbyterian Church, James W. C. Pennington, would later claim that Wright's own life had been shortened by several years because, not being able to depend on public transportation, he had had to cover a far-flung parish, in all kinds of weather, mostly on foot.

Cornish urged his fellow blacks to eschew unnecessary trips. Traveling, "under circumstances of arranged degradation," did more to maintain the system of a caste based on color than anything except the segregation practiced by the church. The editor, of course, knew that sometimes business or personal needs required travel. Indeed, his appointment of Charles Ray to be traveling agent for the *Colored American* meant the constant use of boats and railroads. Wherever Ray met discriminatory practices, he protested publicly and described the unfair treatment in his next report to the home office. On the Hudson River boat *James Madison,* Ray and fellow reporter Philip Bell were told they could not have tea unless served in the kitchen; they refused. On an Erie Canal boat, at mealtime, Ray was refused a place at the first table with whites. When a second

44. *Colored American,* June 10, 1837.

45. Wright's speech of September 27, 1837, in *New York Evangelist,* November 4, 1837.

table had been set, he refused to eat at it. In 1841 Ray reported that there was a Jim Crow car on the New Bedford and Taunton Railroad and that on a Nantucket steamboat, all black men and women had to ride ahead of the wheel, sometimes with the cattle. Where there was good news of genuine equal treatment of black passengers, it too was reported—with relief and gratitude.[46]

The indictments against white racism delivered in speeches and editorials by Wright, Cornish, and Ray in the latter 1830s have been traced. Cornish and Ray also had pivotal roles in arousing and guiding a movement of political protest in New York State during these same years. This protest was largely by petition and had two primary objects. First, it aimed to further the work of the New York Vigilance Committee by securing state legislation guaranteeing a jury trial for blacks arrested as alleged fugitive slaves. Second, it sought to secure for black men the right to vote on the same broad basis as had obtained for whites since the 1820s. Although black people in Ohio, New Jersey, Pennsylvania, Rhode Island, and Connecticut petitioned for the vote during the 1830s and 1840s (black males had been disfranchised by legislation or popular referendum in New Jersey in 1807, in Connecticut in 1814, in Rhode Island in 1822, and in Pennsylvania in 1838), those in New York City and throughout New York State did so with a complexity of organization and a barrage of publicity (in the *Colored American*) unparalleled in other states. In every case except Rhode Island, these campaigns were unsuccessful in gaining or recovering the vote before the Civil War.[47] However, they were the occasion, especially in New York, of at least minimal political involvement on the part of hundreds of free black people who had never before known that such activity was possible or could perhaps make a difference. Samuel Cornish, a primary force in the New York campaign, affirmed the bedrock importance of political equality a few months after the first set of petitions had been tabled by the legislature: "They [that is,

46. *Colored American,* June 10, September 2, 1837; June 16, September 1, 8, 22, 1838; July 20, 27, 1839.

47. Marion Thompson Wright, "Negro Suffrage in New Jersey, 1776–1875," *Journal of Negro History,* XXXIII (1948), 168–224; James T. Adams, "Disfranchisement of Negroes in New England," *American Historical Review,* XXX (1924–25), 543–47; Edward R. Turner, *The Negro in Pennsylvania: Slavery—Servitude—Freedom, 1639–1861* (1911; rpr. New York, 1969), 169–93; "Appeal of Forty Thousand Citizens, Threatened with Disfranchisement, to the People of Pennsylvania, 1838," in Aptheker (ed.), *A Documentary History of the Negro People,* I, 176–86.

whites] must suffer us to be legally and politically men, or never expect us to be morally, religiously or socially such."[48]

The grossest violation of black civil rights was, of course, not disfranchisement but enslavement. It was appropriate, then, that in the New York petition campaign, petitions seeking the ending of slaveholding in the state and protection against reenslavement headed the list of grievances to be remedied. The continued presence of slaves in New York had been permitted by the Constitutional Convention of 1821 in the case of slaves brought into the state with their owners and staying for no more than nine months. Adding to these short-term slave residents was an increasing flow into New York City, in the 1830s, of fugitive slaves, whose masters or their representatives might show up at any time on the city's streets in an attempt to recapture what they felt was their lost property. Finally, even blacks who had been born free were in danger of being kidnapped into slavery. The seizure of blacks, especially young males, for sale into slavery in the South was frequent enough to be a nightmarish possibility for all but the very young and very old. Often the kidnapping would be done pseudolegally by capturing a free black person, taking him before a city magistrate, and producing paid witnesses who would swear that the person was indeed a recent runaway from such and such a southern plantation.

Ever since the 1780s northern states had fitfully tried to prevent kidnappings via such false allegations. The usual protective devices were a mandatory jury trial to determine whether the seized person was indeed a fugitive slave and harsh penalties for kidnapping. In contrast, the federal government had passed a fugitive slave act in 1793 that sought to protect slave owners' rights of recovery. Quick certification of ownership by a local magistrate was profitable for slave owners, for slave catchers, and for city magistrates (through fees paid). New York State legislation in 1828 and a federal court decision in 1834 had tilted the balance in favor of slave owners and slave catchers, facilitating the recovery of slaves without resort to trial.[49]

The growing number of fugitive slaves coming into New York City and the increasing threat of kidnapping had led to the founding, as has been noted, of the New York Vigilance Committee in 1835. Theodore Wright and Samuel Cornish were members of the new organization's

48. *Colored American,* July 22, 1837.

49. Thomas D. Morris, *Free Men All: The Personal Liberty Laws of the North, 1780–1861* (Baltimore, 1974), *passim.*

executive committee, and Wright served as its chairman for several years. Staff worker David Ruggles made it his business to be the eyes and ears of the black community. Ruggles had been brought up in Norwich, Connecticut, where he had attended a free school and had been completely accepted by his white schoolmates. In 1834, after some years in the grocery business in New York City, he had opened a bookshop specializing in abolitionist and anticolonization literature. In September 1835 a white mob had burned down his bookstore. Ruggles ferreted out the presence of blacks illegally detained on shipboard and then reported the captains to the police; he identified slavecatchers by name in articles in the *Emancipator* and the *Colored American;* and he identified their physical persons to blacks on the streets. If these slavecatchers seized a black and took him to the city recorder, with witnesses paid to declare the man a recent runaway, Ruggles would be there with witnesses to swear to the contrary (though at a disadvantage, because the perjured witnesses would usually be white and Ruggles's witnesses, often black).

At its first annual meeting, the vigilance committee reported having "protected from slavery" 335 persons. It had raised over $800, most of it by penny-a-week donations secured by female supporters, but the committee had overspent by nearly $400. Cornish's *Colored American,* which began publication only a couple of months after this annual meeting, helped the vigilance committee in various ways. It publicized the need for funds. It identified and excoriated notorious slave catchers. It announced hearings before the city recorder. And it reported on David Ruggles's activities. In 1839 Ray succeeded Wright as chairman of the committee. Now senior editor of the *Colored American,* Ray used the journal to promote the committee's work, as Cornish had. Although there was some white support for this work (both Garrison and Weld spoke at the first annual meeting), the management of the program and financial support for it in these early years seem to have been primarily Afro-American.[50]

50. *Dictionary of American Negro Biography,* 536–38; Dorothy Porter, "David Ruggles, An Apostle of Human Rights," *Journal of Negro History,* XXVIII (1943), 23–50; *Colored American,* April 15, 22, 29, May 27, July 7, 1837; August 18, 25, 1838. The American Anti-Slavery Society (with Cornish and Wright on its executive committee) and its paper, the *Emancipator,* had given early and extensive coverage to the epidemic of kidnappings and false arrests of free blacks (American Anti-Slavery Society, *First Annual Report* [New York, 1834], 54–57; *Emancipator,* July 28, August 8, October 6, December 1, 15, 1836; January 12, 1837). For details of a number of the cases of assistance and extensive description of the diversity of the committee's program, see *First Annual Report of the New York Committee of Vigilance* (New York, 1837); and *Fifth Annual Report of the New York Committee of Vigilance for the Year 1842* (N.p., May, 1842).

What the vigilance committee needed, however, even more than publicity and funds, was a state law mandating a jury trial for alleged fugitives, thus eliminating the hasty and/or corrupt role of the city recorder. It was clear that such a law would be passed only if there were pressure on the legislature to act on the matter. Black leaders in New York City were convinced that such pressure could come only from those most at risk. Here was a powerful reason for a petition campaign by blacks throughout the state—a campaign spearheaded by those living in New York City, where the protection was most needed. Equally crucial was a matter that affected most adult black males in the state, the gaining of the right to vote on the same basis as for whites.

New York City blacks had used petitioning sixteen years earlier to try to protect their political rights at the 1821 state constitutional convention. New York State's original constitution had made no reference to race as a bar to voting. During the first two decades of the nineteenth century, however, polarization had grown between the Federalists (often former slave owners and present employers of free blacks) and the Democratic Republicans over blacks' being granted the franchise. Convinced that New York elections in 1800 and 1813 had been won by the Federalists by the narrow margin of the black vote in New York City, the opposing party had introduced special requirements for black voting eligibility in the city. As a result the black vote declined from 300 in 1813 to about 160 in 1821, and this in spite of a substantial increase in the city's free black population. The calling of a state constitutional convention in 1821 had led black leaders to suspect a regressive move. A mass meeting of blacks in New York City endorsed a plea to the New York legislature to block laws or constitutional changes that would destroy blacks' political equality. This petition had been tabled. The convention, though effecting an eventual elimination of any property requirement for white voters, had maintained special requirements for black voters, the chief of which was $250 worth of real property.[51]

In late February 1837, a large group of New York City blacks met to start a petitioning process that would continue, more or less vigorously, until the Civil War. At its beginning the petitioning was threefold: to re-

51. Herman D. Bloch, *The Circle of Discrimination: An Economic and Social Study of the Black Man in New York* (New York, 1959), 154–57; Litwack, *North of Slavery,* 76–83. The full requirement follows: (1) having been a citizen of the state for three years; (2) owning a freehold of $250 over and above all debt and encumbrances; and (3) having had one's property rated and having actually paid a tax thereon.

peal the law permitting slave owners to enter the state with slaves and retain that ownership for nine months; to guarantee a jury trial for those alleged to be fugitive slaves; and "to give the right of voting to ALL the male citizens of the State on the same terms, without distinction of color." The petitions were kept at Phoenix Hall for three days to accumulate signatures. When they were delivered to the Albany statehouse, with Cornish's overseeing the transfer, 620 men had endorsed the petition for the vote. Other petitions, from Brooklyn, Albany, Troy, and Oswego County, represented over 400 additional men and women. The routine treatment for such petitions was tabling, yet the one from blacks in nearby Troy threw the House of Representatives into a fever of excitement. Although it was immediately moved that the petition be denied lest it renew earlier turmoil provoked by abolitionists, House members discussed it for a whole day. Opponents urged that universal suffrage for blacks would promote both sedition and "amalgamation," *i.e.*, miscegenation. The House eventually voted one hundred to eleven to reject the petition.[52]

The tabling or denying of black New Yorkers' petitions in March 1837 was merely the end of the first skirmish in what would turn out to be a thirty-year struggle. During the first ten years, Samuel Cornish, Charles Ray, and their younger colleague Henry Highland Garnet had central roles as editors, speakers, traveling promoters of the cause, and lobbyists. The chances of success seemed to grow brighter as equal suffrage for blacks became a major issue between members of the two chief parties emerging in New York State, the Whigs and the Democrats.[53]

During 1837 and much of 1838 Cornish orchestrated the three-issue petitioning through the pages of the *Colored American*. On the question of the vote for blacks, several types of material appeared. Primarily for white readers, of whom there was a significant number, Cornish presented substantive arguments for granting the vote to all black men. After the tabling of petitions in March 1837 and after each successive setback, he urged blacks throughout the state to renew petitions to the legislature, and he pressed blacks who did own $250 worth of real property to exercise their vote and chided those who had the resources to buy that much property but had not done so. The *Colored American* also publicized developments in other states. It attacked the movement toward

52. *Colored American*, March 4, 11, 1837; Quarles, *Black Abolitionists*, 170f.; *Liberator*, March 11, 1837.

53. Phyllis F. Field, *The Politics of Race in New York* (Ithaca, 1982), 41f., 45–47.

disfranchising blacks in Pennsylvania in 1837 and chastised blacks in that state for not organizing their opposition more aggressively. Blacks in Ohio, in contrast, earned Cornish's praise for continued efforts to secure legislative repeal of the whole black code that barred blacks not only from the franchise but also from attending public schools and giving evidence in court trials. Finally, when there was good news, as in New Jersey's and Connecticut's favorable actions on jury trials for so-called fugitives, the *Colored American* made the most of it.[54]

The gathering of signatures on petitions in New York City in December 1837 was more highly organized than it had been a year earlier. Committees were set up in each ward, and they took their work seriously. But again in 1838 the Judiciary Committee in the House recommended tabling and was supported by a vote of the whole House. By the following summer a new black organization had been formed, the Association for Political Improvement of People of Color. One of its goals was support from white abolitionists. It sent a supply of blank petitions to the September meeting of the New York State Anti-Slavery Society, at which Theodore Wright was a featured speaker. That whites did join in on the 1838 petition drive is indicated by the House Judiciary Committee report that during that year it had received petitions for equal suffrage signed by 9,300 persons.[55]

The Whigs took over the governorship and the legislature in the 1838 election. New York black leaders were encouraged and confirmed in their commitment to political activity. William Seward, the new governor, had become convinced that the small but growing antislavery movement could not be stopped. He took stands during his first year in office that confirmed black optimism. One instance involved three black sailors who were citizens of New York State and who had tried, though without success, to enable a slave in Virginia to escape. The governor of Virginia demanded that New York State hand over the black seamen. Seward would not comply, insisting that because New York recognized all men as entitled to personal freedom, the black seamen had broken no law.[56]

The momentum that was developed by the black petition campaign in New York in 1837 and 1838 and by the return of the Whig party to power

54. *Colored American,* April 29, July 15, 22, December 16, 1837; April 12, 1838; April 29, July 15, December 16, 1837; March 3, April 19, December 15, 1838; July 22, 1837; June 17, 1837; June 16, 1838.

55. Freeman, "The Free Negro in New York City," 131; Field, *Politics of Race,* 46.

56. Glyndon G. Van Deusen, *William Henry Seward* (New York, 1967), 11–14, 18, 20f., 25, 45f., 51f., 65f.

in the state government in November 1838 were important elements in the growing cleavage between New York blacks (and eventually most New England blacks) and the Garrisonians, whether in Massachusetts or Pennsylvania. Statements made by Cornish in 1838 reflect the sharpening of focus and the political self-confidence of the editors of the *Colored American*. Cornish editorialized on the situation in Pennsylvania, where court action seemed to have disfranchised all blacks. These threats to black people's basic rights, he declared, proved the necessity of "our brethren of that state throwing themselves upon God and their own efforts." Timid friends of blacks in Pennsylvania had, for forty years, been advising them to avoid trouble by staying away from the polls. The result was unfolding before them, disfranchisement and a general loss of equal opportunity. Staying out of the political arena, fumed Cornish, was "a bad and ruinous policy. No man nor body of men ever gained anything by yielding up their manhood." A month later, addressing himself to the situation in New York, Cornish made clear that black political activism was, as he saw it, mandated by New Testament teaching: "The same inspired volume, which enjoins upon accountable men the harmlessness of the dove, exhorts him to the wisdom of the serpent. It makes no reserve [qualification]. In all lawful things this innocency and wisdom are indispensable. In all moral, civil and domestic concerns, they are equally essential. . . . We recommend this divine injunction to our brethren, in the pursuit of their civil rights." If, wrote Cornish, petitioning turns out to be unsuccessful, then all twelve thousand black males in New York State should do their best to secure $250 worth of real estate. If they succeeded, they would have the balance of power and could force all members of the legislature to repeal that article in the constitution that "graduates civil rights, by human complexions."[57]

In contrast to this firm commitment to political action, William Lloyd Garrison was becoming more of a perfectionist as to the methods he was willing to use to achieve social change. Because the United States Constitution had recognized slaves and slave owning as economic and political entities in the American landscape, Garrison declared the federal government corrupt. He urged his followers to abandon political activity in favor of efforts to convince individuals of the wrongness of slavery. Equally disconcerting to many black leaders was his moving away from single-minded abolitionism to the support of a number of additional

57. *Colored American*, March 3, April 12, 1838.

causes, including women's rights. This last provoked a bitter falling out between Cornish and Garrison in the fall of 1837.

The Grimké sisters had been traveling through New England as public lecturers for the abolitionist cause. Often speaking before "promiscuous" gatherings (that is, groups of men and women) and sometimes occupying pulpits, they had offended more conservative New Englanders, especially many of the Congregational clergy. When these ministers published their criticisms of the Grimkés, Garrison in turn attacked the ministers in the columns of the *Liberator.* Cornish, himself a minister, bridled at Garrison's bitterly anticlerical statements, but most of all he resented the Boston editor's having won over the black community in Boston to his position. Acutely aware of the debt owed by blacks to such white abolitionist ministers as S. S. Jocelyn, Samuel May, and Samuel Cox, Cornish took Garrison to task in the pages of the *Colored American.* Garrison reciprocated, accusing the black journal of having "turned White." Ray stood with Garrison and the blacks of Boston in this confrontation. By the following summer, however, he, too, had come to have serious doubts about the Garrisonians. He feared that their promotion of many causes "important in themselves" would undermine their effectiveness on the main battlefront, "the abolition of American Slavery, and the elevation to equal civil rights [of] the free colored people."[58]

During the annual meeting of the American Anti-Slavery Society in New York City in May 1839, the political activist delegates outvoted the Garrisonians eighty-four to seventy-seven, endorsing the resolution that "this society still holds, as it has from the beginning, that employment of the political franchise, as was established by the constitution and laws of the country, . . . to promote the abolition of slavery is of high obligation." Of the ten blacks voting, only two, both from Massachusetts, held to the Garrisonian position. The eight endorsing political action included two laymen (from Maine and Massachusetts) and six ministers (Charles Gardiner, pastor of Philadelphia's First African Presbyterian Church; Amos Beman, just beginning his pastorate at the Temple Street African Congregational Church in New Haven, Connecticut; and four New Yorkers: Episcopalian Alexander Crummell, Baptist John T. Raymond, Theodore Wright, and Henry Highland Garnet).[59]

58. *Liberator,* October 6, 1837; *Colored American,* October 14, 1837; *Liberator,* October 13, 1837; *Colored American,* July 7, 1838.

59. *Liberator,* May 24, 1839; Robert Dick, *Black Protest: Issues and Tactics* (Westport, Conn., 1974), 85f.

The immediate occasion for the organizational schism in the American Anti-Slavery Society in 1840 was the Garrisonians' insistence on giving several women positions on central committees. However, the secession of some three hundred of over a thousand delegates to form the American and Foreign Anti-Slavery Society was as much because of the Garrisonian disavowal of the federal Constitution as because of the female appointments. Eight black ministers went along with the seceders. Charles Gardiner, Amos Beman, Theodore Wright, and Henry Garnet were among the eight; they remained faithful to the position they had taken the previous year. The four others were Jehiel Beman, AMEZ minister and father of Amos Beman; Christopher Rush, second bishop of the AMEZ denomination; and Stephen Gloucester and Andrew Harris, both young ministers of African Presbyterian churches in Philadelphia.

For Ray, whose personal ties with Massachusetts were still strong, the schism was especially painful. He stayed with the Garrisonian majority as they chose the eloquent Boston Quaker Abby Kelly for the Business Committee and three other distinguished white women for the Executive Committee: Lucretia Mott, influential Philadelphia Quaker; Lydia Maria Child, well-known author; and Maria Weston Chapman, fearless Boston abolitionist. When there was still one vacancy on the Executive Committee, Ray nominated a black woman, Hester Lane, but was talked into withdrawing her name. Ray's acid comment was "Mrs. Hester Lane is well known in this city as a woman of good character and sense, and has been a slave, but the 'principle' could not carry her color—eh!"[60] Ray's heart, however, was not in the strife between white Garrisonians (mostly Bostonians) and white Tappanites (heavily made up of New Yorkers). Before the annual meetings he had deplored the vendetta and doubted that blacks could mediate the differences. Afterward he defined his own position as editor: "We . . . intend to remain perfectly free, as a colored man, for whose rights the entire Anti-Slavery machinery is contending, and through the [journal] of the *colored people,* to reprove all parties in whatsoever in our judgment is wrong."[61]

Ray's editorial declaration of black neutrality in relation to white abo-

60. Quarles, *Black Abolitionists,* 68; *Colored American,* May 23, 30, 1840. Ray had also shown a special interest in the rights of female delegates at the 1839 annual meeting. With David Ruggles, Henry Highland Garnet, and Gerrit Smith, he had voted for women's votes being counted in the tallies. Lewis Tappan, James Birney, Beriah Green, and Peter Williams, Jr., had voted against this move. American Anti-Slavery Society, *Sixth Annual Report* (New York, 1839), 29.

61. *Colored American,* May 2, 9, 1840; *National Anti-Slavery Standard,* June 11, 1840.

litionist infighting was confirmed at a large meeting of New York blacks at Theodore Wright's church a couple of days after the termination of the American Anti-Slavery Society's annual meeting. This gathering at the First Colored Presbyterian Church was called to wish Garrison a bon voyage as he set out for the forthcoming world antislavery conference in London. Wright was chosen chairman of the meeting and Ray, its secretary. A black Garrisonian proposed that the largely black audience endorse Garrison and the other Garrisonians who had been chosen delegates to the London convention by the AASS. An objection was raised that if the meeting were to endorse anyone, it should endorse all delegates chosen for the London conference, including James Birney, Liberty (abolitionist) party candidate for president of the United States, and Samuel Cornish, elected by the new American and Foreign Anti-Slavery Society. Garrison urged passage of the original motion, but Ray spoke for the broader endorsement, saying that approving only part of the whole American contingent implied censure of the others. Cornish vehemently endorsed Ray's position, as did Lewis Tappan. The original resolution was withdrawn.[62]

Ray sent to Birney a detailed report of this meeting, including careful comments on black attitudes toward Garrison: "If the colored people of this City, or any section of the country, do manifest less warmth of feeling, than formerly towards *Mr. Garrison* it is in part oweing to our *Friends* haveing multiplied (who are equally active . . . with *Mr. Garrison*)." So now, wrote Ray, the good feeling is directed toward many whites, not concentrated on the Boston editor. Ray went even further and deplored the party spirit shown in Garrison's *Liberator* since the split had begun to develop among white abolitionists.[63]

These events of May 1840 clarified, especially for black leaders in New York, the fact that blacks had their own agenda and needed to get on with it. To underline this fact, one of the goals of the New York black petition campaign of the past three and a half years was achieved on the very eve of the stormy AASS annual meeting. The state legislature on May 14 passed a law guaranteeing a jury trial for alleged fugitive slaves. What part black petitioning had had in bringing this about is not known. This act of legislation, however, highlighted the fact that for great numbers of blacks, Garrisonian moral purism was a luxury they could not afford.

62. Article from the *Emancipator* reprinted in the *Colored American,* May 30, 1840.

63. Dwight L. Dumond (ed.), *Letters of James Gillespie Birney, 1831–1857* (2 vols.; New York, 1938), I, 575–79.

During the summer of 1840, black leaders in New York State made two important moves to intensify their political activity in support of the vote for all black men. A state convention, for blacks only, was called for August to orchestrate public statements arguing the case for the franchise and to coordinate the gathering of petitions and interviews with key legislators on the eve of decisive voting early in 1841. These same months brought a consolidation of support by black leaders for the Liberty party, whose candidates for federal and state office stood not only for immediate emancipation but also for implementing basic civil rights for free blacks. Charles Ray and his younger colleague Henry Highland Garnet were prominent in these developments.

6. HENRY HIGHLAND GARNET, CHARLES RAY, AND BLACK ACTION PROGRAMS IN NEW YORK STATE IN THE 1840s

That Almighty Being who said, "let there be light and there was light," has called into being the Spirit of this age, to bring out his oppressed poor from under their "task-masters."

—Henry Highland Garnet, 1842

The political efforts of Afro-Americans in New York State in the late 1830s and early 1840s grew out of their previous achievements: the founding of independent black churches, black journalism, efforts to improve black education, black involvement in the movement for immediate emancipation, and organized black assistance for fugitive slaves. The political efforts were also fueled by disillusionment—a recognition of the futility of seeking civil rights for free blacks by exhorting white abolitionists, who turned out, by and large, to be indifferent to the effects of caste prejudice, or themselves distrustful of blacks' abilities, or skittish about socializing with blacks, or all three. Black leaders became convinced that the political process could be more dependable than the attitudes of white liberals. Charles Ray compared the founding of the American Anti-Slavery Society and its impact on blacks with the country's Declaration of Independence in 1776 and the effect of that manifesto "upon the mind and energies of our oppressed nation." By 1840, however, black leaders in New York knew that another declaration of independence was essential, the insistence on independent agitation by blacks to change discriminatory state laws. Both Charles Ray and Henry Highland Garnet saw such agitation as being of one piece with the movement to free the slaves. New legislation and emancipation were parts of "a new creation" being initiated by the Spirit of God and embodied in the imagination, the will, and the energy of leaders of the oppressed themselves.

Independent political efforts by blacks were to falter prior to the Civil

War. Looking at the sweep of Afro-American history from 1776 to the present, however, the decision to organize black petition campaigns, black state conventions, and black lobbying with state legislators did, to use Ray's words, "call forth energies and powers which [blacks] were not aware of possessing."[1] In these historic developments in New York State, Henry Highland Garnet and Charles Ray were central figures.

Garnet, born in 1815, eight years after Ray, continues to fascinate students of nineteenth-century American history.[2] He was a man of unblinking courage, intense emotions, forceful mind, flashing eloquence, and not infrequently, apparent arrogance. His life experiences ran the gamut from slave to distinguished Presbyterian minister. Among the primary influences on him, beyond his own family, was Theodore Wright, his first minister and his revered co-worker in radical reform until Wright's death in 1847. Closest of all in collaboration with Garnet in the crucial 1840s was Charles Ray. The talents of these two were very different. Garnet had a strong desire for center stage, the presence to command it, and the mental and verbal brilliance to keep it. He was also deeply restless and had a volatile temper. Ray's abilities were less obtrusive: warm interest in other people, clarity of expression, whether written or spoken, administrative ability, and a patient determination to promote understanding and united effort among black people. Both men shared a deep commitment to biblical Christianity and to making that Christianity available to the less advantaged of their race. In the 1840s and 1850s, two others became close personal friends of Garnet and Ray and were their co-workers on many fronts: Amos Beman, pastor of a black Congregational church in New Haven, and James W. C. Pennington, Congregational minister in Hartford in the 1840s and successor to Theodore Wright in the First Colored Presbyterian Church (later the Prince Street Presbyterian Church) in New York City.

Information on Garnet's family background and his school days comes from Alexander Crummell, who as a boy lived next door to Garnet in New York City. Crummell and Garnet were schoolmates through their teens, fellow college students at Oneida, and respected friends, even dur-

1. *Colored American*, July 13, 1839.

2. See especially Earl Ofari, "*Let Your Motto Be Resistance": The Life and Thought of Henry Highland Garnet* (Boston, 1972); Jane H. Pease and William H. Pease, *Bound with Them in Chains: A Biographical History of the Antislavery Movement* (Westport, Conn., 1972), 162–90; Joel Schor, *Henry Highland Garnet, A Voice of Black Radicalism in the Nineteenth Century* (Westport, Conn., 1977); and Martin Pasternak, "Rise Now and Fly to Arms: The Life of Henry Highland Garnet" (Ph.D. dissertation, University of Massachusetts, 1981).

ing the many years when Crummell was far removed, doing mission work in Africa. Garnet's grandfather had been a Mandingo chieftain and warrior. Captured in a tribal war, he had been sold to slave traders and bought by the owner of a Maryland plantation. Garnet's father, George, had been born into slavery and given the surname Trusty on that plantation. When Henry was about nine years old, his father secured permission for himself, his wife, his two children, and his brother's family to attend a slave funeral several miles from the home plantation. They all set out, but for Delaware instead of the funeral. They traveled when it was dark and hid when it was light. After arduous nights and days they reached Wilmington and the home of the Quaker Thomas Garrett, a well-known conductor on the Underground Railroad. From there the four Garnets were sent on to Bucks County, Pennsylvania, and a few months later, to New York City.

Soon after arrival the father conducted what Henry Garnet's earliest biographer called a "re-baptism, or baptism to Liberty, . . . simple, solemn, primitive." Each member of the family was given a new surname, Garnet instead of Trusty, perhaps in honor of Thomas Garrett, who had sheltered them. Alexander Crummell remembered George Garnet as "a perfect Apollo, in form and figure; with beautifully moulded limbs, and fine delicate features; just like hundreds of grand Mandingoes I have seen in Africa." He was a grave, awesome, and deeply religious man, who became a class leader and exhorter in the Mott Street AME Church. Henry's mother was equally striking, but in a very different way: "a most comely and beautiful woman; tall and finely moulded with a bright, intellectual face, lit up with lustrous, twinkling, laughing eyes—which she gave as an inheritance to her son."[3]

Henry Garnet entered the African Free School in 1826 soon after his arrival in New York. His schoolmates included boys who would become well-known black leaders: engraver Patrick Reason, educator Charles Reason, Rhode Island resort owner George Downing, actor Ira Aldridge, physician James McCune Smith, and minister and abolitionist-orator (and cousin) Samuel Ringgold Ward—as well as Crummell. Family financial pressures soon forced Garnet in 1829 to go to sea as a cabin boy. While he was away on a run to Washington, D.C., a relative of George

3. James McCune Smith, "Sketch of the Life and Labors of Henry Highland Garnet," *A Memorial Discourse, by Rev. Henry Highland Garnet . . . February 12, 1865* (Philadelphia, 1865), 17–20; Alexander Crummell, *Africa and America: Addresses and Discourses* (1891; rpr. Miami, 1969), 272–74.

Garnet's original master came to the family home to seize them all as recently escaped slaves. By jumping from an upper-story window, the father escaped, as did his wife. Henry's sister was caught by the slave hunters and taken before the city recorder, but she was able to prove herself a resident of the city. When Henry returned, he found the family home abandoned, all its furniture destroyed or stolen, his father in hiding and his mother being cared for by a couple operating a nearby grocery. Young Garnet very nearly went berserk. After spending his earnings on a large clasp knife, he charged up and down Broadway in the hopes that the slave hunters would try to capture him. Friends bore down on the raging youth, and took him to live temporarily with a Quaker minister on Long Island. Here he was indentured to a Captain Smith, but his indenture was cut short after two years by an accident that led to a "white-swelling" in his right leg. He lost the use of the limb for good and had to hobble about on a crutch until the leg was amputated years later.[4]

Crummell was convinced that these events powerfully affected Garnet's subsequent attitudes: "The seriousness which is the fruit of affliction, the melancholy and the reflection which spring from pain and suffering, for he was now a cripple, soon brought Garnet to the foot of the Cross."[5] Garnet began attending Sunday School at Theodore Wright's First Colored Presbyterian Church in 1833, some two years after he had come back from Long Island to live once more with his family. Wright baptized him and had a large share in Garnet's eventual decision to become a Presbyterian minister. James McCune Smith wrote feelingly in 1865 of the strong ties that bound Wright and Garnet together over the ensuing years: "In Garnet's youth, now budding into manhood, and in the maturer years that followed, they were, allowing for the more brilliant gifts of the younger, one in spirit, one in effort, one in all their noble resistance to caste and slavery, one in their manifold and ceaseless endeavor to elevate people of color."[6]

Garnet's first-rate mind and driving curiosity opened doors to his education in spite of the prevailing obstacles against young blacks' being given more than elementary schooling. While he was on Long Island from 1829 to 1831, he was tutored by a scholarly son of the man to whom he was indentured. On his return to New York City, Garnet seems to have attended the Episcopal Collegiate School under Messrs. Curtis and

4. Smith, "Sketch of Garnet," in *A Memorial Discourse by . . . Garnet*, 25–27.

5. Crummell, *Africa and America*, 277.

6. Smith, "Sketch of Garnet," in *A Memorial Discourse by . . . Garnet*, 29.

Leiboldt; there he began the study of Greek and Latin. But black students at this primarily white high school were hampered by not being allowed to sit in the same room with whites. When Peter Williams, Jr., opened a short-lived classical high school for blacks, Garnet was in its student body, as he was in the Phoenix High School opened in 1833 by Theodore Wright, Samuel Cornish, and Peter Williams, Jr.[7]

In 1835 an exciting new opportunity arose for able and ambitious black high school students. New Hampshire abolitionists launched the Noyes Academy in Canaan, New Hampshire, for young people, black and white, male and female. Three blacks from New York City set out for the new school: the seventeen-year-old orator Thomas Sidney, the sixteen-year-old Crummell, and the nineteen-year-old Garnet. It was a long and difficult trip, especially for Garnet, who was both crippled and sick. After a boat trip to Providence, they took the stagecoach to Boston, then to Concord, then to Hanover, and finally to Canaan. Many years later Crummell recalled the four hundred miles of riding on top of the coach. They usually were refused food or shelter at hotel stopovers: "I can never forget his [Garnet's] sufferings— . . . from pain, . . . cold and exposure, . . . thirst and hunger, . . . taunt and insult at every village and town, . . . as we rode, mounted upon the top of the coach. . . . The sight of three black youths, in gentlemanly garb, traveling through New England was, in those days, a most unusual sight . . . [and] brought out universal sneers and ridicule."[8]

The roughly forty white students at the academy warmly welcomed the fourteen young black men and at least one young black woman (Julia Williams, a refugee from the Prudence Crandall School in Canterbury, Connecticut). In spite of an auspicious beginning, trouble soon broke out in Canaan, as it had two years earlier in Canterbury. The three New Yorkers unwittingly precipitated it by delivering stirring antislavery speeches at the July 4 meeting of the New Hampshire Anti-Slavery Society in nearby Plymouth. After weeks of angry muttering among the farmers in the surrounding region, a band of them brought their oxen to Canaan. Reinforced by townspeople incensed over the "nigger-school," these locals seized the main academy building, hitched many yoke of oxen to it, dragged it to a swamp half a mile away, and burned it. Garnet,

7. *Ibid.*, 27f.; Schor, *Henry Highland Garnet*, 9; Crummell, *Africa and America*, 278; Wilson Armistead, *A Tribute for the Negro: Being a Vindication of the Moral, Intellectual, and Religious Capabilities of the Coloured Portion of Mankind . . .* (Manchester, England, 1848), 511.

8. Crummell, *Africa and America*, 279f.

who roomed in the home of the minister-principal, anticipated further trouble, secured a shotgun, and oversaw the making of ammunition by fellow students. In the evening a band of horsemen approached the house where the black students lived. When one rode past and fired at the occupants, Garnet returned fire with his shotgun. The assault was checked, but the black students were ordered to leave the state within two weeks. Again Sidney, Crummell, and Garnet made a long coach trip, this one down the Connecticut River valley and across to Albany. Garnet was so seriously ill that on arrival at home he was confined to his bed for two months.[9]

As already discussed, in the early 1830s the Oneida Institute in upstate New York had opened its admissions to young black nen. During the 1836 academic year Garnet, Crummell, Sidney, and Amos Beman all enrolled at Oneida. Garnet had to spend a year in the institute's preparatory department, presumably because his long spells of earlier illness had prevented continual study. He graduated in the fall of 1839 or in 1840. The years at Oneida were of critical importance for Garnet's development. Although the required study of the Greek and Latin classics had been dropped by 1837, academic discipline was demanding. What Garnet learned about biblical and other literature, logic, rhetoric, economics, government, mathematics, natural science, and moral philosophy would stand him in good stead in subsequent years of preaching and public speaking. Equally important was the mood set by President Beriah Green and other teachers, "an animating mix of Puritan discipline, religious warmth and zealous abolitionism."[10] On campus and off, Garnet was wrestling with two particular questions that remained central for him: How can slaves and free black people effectively resist the evil of white oppression? And what are the intentions of a just and caring God for the human race, the faithful and the unfaithful?

Violent resistance against oppression was no merely theoretical possibility for Garnet. As a fourteen-year-old raging up and down Broadway and as a Noyes Academy student firing at a racist mob, he had embodied

9. *Liberator,* July 25, 1835; Crummell, *Africa and America,* 280f., 283; Smith, "Sketch of Garnet," in *A Memorial Discourse by . . . Garnet,* 30f. For alternative versions of this much-repeated story, see Pasternak, "Rise Now and Fly to Arms," 14–22.

10. *Catalogue of the Officers and Students of the Oneida Institute, 1836* (Whitesborough, N.Y., 1837); *Colored American,* November 4, 1837; Mabee, *Black Education in New York State,* 25; Milton Sernett, "First Honor: Oneida Institute's Role in the Fight Against American Racism and Slavery," *New York History,* LXVI (1985), 101–22; Sernett, *Abolition's Axe,* chap. 4.

it. However, strong forces moved this high-spirited young man to a commitment to Christian nonviolence. In 1834 as a high school student, he, David Ruggles, and other young blacks in New York City founded the Garrison Literary and Benevolent Association for boys from four to twenty years of age. In deciding to name their society after the editor of the *Liberator,* these young men were honoring his relentless attacks on "tyrants and oppressors." They were also endorsing a battle against evil fought by nonviolent means. At the Oneida Institute, Garnet was further imbued with the mixture of Christian nonviolence and aggressive resistance to evil that characterized Garrisonianism. There, however, the leaders were not anticlerical but were themselves clergy, white men whose views and actions paralleled those of Theodore Wright. The Oneida Institute had come under attack by antiabolitionists only a few months after Garnet arrived. This time it was not a local mob, as in New Hampshire, but the New York State Senate that opened fire on Beriah Green's college as a hotbed of abolitionism. New York antislavery men resisted effectively. They gathered in Utica and passed resolutions accusing the Senate and journalists of seeking to destroy the reputation of the college and undermine its financial support merely because its officers and students, as Christians, found slavery to be a sin. Such actions, they declared, were "not only a dangerous infringement of our political compact, but a daring and wicked evasion of God's moral government." This spirited response quieted public criticism for a time.[11]

Garnet, ever restless, was not one to remain confined to his college campus. In the spring of 1837 he was in New York City for the annual meeting of the American Anti-Slavery Society. Writing Crummell, who had stayed at the college, Garnet reported good speeches by several white abolitionists. He also reported on his own growing reputation: "I am quite popular among the people, and were I not so well acquainted with the vanity of the world there would be some danger of being puffed up. I [am] called the poet, and am solicited to write in albums, and so on." Garnet went on to speak of Julia Williams, who had been with him and Crummell during the ill-fated days at Noyes Academy and whom he would marry five years later. She was now one of Boston's delegates to a women's antislavery gathering in New York City: "I had the pleasure of waiting on her six or seven times, and dined and supped with her. O what [a] lovely being she is! Modest susceptible and chaste. She seems

11. Quarles, *Black Abolitionists,* 105; *Liberator,* April 19, 1834; *Emancipator,* May 12, 1836, cited by Schor, *Henry Highland Garnet,* 18.

to have everything which beautifys a female. A good christian, and a scholar." Garnet closed his letter in great haste: "I am going to Brunswick to speechify. . . . I don't know when I shall come up."[12]

Speechify Garnet did and continued to do. A few examples show the range of occasions. In August 1837 he was one of the main speakers at the "monster meeting" of young blacks in New York City that endorsed Philip Bell and Charles Ray's mission to gather petition signatures throughout New York State. The following February, at the Zion Church (AMEZ) in New York, Garnet praised the members of a black women's charitable association for taking seriously the claims of the poor around them. On August 1, the day celebrating West Indian emancipation, in 1838 in Utica and in 1839 in Troy, Garnet was a featured orator. His debut as a speaker to white abolitionists came in May 1840, when, having been recommended by Beriah Green, he addressed the American Anti-Slavery Society.[13]

Garnet was the first former slave to give one of the major addresses to the AASS. In attacking slavery, he knew from boyhood experience what he was talking about. In his speech, he wrestled with the enormity of whites' savage exploitation of blacks. He also tried to understand how his strong belief in God related to this ongoing enormity. White America, Garnet declared, has proved to be a haven for hypocrisy. Settled by pilgrims fleeing religious tyranny and established as a republic with its dearly bought covenant of democratic rights, America has kept millions enslaved long after Great Britain, its former oppressor, freed its own slaves. If citizenship is granted for services rendered, who stands eligible ahead of American blacks? They have made the southern soil fruitful through generation after generation of field labor. They have fought and died for the United States in two wars. And most crucial of all, they have supported the central pillar of American institutions, American religion—that is, true religion, as distinguished from the religion of churches in collusion with slavery. The exercise of such true religion, Garnet insisted, "is the salt that has kept the nation from moral putrefaction."[14]

Garnet was making a case for true black Christians being America's elect, a theme that Pennington and Beman would pick up later. In a suc-

12. Henry Garnet to Alexander Crummell, May 13, 1837, A.L.S. in Schomburg Center for Research in Black Culture, New York Public Library, Astor, Lenox and Tilden Foundations (Microfilm copy in Carter and Ripley [eds.], *BAP,* reel 2, item 53).

13. *Colored American,* September 7, 1837; March 15, August 25, 1838; September 28, 1839; Pasternak, "Rise Now and Fly to Arms," 32.

14. For the full text of Garnet's speech, see Ofari, "*Let Your Motto Be Resistance,*" 127–35.

cession of phrases with clear biblical references, Garnet declared that "the spirit of Christianity" is like sunlight. It is universe-wide, it is blind to color, and it intends good for man. The God of whom this light is a manifestation—the God who hears the raven's cry and the young lion's hungry roar—"most assuredly forgets not the petitions of his chosen people." Blacks, whipped away from natural rights by a distorted church and a distorted government, have sent up prayers from the darkness of their captivity. In consideration of these supplications, "the Lord of Hosts has turned back the fiery waves of the vengeance which a disregard of His law in high places has justly merited." The vengeance has been earned by the North, for its economic support of the slave system, as well as by the South. Garnet's final message to the AASS was itself a prayer. It asked for punishment as well as mercy:

> Avenge thy plundered poor, O Lord!
> But not with fire, but not with sword; . . .
> Chastise our country's locustry;[15]
> Nor let them feel thine heavier ire; . . .
> Let them in outraged mercy trust,
> And find that mercy they deny.

Charles Ray, who had probably known Garnet since 1833, was present for his AASS address. As senior editor of the *Colored American,* Ray reported, "For good sense and rare excellence, [it] has not been surpassed at any anniversary yet held by that Society." And William Lloyd Garrison declared, "Patrick Henry never spoke better." But Garnet's debut was also his farewell; only a few days later he joined seven other black ministers in the secession from the American Anti-Slavery Society.[16]

The American and Foreign Anti-Slavery Society, organized by the seceders, was committed to political activism and to implementing the democratic principles that they found in the federal constitution. The leading black abolitionists who had helped form the new society were convinced, however, that there were more effective instruments by which free blacks could agitate for emancipation and for civil rights than the traditional, primarily white national abolition societies. By 1840 Ray, Garnet, and others settled on two such instruments: all-black state conventions and a national political party committed to immediate emancipation. As

15. *Locustry* has Old Testament reverberations. A plague of locusts, devouring all plants and their fruit, descended on Egypt when the pharaoh refused to let the Hebrews go free. Here human ravagers (that is, oppressors) are the locusts.

16. *Colored American,* May 23, 1840.

they saw it, a state convention for blacks only that focused on the single issue of the black franchise could sharpen their demand and make it more audible to white political leaders. And a national third party for whites and blacks committed to the immediate emancipation of slaves could accomplish more than annual conventions of the already converted.

Ray, who had developed friendships with many white reformers at New York State and other antislavery meetings, at first hesitated to endorse an exclusive black convention. By early May 1840, however, favorable action by the New York legislature and Governor Seward guaranteeing a jury trial for blacks seized as alleged fugitive slaves convinced Ray that a conclave composed exclusively of blacks made sense. Late in May at a meeting in New York City chaired by Ray, forty-one blacks endorsed the call for such a state convention. Ray's and Theodore Wright's names headed the list. The rationale for the convention echoed Cornish's words of fifteen months earlier: "We are convinced, fellow citizens, that not only our political, but our depressed condition in all other respects in the State, owes itself . . . to the fact that we are politically weak. . . . The body politic sees in us, therefore, no favors to court, and nothing to fear." Garnet also signed the call as a delegate from Troy, which was next door to Albany, the proposed site of the convention. Garnet himself had composed an earlier and similar manifesto from Troy blacks meeting in the Liberty Street Presbyterian Church, where he had been pastor for some six months.[17]

To some white abolitionists, however, this black separatism seemed dangerous, more so than that of the earlier national black conventions, which had been less action oriented. The *National Anti-Slavery Standard,* mouthpiece of the American Anti-Slavery Society, came out strongly against blacks' excluding sympathetic whites from their gatherings. Such a policy would strengthen segregation in churches and schools and thereby impede the progress of free blacks. Rather, invite white abolitionists: "Teach them to forget, and forget yourselves as fast as possible, that you are colored men and women. Do not give 'color to the idea.'" The *Standard*'s editor further urged blacks not to push too fast. Ray disagreed; courteously but decisively, he insisted that blacks had taken their time in pressing for justice. If whites had not yet understood that the United States was the blacks' home and country as much as the whites', it was the whites' fault for not listening. Black political action was now in order, not more talk between blacks and whites. Moreover, an exclusively black

17. *Ibid.*, May 2, 1840; *National Anti-Slavery Standard,* June 18, 1840; *Colored American,* June 6, 27, 1840.

convention would be good for the black image, blacks' views of themselves, and whites' views of them. Ray agreed that white friends might come as spectators, but they should stay in the background. Otherwise, "such is the public disposition, they will regard the proceedings of the Convention as theirs, and not as ours."[18]

Over against Ray's confident separatism stood a black New Yorker whose words carried great weight. James McCune Smith, trained in medicine in Glasgow, had been for a time on the editorial staff of the *Colored American*. He was an articulate and energetic supporter of black advancement, but he feared a strong white counterattack against what might seem a threatening assertion of black political rights. Writing in the *Colored American*, Smith attributed the total disfranchisement of Pennsylvania blacks in 1838 to white anger against widespread black pressure for political equality. Moreover, said Smith, there was a principle at stake. He did not believe in banning anyone from any voluntary gathering on account of color. Smith's position was supported by William Whipper of the American Moral Reform Society and David Ruggles, secretary of the New York Vigilance Committee. On the eve of the convention, Ray tried to answer Smith's objections. He pointed out that Pennsylvania blacks had never organized as New York blacks were doing. The disfranchisement in Pennsylvania, Ray insisted, was due to other factors. Moreover, he was convinced that a tide of white support for unrestricted black franchise was building. He cited as evidence word "from high and respectable political sources" and the favorable notice given the convention by two influential newspapers that could never be accused of favoring abolition.[19]

For the success of the state convention and of the accelerated petition campaign, the position taken by large black denominations, especially the AMEZ and the AME churches of New York State, was important. It was, accordingly, gratifying to Ray and to Philip Bell, himself brought up in the AMEZ church, when the annual AMEZ conference strongly endorsed the *Colored American*'s position. The AME denomination, with the bulk of its membership in Philadelphia and further south, tended to keep a greater distance between itself and the political activism of Cornish, Wright, Ray, and Garnet than did the New York City–based AMEZ denomination. Ray had tried, in a June editorial on the forthcoming AME conference, to rouse that group to interest in secular politics:

18. *National Anti-Slavery Standard*, June 18, 1840; *Colored American*, May 2, July 8, 1840.

19. *Colored American*, August 15, 1840; Jane H. Pease and William H. Pease, "Black Power—The Debate in 1840," *Phylon*, XXIX (1968), 19–26.

"The ministers of this body are mostly from the South and West, and while they are men of worth and piety, they exhibit, perhaps, less of liberality and public spirit, and of interest in the great questions of the day, than the ministers of the [AMEZ church]." Ray wondered whether the difference lay in part in the advanced age of AME ministers. AME leaders took offense at these invidious comparisons, and Ray agreed to withdraw any aspersions cast on them if they were unwarranted. He had, however, accomplished his purpose of provoking them to more attentiveness to New York black political activities.[20]

The much-publicized New York State black convention took place from August 18 to 20, 1840, in Albany. It was the first of its kind in the country. Black clergy were prominent in its proceedings. Theodore Wright called the convention to order and gave the closing prayer. Among the vice-presidents was John T. Raymond, pastor of the Zion Baptist Church in New York City from 1832 to 1839 and a strong supporter of Ruggles in the vigilance committee of that city. Garnet was one of three secretaries. Charles Ray chaired the Business Committee, which established convention agenda from day to day. Two addresses were to be composed: one to the colored people of the state and the other to the state's citizenry at large. Garnet, Ray, and Wright were deputed to compose the former; Crummell, Wright, Ray, and others drew up the latter. Garnet was to chair the central committee of seven, all of whom lived near the state capitol, to coordinate black petitions to the legislature during the fall and winter.[21]

Nearly 140 delegates, representing communities all the way from Long Island to Buffalo, had come to the convention. Ray was immensely heartened: "If the Convention was a fair representation of our people in the State, then we are a more talented, a better educated, more improved people . . . than we had any anticipation we were." The best of it was that a majority of the attendees were young men. There also were many spectators, both men and women, from the greater Albany area. Among these were a number of the white leaders of the Whig party in Albany. Their consistent attendance, morning, afternoon, and evening, and their respectful attention suggested that they realized they were listening to their equals.[22]

20. *Colored American*, June 13, 20, 27, July 1, 1840.

21. Philip S. Foner and George E. Walker (eds.), *Proceedings of the Black State Conventions, 1840–1865* (2 vols.; Philadelphia, 1979–80), I, 5–26.

22. *Colored American*, August 29, 1840.

The dream of the convention's organizers and delegates was that this respectful attention on the part of white auditors would become contagious among New Yorkers at large. In retrospect, however, it can be seen that this hope was illusory. From election day in November 1840 until May 1841, when the state assembly decisively settled the question of a black vote for that session, Ray and Garnet orchestrated the most intensive and extensive black political effort of the country up to that time. The pages of the *Colored American* were sprinkled weekly with accounts of local meetings in dozens of New York communities, each exhorting its citizens to participate in the petitioning for the franchise. Frequent editorials by Ray repeated the message.

All that was left to do was for Garnet to deliver the petitions to the appropriate assemblymen and to do whatever further lobbying seemed wise. However, Garnet had again fallen desperately ill with his recurrent leg infection. In December the limb that had brought him so much pain was amputated. His recovery was rapid. By early January he reported to Ray that he was once more able to turn his attention "from the chamber of affliction, to other important things." By mid-February he delivered the petitions and was highly optimistic. Late in March, Ray, too, sensed victory in the offing: "The mistiness of night is receding. Light and truth are springing up, and justice is seemingly about to take possession of the throne."[23]

Prospects for ending black disfranchisement in New York in March 1841 were substantially improved over the situation four years earlier when Cornish, Bell, and others had launched their campaign. The number of black signatures on petitions delivered to the legislature had risen to 2,093, as compared with 620 in 1837. The climate of white opinion also seemed to be changing, undoubtedly influenced by the recent visibility of responsible black leaders, as well as by the growth of antislavery convictions. Garnet had been courteously received when he delivered petitions to individual assemblymen, and they had assured him that they would speak for the black franchise when the matter came to the assembly floor.

When the issue of the black vote was referred to the assembly's judiciary committee, Garnet was invited to appear. On the evening of February 18 he delivered an address stressing the blacks' claim to full citizenship by virtue of services rendered the country in wartime and peacetime, and "re-

23. *Colored American*, January 16, March 27, 1841.

publican and loyal" use of the franchise when blacks had it; the damaging effects of disfranchisement ("discouragement, pauperism and crime"); and the openness of voters at large to see justice done blacks in this matter. Garnet asserted blacks' "determination not to cease blowing the ram's horn (like Joshua marching around Jericho) until the massive walls of injustice shall fall and crumble into dust." In his report for the *Colored American,* Garnet included the informal word around the Albany capitol that a bill endorsing reenfranchisement would pass the House by a large majority and the Senate almost unanimously. Pleased indeed that "one so young and humble" had had an impact on "the wise and learned judiciary committee," Garnet tried to temper his pride: "God blessed the *truth for its own sake.*"[24]

Assembly action in April on reenfranchising New York blacks proved Garnet very wrong; the measure was defeated by a vote of forty-six to twenty-nine. How could the black leaders have been so far off the mark? Presumably they were lulled by the statements of a liberal governor, some liberal legislators, and liberal journalists into greatly underestimating the degree of antiblack prejudice in the constituency. For example, Governor Seward, in his annual message to the legislature in January 1841, had deplored the property requirement for black voters as "arbitrary" and "incongruous with our institutions." Also immensely heartening to Ray and Garnet was the statement by the Whig editor of the influential Albany *Evening Journal,* Thurlow Weed, taking a stand in March 1841 for ending restrictions on black voting rights. Weed spoke of "the spirit of our age and the genius of our institutions." He reiterated the arguments of black leaders themselves: the independence and devotion to democracy of blacks who had voted, as well as the notable efforts by blacks to improve their condition in spite of often being barred from common schools and the higher-paying jobs of skilled workers. Indeed, the assembly's own judiciary committee had reported to the House that judging by petitions submitted, "public sentiment in all quarters is strongly indicated in its [equal franchise for blacks] favor."[25]

After the defeat in the legislature, Ray's public words were resolute

24. *Ibid.,* March 13, 1841.

25. Field, *Politics of Race,* 48; *Colored American,* January 16, March 27, 1841; New York State Assembly, *Documents* (1841), no. 183, p. 4, cited by Field, *Politics of Race,* 46. Since the Judiciary Committee in 1838 had reported receiving petitions for equal suffrage from 9,300 persons, it seems likely that the petitions delivered by Garnet to the assembly in 1841 had been swelled by many from whites.

regarding the long run: "The Legislature have gone far ahead . . . of any previous one, upon this subject, though they have not done all they ought to have done, nor all we expected them to do. We shall see that the matter does not rest here." Five weeks after this statement, Ray addressed the New York Vigilance Committee, which was meeting in celebration of the legislature's repeal of the Nine Months Law, which made it illegal any longer for slave owners to bring slaves into the state even for nine months and keep them enslaved. The black editor used this occasion to plan for another state convention the following August. This time the exclusion of whites was modified: "Bring with you, also, your white friends, who regard the objects of the convention as of paramount importance."[26]

The 1841 black convention was held in Troy, in Garnet's church. There were thirty delegates from the Albany area and sixty-eight from New York City. Garnet, Ray, Wright, and Crummell were again prominent in the proceedings. This year Ray chaired the committee to prepare an address to New York voters. The result was a crisply written document with arguments addressed directly to white anxieties. First, blacks have committed no crime to deserve disfranchisement. The higher proportion of blacks arrested results from many being apprehended for trifling crimes—the types of misdemeanors for which whites are generally not even detained by the police. Second, blacks can be politically equal but socially distinct, as are Jews or Quakers or blacks in Massachusetts, where they do have the vote. Third, whites can rest assured that blacks will not vote in a bloc for one party; witness the record in Massachusetts. Finally, blacks are as literate as whites; in New York City, one black is in public schools for every seventeen whites, whereas there is one black to every eighteen whites in the overall population.[27]

Of special significance in the business of this state gathering was a declaration supported in speeches by Wright, Garnet, and Ray and aimed at politically quiescent black clergy in the state. This time the declaration, however, avoided citing any specific denomination: "The colored ministry of New York, who withhold their influence and cooperation in furthering the efforts which are now being made for the restoration of the political rights of their brethren, fail to discharge their duty to God, and to sustain the relations which exist between them and their brethren."[28]

During the closing months of 1841 there were major setbacks in New

26. *Colored American,* May 8, June 19, 1841.

27. Foner and Walker (eds.), *Proceedings of the Black State Conventions,* I, 27–30.

28. *Colored American,* September 11, 1841.

York blacks' political prospects. In the November election the Whigs lost control of both houses of the legislature, and the comparatively progressive Governor Seward decided not to enter the 1842 race for reelection. Ray, after years of staving off financial collapse for the *Colored American,* finally closed the paper at the end of December 1841. New York State black conventions were held annually for the next several years, and petitions for the vote were gathered year by year. However, it was not until 1846, when a convention was called to revise the state constitution, that new life was infused into the struggle for the black franchise. In the meantime Ray and Garnet remained active in the other major crusades for Afro-American rights: the concerted effort to assist fugitive slaves and the emergence of a third national political party committed to immediate emancipation.

Ray had been an active abolitionist from the time of the founding of the American Anti-Slavery Society, shortly after his first arrival in New York City. He also had become closely identified with the work of the New York Vigilance Committee at the start of its program in 1835. Some fifty years later, after Ray's death, his daughters described three types of workers in the movement to liberate slaves: those who wrote or spoke eloquently on their behalf, those who gave generously to enable the purchase of freedom, and "those who not only went about quietly awakening an interest in the bondman, but actually came in contact with him, aiding him with counsel, sympathy, and often with shelter." To this last group they felt their father had belonged, and they quoted him to support their contention: "Many a midnight hour have I, with others, walked the streets, their [that is, the fugitive slaves'] leader and guide; and my home was an almost daily receptacle for numbers of them at a time."[29]

As soon as Garnet had finished his academic work at Oneida in the fall of 1839 and had settled in his pastorate in Troy next door to Albany, he became active in aiding fugitives.[30] By the early 1840s Wright and Ray (who had succeeded Wright as president of the New York Vigilance Committee) often worked in tandem with Garnet in forwarding runaways. Ray described one such mission:

> We had here, on one occasion, a party of twenty-eight persons of all ages, from the old grandmother to a child of five years. We destined them for Canada. I secured passage for them in a barge, and Mr. Wright and myself spent

29. Ray and Ray, *Sketch of Charles B. Ray,* 23f.

30. Garnet later claimed to have given hospitality to 150 runaways in one year. *Weekly Anglo-African,* September 17, 1859.

> the day in providing food, and personally saw them on the barge. I then took the regular passenger boat [at the] foot of Cortlandt Street, and started. Arriving in the morning, I reported to the Committee at Albany, and then returned to Troy and gave Brother Garnet notice, and he and I spent the day in visiting friends of the cause there, to raise money to help the party through to Toronto, Canada, *via* Oswego. We succeeded, with what they raised in Albany, in making up the deficiency in my hands, to send them all the way from here with safety.[31]

There is no record of Ray's or Garnet's losing any of their "passengers" on the Underground Railroad to slave catchers or federal marshals. However, the very success of the operation rested on an absence of publicity, so not much is known about it.

The legitimacy of resorting to violence to aid captives was debated early in the New York Vigilance Committee. Cornish and Ray parted company with the committee's staff member David Ruggles over his encouraging black crowds to use force if need be to gain the release of those arrested as alleged fugitives. However, Carleton Mabee is right in describing Wright, Cornish, and Ray as belonging to the "limited nonviolence" school, as contrasted with the categorical nonviolence of the Garrisonians. As early as 1837 Cornish, criticizing the blanket commitment to "Peace" of Whipper and his American Moral Reform Society, observed that he had "yet to learn what virtue there would be in using moral weapons . . . against a kidnapper." Sixteen months later he repeated his justification of physical force and even "offensive aggression" in defense of "personal liberty and rights." At a mass meeting of blacks in December 1837, however, in a discussion of the legitimacy of violent resistance against kidnappers, the defense of nonviolence, which won the debate by a small margin, was led by Wright and Ray. They clearly feared provoking an antiblack riot.[32]

Between 1839 and 1841 there was a dramatic development in the battle for the freeing of slaves. It was the result of a successful mutiny on a slave ship and became a spectacular expansion of the year-to-year work of the

31. Ray and Ray, *Sketch of Charles B. Ray,* 35f.

32. Mabee, *Black Freedom,* 58; *Colored American,* September 9, 1837; Mabee, *Black Freedom,* 277; *Colored American,* December 9, 1837. On January 22 and February 5, 1838, there was further discussion, led by Garnet and Ruggles, of the use of force against physical aggression. *Colored American,* February 3, 1838. For the range and ambivalence of white abolitionists' positions on the resort to violence, see Lawrence J. Friedman, *Gregarious Saints: Self and Community in American Abolitionism, 1830–1870* (Cambridge, England, 1982), chap. 7.

vigilance committees in New York City and elsewhere. The *Amistad* was a ship chartered by two Spaniards to carry roughly fifty recently purchased enslaved Mendi, a West African people, from Cuba to Príncipe. Led by Joseph Cinqué, son of a Mendi chief, the slaves overpowered the ship's crew, seized their weapons, killed the captain and the cook, and set the sailors adrift in a small boat. The two owners' lives were spared on the condition that they steer the ship back to Africa. After the *Amistad* followed a zigzag course, lasting sixty-three days, a United States Navy brig sighted it off Long Island. It was boarded and taken to New London, Connecticut. The Africans were imprisoned and charged with the murder of the ship's captain.

The story of the *Amistad* and that of the ensuing trial before the United States Circuit Court in New Haven received extensive press coverage. Abolitionists rose to defend the Mendi, declaring them kidnapped from Africa and justified, as any free people, in using force to recover their freedom. Lewis Tappan and S. S. Jocelyn formed the Amistad Committee to raise money for the Africans' defense. Contributions poured in over the next eighteen months from both blacks and whites. Two able lawyers, Theodore Sedgwick and Roger Baldwin, took on the case in its early stages.[33] When the circuit court judge decided for the release of the Mendi, the local district attorney, pressured by the angry president Martin Van Buren, appealed the case to the United States Supreme Court. Former president John Quincy Adams, now a Massachusetts senator seventy-three years old and nearly blind, agreed to argue the case before the Court. In March 1841, after a marathon argument by Adams, the Court ordered that Cinqué and his fellow Africans be freed.[34]

One final task remained for American supporters of the Africans: to raise the funds needed to return them to their homeland. Meetings for this purpose were held in black churches in New England, New York, and Philadelphia, the star attractions at each being a contingent of the Mendi, some of whom could now sing a hymn in English or read a Bible passage. Ray reported at length on one of the New York meetings, held in the large Zion Church (AMEZ). Several resolutions were introduced and spoken to by James McCune Smith and Ray. The first was a crisp

33. Theodore Sedgwick was the grandson of the lawyer and congressman after whom Theodore Sedgwick Wright had been named. Roger Baldwin had been one of the four who, in 1831, had voted for the founding of the New Haven manual labor college for blacks, in the face of some seven hundred opponents.

34. Wyatt-Brown, *Lewis Tappan,* 205–12; Quarles, *Black Abolitionists,* 76–78.

exoneration of the Africans' killing of the captain and cook of the *Amistad:* "The Mendi people did no more than exercise that natural resistance against tyrannical oppression, which the consent of all ages of mankind, and the example of the American Revolution has sanctioned as both right and lawful." The last resolution was a tribute to the Africans. It pointed to the "intelligent sympathy" aroused among Americans by the Mendi, as well as to the latter's "singular aptness of intellect," as powerful and irrefutable evidence of "the common humanity of the natives of Africa, and of these United States." All these resolutions were unanimously adopted by the large assembly. Toward the end of this unforgettable occasion, Theodore Wright prayerfully sounded the note of "African redemption," one that was to become a compelling call for a growing number of Afro-American leaders, both clerical and lay, during the next two decades. Wright thanked God that the Mendi, having been introduced to "the truths of the gospel," would be returning home eager to share these truths with their people. Thus an opportunity was providentially offered to friends of missions "to unite for the evangelization of Africa."[35]

Two months later, in July 1841, Garnet sent a letter to the *Colored American* entitled "Shall Africa Have the Gospel?" It foreshadowed his special sense of mission to that continent during the 1850s and to the end of his life.[36] That same summer forty-three black delegates from Massachusetts, Rhode Island, Connecticut, New York, and Pennsylvania met in Hartford to found the Union Missionary Society (UMS), an organization committed to carrying the Christian gospel to Africa.

It would be difficult to overestimate the importance of escaped slaves and of the efforts made on their behalf in moving larger numbers of whites in the North toward support of universal and immediate emancipation. However, successful slave escapes, whether by individuals, families, or shiploads, left the mass of the enslaved no better off. During the 1840s two visionary programs were advanced to effect the emancipation of slaves at large. One rested on nationwide political action, the other on slave revolt. Ray and Garnet strongly supported the former. Garnet, at certain moments, also invited the latter, an enactment on a grand scale of what the crew of the *Amistad* had accomplished.

35. *Colored American,* May 22, 1841. Ironically enough, once Cinqué arrived back in his homeland, he established himself as a slave trader. Samuel E. Morison, *The Oxford History of the American People* (New York, 1965), 520.

36. *Colored American,* July 24, 1841.

Serious talk of forming a third national political party committed to immediate emancipation began in the summer of 1839. Cornish opposed it, fearing the corrupting effect of positions of power in even a minority political party. Moreover, an advance commitment to vote only for abolitionists, he argued, would destroy any black leverage with a major party such as the Whigs. Garnet and Ray, in contrast, strenuously supported the third party movement. Ray's rationale was simple. The slave system was the single great evil. No black could rest easy in his conscience if he helped elect someone who was going to make peace with slave owners. Ray took sharp issue with Cornish for shying away from abolitionist party politics: "Brother Cornish . . . stands by the old paths, but does not enquire for the new. He embraces every true principle, but goes but JUST HALF WAY. There is not a feature of what people falsely call, ultrism in his character, nor of a real reformer."[37]

Although Ray sounded here like a third party purist, he and Garnet were quite willing to work both sides of the political street. The very next week, after committing the *Colored American* to the support of a third party, Ray was wooing New York Whigs, who had again done well in the fall election. Addressing an editorial to "the Powers that be in the State," he urged them to keep in mind during the coming legislature that amending the state constitution to restore political equality to blacks would be a politically shrewd move. It would, he estimated, add twenty thousand voters to the state's lists, almost all of whom would vote the Whig ticket in recognition of that party's "high regard for human rights." But would Whigs not pay a heavy price in losing former white supporters by such a move? Ray dismissed this as "a MOON-SHINE objection." He added that voters alienated by recognition of blacks' rights would be men who did not really believe in Whig principles. Besides, restoring the franchise to blacks would gain the votes of other whites, "the existing friends of the colored people." For several years Ray, Garnet, and others followed this two-sided policy, strong support for a third party and cultivation of major party votes for black suffrage.[38]

On April 1, 1840, 121 abolitionists (104 from New York State) gathered in Albany to consider forming a third national party committed to immediate emancipation. Many abolitionists felt that the movement was not yet ready for such a bold move. The vote was forty-four to thirty-

37. Richard H. Sewell, *Ballots for Freedom: Antislavery Politics in the United States, 1837–1860* (New York, 1980), 52f.; *Colored American,* August 17, November 9, 1839.

38. *Colored American,* November 16, 1839.

three, with over a third of the delegates abstaining. The party would not be formally designated the Liberty party until 1841. The convention nominated James Birney for president of the United States.[39] Birney, a southern lawyer and small-scale slave owner, had practiced law in Alabama and Kentucky, had freed his slaves, and had shifted from colonizationism to immediatism under Theodore Weld's influence. Birney became editor of the *Philanthropist,* and his editorial offices in Cincinnati were wrecked by mobs that also sought his life. In 1837 he was chosen corresponding secretary of the American Anti-Slavery Society.

Charles Ray promptly and enthusiastically endorsed Birney's nomination, declaring, "We go for thorough-going political action." Only the clear commitment of the August 1840 New York State black convention to exclude issues other than the black vote from its agenda prevented Ray, Garnet, and Wright from seeking that body's endorsement of Birney and his party. As the fall election drew near, Ray's *Colored American* urged blacks to vote the whole abolitionist party ticket, with the possible exception of supporting Whig Seward for state governor, since he continued to seem inclined toward antislavery and equal voting rights for blacks. On the very eve of the election, Ray reminded his readers of the awesome importance of the vote: "Act independently, from a sense of your own rights, and the rights of our oppressed brethren in the South. . . . Cast that vote, then, as you would wish you had done, should you soon follow that act to judgment."[40]

When the votes were counted in November 1840, Birney received slightly over seven thousand, over a third of them from New York State, where Gerrit Smith had been on the ticket as a third party candidate for governor. Although Ray had not been sanguine before the returns were in, he was clearly disappointed. He attributed the poor showing to the paucity of truly sincere abolitionists and the hostility of Garrisonian abolitionists to political efforts. Birney and other leaders of the Liberty party, for their part, were quite aware of the importance of black support. Indeed, they had asked Ray and another black to run on their ticket. Both had declined in protest against the constitutional disfranchisement of most blacks in New York State. By February 1841 Birney publicly endorsed equal voting rights for blacks as one of the party's principles.[41]

39. Sewell, *Ballots for Freedom,* 66–72.

40. *Colored American,* April 18, October 31, 1840.

41. *Colored American,* December 5, 1840; James Birney to Lewis Tappan, February 5, 1841, in Dumond (ed.), *Letters of Birney,* II, 623.

When the Liberty party's central nominating committee met in New York City in mid-May 1841 to choose candidates for the 1844 election, three prominent blacks were on the committee: Theodore Wright, Charles Ray, and the well-known layman John Zuille. At the ensuing convention, Birney was again chosen to be the presidential candidate. Ray exulted that this convention drew many more delegates than did the business meetings of either national abolition society.[42]

Of the black clergy, it was Henry Garnet and another fugitive slave, Garnet's cousin Samuel Ringgold Ward, who did the most actual campaigning for the Liberty party between 1840 and 1844. Although Ray did not become a stump speaker for the Liberty party, he continued to be recognized by the party as a leading black supporter. Garnet, Ray, Wright, and nearly fifty others at the national black convention in August 1843 voted to endorse the third party; only seven dissented. Garnet proudly reported this to the national convention of the party two weeks later. He was put on the committee to nominate officers, Ray was elected one of the convention's secretaries, and Garnet and Ward gave major addresses.[43] In 1844 the party polled over sixty-two thousand votes, almost nine times as many as in 1840.

Garnet's most celebrated speech for the cause was delivered in 1842 at the Massachusetts Liberty party convention held in Faneuil Hall in Boston. He began with a tribute to the consistent purpose and toughness of the abolitionists. But he reminded his audience, "All our success is of God; . . . yes, that Almighty Being who said, 'let there be light and there was light,' has called into being the Spirit of this age, to bring out his oppressed poor from under their 'task-masters'; and it is enough for us to be used as instruments in the hand of God, in accomplishing his glorious purpose." Garnet predicted that the Liberty party would soon be the country's most powerful party and compared the "mighty current of Anti-Slavery feeling" with the vast and irresistible flow of the Mississippi River.[44]

The last half of this address drew Garnet's listeners back to the dreadful present. Despite growing abolitionism, there was nationwide subservience to slave owners' interests and no sign that slavery was dying out.

42. *Colored American,* May 22, 29, 1841.

43. George Walker, "The Afro-American in New York City, 1827–1860" (Ph.D. dissertation, Columbia University, 1975), 157; Quarles, *Black Abolitionists,* 184f.

44. *Emancipator,* March 4, 1842 (Microfilm copy in Carter and Ripley [eds.], *BAP,* reel 4, item 75); Ofari, "*Let Your Motto Be Resistance,*" 139, 141.

Invoking the terror of Nat Turner's revolt a decade earlier, Garnet declared that only the slaves' faith that abolitionists would achieve their goal kept in check "those heaving fires that formerly burst forth like the lava of a burning volcano, upon the inhabitants of Southampton and elsewhere." Like many others, black and white, Garnet was fully aware that a national civil war might well be in the offing. Although his hope was for a nonviolent solution, his words were ominous: "I cannot harbor the thought for a moment that their deliverance will be brought about by violence. No; our country will not be so deaf to the cries of the oppressed. . . . No, the time for a last stern struggle has not yet come (may it never be necessary.) The finger of the Almighty will hold back the trigger, and his all powerful arm will sheathe the sword till the oppressors' cup is full. [Hear, hear.]"[45]

Although Garnet, in the enthusiasm of this speech for the Liberty party, predicted that it would become the most powerful party in the country, he was not about to depend solely on national political action to end southern slavery. Eighteen months after Garnet's Faneuil Hall speech, the first national black convention in eight years was held in Buffalo. Here Garnet delivered an address to the slaves themselves, placing squarely upon their shoulders the responsibility of destroying the system. The "Address to the Slaves of the United States of America" moved his immediate audience to tears by a description of the destructive curse of slavery. Garnet went on to transfix the listeners by a call for a general work stoppage by slaves and, if need be, violent insurrection:

> *Slavery!* How much misery is comprehended in that single word. . . .
>
> Millions have come from eternity into time, and have returned again to the world of spirits, cursed and ruined by American slavery. . . .
>
> They endeavor to make you as much like brutes as possible. . . .
>
> *To such Degradation it is sinful in the Extreme for you to make voluntary Submission. . . .*
>
> You should therefore now use the same manner of resistance, as would have been just in our ancestors, when the bloody foot-prints of the first remorseless soul-thief was placed upon the shores of our fatherland. . . .
>
> Brethren, the time has come when you must act for yourselves. . . . Then go to your lordly enslavers and tell them plainly, that you *are determined to be free*. Appeal to their sense of justice. . . . Tell them . . . of the exceeding sinfulness of slavery, and of a future judgment, and of the righteous retributions of an indignant God. . . . Do this, and for ever after cease to toil for the heart-

45. Ofari, "*Let Your Motto Be Resistance,*" 141–44.

> less tyrants. . . . If they then commence the work of death, they, and not you, will be responsible for the consequences. . . .
>
> However much you and all of us may desire it, there is not much hope of redemption without the shedding of blood. If you must bleed, let it all come at once—rather *die freemen, than live to be slaves*. . . .
>
> Brethren, arise, arise! Strike for your lives and liberties. Now is the day and the hour.
>
> Let your motto be resistance! *resistance! resistance!* . . . Brethren, adieu! Trust in the living God. Labor for the peace of the human race, and remember that you are *four millions*.[46]

The wonder in this address is that 145 years later, for those who have never known enslavement, and even in cold print, it remains a volcanic combination of intense feeling, irresistible determination, and conviction that even by the road of bloodshed, tyranny will indeed be destroyed.[47] Garnet, responding to the many forms of unjustified white violence that he had experienced, was glorifying violent black resistance. A considerable part of his speech was devoted to four past episodes of heroic black revolt or conspiracy to revolt: Denmark Vesey's 1822 slave conspiracy in South Carolina, Nat Turner's 1831 slave revolt in Virginia, Joseph Cinqué's successful slave ship mutiny in 1839, and the slave Madison Washington's comparable success in 1841 in seizing the bark *Creole,* which was carrying slaves from Virginia to New Orleans. Garnet made clear that although Vesey's conspiracy had failed, the near miss had had powerful results: "That tremendous movement shook the whole empire of slavery. The guilty soul-thieves were overwhelmed with fear. . . . And in consequence of the threatened revolution the slave States talked strongly of emancipation."[48]

The names of those who had plotted revolt, said Garnet, whether they had failed or succeeded, would be revered down through history, as would those who might lead revolt in the 1840s. Although Garnet's ad-

46. For the complete text of the address, see Ofari, "*Let Your Motto Be Resistance,*" 144–53.

47. A careful reading of Garnet's address alongside David Walker's 1829 *Appeal to the Colored Citizens of the World,* discussed earlier, suggests that Garnet had been powerfully affected by Walker's work. When Garnet published his address in 1848, the volume also included Walker's *Appeal* and a brief, admiring sketch of Walker's life. Aptheker, "*One Continual Cry,*" 40–44.

48. Similar, and even more visible, results had come from the Nat Turner revolt. The 1832 legislature of Virginia had debated for several weeks the ending of the slave system in that commonwealth as a result of the recent nightmare of bloodshed. Emancipation had lost by a narrow margin.

dress never promised insurrectionists victory or even survival, he seems to have believed that a large-scale uprising of slaves in the South was possible. There is evidence that John Brown, already fleshing out plans for a major escape route for slaves from the South through the Alleghenies, knew Garnet and was drawn to him. Some say that Brown was so impressed with Garnet's "Address to the Slaves" that he paid for its publication in 1848. Likewise, it has been suggested that talk with Garnet was one element fueling Brown's growing conviction during the 1850s that slaves throughout the South were in a fever of hatred against their owners, were on the brink of revolt, and would respond at once and in large numbers to his 1859 raid.[49]

Garnet may have had a political reason for delivering his "Address to the Slaves" and seeking its broad distribution. The piece may have been, like David Walker's *Appeal . . . to the Colored Citizens of the World,* addressed as much to whites as to slaves—to whites in both the South and the North, most of whom still seemed to be unfazed by abolitionist argument. Perhaps, as in Virginia over a decade earlier, fear would bring more action than reason or appeal to conscience. And perhaps, if the blacks meeting in Buffalo endorsed Garnet's call to insurrection, the Liberty party, whose convention was to meet a few days later, would do likewise. The party might gain new members by stressing that there were only two real options: political action or large-scale violence.

It is a mistake to see Garnet's Buffalo "Address to the Slaves" as fundamentally different in tone from his earlier speeches. He had begun his 1840 "Address of the New York State Convention to Their Colored Fellow Citizens" with the quotation "Hereditary bondsmen, know ye not, who would be free, themselves must strike the blow!" The same quotation appeared again at the midpoint of his 1843 address. As has been described, at the Boston Liberty party gathering in early 1842, Garnet had reminded his hearers that what had ignited the Turner revolt was still fatefully present and only kept in check by abolitionist efforts and the will of the Almighty to restrain the trigger finger and to leave the sword sheathed "till the oppressors' cup is full." The question was not whether bloody retribution could be prevented, but for how long it could be prevented.[50]

49. Stephen Oates, *To Purge This Land with Blood: A Biography of John Brown* (New York, 1970), 61, 211f.

50. Foner and Walker (eds.), *Proceedings of the Black State Conventions,* I, 15. For other analyses of Garnet's Buffalo address, see Mabee, *Black Freedom,* 55–63; and Schor, *Henry Highland Garnet,* 49–61.

Garnet's "Address to the Slaves" was considered at length by the Buffalo national convention. After it had been read aloud, Ray moved that it be referred to a committee chaired by Garnet for consideration of changes in wording so as to render some of its points less objectionable when it appeared in print. Garnet, fearing that the cental message would be watered down in committee consideration, spoke at length against referral. When he had finished, the whole gathering was in tears. Frederick Douglass spoke in support of Ray's motion, declaring that there was "too much physical force" in the address and in Garnet's supporting remarks. They would lead to insurrection, a catastrophe to be avoided. After more discussion Ray's motion to refer the address for reworking was approved by a large majority.

After the lapse of a day, the committee on Garnet's address reported back, having made "some very slight alterations." A delegate from Cincinnati spoke against endorsement, declaring that the address would be fatal to the safety of free blacks in the slave states, as well as in Ohio, a border state. That afternoon a vote was taken; eighteen endorsed the address and nineteen opposed endorsement.[51] Wright endorsed it. Ray, too busy expediting other convention business to hear much of the debate, abstained and then asked to change his vote to endorsement. When an objection was raised, he withdrew the request. During the evening session a delegate who had helped defeat endorsement moved and secured reconsideration. Amos Beman, who had been elected president of the convention, stepped down from his chair and spoke at length and with great effect against endorsement. Garnet replied. Douglass and Remond (representing Massachusetts) and Ray spoke in support of Beman. In the final vote, nine favored endorsement and fourteen opposed it. The opposition included Wright, Ray, and Beman.[52]

Although Garnet's militant "Address to the Slaves" was narrowly rejected by the 1843 convention, he would bring it up again at the 1847 convention and publish it in 1848. Meanwhile, he secured the backing of many black leaders in pressing for blacks' being allowed to join state militias. Garnet brought the matter up at the New York State convention in Syracuse in 1845. Arguing that learning to use arms was as basic a right as voting or jury duty, he won the nearly unanimous support of the convention and strong support at the 1847 and 1848 national black conventions.

51. "Minutes of the National Convention of Colored Citizens . . . 1843," in Bell (ed.), *Minutes of the National Negro Conventions,* 13, 17, 10, 18f.

52. *Ibid.,* 23f.

No state governments proved willing to implement these resolutions, but during the 1850s some private black militia companies were organized. The one in Harrisburg, Pennsylvania, was named the Henry Highland Garnet Guards.[53]

Both Garnet's "Address to the Slaves" and black agitation for inclusion in state militias played a part in preparing northern black leaders eventually to urge black enlistment in the Union forces during the Civil War. However, for most black activists in New York State in the mid-1840s, the primary goals remained to maximize black and white support for the Liberty party and to secure the vote for free black males. (New York City leaders such as Wright, Ray, and James McCune Smith, however, resisted some of the steamroller tactics Garnet used in getting the New York State conventions, heavily made up of upstate New Yorkers, to endorse the Liberty party.)[54] The Liberty party and the black franchise were becoming important issues in New York State politics in 1845 and 1846. Liberty candidates won their highest percentage of the total state vote, 4.7 percent, in 1845. Some Whig politicians concluded that votes cast in 1844 for Liberty's presidential candidate, James Birney, had cost Whig Henry Clay the election in New York State and in the nation. Late in 1845 a combination of Whigs and radical Democrats in the General Assembly forced passage of a bill calling for a state constitutional convention the following year.[55]

Because the Liberty party had officially endorsed equal voting rights for blacks, and because in some New York counties the Liberty party seemed to hold the balance of power, black voting rights had to be addressed both by candidates for election in April 1846 as delegates to the convention and by newspapers with Whig or Democratic orientation. The New York *Tribune* in January 1846 strongly endorsed blacks' renewed plea for equal voting rights. Whig candidates in counties where antislavery and the Liberty party had shown strength tried to draw former Liberty voters over to their ranks by promising support for the black franchise. However, Whig candidates in counties such as New York (that is, New York City), where there were few Liberty party voters and general white opposition to the black franchise, often opposed any voting by blacks. And Democratic candidates in strongly antislavery counties such as Clinton (bordering on Vermont) and Cortland (in central New York)

53. Pease and Pease, *They Who Would Be Free,* 158–60.

54. Foner and Walker (eds.), *Proceedings of Black State Conventions,* I, 31–42.

55. Field, *Politics of Race,* 44, 46.

often endorsed equal suffrage for blacks. As a result of Whig blandishments and that party's previous history of liberalism toward blacks, one segment of Liberty party voters broke away from the minority party to support the only party able to win control of the convention, the Whigs. In contrast, Liberty party leader Gerrit Smith and his staunch supporter Henry Garnet strongly urged continued support of Liberty party candidates, insisting that even liberal Whig candidates had proved to be willing to compromise with slave interests.[56]

When the constitutional convention gathered on June 1, 1846, the Democrats controlled it, with seventy-eight delegates to the Whigs' fifty-three. Judging from the two official reports on delegate debate, supporters of liberalization of black voting rights occupied far less time than did opponents. Delegates' arguments for equal political rights for blacks had, in almost all cases, already been presented by black leaders such as Ray, Wright, and Crummell in their addresses to New York State voters from the New York State black conventions in 1840 and afterward. The Declaration of Independence, with its words about all men being "created equal" and "with certain inalienable rights," was frequently cited. The Revolution's battle cry "no taxation without representation" was placed alongside the fact that thousands of New York blacks paid taxes but were disqualified from voting. Blacks, some delegates said, have served their country valiantly in combat, especially in the War of 1812, but how miserably they have been treated since then. Blacks are every bit as intelligent as immigrants into the United States from foreign countries. The alleged high rate of criminality among blacks is a direct result of the degrading conditions under which they are forced to live. Vermont, Massachusetts, and Rhode Island have proved that equal political rights for blacks do not have injurious consequences.

The delegates opposing equal voting rights for blacks did not indulge in the Negrophobia of the New York journalists two decades earlier whom Cornish had entered the public arena to combat. The major premise of these delegates was that the black race had been created inferior to whites and would remain so. The acting chairman of the convention committee charged with reporting out a recommendation on the black franchise was John Kennedy, from New York County and born and brought up in Maryland. He declared that the inalienable rights referred to in the Declaration of Independence were natural rights, not civil

56. *National Anti-Slavery Standard,* January 29, 1846; Field, *Politics of Race,* 46–50.

rights. If voting were a natural right, then women and children should have it. Physiologists, declared Kennedy, have taught us that there are five races, each with distinctive characteristics, and that the Caucasian and Ethiopian races are the farthest apart and have the fewest similarities. Rejecting as undemocratic any property requisite for voting, Kennedy urged that if the franchise were to be broadened, it should be modified to include white females, not blacks. Delegate Russell from Saint Lawrence County supported Kennedy's assertion of black inferiority, saying that over a period of four thousand years blacks "have never yet been found capable of sustaining our political institutions, under any circumstances, or in any country." He warned that if New York gave the vote to all blacks, it would soon be flooded with emancipated slaves, since New Jersey and Pennsylvania, the only states between New York and the South, granted no such privilege. Such an influx of former slaves, Russell declared, would reduce white working mens' wages and either force them out of the state or reduce them "to the same servile conditions" as laborers in other countries.[57] Delegate Hunt from New York City insisted that "all sane negroes . . . knew . . . that they were negroes and aliens by the act of God, and there was no remedy." He promised that if black suffrage were approved, blacks as a body would be excluded from Manhattan.[58]

On the initial convention motion to eliminate racial distinction in voting rights, the vote was negative, 63 to 37. Eventually a large majority was in favor of submitting the issue to the electorate for a referendum separate from that for the recommended revised constitution as a whole. In the November election equal suffrage was defeated by a vote of 224,336 to 85,406. Only 27.5 percent of the voters favored equal suffrage, in comparison with 37 percent of the constitutional convention delegates. In spite of heavy voting in New York City, with its large black population, against broadening the franchise, there was no clear correlation

57. For a similar point of view from a New York city cartman, see a letter to the New York *Globe* that claimed that getting the vote would lead to blacks being given cartmen's licenses. Accordingly, the writer urged that convention delegates be chosen who were "opposed to taking the bread from the mouths of our wives and little ones, in order to give it to the Negroes of the South, who . . . are invited hither." Letter cited by Pease and Pease, *Bound with Them in Chains,* 173.

58. The arguments made at the convention discussed in the preceding paragraphs are from William G. Bishop and William H. Attree (eds.), *Report of the Debates and Proceedings of the Convention for the Revision of the Constitution of the State of New York* (Albany, 1846), 1018f., 1026ff., 1030f., 1034.

statewide between the presence of blacks and white attitudes on black voting rights. Nor was there significant correlation between Whig membership and being prosuffrage. The points of high correlation with the prosuffrage position were (1) having voted for the Liberty party in the 1840s and (2) having come from New England, especially if the voter resided in western New York State, which had been profoundly affected by Christian revivalism.[59]

The results of this referendum were a harsh blow for black activists, as well as for white liberals. Nine years later Horace Greeley, Whig editor of the New York *Tribune,* would wearily recall, "We did what we could for Equal Suffrage in 1846, with feeble hopes of success, but with a perfect consciousness that we incurred general obloquy and injured our political associates by so doing."[60] The hopes of Ray and other black leaders had been far from feeble, yet their subsequent public mood had no defeatism in it. Ray, Wright, and James McCune Smith, in correspondence with Gerrit Smith, commented on the recent referendum: "We feel that from man we have not merited this rebuke; to God we bow in meek submission. The future is ours—and we advance toward it, with unbroken faith in Him, who will not forsake us."[61]

Garnet's reaction to the political defeat for New York blacks in the fall of 1846 was to step up his assault on slavery and the North's share in maintaining it. He also staged costly protests against segregated seating on northern railroads. For him the annexation of Texas in 1845 and the ensuing war with Mexico seemed to make clear that national policy was being controlled by slave-owning interests, not by abolition-minded northerners. At the anniversary meeting of the American and Foreign Anti-Slavery Society in May 1847, Garnet spoke the minds of most present: "We hear much said . . . of the horrors of war. . . . Who makes the very bullets that we are now mowing down the poor Mexicans with? These very pirating Yankees . . . who with their lips deprecate the war. They admit that Slavery is wrong in the abstract, but when we ask them to

59. Field, *Politics of Race,* 52–57, 61–72, 76–78. Field notes New Englanders' "traditionally high regard for equal opportunity and individual effort" (*ibid.,* 77). Also see John Stanley, "Majority Tyranny in Tocqueville's America: The Failure of Negro Suffrage in 1846," *Political Science Quarterly,* LXXXIV (1969), 412–35.

60. Field, *Politics of Race,* 80.

61. Quoted by Gerrit Smith from a recent letter to him by Ray, Wright, and James McCune Smith. Gerrit Smith to Rev. T. S. Wright, Rev. Charles B. Ray, and Dr. James McCune Smith, November 14, 1846, in Gerrit Smith Papers (Microfilm copy in Carter and Ripley [eds.], *BAP,* reel 5, item 285).

help us overthrow it, they tell us it would make them beggars. . . . Patriotism or morality, with a Yankee, means *Money*."[62]

At the national black convention of October 1847, held in Troy at the Liberty Street Presbyterian Church, Garnet again read his "Address to the Slaves," which had caused such a sensation four years earlier. Far from endorsing Garnet's piece, this convention unanimously adopted a report by Frederick Douglass on how to end slavery and caste. This report labeled any plan involving insurrection and bloodshed suicidal and wicked. Six months later Garnet had his address published in a volume that also included David Walker's *Appeal . . . to the Colored Citizens of the World,* originally printed in 1829. Garnet had composed a brief and admiring introduction to the *Appeal*. For his own *Address to the Slaves of the United States of America,* there was a preface, in which he proudly noted that, though rejected by the 1843 national black convention, "the document elicited more discussion than any other paper that was ever brought before that, or any other deliberative body of colored persons, and their friends."[63]

There was one significant change in the text of Garnet's published address as compared with the speech of 1843. Surprisingly, it has passed largely unnoticed. In place of the earlier passage "Brethren, arise, arise! Strike for your lives and liberties. Now is the day and the hour," more cautious words were substituted: "We do not advise you to attempt a revolution with the sword, because it would be INEXPEDIENT. Your numbers are too small, and moreover the rising spirit of the age, and the spirit of the gospel are opposed to war and bloodshed."[64] This important shift reflected the point of view of Wright, Ray, Amos Beman, and others close to Garnet. Despite this note of prudence, Garnet's basic position—his defense of slaves' resorting to violence to gain their freedom—remained unchanged. Indeed, that position was gaining ground among northern black leaders in the latter 1840s. The Ohio convention in January 1849 passed a resolution recommending that five hundred copies of Garnet's volume be secured for distribution. A few months later Doug-

62. *Emancipator,* May 19, 1847.

63. *North Star,* December 3, 1847; "Proceedings of the National Convention of Colored People . . . 1847," in Bell (ed.), *Minutes of the National Negro Conventions,* 13–15; *Walker's Appeal, with a Brief Sketch of His Life, by Henry Highland Garnet, and Also Garnet's Address to the Slaves of the United States of America* (1848; rpr. New York, 1969). The preface to Garnet's *Address to the Slaves of the United States of America* was dated April 12, 1848.

64. *Walker's Appeal . . . and Also Garnet's Address to the Slaves,* 96. Compare with the 1843 version in Ofari, *"Let Your Motto Be Resistance,"* 152.

lass, the stalwart Garrisonian committed to ending slavery by moral suasion and not violence, told a packed audience in Boston that Americans should welcome a successful slave uprising.[65]

About the time Garnet published his *Address to the Slaves,* which urged slaves to refuse any longer to work for their masters, he renewed his physical resistance against Jim Crow arrangements (de facto, not de jure) on railroads. The pioneer in this kind of protest was David Ruggles, the secretary of New York City's vigilance committee. In 1841 Ruggles had to be dragged from his seat in a white car of the New Bedford Railroad because he refused to obey orders to move. Later that same year Frederick Douglass and two white abolitionists refused compliance on the Eastern Railroad, clung to their seats when several employees tried to drag them out, and eventually were removed from the train after some manhandling. Soon thereafter Garnet made a similar protest on the Utica and Schenectady Railroad and was pulled from the car in which he had been sitting. Years later he recalled the episode: Although he had been on crutches because of his recent amputation, "it had required four stout men to do it." The struggle was worthwhile, however, for soon afterward the railroad eliminated Jim Crow seating. Garnet advised a crowd in Providence in 1848: "Always remonstrate, and resist in some way or other, when abused in this manner. Resistance [will] secure respect from friends and foes." As to the method of resistance, Garnet did not recommend fighting but suggested hugging the seat, as he had done, until it, too, was dragged away, or giving the assailants a grizzly bear embrace.[66]

Two months after his speech in Providence, Garnet followed his own advice. Boarding the Buffalo and Niagara Railroad in Buffalo, on his way to give some temperance lectures in Canada, he was ordered by the conductor to move from the third car to the one immediately behind the engine. Garnet quietly refused to comply. The conductor seized him by the throat and choked him severely. Then, with another man's help, the conductor dragged Garnet off the train, beating him so severely on the head and chest that he had to call a physician. His detailed account of this episode was printed in the Buffalo *Daily Propeller* and picked up by the *Liberator* and Douglass's *North Star.*[67] Having advised slaves to resist, Garnet was doing his best, as a "free" black, to do the same.

65. Quarles, *Black Abolitionists,* 227–28.

66. Mabee, *Black Freedom,* 113f., 119f.; *North Star,* April 14, 1848.

67. Garnet's letter to the editor of the Buffalo *Daily Propeller* is reproduced in Carter and Ripley (eds.), *BAP,* reel 5, item 697. *Liberator,* July 14, 1848; *North Star,* June 3, July 7, 1848.

Garnet had begun the 1840s as newly installed pastor of the Liberty Street Presbyterian Church. By the end of the decade he had washed his hands of Presbyterianism for its accommodation with slave owning and undertook mission work with unchurched blacks in western New York State. After the demise of the *Colored American,* Ray had also turned to a mission post. His work was with the unchurched, poor, and uncared-for blacks in New York City. Stalled for the time being in their political efforts, both men poured their energies into ministry among Afro-Americans who seemed to have been forgotten.

SAMUEL CORNISH
Courtesy Presbyterian Historical Association, Philadelphia

CHARLES B. RAY
Courtesy Schomburg Center for Research in Black Culture, New York Public Library, Astor, Lenox, and Tilden Foundations

HENRY HIGHLAND GARNET
Courtesy Presbyterian Historical Association, Philadelphia

AMOS G. BEMAN
Courtesy Yale Collection of American Literature, Beinecke Rare Book and Manuscript Library, Yale University

JAMES W. C. PENNINGTON
Reprinted from William Franklin Henney, Hartford: Commonwealth of Connecticut

7. HUMAN BETTERMENT THROUGH CHURCH AND THE BIBLE: GARNET'S AND RAY'S MINISTRIES IN THE 1840s

We shall acknowledge no other creed than the Bible, and no other Head than God and his Son Jesus Christ.

—Henry Highland Garnet, *Pennsylvania Freeman*, April 6, 1848

I entered upon this work to reach first the outcast portions of the people seldom reached with the Gospel and the means, motives and blessings of a higher material, moral and spiritual life.

—Charles Ray, about 1865

Henry Highland Garnet's and Charles Ray's roles as ministers presented as great a contrast to each other as their respective contributions to action programs. Garnet, with an excellent education and native brilliance as a speaker, became a superb preacher. His authoritative, if not arrogant, manner made him a forceful, though controversial, pastor. Prestigious pulpits became available to him. But he also felt a strong pull toward mission work with the unchurched or with non-Christians. This had, after all, been the quintessential Christian calling since the time of Paul the Apostle. After several years of building a solid Presbyterian church in the small black community of Troy, New York, he became a preacher among the spiritually shepherdless black people in the western part of the state. This work lasted only two years. Then a post lecturing in Great Britain to promote the boycott of slave-grown produce drew him into greater prominence and offered fuller scope for his forensic abilities. After roughly two years in this position, he again responded to the call to the mission field, this time to Jamaica. Family illness cut this service short after three years. Returning to the United States, he accepted the most influential black Presbyterian pulpit, that of New York City's First Colored Presbyterian Church, founded by Samuel Cornish and built up by Theodore Wright. Here he stayed for eight years before moving to the Fifteenth Street Presbyterian Church in Washington, D.C., in 1864. Those eight years brought striking success as a pastor, but also bitter friction with trustees over salary demands and involvement in the controversial African Civilization Society.

Ray's ministerial career was of a different order. Deprived of college training, employed for four years as a shoemaker, and absorbed for another five years in journalism and political action, he did not follow up his original call to the ministry until 1844, when he was thirty-six years old. With neither the education nor the power in the pulpit of a Wright or a Garnet, Ray went where he sensed that he was most needed and became a New York City missionary. He also gathered a small Congregational church, drawing from the less advantaged class of black people. He stayed in these twin roles until the late 1860s. Along with this pastoral work he remained an activist as to political rights and educational and employment opportunities for blacks. The remarkable tributes to him that poured in at his death in 1886 showed that his quiet devotion over many decades to the welfare of his people in New York City and beyond had won him a special esteem.

Garnet's first pastorate was the Liberty Street Presbyterian Church in Troy, which Ray had visited in 1837 and 1838, and of which Daniel Payne had been pastor from 1837 to 1839. When Garnet came to Troy, this was a nondenominational black community church. Founded in 1834 and provided a building by the city government, it had drawn roughly a third of the black community of three hundred by the time of Ray's first visit. An active congregation gave strong support to the *Colored American* and was vigorously involved in antislavery and self-improvement. Wright knew the church well and must have thought it an ideal initial pastorate for the brilliant young activist Garnet.[1]

Garnet began ministry in Troy immediately after completing academic work at Oneida in the early fall of 1839. By December he had led the Liberty Street congregation to apply to the presbytery of Troy to be recognized as a formally constituted Presbyterian church. Some four months later William P. Johnson, superintendent of the Sunday school in Wright's church and agent of the *Colored American,* visited Troy and sent

1. Will Gravely has spelled out the rich significance of the early black community churches in Philadelphia, New York, Boston, and Newport. Many of his comments apply also to the early phases of churches like those on Liberty Street in Troy, Temple Street in New Haven, and Talcott Street in Hartford: "The Union Church, as a racially separate institution, embodied the elusive dream of black communal unity. It . . . demonstrated the persistent symbiosis between churches and other voluntary associations in black life." "The Rise of African Churches in America (1786–1822): Re-examining the Contexts," *Journal of Religious Thought,* XLI (1984), 58–73.

an enthusiastic report back to New York City. Having attended Garnet's church several times, the visitor knew it to be a place "where the Lord in a copious manner has poured out his spirit." He praised the school managed by the church and thought highly of Garnet's female assistant who was running it. Garnet himself evidently intended to be away from the church for the whole summer, devoting himself full-time to preparation for the August black state convention on the franchise.[2]

The young graduate of Oneida was ordained a ruling elder in 1841, was licensed to preach in 1842, and was ordained and formally installed as Presbyterian minister at Liberty Street in 1843. Between his arrival in Troy in 1839 and his ordination in 1843, Garnet was given theological training to supplement his schooling at the Oneida Institute. His chief tutor was a prominent white clergyman, Nathan S. S. Beman, a graduate of Middlebury College and a college teacher prior to coming to Troy in the early 1820s as minister of the First Presbyterian Church. In the course of Beman's pastorate, the First Presbyterian Church became famous for the eloquent substance of his sermons, the elegance of the church's appointments, and the high income level of its white members.

There must have been much about N. S. S. Beman that appealed to Garnet. He initiated a series of revivals in his church soon after he came that aroused criticism from conservative clergy, yet he was chosen moderator of the Presbyterian General Assembly in 1831. By the time Garnet entered the Oneida Institute, Beman was known as one of the leaders of New School Presbyterianism and a forthright abolitionist. What better tutor could Garnet have had? However, the blacks in Beman's church had a serious problem, and Ray had publicized it in a report to the *Colored American* in 1838, some nine months before Garnet came to Liberty Street. After a brief visit to the building when no service was going on, Ray concluded that it was too ornate for a "temple of God" and that it was clearly catering primarily to the wealthy. Most offensive to him were the Negro pews. After viewing them he had a sarcastic recommendation: "I would suggest one thing to carry the principles out farther, that they hang up curtains before the negro seats, to shut the colored people from the view of the white people entirely, and from the Dr. also."[3]

On another matter besides segregated seating in churches, Garnet disagreed vehemently with the man who tutored him in theology. Beman strongly opposed a third national political party committed to immediate

2. William P. Johnson to Charles Ray, June 3, 1840, in *Colored American*, July 11, 1840.

3. *Colored American*, December 15, 1838.

emancipation. He did his best to scuttle the Albany convention in the spring of 1840 that had been called to make Liberty party nominations for top national and state offices. However, the convention persisted toward the goal of the majority, and Garnet, Wright, and Ray strongly supported the nominees, who included Gerrit Smith for governor of New York.[4]

If there was sharp political disagreement between Beman and Garnet during the latter's first year in Troy, what must their divergence have been three years later, when Garnet was delivering his "Address to the Slaves" and trying to maneuvre general black support for the growing Liberty party? It was in this same year, however, that Garnet was ordained and formally installed as pastor of the Liberty Street Presbyterian Church. As Garnet's primary tutor, Beman must have supported Garnet's ordination by the presbytery. It was a vivid example of New School Presbyterian appreciation of able black clerical leadership, even though such a leadership was committed to methods of radical social change disapproved of by white clergy in the presbytery.

Established in a church of his own, by 1842 Garnet felt free to marry Julia Williams, the young woman he had known during the chaotic weeks at the Noyes Academy and with whom he was deeply in love by 1837. Theodore Wright came up to Troy for the ceremony that united in matrimony a remarkable young man and a remarkable young woman who would work effectively alongside her husband in his pastorates and share with him good times and bad. Early in 1844 their son James was born and less than a year later their daughter Mary, a frail child who nevertheless would outlive her father.[5]

Garnet's abilities as a minister are reflected in the minutes of the session (made up of the minister and two or three lay members) of the Liberty Street Presbyterian Church, as well as in occasional reports to missionary agencies providing financial support for the church and its pastor. By 1843 church membership had more than doubled from what it was upon Garnet's arrival. Over the years most new members entered the church on confession of faith, but not a few came with letters from other churches, including Presbyterian, Baptist, and Methodist. The congregation was steadily growing and promised soon to outgrow its meeting place. The Sunday school had over seventy in attendance. Many of these were adults: "Many an aged man or woman has learned to read the sacred

4. Sewell, *Ballots for Freedom,* 70.

5. Pasternak, "Rise Now and Fly to Arms," 54ff., 75, 78.

scriptures in that school." Each year since Garnet's arrival there had been "a season of the outpouring of God's spirit." Whites in the area, impressed by the vitality of the church, promised assistance.[6]

The session minute book provides another indication of the church's health. During the eight years of Garnet's ministry, only four cases concerning moral discipline came before the session. In 1842 a Miss Jones charged a Mr. Selden with slander for accusing her of having had a child. Witnesses were heard, and there was amicable agreement that the report was untrue. The next year Catharine Thompson was summoned to answer the charge of covenant breaking (not defined). At a meeting six months later, she acknowledged that she had "done wrong and promised to do better hereafter." In 1845 a female member was summoned to answer the charge of adultery; she confessed and begged forgiveness. She was "admonished" and suspended from the church. Concurrently, a male member was summoned and charged with "habitual intemperance." The session remonstrated with him and asked him to sign a temperance pledge. When he refused, he was dismissed from membership. (By 1844 ninety-six persons connected with the church had taken the temperance pledge.)[7]

In dire need of additional income, Garnet applied in the spring of 1843 to the American Home Missionary Society (AHMS) for appointment as a missionary within the United States and for an accompanying stipend. The AHMS had been organized in 1826 as an amalgam of Congregational and Presbyterian efforts to establish new churches and help struggling ones, especially in New York and Ohio. Garnet's appointment was approved, and though the stipend was minuscule, he gratefully accepted it: "Sometimes a very small act of kindness . . . is like a balm to the soul. . . . I believe that the Lord has made use of the commission as an instrument to inspire me with new courage." In securing the AHMS appointment, Garnet had been interested in far more than financial help. His missionary commitment was both intense and far-reaching: "I hope I may yet see the day when many missionaries from among our own people shall be sent abroad through this and every other state . . . to publish the doctrines of the Bible in a proper manner."[8]

6. Henry Garnet to Milton Badger (secretary of the American Home Missionary Society [AHMS]), July 25, November 22, 1843, both in AHMS Archives, Amistad Research Center, Tulane University, New Orleans; Liberty Street Church Session Minutes, 1840–1921.

7. Liberty Street Church Session Minutes, March 1, 4, 1842; March 6, October 10, 1843; March 21, April 4, 1845.

8. Henry Garnet to Milton Badger, July 25, 1843, in AHMS Archives.

It was not long before doubts surfaced for both parties as to whether the Garnet-AHMS connection was a sound one. In the fall of 1843 Garnet received a letter from Lewis Tappan and Charles Ray that invited him to become temporary agent for the Union Missionary Society, founded by blacks in the wake of the return of the *Amistad* Mendi to Africa. Garnet regretfully replied to Tappan and Ray that his AHMS appointment precluded work for any parallel organization, but it was clear where his heart was: "My prayer to the Good Shepherd of Israel is that the Mendi Mission may be blessed, and may be the means of doing good to the poor benighted people of my father land."[9]

Garnet applied in May 1844 for a renewal of his AHMS commission and stipend. The society, however, had become uneasy about him. During his first year as its representative, Garnet delivered his "Address to the Slaves" at the national black convention in Buffalo, nearly secured convention endorsement of the address, secured convention endorsement of the Liberty party ticket, was a delegate to the summer 1843 national convention of the Liberty party, and in January 1844 delivered a four-hour address to the New York State legislature urging the ending of voter discrimination. Also, the AHMS, in large measure an agency of New School Presbyterians, fell upon hard times in the latter 1830s as a result of strife between the New School and the Old School, the schism in the denomination in 1837, and the deep economic depression of the same period.[10]

Secretary Charles Hall of the AHMS wrote to the Troy Presbytery to report hesitation over renewing Garnet's commission because of reports that he had been "much engaged in *political action*." After Garnet heard the letter read aloud at a meeting of the presbytery, he wrote Hall, withdrawing his request for renewal of his commission. Garnet added, "It is true that I am an abolitionist. . . . I have lifted up my feeble voice for my oppressed brethren—and what more or less could I do? My own kindred are this moment in slavery—and I must speak for them—and do all that I can to break off their chains. This is all my crime." Garnet went on to hope that the AHMS would pass beyond such fearful caution, and he pledged himself to continue as in the past: "If I had a thousand lives I

9. Henry Garnet to Lewis Tappan and Charles Ray, October 2, 1843, in American Missionary Association (hereinafter cited as AMA) Archives, Amistad Research Center, Tulane University, New Orleans.

10. Letter of May 13, 1844 (including an application for the grant renewal by three elders and four deacons of Liberty Street Presbyterian Church), AHMS Archives (Microfilm copy in Carter and Ripley [eds.], *BAP,* reel 4, item 805); Schor, *Henry Highland Garnet,* 68; Nichols and Nichols, *Presbyterianism in New York,* 145–47.

would spend them all for my bleeding people." Hall tried to mollify him with double-talk. The society's quarrel, he wrote, was not with abolitionism, particularly in a black man, but with "a species of public action inconsistent with regular attendance on your pastoral duties and with those proprieties of the ministerial office which the church requires their pastors to observe." Garnet evidently stood by his withdrawal and thereby ended his relationship with the AHMS.[11]

Freed of AHMS restraints, Garnet campaigned for the Liberty party prior to the election in November 1844. Having returned home from one trip exhausted from long days of travel and speech making "among the honest farmers," he wrote to one of his hosts and companions in the crusade: "It will be a long day before I shall forget your hospitality. Never fear. The Lord is on our side. Although clouds may hang over us, and a mighty tide of opposition set against us yet a brighter day is coming." Garnet warned his friend against hoping for early success. He would thank God if this great work, the coming of "Emancipation Day," were to be achieved in twenty years. Then came a short statement packed with military imagery: "Since my return I have put on my armour—joined the "*Neucleus* of *Liberty*"—and hoisted my banner with this motto inscribed upon it 'The Sword of the Lord and Gideon.' Pass around the Constitution—it is short and plain. . . . 'Enlisted during the War.'"[12]

By 1845 Garnet was seriously considering missionary work in western New York State, where the need seemed greater than in the small black community in Troy. Such a move, moreover, would bring him closer to his longtime friend Gerrit Smith and to the ardent black Methodist helper of fugitive slaves, Jermain Loguen, both of whom lived near Syracuse. Freed from the supervision of the Troy Presbytery, Garnet would find it easier to combine Christian ministry with militant antislavery evangelism.[13]

From 1843 to 1845, when Garnet was cutting his ties with the heavily Presbyterian American Home Missionary Society and weighing a move from Troy to western New York State, Charles Ray was making a shift in

11. Henry Garnet to Rev. Charles Hall, June 28, 1844, A.L.S. in Amistad Research Center, Tulane University, New Orleans (Microfilm copy in Carter and Ripley [eds.] *BAP,* reel 4, item 832); Rev. Charles Hall to Henry Garnet, July 1, 1844, in Carter and Ripley (eds.), *BAP,* reel 4, item 835.

12. Henry Garnet to G. A. Thacther, from Troy, September 3, 1844, in Black History Collection, Manuscripts Division, Library of Congress.

13. Henry Garnet to Gerrit Smith, from Troy, September 9, 1845, in Gerrit Smith Papers.

vocation from journalist to city missionary and Congregational pastor. In fact, it was a return to the calling that had originally sent him to the Methodist academy in Wilbraham, Massachusetts, and to Wesleyan University over a decade earlier. Ray had been forced to close down the *Colored American* at the end of 1841. During that last year the paper, along with having a central preoccupation with the New York black campaign for the franchise, devoted considerable space to the successful conclusion of the trial of the *Amistad* crew. It also publicized the prospective return of these Mendi to Africa, their interest in evangelizing their homeland, and the need for funds to enable both. From April through November 1841, Ray ran at least eighteen pieces on Christian missions in Africa, whereas only one had been published in the preceding year.[14] Most of these letters and articles clearly distinguished between the questionable assumptions of the American Colonization Society and what the authors saw as true Christian evangelism in Africa, preferably carried on by black missionaries.

After the founding of the Union Missionary Society, specifically committed to the evangelization of the Mendi, Ray was active in its management. He and Garnet could not attend the meetings that launched the society in the summer of 1841, because they occurred on the eve of that year's New York State black convention. By early 1843, however, Ray was not only on the Executive Committee of the UMS but also was its secretary. It was presumably in this capacity that he joined with Lewis Tappan in the fall of 1843 in asking Garnet to serve as part-time agent for the UMS. Ray seems to have remained secretary of the Executive Committee of the UMS until that organization merged with several others in 1846 to form the American Missionary Association (AMA).[15]

In 1844 Ray himself undertook ministerial responsibilities that were in part financed by the UMS and later by the AMA. He began work as "City Missionary to the Destitute Colored Population," reaching out to poor and unchurched blacks somewhat as Cornish had done over twenty years earlier. And like Cornish, Ray gathered the nucleus of a church from those he visited. His Bethesda (black) Congregational Church wor-

14. Donald M. Jacobs (ed.), *Antebellum Black Newspapers: Indices to New York "Freedom's Journal" (1827–1829), "The Rights of All" (1829), "The Weekly Advocate" (1837), and "The Colored American" (1837–1841)* (Westport, Conn., 1976), 248f.

15. Notice to UMS Executive Committee members, dated February 1843 and signed by Charles Ray, in *Christian Freeman,* April 18, 1843 (Microfilm copy in Carter and Ripley [eds.], *BAP,* reel 4, item 560); Notes from Ray to a staff member of the UMS, written in 1845 (AMA Archives, nos. F1-5576, F1-5608).

shiped in a hall on Grand Street. Two white churches, First and Second Congregational, gave early financial support.[16] Seeking out the unchurched was characteristic of the Evangelicalism of the Second Great Awakening, but Ray was notable for the durability of his commitment to the work of an urban missionary. He would continue it either as city missionary or on his own until after the Civil War. His comments made after visiting N. S. S. Beman's church in Troy in 1838 pointed toward his later ministry: "The house is a splendid, costly building, with too much ornament for a temple of God, and we think God is displeased with it. . . . We read 'to the poor the gospel is preached,' this cannot be the case in such churches,—there the rich only can hear very advantageously; the rich sitting in the most eligible positions, as in an easy chair, while the poor . . . are driven to sit where they can, or not come at all. Rich professors [that is, those who profess Christian belief] and fashionable Christianity, are becoming a curse to the world." Ray compared this fashionable Christianity with "the Jewish church," which had rejected Christ. He doubted that half of Beman's congregation would accept the Lord should he reappear.[17]

When Ray was formally installed as minister of the Bethesda Congregational Church in 1845, the white pastor of the Crosby Street Congregational Church, which Ray had been attending, preached the sermon. Simeon Jocelyn, who had organized and ministered to the African Congregational Church in New Haven, gave the right hand of fellowship. And Lewis Tappan, co-worker with Ray in the Union Missionary Society and many other enterprises, addressed the congregation.[18]

Why did Ray, an ordained Methodist minister and a close associate of black Presbyterian ministers, found a Congregational church? Because Congregationalism was a highly decentralized denomination, Ray could count on the independence of the local congregation and pastor. Moreover, less distracted by the demands of denominational churchmanship than if he were an African Methodist Minister, he would have the freedom to continue his social and political activism. However, to be acceptable to one of the New York presbyteries, he would have to undergo a regimen of tutoring comparable to Cornish's in Philadelphia. Because he

16. George E. Walker, "The Afro-American in New York City" (Ph.D. dissertation, Columbia University, 1972), 137.

17. *Colored American,* December 15, 1838.

18. Freeman, "The Free Negro in New York City," 418; Ray and Ray, *Sketch of Charles B. Ray,* 17.

had married again in 1840, four years after his first wife's death, and there were now children in the family, it was important that he secure a regular income as soon as possible after the demise of the *Colored American*.

Ray's choice of Congregationalism, however, was more than a last resort. He knew well three black ministers who had had favorable experiences in black Congregational churches, as well as in relations with white Congregational clergy in their respective communities: James Pennington in Hartford, Amos Beman in New Haven, and Amos Freeman in Portland, Maine. Ray himself had found a true church home in the primarily white Congregational church on Crosby Street. Over forty years later his daughters recalled it as "a heroic band of men and women whose principles were in accord with the sacred idea that all men are brothers."[19]

Ray's experience with white Congregational ministers in New York City bore out the early favorable impressions. He regularly attended the Monday meetings of the Congregational Clerical Union and found the discussions of topics relating to pastoral work helpful. Later, when the Manhattan Congregational Association was formed, he at once became an active member. This association's discerning minute at the time of Ray's death was proof of his having been appreciated.[20]

Detailed knowledge of Ray's work as city missionary and pastor of Bethesda comes from his periodic reports to the American Missionary Association during the years when he was receiving small cash grants to supplement his annual receipts from church members and other individuals he solicited. Along with Wright, Cornish, and Pennington, Ray was placed on the AMA's twelve-man Executive Committee at its founding in 1846. The AMA was supporting four home missionaries in 1847 and fifty-one by 1853. Ray was evidently one of the first missionaries to receive a grant from the new organization, which had been founded in protest against the leniency toward slavery of both the American Home Missionary Society and the heavily Congregational American Board of Commissioners for Foreign Missions. Because the Tappans were a power in the new organization and Simeon Jocelyn was one of its earliest staff members, Ray had warm white allies as well as close friends of his own race in the AMA inner circles. Moreover, Ray's political convictions agreed with the AMA's. Although the organization never officially endorsed a political party or candidate, it stood with the principles of the Liberty party.[21]

19. Ray and Ray, *Sketch of Charles B. Ray*, 17.

20. *Ibid.*, 19, 78.

21. Clifton H. Johnson, "The American Missionary Association, 1846–1861: A Study of

The AMA commissioned Ray primarily as city missionary rather than as pastor of Bethesda. The two enterprises, however, could hardly be separated. By 1848, when Bethesda was three years old, church membership had grown from thirteen to thirty. "Our meetings on the Sabbath," Ray said, "have been generally interesting, and in the evening especially well attended, the house better filled than it has ever been." There were sixty-six registered in the Sunday school, but attendance in the winter suffered because many children did not have warm clothing. Ray tried to bring alive for the AMA what it meant to be a city missionary, to do something "towards reforming the outcast, and saving the souls, of at least the sick, and dying." He cited at length the cases of two of those "for whose souls men care seemingly but little." In one family that he often visited, the eight-year-old son had died. Ray was summoned to conduct the funeral. He saw this as an opportune time to make a lasting impression on the parents, especially the father, who was "given to intemperance, and had several times abandoned his family." Ray's words at the funeral seemed to make a difference. Almost every Sunday, for two months, both parents attended church, sometimes for both services and the lecture: "The father is thus far another man, & seems determined to lead another life."[22]

Another fruitful encounter grew out of Ray's habit of random conversation with men in the streets: "I stopped . . . to converse with a group of men, and to give them some tracts. In the course of my conversation [a] Sailor on taking a tract, remarked that he could not read, but that his wife could, and he wished he could get her a Bible." She had often asked him for a Bible, and he had promised to get her one but had been so hard-pressed "to buy bread, & pay rent" that he seemed never to have the extra two shillings for a copy of the Scriptures. Ray offered to give the sailor a Bible if he would walk home with him. As they traveled the half mile through the dusk, Ray's companion told of having been wrecked at sea on his way home from Europe. He was marooned on the wreck for seventeen days and watched three of his black fellow seamen washed away, unable to hold on longer. He was rescued just before the ship sank. Disinclined to go to sea again, the sailor was sorely pressed for even minimal income: "On giving him the Bible with remarks, he seemed to feel that he was receiving a message from heaven. He thanked me and stated

---

Christian Abolitionism" (Ph.D. dissertation, University of North Carolina, 1958), 29ff., 93, 210–12.

22. Report of February 1848 to AMA Executive Committee (MS in AMA Archives).

that he loved to hear the Bible read, and that his wife took great comfort in reading it also. I commended him to the God of the Bible, and we parted."[23]

Being with people through their last days and hours was a large part of Ray's work, more so than for most ministers, for his constituency had a high mortality rate. In February 1848 Ray reported constant visits paid to five very ill people, three of them near death: "One is calmly waiting in the Lord till her change come, in certain hope of then being forever with him. Three of the others are exceedingly anxious to know that all is well with them, and are striving to commit themselves to God through his Son." A month later Ray told the AMA that one of those he had been visiting had sent for him on the day she died. Greatly "distressed about her soul," she asked Ray to sing with her. The two then prayed together "that God would take her to himself," and she died just as the prayer ended. In the same report Ray told of conducting six funerals of young people. All had died of consumption.[24]

Another part of Ray's task as city missionary was to pay a weekly visit to the Colored Home, which was maintained by the city and private contributions as a haven for about two hundred indigent and handicapped people. Ray conducted a service of worship and stayed to talk with those who were eager for spiritual sustenance and Christian counsel.

Securing his $600-a-year income continued to be problematic for Ray. In February 1848 he reported that he received some $450 in contributions for the year beginning April 1847, and $51.50 was due to come in by April 1, 1848. He requested an AMA grant of $70 to $100 "to carry him through the winter." Ray based his request on his family's need and his inability to raise the money elsewhere. The AMA promptly sent him a check for $50. Two years later the situation was no better. Ray petitioned the AMA for enough to bring his total annual income up to $600.[25]

There were other problems. By 1849 the Bethesda Congregational Church had only thirty-seven members, but the congregation for Sunday service had grown substantially. Ray was looking for more adequate quarters but found himself blocked: "The colored population of a large city . . . cannot like their brethren among the whites, even when possessed of equal wealth, secure an eligible location for their assembly to-

23. *Ibid.*

24. Report to AMA, March 14, 1848 (MS in AMA Archives).

25. Charles Ray to AMA Executive Committee, February 1848, March 12, 1850, and receipt signed by Ray acknowledging $50 paid to him by Lewis Tappan, AMA treasurer, all in AMA Archives.

gether. . . . Prejudice follows them as they seek to purchase or rent a place in which to worship God." The price of a property, he complained, which was already almost beyond the reach of a black congregation, was boosted further, or objections were raised to black congregations' occupying a chosen site. In spite of these obstacles, sometime in the 1850s Ray was able to move the Bethesda Congregational Church from its original hall on Grand Street to a roomy church on Sullivan Street.[26]

After roughly five years of occasional small grants in support of Ray's ministry, the AMA asked a three-man committee to evaluate his work, both as a city missionary and pastor. Their report was positive in both areas: "Such labor is of decided advantage to the colored population of the city among whom it has been put forth." The committee doubted the wisdom of continued AMA support, however, fearing that it would lead to a flood of requests for aid from other urban missionaries. Accordingly, the AMA terminated its grants to Ray. He somehow managed to support his family into the late 1860s on an income gained from church members' contributions, donations from other individuals he solicited year by year, and a small return on property originally owned by his wife.[27]

Ray's undertaking mission work and ministry during the 1840s did not preclude his continuing help for fugitive slaves and prominence in efforts for free blacks' education and civil rights. Concerned for the material progress of the whole of the city's black community, Ray particularly hoped to see a substantial number move to the country and make a living based on agriculture. Samuel Cornish and many other black promoters of the elevation of the race had had a similar hope. Ray's own early experience in farming gave concreteness to his vision. At the national black convention of 1843, where Garnet delivered his "Address to the Slaves," Ray chaired the Committee on Agriculture. Its substantial report, undoubtedly written by him, defined wealth as independence and assurance of the necessities of life. The report declared that both of these are more readily available where the soil is the means of production; from soil come both the food and the clothing needed by all human beings. And assets expand; the savings that might earn 5 percent in a city bank are likely to earn 25 percent if invested in land in the western territories.[28]

26. *American Missionary,* November 1849; Freeman, "The Free Negro in New York City," 407; Ray and Ray, *Sketch of Charles B. Ray,* 17.

27. Report of the "Committee on Report & Labors of City Missionary," 1851 (MS in AMA Archives, no. 80127); Freeman, "The Free Negro in New York City," 408.

28. "Minutes of the National Convention of Colored Citizens . . . 1843," in Bell (ed.), *Minutes of the National Negro Conventions,* 30–32.

Ray's committee report cited the experience of blacks in Mercer County, Ohio, since the latter 1830s. The moving spirit behind the Ohio experiment had been Augustus Wattles, a white radical who had been with Theodore Weld at Lane Theological Seminary in Cincinnati. After the student exodus from Lane over the abolition question, Wattles turned to promoting a black farming community where adults could prosper through hard work uncorrupted by urban vice, and where children could grow up in a healthy environment. By 1838 blacks in Mercer and surrounding counties owned thirty thousand acres. Men who had lived there only a year had cleared and put into cultivation fifteen to thirty acres. The best corn crops that season were in the black settlement. Land bought by blacks for $1.25 an acre was now worth $10 an acre. When Ray visited Ohio in 1839, he went to Mercer County and other black farming settlements. He reveled in the fact that more land was owned by blacks in Ohio and more of them were making a living on their farms than in all the rest of the states combined. The situation was the more encouraging because a manual labor school set up by Wattles and open to whites as well as blacks seemed solidly established, with one hundred students and two regular teachers.[29]

A cardinal conviction of the Committee on Agriculture at the Buffalo convention was that in the country, blacks could escape the curse of prejudice: "The business of farming is the shortest, surest road to respectability and influence." The black farmers in Mercer County had testified: "In our present residence in this county, we have never in any manner been injured by our white neighbors; but on the contrary we have been treated in a kind and friendly manner. They attend our meetings, come to our mill, employ our mechanics, and day laborers, buy our provisions, and we do the same by them. That is we all seek our own convenience and interest without regard to color." Ray's committee strongly recommended the migration of black families from the large cities to the country, especially to Michigan, Ohio, Indiana, Illinois, and the territories of Wisconsin and Iowa. A resolution to that effect was adopted by the 1843 convention without dissent.[30]

Three years after the Buffalo convention, the white philanthropist Gerrit Smith proposed a large-scale land grant program to hasten the emigration process for three thousand black people in New York State.

29. William H. Pease and Jane H. Pease, *Black Utopia: Negro Communal Experiments in America* (Madison, Wis., 1972), 38–40; Mabee, *Black Freedom*, 154f., 403; *Colored American*, December 15, 1838; November 2, 1839.

30. *Minutes of the National Convention . . . 1843*, 30–36.

When Smith's father died in 1837, Smith became owner of over a half million acres. In 1846 he announced, "For years I have indulged the thought that, when I had sold enough land to pay my debts, I would give away the remainder to the poor. I am an Agrarian. I would that every man who desires a farm, might have one." Smith, eventually one of the richest men in the country (he may have donated as much as eight million dollars during his life), decided to give land to the poor of his home state, and to the blacks as the poorest of the poor. Cruel prejudice, he declared, blocked from them "the avenues to riches and respectability—to happiness and usefulness." He cited the restriction of the black vote as a glaring example of the handicaps faced by poorer blacks.[31]

Smith wrote to three long-time friends in New York City: Wright, Ray, and James McCune Smith. He asked them to choose two thousand black men worthy of receiving grants of roughly forty acres of moderately good farmland. They must be twenty-one to sixty years of age, of modest means, and not addicted to liquor. The land to be allotted lay in the northeast and central counties of the state. Six weeks later, Smith again wrote his black associates. He was alarmed by reports "respecting the intemperance of colored men." He urged his correspondents to prepare a letter to the recipients of land grants that advised them "respecting their habits, their use of the lands I give them, etc. etc." Smith also hoped that such a circular might have a good effect on the constitutional convention sitting in Albany: "It might contribute to shame [the delegates] out of the wicked & mean purpose of robbing colored men of their rights."[32]

Because Theodore Wright was seriously ill, it is likely that Ray took the lead in preparing the document suggested by Smith. This *Address to the Three Thousand Colored Citizens of New York* . . . hailed the grand opportunity offered by Gerrit Smith for two thousand black individuals or families to leave behind uncertain and poorly paid employment for a life in which hard work could bring a decent livelihood, freedom from racist attitudes, and true community. The authors of the *Address* foresaw the possibility that recipients of the grants would be discouraged by rumors that the land was too poor for farming and urged their fellows not to sell the land. Instead, the authors advised, settle on the land, clear it, practice rigid economy, avoid mortgaging the farm, put away distrust of one another, help one another, and abstain from all intoxicating drinks.

As a final incentive to positive response by urban blacks to this agri-

31. Harlow, *Gerrit Smith*, 242; Friedman, *Gregarious Saints*, 100.

32. Gerrit Smith to Theodore Wright, Charles Ray, and J. M. Smith, September 10, 1846, in Gerrit Smith Papers.

cultural opportunity, Ray, Wright, and Smith stood back and looked at the whole Afro-American experience and God's relation to it. It was a classic statement of faith in the ultimate primacy of divine will's working through human suffering and responsible human effort:

> The good God, when He suffered the first swarth man to be inveigled, entrapped, and stolen from Africa, when He suffered untold thousands of such, to perish in the agony of the way to the sea coast, . . . when He meted out the cruel sufferings of the sugar and rice plantations, when He gave to us the better [*sic*] fate of Tantalus, in this land of Christian light and Christian glory—He overruled the evil intentions of men for the benefit of mankind, by placing us in the midst of the path of progress, that we might work out the great problems of human equality."[33]

It was several decades before it became clear that the Smith land grant program was a debacle. During late 1846 and the following two years, there was heavy correspondence between Peterboro and New York City. Ray and J. M. Smith sent recommendations of persons who would use land well, and Gerrit Smith forwarded some two thousand individual deeds. By the fall of 1848, however, two years after the original grant, only twenty to thirty black families had moved to their farmland. And the number of black settlers did not grow over the next years. As Leon F. Litwack, a historian of antebellum free blacks' vicissitudes, has put it, by the 1850s it was clear that "the virtues of agrarian life had made little impression on urban Negroes."[34]

In March 1847 the black community in New York City and black leaders throughout the state and beyond suffered a major loss in the death of Theodore Wright. Like John Gloucester in Philadelphia and Samuel Cornish in New York City in the 1820s, Wright had been forced again and again to wrestle with his church's indebtedness. In 1840, some six months after joining the Third Presbytery, he had laid the problem before that body. He was directed by the presbytery to work with white member churches (as he had in 1831 in the New York Presbytery) to secure contri-

33. Theodore S. Wright, Charles B. Ray, and James McCune Smith, *An Address to the Three Thousand Colored Citizens of New York Who Are the Owners of One Hundred and Twenty Thousand Acres of Land in the State of New York, Given to Them by Gerrit Smith, Esq. of Peterboro, September 1, 1846* (New York, 1846), 18. For an excellent review of antebellum black leaders' views on "the destiny of black Americans," see Leonard I. Sweet, *Black Images of America, 1784–1870* (New York, 1976), 69–124.

34. Charles Ray to Gerrit Smith, December 6, 1847, January 20, March 31, May 18, June 5, July 4, 1848, October 14, 1850, all in Gerrit Smith Papers; Harlow, *Gerrit Smith,* 245f.; Litwack, *North of Slavery,* 177.

butions. A board of trustees made up of lay elders from the white churches was to hold the deed to the black church and oversee the liquidation of its debt.[35]

In spite of this burden and though plagued by serious illness during his last years, Wright had remained an effective pastor during the early 1840s. His First Colored Presbyterian Church gained 130 new members between 1840 and 1843. Moreover, Wright had continued to participate actively in such extrachurch causes as the Executive Committee of the American and Foreign Anti-Slavery Society, the New York Vigilance Committee, the annual state black conventions campaigning for the franchise, and the Liberty party.

Wright was distinctive in a number of ways. He built the First Colored Presbyterian Church into much the largest black Presbyterian church in the country. The quality of the preaching, the Sunday school education, and the pastoral care in this church was high. That the Third Presbytery chose Wright as its moderator in 1845 cannot be dismissed as a mere token gesture. However, something of the true nature of Wright's relations with his white presbyterial colleagues was reflected in the bitter comments on this moderatorship by Amos Beman, Congregational minister in New Haven: "Perhaps it may relieve fears . . . lest the 3d Presbytery, to which Br. Wright has for so many years belonged, should shower too many honors upon him, . . . to know the *fact,* that notwithstanding he had been sick, and for most of the time for several months confined to his house, *only one of the members of the Presbytery ever called to see him.*"[36]

The primary bases of Wright's influence and the roots through which he drew nourishment had lain not in the white presbytery but in the overall black community. On scores of occasions recorded in the newspapers of the 1830s and early 1840s, Wright and other black ministers had presided over important public events having to do with church life, abolition, the franchise, aid for fugitive slaves, emigration, and temperance. For example, when Zion Church, the mother church of the AME Zion denomination, was destroyed by fire and a grand replacement had been built, a service was held to consecrate this new church, which was able to accommodate nearly two thousand worshippers. The dedicatory prayer

35. Minutes of Third Presbytery of New York, April 10, 13, May 5, 1840; November 2, 1846.

36. Amos Beman to James W. C. Pennington for publication in the *Clarksonian,* which Pennington edited, in Amos Beman Scrap Book (Amos G. Beman Papers). The one who had visited Wright was Rev. William Patton.

was offered by Bishop Christopher Rush. The Scriptures were read by Assistant Superintendent William Miller, pastor of the Wesley AMEZ Church in Philadelphia. And the address and concluding prayer were given by Wright.[37] Paralleling such public instances of black interdenominational cooperation were Wright's close personal friendships with some black Episcopal, Methodist, and Baptist clergy. He had an early and many-sided association with Peter Williams, Jr. From 1835 on Wright and Daniel Payne, the dedicated apostle of education within the AME denomination, were close friends. Closer at hand was John T. Raymond, pastor of the Zion Baptist Church in New York City during the 1830s and then of the Hamilton Street Baptist Church in Albany. Wright and Raymond were ardent fellow workers for the vigilance committee and the expansion of the black franchise. To a lesser extent Wright had warm and frequent associations with most of the other black clergy in New York City and with men such as Baptist Nathaniel Paul in other cities. However, his ties with black Presbyterian and Congregational clergy were the closest.[38]

By the late weeks of 1846 Wright was very feeble. Physicians advised a trip to Nassau. Before Wright sailed, Amos Beman traveled to New York City for a glimpse of him and a farewell service in the First Colored Presbyterian Church. Wright himself was too weak to say much to his congregation: "I cannot talk much—you know my advice—fear God and keep his commandments—prepare to meet thy God—live in peace—in love—in faithfulness—and if we meet no more *here,* may we all meet, where parting is unknown." Wright survived his trip to the West Indies but barely lasted out the winter. He died on March 25. William Lloyd Garrison published the most complete obituary. Although the editor of the *Liberator* made reference to "sectarian feelings . . . [which Wright] allowed to bias his judgment" at the time of the schism of 1840, the general tone was appreciative: "Mr. Wright was distinguished for his amiable qualities, his devotional spirit and his persuasive eloquence. . . . He was active and useful in his ministrations to the colored people of New York, by whom he was generally beloved and will be much lamented."[39]

37. *Colored American,* May 2, 1840; William J. Walls, *The African Methodist Episcopal Zion Church: Reality of the Black Church* (Charlotte, N.C., 1874), 129; *Colored American,* January 23, 1841.

38. Daniel A. Payne, *Recollections of Seventy Years* (1888; rpr. New York, 1969), 49.

39. Communication sent by Amos Beman to James Pennington for publication in the *Clarksonian,* in Amos Beman Scrap Book (Amos G. Beman Papers), II, 66; *Liberator,* April 2, 1847.

Wright's funeral included a mammoth procession following the casket from Wright's home up to Canal Street, then downtown and across town to the First Colored Presbyterian Church. Lewis Tappan and three clerical representatives of the Third Presbytery, Samuel Cox, Edwin Hatfield, and William Patton, were among the pallbearers. A half dozen other white clergy were in the procession. Ebenezer Davies, a Welsh missionary visiting America from British Guiana, happened to be in New York City at this time and was pressed into service as a pallbearer. He later described the remarkable event. He spoke of "crowds of coloured people . . . hastening . . . from all quarters" toward Wright's house: "The immense procession starts. . . . As we pass on from street to street, all sorts of people seem to regard the procession with utmost respect. The cabmen, 'busmen, and cartmen behave exceedingly well. But did you overhear what those three or four low dirty men said as we approached? . . . Those men are not Americans, but *Irishmen*." Back at the church a crowd far too vast to be accommodated tried to press into the sanctuary. Davies estimated six hundred inside and over five thousand outside. A black man gave out a hymn; Samuel Cox read the Scriptures and spoke a few words. William Patton gave the main address. Speaking of Wright's ministry, Patton noted the extra burden the black man had borne as he traveled about the city "to beg money in order to extricate this [church] from pecuniary difficulties." This task had been made far more laborious because public transport so often refused to serve black customers. Seeing a prospective donor often meant walking for miles uptown and then more miles back downtown. Exhaustion from such efforts "under the full muzzle of the July or August sun" had brought on Wright's fatal illness.[40] In spite of Wright's many gifts and accomplishments and all the respect and affection he had aroused in thousands of blacks and many whites, he proved to be as vulnerable to the special obstacles facing a black minister as John Gloucester had been a quarter century earlier.

In the three years after Wright's death, Garnet searched for new directions and further protested against Christian churches that had made their peace with the slave system. The 1843 national black convention, which had refused to endorse Garnet's "Address to the Slaves," had also spent much time discussing a resolution that "the great mass of American sects, falsely called churches, which apologize for slavery and prejudice, or prac-

40. Ebenezer Davies, *American Scenes and Christian Slavery: A Recent Tour of Four Thousand Miles in the United States* (London, 1849), 239–42.

tice slaveholding, are in truth not churches, but Synagogues of Satan." Garnet and Ray joined Bostonians Frederick Douglass and Charles Remond in speaking for this resolution. It was endorsed by a vote of twenty-three to ten.[41] As has been discussed, Garnet lived up to this vote the following year when he resigned his American Home Missionary Society commission rather than limit his public speaking against slavery and for the Liberty party.

Stung by the AHMS rebuke and searching for a post where his work could accomplish more dramatic changes than in Troy, Garnet wrote Gerrit Smith in 1845 that he hoped soon to be living in western New York: "Then I shall be able I trust to enjoy frequently what I have much longed for—the soul cheering influence of the Preacher—the unflinching friend of my people."[42] It took three years of canvassing the black communities in Syracuse and to the west before Garnet was ready to make the break from Troy to found a school and be pastor of a small church in Geneva.

Before Garnet left Troy, however, he cut the ties of his Liberty Street church with Presbyterianism. His public explanation of the move must have pleased Gerrit Smith, who had withdrawn from the Peterboro Presbyterian Church, organized a nondenominational one, and served as its minister. Garnet stated:

> Whereas, Sectarianism is at variance with the spirit and the letter of the Gospel . . . and is a most prolific source of wars, and slavery . . . therefore, Resolved, that the members of Christ's body, heretofore denominated "The Liberty St. Presbyterian Church of Troy, N.Y.," do hereby solemnly repudiate all Sectarianism, sincerely regretting . . . that we ever gave countenance to that destructive devise of Satan.
>
> Resolved, that we shall hereafter be known as "the Church in Liberty St., Troy, N.Y.," and that we shall acknowledge no other creed than the Bible, and no other Head than God and his Son Jesus Christ.[43]

Six months later Garnet and several Philadelphia blacks were asked to prepare an address for a black antislavery convention in that city. The

41. *Minutes of the National Convention . . . 1843,* 10–12, 15.

42. Henry Garnet to Gerrit Smith, from Troy, September 19, 1845, in Gerrit Smith Papers. Garnet called Gerrit Smith "the Political Preacher."

43. Alan K. Kraut, "The Forgotten Reformers: A Profile of Third Party Abolitionists in Antebellum New York," in Perry and Fellman (eds.), *Antislavery Reconsidered,* 119–45; *Pennsylvania Freeman,* April 6, 1848 (Microfilm copy in Carter and Ripley [eds.], *BAP,* reel 5, item 608).

themes of this address mirrored the Troy Liberty Street church's manifesto. Presbyterians, Baptists, Episcopalians, and Methodists were described as "connected with the gory institution of slavery in [their] ecclesiastical relations." The authors of the address pleaded with blacks who were members of churches belonging to primarily white denominations, that is, blacks in African Presbyterian and African Episcopal churches and those continuing as minority members of white Methodist and Baptist churches: "Forsake these murderers and destroyers of your people, and let the world know why you do it." They urged blacks to withdraw support from the American Board of Commissioners for Foreign Missions and from the Bible and tract societies, "all of which, in this country, are pro-slavery." Let the "teaching and discipline of the Bible," they urged, "supercede the dogmas of men." Let Christian churches be simply the churches of Christians in a given community.[44]

At the time of this convention in Philadelphia, Garnet and his family were already living in Gerrit Smith's home near Syracuse. Garnet had been commissioned by the resolutely abolitionist and nondenominational American Missionary Association to open a school and build up the Union Colored Church in Geneva's community of three hundred blacks. The AMA initially paid Garnet a stipend of $200 a year and contributed funds toward the upkeep of the school. By December 1848 the school was filled to its fifty-pupil capacity. The church had only fifteen members, but within three months that number had swelled to seventy. Because of his daughter Mary's frail health, Garnet, his wife, and the two children continued for some months to live with the Smiths. Garnet made the round trip of seventy-five miles to Geneva as school, Sunday school, and church services required.[45]

In August 1849 Garnet reported to Lewis Tappan as officer of the American Missionary Association, "The house which holds about 200 is too small for the Congregation. At our last the emblems [the bread and wine of the communion] were handed out out of doors, to those who were unable to enter in." The congregation was generally poor, and Garnet estimated that they could only provide $200 of the $300 needed to

44. "An Address from the Anti-Slavery Convention, Assembled in the Brick Wesley Church, October 2d and 3d, 1848, to the Colored Citizens of the City of Philadelphia," *Pennsylvania Freeman,* October 5, 1848 (Microfilm copy in Carter and Ripley [eds.], *BAP,* reel 5, item 801).

45. Henry Garnet to Lewis Tappan, August 25, 1849, in AMA Archives; Pasternak, "Rise Now and Fly to Arms," 90f.

maintain the mission station. He asked Tappan for counsel as to "any way in which this field can be kept open, and cultivated," saying he had a young man in mind who could usefully occupy the post.[46]

Garnet saw himself as the explorer for, and founder of, a number of new churches like the one in Geneva. Hoping to rouse the support of the AMA, he described the black population in that area. Originally from other states, and especially from the South, they were as prosperous as blacks of a similar sort in other parts of the country, but they were in a deplorable religious state. The usual "powerful temptation to abandon God" had been strengthened by "the souring influence of prejudice on their minds." Garnet saw no hope of traditional "sectarian" preachers helping them, and his view of Garrisonians was equally harsh. Blacks disillusioned with the traditional church are "rushing headlong into . . . the looseness and folly and sugar-coated Sin which is peculiar to the preaching of the Garrisonians."[47]

Garnet proposed that a New York State society be formed "and agents and missionaries be employed to go forth into the hedges and highways, and entreat these neglected ones to turn into the paths of rectitude and virtue." Neither the American Missionary Association nor the editors or readers of the *North Star* picked up on Garnet's grandiose proposal. Instead, the AMA offered him a commission and stipend if he would continue on at the church he had founded in Geneva. By January 1850 Garnet accepted the AMA offer and seemed full of hope for what this new church could accomplish. Two-thirds of the black population of Geneva and its environs were coming to this place of worship. The church was incorporated as the Geneva Tabernacle, and its members and friends were trying to gather the $500 needed to put up a new building: "The Church is orthodox but not sectarian. The advance of the people religiously has been such as to astonish their foes, and amaze their warmest of friends. . . . We know that the purposes of our Lord will ripen, and neither man nor devils can thwart them. The waste places shall yet be rebuilt. And the wilderness . . . shall be glad for us. And the desert shall rejoice and blossom as the rose."[48]

It must have come as a shock to the AMA to receive word from

46. Henry Garnet to Lewis Tappan, from Peterboro, August 25, 1849, in AMA Archives.

47. *Ibid.*

48. *North Star,* January 19, 1849; Henry Garnet to George Whipple (secretary of the AMA), December 12, 1849, January 16, 1850, both in AMA Archives. The final sentence is a quotation from the Bible, Isa. 35:1.

Garnet in early July 1850 that he was resigning his commission and would shortly be leaving Geneva for England. Garnet's departure was the more frustrating for the AMA because he had accomplished so much in his two years in this small community. Not only had Garnet provided invigorating preaching ministry, the oversight of a large Sunday school, and continued teaching in a weekday school for black children; his enthusiasm for getting black people back on the soil had proved contagious. By the summer of 1850 blacks owned sixty acres within the village limits, and a number of others in the township owned small farms. But Garnet had a powerful urge to go to Great Britain. He had been invited to become a salaried agent of a favorite cause, the Free Produce Movement, having been recruited by the movement's British leader, the Quaker Henry Richardson of Newcastle. The Free Produce Movement and its American analogue, the American Free Produce Association, were trying to advance the abolition cause by reducing the market, on both sides of the Atlantic, for slave-grown produce. These products included cotton bought by textile manufacturers; clothing made from these textiles; and sugar, coffee, or rice purchased by individuals.[49] Garnet weighed Richardson's offer for a year before he finally accepted. He was drawn to a crusade that gave promise of becoming an economic flanking movement against the whole American slave system. "Domestic affairs and public relations," however, forced him to decline the initial British offer.[50] A year later the picture had changed. On the one hand, the Geneva church was more solidly established. On the other, a more threatening Fugitive Slave Act was about to become law. Garnet, as a widely known and highly effective antislavery lecturer, must have wondered whether his high visibility would constitute protection or vulnerability under the new, more aggressive program of recapturing fugitives.

Because of this specter of reenslavement, but also because of other disillusioning factors, when Garnet left the United States he did not intend to return. His mood upon departure was the culmination of a gradual two-year shift toward a more favorable view of black emigration out of the United States.

By 1856, however, Garnet was back again in New York City, his whole family debilitated by illness incurred at the end of his three years as

49. R. J. M. Blackett, *Building an Antislavery Wall: Black Americans in the Atlantic Abolitionist Movement, 1830–1860* (Baton Rouge, 1983), 118–21.

50. Henry Garnet to Lewis Tappan, August 25, 1849, in AMA Archives.

a missionary in Jamaica for the Scottish United Presbyterian Church. When offered the pastorate of his mother church, now named Prince Street Presbyterian, he accepted. His immediate predecessor in that post was James W. C. Pennington, originally pastor of the Colored Congregational Church on Talcott Street in Hartford, Connecticut, and close friend of Amos Beman, pastor of the Temple Street African Congregational Church in New Haven. The following chapters turn to these two Connecticut activists, whose concerns and efforts in the 1840s had so closely paralleled those of Wright, Ray, and Garnet.

8. AMOS G. BEMAN, NEW HAVEN PASTOR AND CONNECTICUT ACTIVIST

Most firmly do I believe the elements of substantial good exist among our population, which the patient hand of Christian culture can under God marshal into a scene cheering to every virtuous mind.

—Amos G. Beman, 1843

During the 1840s, while Henry Garnet and Charles Ray were campaigning for blacks' political rights in New York State and were beginning their work as Christian ministers in Troy and New York City, two other black pastors were emerging as influential activists in Connecticut. James W. C. Pennington began informal and unlicensed ministry in the Temple Street African Congregational Church in New Haven in 1835. Amos Beman was chosen full-time pastor of this church in 1838. His ministry there lasted nineteen years—as long as Theodore Wright's in New York City. Pennington's ministerial career, like Garnet's, was more episodic. His eight-year pastorate in Hartford was interrupted by a trip to England and a two-year leave of absence.

There had been an important forerunner of Beman and Pennington in Connecticut: Lemuel Haynes, born in 1753 in West Hartford of a white mother and a black father. He was brought up as an indentured servant in a white family active in the Middle Granville Congregational Church. A bright and devout young man, Haynes was encouraged toward the ministry. He was ordained at the age of twenty-two in Litchfield County. His ministry in several white churches in Connecticut, Vermont, and New York was effective and did much to open whites' eyes to the capacities of at least this Afro-American. In 1805 he became truly a celebrity in composing and delivering a deft sermon satirically refuting the tenets of the prominent Universalist, Hosea Ballou. This sermon was reprinted dozens of times prior to Hayne's death in 1833, and thereafter. Though he was not a political activist, Haynes startled many whites in New England and educated them toward a broader view of his race. And he must have inspired not a few blacks by his record of achievement.[1]

Just as there was a parallel between Beman's long pastorate and Wright's, there were also similarities between Beman's and Ray's careers. Both served the black community in many different roles. Both were Congregational ministers who were drawn into significant colleagueship with white clergy of that denomination. And both were at the center of black people's efforts to recover the franchise, Ray in New York and Beman in Connecticut. Beman and Ray first met in the fall of 1832 during Ray's short stay at Wesleyan University. Beman was a high school student at the time, his father the pastor of the only black church in Middletown. Young Beman and Ray kept in touch with each other during the nearly seven years until Ray visited New Haven as an itinerant preacher and reporter for the *Colored American*.

The 1830s and 1840s were notable for Connecticut blacks. The birth and development of black churches, the spread of the temperance movement, blacks' efforts to improve the schooling available to their children, and the drive for restoration to blacks of the right to vote all spelled an enrichment of community life, a heightening of expectation, and some improvement in the economic standing of a significant number of the state's black people. No other black leader contributed as much to this growth as Amos Beman. As spokesman, model of achievement, and black pastor respected by his white ministerial colleagues, Beman's position was as demanding as it was influential. Visits and correspondence with his black friends and fellow ministers—Ray and Wright in New York City, Garnet in Troy, and Pennington in Hartford—strengthened him for his work.

Amos Beman's father, Jehiel, had been a persuasive example in the son's development. Jehiel Beman was the son of a freed slave and had worked as a shoemaker in Colchester for many years before he was sent to Middletown by the AME Zion denomination in 1830 to serve as pastor of its newly founded Cross Street church. He and his family were soon active in wider efforts at improving the situation for blacks. During the summer of 1831 there were meetings of black people in Hartford, New Haven, and Middletown to protest the continuing promotion by the American Colonization Society of black American settlement in Li-

1. Richard Newman, *Lemuel Haynes: A Bio-Bibliography* (New York, 1984) 11–17.

beria. The Middletown meeting was in the Cross Street church, and nineteen-year-old Amos Beman was chosen secretary. The meeting endorsed Garrison's *Liberator,* founded the previous January, and chose the elder Beman as agent for the paper in the area. In 1833 the black Home Temperance Society of Middletown was founded, with Jehiel Beman as president, Amos as secretary, and Amos's older brother Leverett as treasurer. Three years later, by virtue of Jehiel Beman's efforts, a state temperance society held its organizing meeting in Middletown. In 1834, in the face of mob harassment, the largely white Middletown Anti-Slavery Society was founded. Jehiel Beman was present at the first meeting and was chosen one of five managers.[2]

Amos Beman's most vivid memory of his years in Colchester was of his schoolteacher Huldah Morgan. When he was sixty years of age, he recalled her as one of the "noble women" he had known, "an *impressive* teacher."[3] In Middletown, when Beman was between eighteen and twenty-one years old, there were other powerful influences besides those of family. One day while Amos was employed with others in a shop, a black man from Hartford came in with a speech by Henry Clay on colonization and free blacks. The visitor read it aloud and criticized it "with a logical acumen and indignant eloquence the burning power of which fell like fire upon every heart present." A similar message came from the *Liberator.* Later Beman remembered that "its clarion voice sank deep into our mind." The *Liberator,* David Walker's *Appeal . . . to the Coloured Citizens of the World,* and William Lloyd Garrison's *Thoughts on African Colonization* "were read and re-read until their words were stamped in letters of fire upon our soul."[4]

By 1833 young Beman was restive for more advanced education. Trustee action at Wesleyan University in the fall of 1832, following the uproar over Charles Ray's presence, precluded Beman's admission, but he found another way. Samuel Dole, who had relayed to the *Liberator* the information about Ray's treatment in Middletown, was now himself a student at Wesleyan. He and Beman arranged for tutoring sessions in Dole's room. Trouble soon developed: student insults aimed at Beman as he came and went, water thrown from upstairs windows, and a student

2. *Liberator,* July 23, 1831; May 11, 1833; Jesse Baldwin Collection, Middlesex Historical Association, Middletown, Conn.

3. Amos Beman to an unnamed editor, October 1868, in Amos Beman Scrap Book (Amos G. Beman Papers), II, 113.

4. Report by Amos Beman of the 1854 black state convention, which had met in Middletown, in *Frederick Douglass' Paper,* October 13, 1854.

meeting that asked Dole to tutor Beman off the university grounds. Even though Dole yielded to the pressure and met Beman off campus, student hostility followed them and issued in a letter to Beman: "A no. of the students of this university, deeming it derogatory to themselves as well as to the university, to have you and other colord people recite here, do hereby warn you to desist from such a course, and if you fail to comply with this *peacable* request, we swear, by the ETERNAL GODS! that we will resort to forcible means to put a stop to it." According to Dole, President Fisk had been absent at this time, and Dole had shown the threatening note to two professors. One had "passed by on the other side." The other had cited the trustee by-law as justifying the student harassment.[5]

Almost a year after Ray left Middletown in defeat, Beman did the same. However, his prospects were brighter as he traveled the twenty miles to Hartford on foot. He carried with him a letter from Dole certifying that "Mr. A. G. Beman has, for the last six months, been under my instruction, . . . has conducted himself with propriety and has likewise made commendable progress in his studies."[6] Certified to teach in Hartford's district school system, he was employed at once in the city's one school for blacks, which was conducted in the African Congregational Church. This church had originated in 1826, when a number of black people who had left several of the city's primarily white churches formed the African Religious Society, where they could worship as they pleased, free from the humiliation of the Negro pew. In 1828 a building had been put up on Talcott Street, near the city's center. By the time Beman began teaching there, the worshipers had separated into Congregational and Methodist groups, each with its own services. In 1830 Hartford blacks had asked for and been given a separate school, located in the Talcott Street church. Beman was its first regular teacher.[7]

Within a few months of Beman's arrival in Hartford, Hosea Easton came to the city. He would point the way for Beman somewhat as Beman's father had. Easton was from a Boston black family remarkable for its mechanical ingenuity, economic enterprise, and aggressive protest

5. Communication from "Truth" in Middletown, dated September 1833, in *Liberator,* November 2, 1833. Beman's own account was published twenty-one years later in *Frederick Douglass' Paper,* October 13, 1854.

6. Testimonial from Samuel Dole, November 1, 1833, in Amos Beman Scrap Book (Amos G. Beman Papers), III.

7. David O. White, "Hartford's African Schools," *Connecticut Historical Society Bulletin,* XXXIX (1974), 48; D. O. White, "The Fugitive Blacksmith of Hartford: James W. C. Pennington," *Connecticut Historical Society Bulletin,* XLIX (1984), 10.

against white racism. Hosea worked for many years in his father's factory, but the business failed, and the younger Easton turned to the Methodist ministry. In 1832 he applied for membership in the New York Conference of the AME Zion church. Two years later he was ordained deacon and elder by Bishop Christopher Rush and was sent to Hartford. By 1836 he persuaded the black Methodists who were using the Talcott Street building jointly with the Congregationalists to buy land and put up their own building on Elm Street, later known as the Metropolitan AME Zion Church.[8]

Of special interest to young Beman, whose district school took its black pupils only through elementary subjects, was the fact that Easton began a movement almost from the day of his arrival in Hartford to establish and raise funds needed to support a black high school. In June 1834, at the national black convention meeting in New York City, Easton won endorsement of his project as "praiseworthy [and] fully entitled to liberal public patronage." He took to the road to secure the contributions needed to turn this idea into a reality but was forced by the disastrous riots of the summer of 1834 to abandon his fund-raising travels.[9]

Near the conclusion of Beman's four years of teaching in Hartford, Easton published a major work, *A Treatise on the Intellectual Character, and Civil and Political Condition of the Colored People of the U. States; and . . . the Duty of the Church to Them,* which Vernon Loggins, historian of Afro-American writing, has labeled equal in radical thrust to David Walker's *Appeal . . . to the Coloured Citizens of the World.*[10] The appearance of this book in 1837 was a landmark event for Hartford's black community and its white friends. As the issues of the *Colored American* did, Easton's book aroused in Beman the ambition to be a writer.

For Amos Beman the examples of his father and Hosea Easton made

8. William C. Nell, *The Colored Patriots of the American Revolution with Sketches of Several Distinguished Colored Persons . . .* (1855; rpr. New York, 1968), 33f.; Rev. H. Easton, *A Treatise on the Intellectual Character, and Civil and Political Condition of the Colored People of the U. States; and . . . the Duty of the Church to Them* (Boston, 1837), 45; Walls, *The African Methodist Episcopal Zion Church,* 146.

9. "Minutes and Proceedings of the Second Annual Convention . . . of the Free People of Color . . . 1832," p. 4; "Minutes and Proceedings of the Third Annual Convention . . . of the Free People of Colour . . . 1833," p. 4; "Minutes of the Fourth Annual Convention of the Free People of Colour . . . 1834," pp. 16–18, 26f.; *Emancipator,* February 17, 1835. The minutes of all three of these conventions are in Bell (ed.), *Minutes of the National Negro Conventions.*

10. Vernon Loggins, *The Negro Author: His Development in America to 1900* (Port Washington, N.Y., 1964).

clear how pivotal the role of the black minister could be both in the life of a local black community and in movements for the elevation of the race throughout a given state. But becoming a minister of the sort he wanted to be necessitated more education. After two years of teaching he entered the Oneida Institute and was one of four Afro-Americans in a first-year class of thirty-three students. The others were Alexander Crummell and Henry Highland Garnet, fresh from the Noyes Academy fiasco in New Hampshire, and Amos Freeman, close friend of Beman.[11] Although Beman was listed in the 1836 catalog (that is, for 1836 to 1837), and was slated to room with Garnet, Beman evidently withdrew after only one year of study. The only record of this brief college career is letters of reference, presumably written after Beman had withdrawn. A professor of mathematics and one who taught languages jointly testified, "Mr. Amos G. Beman has sustained the character of good and regular student since he has been connected with the institution." And President Beriah Green wrote, "Mr. A. G. Beman has won the confidence, secured the love and raised the hopes of his affectionate instructors."[12] In light of these testimonials, it seems likely that only financial pressure forced the young Hartford teacher to resign and resume his post in the Hartford district school.

Less than two years after Beman's return to his teaching, the Hartford North Association of Congregational ministers examined him as a candidate "for license to preach the Gospel." The association questioned Beman in four areas: natural and revealed religion, ecclesiastical history, biblical science, and pastoral theology/personal piety. It was unanimously voted that he be licensed to preach for the customary four years, presumably before ordination and installation as a settled pastor.[13] A few days later Beman left for New Haven, where he intended to teach school and minister to the Temple Street African Congregational Church, which had been left without a pastor when Pennington returned to Long Island. Beman carried with him attestations to his character by two white ministers of Hartford: Horace Bushnell, who was entering on what would be a long and distinguished pastorate at North Congregational Church, and John

11. Sernett, *Abolition's Axe,* chap. 4.

12. The first of these letters was dated October 27, 1836; the second is undated. Amos Beman Scrap Book (Amos G. Beman Papers), III.

13. Minutes of Meeting on June 5, 1838, in East Windsor, "Votes and Proceedings of the North Association of Hartford County," Vol. 2, 1801–1843 (Connecticut Conference of United Church of Christ Archives, Hartford), 276f.

Hempstead, stated supply pastor for the African Congregational Church during Beman's last year in Hartford. The committee that had overseen Beman's teaching also supplied him with a letter of reference.[14]

New Haven was a bustling city, both promising and threatening for black people when Beman arrived. Connecticut's economy had expanded and diversified between 1820 and 1840. To the state's ongoing agricultural and commercial activity was added a slow-starting but eventually vigorous industrial revolution, substantially augmented by the inventive abilities of Connecticut citizens. Another important dimension of the state's economic growth was the construction of canals and railroads, facilitating the transportation of agricultural goods to the cities and of manufactured articles to distant markets. In light of these developments, it is not surprising that the population of New Haven almost quintupled between 1820 and 1860. The black population also increased, but proportionately far less. Constituting 7.5 percent of the city's inhabitants in 1820, blacks made up only 3.8 percent of the total in 1860.

As in New York City, black hopes for sharing in the expanding economic opportunities in New Haven remained largely unrealized. The reasons are familiar. The most successful merchants and mechanics refused to take on black apprentices, thus preventing most young blacks from securing the training needed to enter the trades. New skilled work opening up in textile and carriage factories was also monopolized by whites. Even unskilled work in canal and railroad construction diminished for black people with the influx of Irish immigrants. The net result in New Haven was that nine out of ten adult black workers were in menial labor as house servants, or in dirty or heavy common labor as sailors, stevedores, washerwomen, porters, and "helpers." The 10 percent of the black population doing work requiring training included blacksmiths, carpenters, shoemakers, dressmakers, farmers, teachers, and clergymen.[15]

Along with these discouraging aspects of the economic situation for blacks, there were positive developments. About the time of the War of 1812, the expanding black male population of Connecticut began to exercise its right to vote in considerable numbers. Although this provoked

14. Amos Beman Scrap Book, III.

15. Jarvis M. Morse, *A Neglected Period of Connecticut's History, 1818–1850* (New Haven, 1933), 233–45, 261–66, 269–79; Robert A. Warner, *New Haven Negroes: A Social History* (1940; rpr. New York, 1969), 12–26, 301; Lawrence Bruser, "Political Anti-Slavery in Connecticut, 1844–1858" (Ph.D. dissertation, Columbia University, 1974), 23f.; "Proceedings of the Colored National Convention . . . 1855," in Bell (ed.), *Minutes of the National Negro Conventions,* 20f.

the state legislature to disfranchise blacks in 1814 and to confirm that action in the new state constitution of 1818, black political awareness remained. There was also religious ferment in the state that was beneficial to black people. The 1818 state constitution reflected the growing power of dissenters from tax-supported Congregationalism. The constitution disestablished the church of the "standing order"—that is, it ended the use of tax money to maintain the Congregational churches, to which the majority of church members belonged. (Only Massachusetts maintained a religious establishment longer than Connecticut, until 1833.) The way was thereby opened for the founding of dissenting churches, and of schools and colleges of their persuasion, with no financial disadvantage vis-à-vis Congregational institutions. Baptists, Methodists, and Episcopalians, whether white or black, were the chief beneficiaries of this broadening of freedom of religion. Roman Catholics were soon also helped by it.

During the 1820s independent black religious societies were founded in Connecticut's three largest black communities, Hartford, New Haven, and Middletown. In all three cities active assistance was given these fledgling churches by liberal or radical white Evangelical clergy. Within Connecticut Congregationalism, an activist, revivalist wing was emerging, paralleling the rise of the New School party within Presbyterianism in Pennsylvania, New Jersey, and New York. Lyman Beecher, the influential Congregational minister in Litchfield, was a force in this movement prior to his leaving for Cincinnati in the mid-1830s. At Yale Divinity School, Nathaniel Taylor became the chief theoretician of the New Divinity. To orthodox Calvinists, either Presbyterian or Congregational, Taylor's insistence that sin was man's own free choice of some good other than God as his primary goal undermined the traditional doctrine of man's natural depravity. New Divinity men, like New School Presbyterians, were ardent supporters of missionary work in the United States and overseas. From 1820 to 1860 Congregational ministers sympathetic to Beecher's and Taylor's emphases were important friends of black religious societies and churches in Hartford, New Haven, and Middletown.

Like Philadelphia and New York City whites, some Connecticut whites grew more hostile when black people began organizing their own churches, schools, and societies for moral reform. Prior to industrialization, New Haven whites had thought of black people in three primary roles: as household servants who often lived in their employers' homes and seemed thoroughly domesticated in attitude; as poorly paid doers of dirty jobs who lived in miserable quarters; and as central figures in the "vice section" of the city, where they were prostitutes, pimps, or landlord managers of this enterprise. When black efforts to "elevate the race" took hold in Connecticut, assisted by white abolitionists, white opposition was occasionally vehement and violent. The nearly unanimous rejection by New Haven citizens of a proposed manual labor college for blacks and the violent closing down of Prudence Crandall's school for black girls in 1833 were cases in point. Antiblack and antiabolitionist violence, comparable to that in Canterbury, broke out in New Haven in 1834 and 1837, in Norwich in 1834, and in Hartford in 1835. Indeed, one historian, citing sixteen antiabolition and antiblack mobs in Connecticut between 1833 and 1837, has concluded that this was the most hostile state in New England toward abolitionists and blacks.[16]

In this volatile racial situation, being a black leader in movements to better the condition and secure the rights of black people required a rare mix of native ability, indignation, courage, and prudence. Perhaps above all, it required the perseverance born of a deeply hopeful attitude. That Amos Beman labored in New Haven for nearly twenty years without ever himself becoming the occasion for public turmoil does not negate the fact that his career required the steady presence of all of these traits. The same was true of James Pennington's much briefer career in Hartford.

Beman's ministry at the Temple Street African Congregational Church had been solidly prepared for by Simeon Jocelyn, sponsor and public defender of the ill-fated proposal to establish a black manual labor college in New Haven. A dozen or so years older than Beman, Jocelyn had been brought up in New Haven and studied theology with Nathaniel Taylor. As early as 1820, about the time Cornish began work in New York City, Jocelyn was working informally with New Haven's black community, encouraging regular worship and Christian education. As a result, the African Ecclesiastical Society was formed with a score of members. Many New Haven whites were hostile toward Jocelyn's efforts. In the words of a later black minister of the Dixwell Avenue Congregational Church, the successor to the Temple Street African Congregational Church, which in turn was descended from this African Ecclesiastical Society, Jocelyn "was much abused, frequently disturbed, and threatened

16. L. L. Richards, *Gentlemen of Property,* 40.

with bodily harm. On more than one occasion the men of his congregation felt constrained to act as a bodyguard to him in going to and from the place of meeting."[17]

In August 1829 the society was formally organized as a Congregational body under the direction of the Western Consociation of New Haven County. Between twenty and thirty black people were examined and approved for membership by the white clergy and were constituted a church. On the same occasion Jocelyn was ordained as an Evangelist by the laying on of the hands of the consociation's clergy. Over the next five years Jocelyn never asked for or received any salary. This early white philanthropy was harmful in that it established a tradition of unpaid ministry, which would be one factor in Beman's recurrent difficulty in getting his salary paid on time.[18]

During the fall of 1831 it became clear that New Haven whites' hostility went far beyond opposition to higher education for blacks. A letter to the *Connecticut Journal,* reminiscent of those written by Mordecai Noah in New York City, cited reasons for white alarm as not only the recent revolt of Nat Turner in Virginia but also "the impudent and insolent bearing of many blacks in this city, as you daily meet them in the streets and in places of public resort." The author blamed it all on a recent visit by William Lloyd Garrison. The city's newspapers publicized riots in Providence and lurid goings-on in a hotel, the New Liberia, in the vice section of New Haven. Blacks were insulted, and one was assaulted. Arthur Tappan's house on Temple Street was stoned. A black-occupied shack on Sodom Hill was torn down and the New Liberia raided by self-appointed law officers. Violent episodes continued, and in 1834 Jocelyn gave up his post at the Temple Street African Congregational Church.[19]

By the early 1830s there was another kind of white presence in New Haven, one friendly toward blacks' efforts at improvement but not so radical as Jocelyn. The so-called African Improvement Society, with a board of managers of blacks and whites in "expedient" proportions, had been organized three years before the Temple Street African Congregational Church was formally constituted by the consociation. The primary architect of this arm of Christian benevolence was Leonard Bacon, the

17. Edward F. Goin, "One Hundred Years of Negro Congregationalism in New Haven, Conn.," *Crisis,* XIX (1920), 177–81.

18. Handwritten account, presumably by Simeon Jocelyn, in Amos Beman Scrap Book (Amos G. Beman Papers), III.

19. Warner, *New Haven Negroes,* 57f., 64f.

newly chosen brilliant young minister of Center Congregational Church. Bacon was fresh from Andover Theological Seminary, where he had developed a deep interest in Christian missions in Africa and in the founding of an American college financed by the American Colonization Society to train Afro-Americans to take the lead in these missions. Although the ACS had no funds for such a project, after two years in New Haven Bacon accepted appointment as agent to promote the Colonization Society of New England. However, he was also eagerly supportive of efforts to improve black schools and churches in the United States at large and in New Haven in particular.[20]

Accordingly, when Amos Beman came to New Haven in 1838 as the first full-time licensed black minister serving a black church in the city, he entered a white community with some members having shown their desire to help black people and others having brutally demonstrated their contempt for blacks and the whites who worked with them. Beman wrote the following in his diary on arrival: "This day I landed in this city from Hartford—how long I shall stay I know not. Resolved that I will, while in this city endeavor to glorify God—and seek the good of immortal soul. I will watch over me self *strict,* pray much—and endeavor to make good use of my time."[21]

The young black pastor maintained his ties with Hartford, going there in August 1838 to deliver an address on moral improvement and in January 1839 to attend the annual meeting of the African (renamed Colored that same year) Congregational Church. He preached five times in Hartford, evidently hoping for a call from the church there. That call went to James Pennington instead. In March 1839 the Temple Street African Congregational Church gave Beman an official invitation "to settle over us as our pastor." The vote was unanimous, and he was offered a salary of $400 a year, a large amount for a black minister of his era. That same month Leonard Bacon and three other white ministers of New Haven met with Beman as an ecclesiastical council to examine him for ordination as evangelist in the Temple Street African Congregational Church. The council's being satisfied with Beman's answers and attitude, there was a public service of ordination in the evening of the same day at the black church. Each member of the council participated in the service. Bacon, who gave

20. *Ibid.*, 46f.; letters from and to Leonard Bacon, 1823 and 1824, in Special Collections, Franklin Trask Library, Andover Newton Theological School, Newton Centre, Mass.

21. Amos Beman Scrap Book (Amos G. Beman Papers), June 9, 1838.

the charge to the young minister, wrote to his own wife, who was on a visit in Florida: "The house was quite full with a very decent congregation of as many shades of color as you can find in St. Augustine. The occasion was a very interesting one. I think this young man is uncommonly well qualified to do good. I charged him among other things always to instruct his hearers in their own duty rather than in other people's." Although Beman would not remain entirely faithful to Bacon's charge that he and his people mind their own duties and not white people's, he was deeply affected by the occasion: "This day I have been examined and ordained as an Evangelist—Oh! how solemn!"[22]

Some three months later Charles Ray came to New Haven, invited to speak to the city antislavery society. In reporting to the *Colored American,* he spoke of Beman as "an old friend, whom we have long dearly loved for his manly dignity, his piety, his talents, and his philosophic mind." Beman persuaded Ray, who had never been in New Haven before, to stay for five days. During this time the New Yorker gave three lengthy speeches to large audiences in the "Union meeting house" (the Temple Street African Congregational Church). As usual on his speaking tours, Ray's addresses emphasized economic, moral, and intellectual development. Twenty new subscribers for the *Colored American* came forward. On Sunday Ray preached twice to Beman's congregation. He pronounced them "neat and respectable" and their singing, a tribute to them.[23]

Two and a half years after Beman's ordination as evangelist, the ecclesiastical council of New Haven confirmed him as an ordained minister. At the installation service, Theodore Wright and James Pennington were center stage. Leonard Bacon and two other leading New Haven ministers also participated.[24]

By the mid-1840s Beman had quietly grown into a force to reckon with in the city of New Haven and among black leaders at large. His church on Temple Street was the center of a varied program of educational, mutual assistance, and protest meetings that ran right through the week. He was a leader in statewide black gatherings to promote temperance and civil rights. And his influence at national and regional black

22. Amos Beman Scrap Book (Amos G. Beman Papers); Leonard Bacon to his wife, March 6, 1839, in Bacon Family Papers, Yale University Library, New Haven; Robert A. Warner, "Amos Gerry Beman (1812–1874): A Memoir on a Forgotten Leader," *Journal of Negro History,* XXII (1937), 201.

23. *Colored American,* June 29, 1839.

24. Account of Beman's ordination and installation in Amos Beman Scrap Book (Amos G. Beman Papers).

conferences became comparable to that of Ray and Garnet. His great strengths as a public servant lay in his passion for black advancement, his clarity of mind, and his facility with words.

Beman was serving as secretary for gatherings of blacks in Middletown at the age of twenty. Over the years he recorded proceedings and formulated committee reports for dozens of meetings. He was also master of the spoken word. In the absence of printed sermons, our best clue to his power as a preacher lies in the response to his public addresses, which evoked extravagant praise from both black and white listeners. At the age of thirty-one he was chosen president of the 1843 national black convention in Buffalo. In the intense debate over endorsement of Garnet's "Address to the Slaves," he stepped down from the presiding chair to speak for an hour in convincing opposition to such endorsement. At many other large gatherings through the 1840s and 1850s to aid fugitive slaves, promote temperance, combat the Fugitive Slave Bill, and review the progress of free blacks, he spoke with equal effectiveness.

Inspired by the examples of Samuel Cornish, Hosea Easton, and Charles Ray, Beman longed also to be a notable writer. When Ray became senior editor of the *Colored American,* Beman submitted a series of articles on temperance that appeared almost weekly during the summer of 1839. In the fall of 1840 he sent to Ray's paper reports of his travels to Maine; these were modeled on Ray's accounts of his extensive visiting among black communities from 1837 to 1839. From July 1840 through August 1841, sixteen articles by Beman appeared in the *Colored American* under the broad banner of "thoughts."[25] In these articles he was attempting the role of editor-preacher that Cornish had played to such good effect in 1837 and 1838. Beman wrote clearly and correctly, but his overblown style lacked the force of Cornish's editorials. When the *Colored American* ceased publication, Beman launched his own paper, the *Herald of Justice,* but it was short-lived. Thereafter he gave generous support and written contributions to other black editors.[26]

In the complex web of activities aimed at black improvement that

25. *Colored American,* July 4, November 21, December 5, 12, 1840; January 2, 23, February 6, March 6, June 12, 19, July 3, 10, 17, August 2, September 18, October 2, 1841.

26. Beman's work was published in James Pennington's *Clarksonian* (1843), Samuel Ringgold Ward's *Impartial Citizen* (1848–51), Henry Bibb's *Voice of the Fugitive* (1851–52), Frederick Douglass's papers (from 1847 through the 1850s), William Howard Day's *Aliened American* (1853), the *Anglo-African* (magazine and weekly, from 1859 into the mid-1860s), and the *Christian Recorder,* journal of the AME denomination. Beman sometimes used the initials *G. B. A.* to identify his articles.

Beman promoted, three causes were primary: antislavery, including aid to fugitive slaves; temperance; and the reenfranchisement of Connecticut's blacks. On August 1, 1839, Beman addressed Hartford's black community as it celebrated West Indian emancipation. He urged free blacks to make the most of their freedom and thereby hasten general emancipation. A year later he spoke in Boston, and his tone was more bold. Harking back to the American Revolution, he noted how mild the bondage forced on "our fathers" by British taxation had been compared with bodily enslavement, "the vilest system of evil that ever saw the sun." Accordingly, celebration on August 1 should be far greater than on July 4. Beman concluded his address with an invocation of Samson's heroic destruction of his tormentors: "Sympathy [with the West Indians] should unite all intelligent creatures as one, to grasp the pillars of despotism, and to bow themselves till they fell, though they died with the Philistines. Out of the ashes, even, of such, a phoenix would arise—a host by whom the work should be carried on, and the battle pushed to the gate."[27]

The extended trial of the *Amistad* rebels and their acquittal in March 1841 had a special effect on Beman and the members of his church. The proceedings in the New Haven court highlighted for the city's black people what courage and determined will could accomplish toward liberation. It also dramatized the native intelligence of Africans and their readiness to respond to the Christian message. For the grandson of a slave, as Beman was, as well as for the former slaves Garnet and Pennington, Africa thereafter had a new claim. Years later Beman recalled the Mendi mission in Africa: "Familiar with it from the beginning—having had a personal acquaintance with Cinque and the Amistad Africans, and the friends who gathered around them in those perilous hours when danger and death threatened them—having seen the arm of God made bare for their deliverance, and his Providence as a 'wall of fire around' the Mission in Africa for its defence—my soul always quickens with new zeal, whenever I have the unspeakable pleasure of presenting its claims."[28]

While the Mendi prepared to return to Africa, Beman helped the New York Vigilance Committee celebrate its fifth anniversary in the huge (AME) Zion Church. He was one of the featured speakers. The aim was

27. Summary and excerpts from Beman's address given in "the Colored Congregational Church" in Hartford, August 1, 1839, reprinted from the *Connecticut Observer* in the *Emancipator,* November 1, 1839 (Microfilm copy in Carter and Ripley [eds.], *BAP,* reel 3, item 260); *Liberator,* August 14, 1840. For the story of Samson's pulling down the temple to crush his Philistine captors and himself, see Judg. 16:13–30.

28. Amos Beman to the *Weekly Anglo-African,* from Portland, Maine, March 1, 1859.

to inspire listeners to give enough to liquidate the vigilance committee's $1,000 debt and to proceed to help as many needy fugitives in the coming year as in the year just past (178 had been aided). Beman's speech, reproduced in full in the *Colored American,* defined the principles of the committee as those of the Declaration of Independence; of William Blackstone, Thomas Clarkson, and William Wilberforce in England; of William Ellery Channing and Jonathan Edwards in America; and of the Bible. Addressing the antiabolition argument that enslaved Afro-Americans were not fit for freedom, Beman spoke from his experience with the Mendi: "No minds for elevation in this country [?], but in *Africa they have!*" The speech was part sermon. Beman cited Thomas Jefferson's having trembled "for his country when he reflected that God was just, and that his *justice* could not sleep *forever.*" "God," Beman declared, "measures our love to him . . . by our efforts to do good to the bodies and souls of our fellow men, by our 'remembrance of those in bonds, as bound with them.'"[29] In New Haven during the next fifteen years, Beman put what he had preached into practice by involving his church more and more with the work of the Underground Railroad.

In the view of American Evangelical Protestants in the 1830s and 1840s, there was a form of bondage among whites and free blacks paralleling physical enslavement. It was addiction to alcohol. Black leaders had emphasized temperance as far back as the 1780s, in the Free African Society of Philadelphia.[30] The 1840s brought the high tide of antebellum black involvement in the temperance movement, and Beman was one of the most energetic black crusaders on this issue. Temperance, and often total abstinence, had been a central theme in Cornish's editorial work and in Ray's, Garnet's, and Jehiel Beman's social messages to their people. This was a matter of economic realism as much as of proper Christian behavior. Only with sobriety could money be saved; families fed, clothed, housed, and educated; and church responsibilities taken seriously.

For both Ray and Beman this reform became a passion by 1840. In that year Ray ran eight articles in the *Colored American* on the evils caused by liquor and on the blessings of temperance. In 1841 there were sixteen articles on these subjects. As Beman entered his third year of ministry in 1840, he was chosen vice-president of the Connecticut State Temperance Society of People of Color. Soon he was president of the organization. In 1842 he was one of the founders of the Delevan Union Temperance So-

29. *Colored American,* May 15, 22, 1841.
30. Quarles, *Black Abolitionists,* 93f.

ciety of Colored People, a vigorous enterprise promoting the formation of local temperance groups in New York, New Jersey, Connecticut, and Massachusetts. Its annual gatherings drew as many as a thousand black people. Beman, Wright, Ray, and Garnet were prominent in these meetings; Wright served as president in 1843 and Garnet, in 1846. Beman was principal speaker in 1845.[31]

Evangelical Protestants made much of abstinence from liquor as a moral good. For black people abstinence had special significance. Many of them lived in poverty or close to it. Following the examples of whites, it was easy for blacks to turn to drink as an escape and thereby confirm colonizationist whites' expectations. Again and again black leaders linked sobriety with striking blows against slavery. At the huge gathering of the Delevan Union in 1843, the central theme of the speeches by Garnet and others was that temperance furthers true democracy by striking off the fetters that society imposes on working people of both races. Abstinence brings them more food and less unnecessary labor, more knowledge, moral behavior, and self-respect, and less of society's contempt and persecution.[32]

Because of their emphasis on moral self-discipline, black temperance crusaders were as much lauded by middle- and upper-class whites as they were jeered at and attacked by Catholic immigrants. A letter by a white person that was published in the New York *Tribune* in June 1846 surely spoke the mind of Leonard Bacon and other white ministers acquainted with Beman. It was read aloud at the Delevan Union convention that summer. The writer noted the handicaps that faced the freed slave who had been denied education, owned no property, and was constantly exposed to the example of white drunkenness. Afro-American temperance pioneers, the letter went on, had emancipated the minds of their fellows. As a result blacks had progressed remarkably: "They have built schoolhouses, erected churches, and educated their own pastors & physicians; and whether viewed in their private dwellings or their public assemblies, (Africans though they be,) they have presented as peaceful, orderly and prosperous a community, as is presented in white communities around them."[33]

31. Jacobs, *Antebellum Black Newspapers,* 538f.; Amos Beman Scrap Book (Amos G. Beman Papers), II, 143, and scattered clippings. *Christian Freeman,* July 24, 1845; Quarles, *Black Abolitionists,* 92ff.

32. Amos Beman Scrapbook (Amos G. Beman Papers), II, 143.

33. Letter dated June 27, 1846, read at the Delevan Union convention, July 8, 1846, in Amos Beman Scrap Book (Amos G. Beman Papers), II, 131.

At the Temple Street African Congregational Church, as at many other black churches, abstinence from the use of alcohol was a requirement of church membership. Beman's implementation of abstinence among his church members was an integral part of their growing ambition for a whole range of advances—educational, economic, and eventually, political. This change wrought by "the patient hand of Christian culture" in the Temple Street church had been paralleled in the pastorates of Cornish, Wright, Ray, and Garnet. It was especially dramatic in Beman's work because the black community of New Haven, numbering around nine hundred, was small enough to be largely affected by one able pastor's long service in the city, as well as large enough to be highly visible.

Beman had had good reason to be elated after his installation as the ordained minister of the Temple Street church in 1841. He was now the settled pastor of the strongest black church in the community (to be sure, there had been an AME Zion congregation worshiping in New Haven since the early 1820s).[34] Moreover, he was married, had a daughter and son, and had been guaranteed a $400-a-year salary, which was enough to provide a fairly comfortable living. However, the following years of notable contribution to his parish and his city were to bring an unending succession of financial dilemmas. Although the congregation included many of the most prominent people in the city's black community, most of the church's members were waiters, janitors, truckers, servants, or common laborers, with here and there a barber or neighborhood grocer. After visiting many members of the Temple Street church in their homes in 1839, Ray had reported, "A few perhaps may be termed rich, *none* poor, all comfortable. Most of those who have been there some time, live in their own neat, commodious dewellings, have their own productive gardens. . . . All find enough to do, and are in circumstances to enjoy life.[35]

In spite of this solid membership numbering 101 by 1841, Beman's church was faced with serious financial problems. The church owned its frame meetinghouse but this was dilapidated. The addition that had been built to accommodate the Sunday school was flimsy. And church members had never developed the disciplined giving that could assure a minis-

34. Warner, *New Haven Negroes,* 84ff.; *Colored American,* June 29, 1839.

35. *Colored American,* June 29, 1839. The only truly well-to-do man associated with the church was William Lanson, a successful contractor who had built part of New Haven's wharf. He was, however, also the owner of much of the city's vice section and had been dropped from the Temple Street church's membership soon after Beman came to the city. Warner, *New Haven Negroes,* 26, 28, 56, 80.

ter his annual salary. Fifteen months after his installation Beman was so hemmed in that he was ready to resign. Convinced that he had done his work well for four and a half years, he wrote to the ecclesiastical council that had ordained him: "Stern duty to myself and family [by this time the Bemans had a third child] compels me quite reluctantly to lay my necessities before you, or else I would do as on previous occasions, and act upon a sentiment long since adopted, and make: 'silent grief my glory.'" Small debts were accumulating daily and now added up to $100. Because the church owed Beman so much back salary, he could not discharge these obligations. He was "unwilling longer to labor here under these trials." However, he hated to leave the parish: "For most firmly do I believe the elements of substantial good exist among our population, which the patient hand of Christian culture can under God marshal into a scene cheering to every virtuous mind."[36]

The church and New Haven's Congregational council persuaded Beman not to resign by promises of action on two fronts, raising money to build a new church and paying the salary owed him. In the spring of 1844, on the strength of assurances of support from the city's white clergy, the church tore down its old building, bought an adjacent strip of land to enlarge its building lot, and secured permission from the city's mayor and aldermen to put up a simple brick church. The need for some $2,500 to pay for this construction was endorsed in the public press by prominent whites, including Leonard Bacon and Nathaniel Taylor. The language was reminiscent of Benjamin Rush's in Philadelphia thirty years earlier: "The Christian order and sobriety of their assemblies, and the high stand on the subject of temperance, . . . are exerting a most salutory influence on that portion of our population; and the interests of all classes are advanced by their elevation and improvement."[37]

Beman was sent by his church and the white clergy of New Haven on a fund-raising mission to Congregational churches in other Connecticut communities. He carried with him a strongly worded letter from New Haven's ministers, who assured potential donors that the black church's building project had "the sanction and encouragement of the enlightened, virtuous and benevolent among us." In April 1845 the building was

36. Amos Beman to Leonard Bacon, Roger Baldwin, and three others, January 5, 1843, in Amos Beman Scrap Book (Amos G. Beman Papers), III. Bacon and two more of the five had been on the council that had examined Beman in September 1841 preparatory to installation. Also see Amos Beman to "the Colored Congregational Church and Society of New Haven," April 1, 1843, *ibid.*

37. Amos Beman Scrap Book (Amos G. Beman Papers), III.

completed and dedicated. Two-thirds of the monies raised to meet the construction cost came from white people, but the total was well short of the goal, and a heavy mortgage had to be signed.[38]

At the end of 1843 Beman, discouraged by the overall financial picture in New Haven, was seriously considering overtures from the Second African Presbyterian Church in Philadelphia. This church had been formed in 1824 after a division within the First African Presbyterian Church over who should be John Gloucester's successor. The new church had prospered, reaching a membership of over two hundred by 1840. Moreover, an able young black graduate of the University of Vermont, Andrew Harris, like Garnet a protégé of Theodore Wright, was preparing for ministry in the church. Spurred on by the prospect of Harris as their pastor, the church paid up the interest on its mortgage, along with some of the principal. They had realistic plans for retiring the rest of the debt within fifteen months.

In 1842, however, a twofold disaster struck this Philadelphia church. In April Harris was suddenly stricken with a severe illness, and he died. And at the end of July another race riot broke out in the city. Whites, many of them Irish, attacked a parade being staged by Philadelphia blacks as part of their customary celebration of the West Indies emancipation. Banners for temperance especially angered assailants, who used clubs and stones on black men, women, and children; raided private homes; threatened a Methodist church; and burned down the Second African Presbyterian Church. There were several unsuccessful attempts to set fire to Temperance Hall, the focal point of a successful temperance campaign in the Moyamensing black community. Some 1,040 blacks were said to have taken a temperance oath in the hall, and the number of liquor salesmen in the area had dramatically declined. White businessmen, including many liquor dealers, finally persuaded the city council to destroy the building as a threat to public safety. The trustees of the Second African Presbyterian Church sought restitution from the state supreme court, but finding a place to worship, reconstituting a scattered Sunday school, and raising money to pay for rented space were major challenges.[39]

38. *Christian Freeman,* June 29, 1843; Amos Beman Scrap Book (Amos G. Beman Papers), III; Warner, *New Haven Negroes,* 88f.; Warner, "Amos Gerry Beman," 205.

39. Adam D. Simmons, "Ideologies and Programs of the Negro Anti-Slavery Movement, 1830–1861" (Ph.D. dissertation, Northwestern University, 1983), 34f.; "The Report of the Board of Trustees of the Second African Presbyterian Church, for the Year 1842" (MS at Presbyterian Historical Association, Philadelphia); Amos Beman Scrap Book (Amos G. Beman Papers), I, 76–78.

It was at this juncture, probably at Theodore Wright's suggestion, that the Philadelphia church opened negotiations with Amos Beman as an able and experienced minister under whose leadership the church might recover its former momentum. The session wrote Beman in December 1843; it urged him to come to Philadelphia, preach several times, and participate in a communion service. Beman's own illness and that of his family forced him to postpone the trip until early May. Stopping over with Wright in New York City on his way to Philadelphia, he learned of a fierce riot with nativist and Irish participants that had exploded in the Kensington section of greater Philadelphia.[40] Although black people were not primary targets in this violence, Beman remembered what had happened in Philadelphia in the summers of 1834 and 1842.[41] He also had in mind the racial violence that had broken out in Hartford in 1835 while he was teaching school there. A fight had been started by some whites on Front Street. The following evening a crowd of whites harassed black people who were leaving the Talcott Street church. A black man ran for a gun, fired it at the mob, and wounded one of the whites. The following day there was general rioting, and several buildings where blacks lived were destroyed. Only when special police were called out was the violence quelled. Beman wrote to the session of the Second African Presbyterian Church: "I . . . can easily conceive the effect which such a state of thing must have upon the minds of all classes of the community and how *unfavorable* it must be for a religious point of view; and I have therefore concluded that the voice of duty does not call me there at present."[42]

There was a change for the better for Beman after he declined the pastorate in Philadelphia. He was drawn more substantially into the periodic gatherings of white Congregational ministers and attended the annual meeting of the clergy of the New Haven East Consociation for the first time in May 1843. He attended again in 1844 and 1845. In 1845 he was chosen scribe. The result was a beautifully legible set of minutes. He was also selected to be preacher for the gathering in 1846. In both 1846 and 1847 he was chosen one of three delegates from the local association to the General [State] Association.[43]

40. Michael Feldberg, *The Philadelphia Riots of 1844: A Study of Ethnic Conflict* (Westport, Conn., 1975).

41. At some point Beman had clipped out a newspaper article describing in detail the Philadelphia riot of August 1, 1842. Amos Beman Scrap Book (Amos G. Beman Papers).

42. Morse, *A Neglected Period of Connecticut's History,* 196f.; Amos Beman Scrap Book (Amos G. Beman Papers), III.

43. Congregational Church, "New Haven East Consociation Records, 1731–1893" (Connecticut Conference of United Church of Christ Archives, Hartford), XV, 608a, 610a, 612a–f.

Racial integration at clergy meetings, however, did not spill over into attitudes and practices at worship services in white churches. Vivid evidence was supplied by Ebenezer Davies, the Welsh missionary to Africa who was visiting the United States in 1847 and who had attended Theodore Wright's funeral. He came to New Haven from New York City and attended an evening service at the Temple Street African Congregational Church. He was delighted by the hymn singing, and he found Beman's prayer "very judicious, sensible and pious." The service was part of a series of revival meetings in the course of which a number claimed to be converted. Davies approved of the caution whereby none of these had yet been admitted to membership in the church. The missionary urged Beman and his congregation to come Sunday evening to North Congregational Church, where Davies was to speak on the work of the London Missionary Society in British Guiana. Beman answered, "We should be glad to come; but the fact is they would pack us, myself and all—into some negro pew, and we should feel it keenly."[44]

In addition to the broadening of Beman's give and take with Congregational ministers in New Haven in the latter 1840s, there was an increase in the vigor of black church life in other denominations. By 1841 the Varick Memorial AME Zion Church had its own building, and by 1848 its members numbered eighty. An independent Baptist church had been founded by black members uneasy in the First and Second Baptist churches. Like the AME society begun in the 1820s, it struggled with poverty and changing leadership, but all three groups added to the diversity of black institutional life in the city. Most important as a sister church and rival of the Temple Street Church was the Saint Luke's Episcopal black parish. It was organized in 1844 and was promptly recognized by the diocese of Connecticut. A long search for a suitable rector finally found an able black man, James Holley, who took the leadership of Saint Luke's in 1856 and, during a five-year pastorate, did much to strengthen the church.[45]

The Temple Street African Congregational Church and its pastor were influential models inspiring these black Methodists, Baptists, and Episcopalians to develop their distinctive strengths and compete for the city's black constituency. While these new churches were emerging, Beman's own church membership was increasing—and in a decade dur-

44. Davies, *American Scenes,* 262f.

45. Warner, *New Haven Negroes,* 85–88; Randall Burkett, "The Rev. Harry Croswell and Black Episcopalians in New Haven, 1815–1858" (Paper read at Northeastern Seminar on Black Religion, New Haven, February, 1986).

ing which the city's black population stood still. Between 1839 and 1848, 125 new members were added to the Temple Street Church, and its roster stood at 177 in spite of over twenty excommunications. Thus the Temple Street church had close to 20 percent of the adult members of the city's black community.[46]

During the six years after 1844, when Beman had declined the Philadelphia pastorate, his church's and his own financial situation improved only marginally. In 1849 black Presbyterians in Philadelphia again tried to lure Beman away from New England. This time it was the First African Presbyterian Church, long since recovered from the schism suffered after Gloucester's death and now substantially larger than the Temple Street church in New Haven.

Beman went to Philadelphia for an extended visit early in 1850 and received a firm call in late March. The proposed salary was $350, with a probable $150 more from the Presbyterian Board of Missions. After two months of prayerful consideration and advice from his ministerial associates in New Haven, Beman wrote declining the offer, in spite of its being a field of labor ten times larger than the New Haven black community. A major drive for funds among New Haven's white and black people in 1849 had netted $1,100, of which $800 came from whites. The Temple Street church's indebtedness was wiped clean. In the spring of 1850 Leonard Bacon requested enough more money from the whole New Haven community to pay Beman what was owed him.[47]

Such financial dependence upon whites could well have bred social conservatism in an aspiring young preacher like Beman. However, his deepest ties were with his people and his fellow black clergy. He followed a course primarily dictated by his assessment of his people's primary needs. And he continued to be prized by influential whites in New Haven for his intelligence, ambition, Christian conviction, and success as a pastor. In the late 1840s and the 1850s he grew more aggressive in his criticism of white racism and of at least one prominent Hartford Congregational minister, Horace Bushnell, whose racist phrases Beman repeated and excoriated. However, when Beman left New Haven in 1858, he still had the confidence of white clergy.

For Beman the religion, culture, and economic stability of New Haven's middle- and upper-class whites were most concretely experi-

46. Amos Beman Scrap Book (Amos G. Beman Papers).

47. Amos Beman Scrap Book (Amos G. Beman Papers), III; Warner, "Amos Gerry Beman," 206; Warner, *New Haven Negroes,* 89.

enced in the person of Leonard Bacon. To give vent to resentment against him would have been difficult. Bacon's role in Beman's ordination as an Evangelist in 1839 has been noted. What views as to blacks' proper behavior had lain back of Bacon's charging Beman at that ordination "to instruct his hearers in their own duty rather than in other people's"? Bacon shared in the general social conservatism of the Evangelical "benevolent empire." Blacks should "elevate" themselves, not demand changes in the structure of society. However, a close association with Jocelyn and Beman between 1825 and 1855 slowly broadened Bacon's understanding of American racism.[48]

Through the early 1830s Bacon was an influential, yet critical, supporter of the American Colonization Society. By 1839 major doubts about the efficiency of the society's staff and the industry of leaders and workers in Liberia substantially lessened his involvement. Like many others in New Haven, Bacon was deeply affected by the trial of the Mendi who had revolted on the *Amistad.* By the year of Beman's ordination, Bacon had warm relations with Lewis Tappan and was cooperating in efforts to raise money for the defense of the *Amistad* crew. However, Bacon was never an abolitionist of Tappan's stamp. He was too much concerned about maintaining effective relations with upper-class whites in his Center Congregational Church congregation and too much alarmed by North-South polarization to become a crusader. He did move far enough, however, to remain Beman's champion when the black minister emerged as a civil rights activist.[49]

The high tide of the antebellum black campaign for the vote in Connecticut came in the 1840s, but it gathered strength slowly. With no large concentration of black population and no tradition of activism comparable to that in New York City, Beman in New Haven, Pennington in Hartford, and members of their respective churches learned much by personal contact with Wright, Ray, and Garnet, as well as by reading the *Colored American.* The disfranchisement of Connecticut blacks had come

48. Bacon to his wife, March 6, 1839, in Bacon Family Papers, Yale University Library.

49. Leonard Bacon to his wife, January 20, 1832, January 16, 1834, Leonard Bacon to R. R. Gurley, February 3, 4, 25, 1835, Leonard Bacon to Gerrit Smith, February 3, 1834, all in Bacon Family Papers, Yale University Library; Theodore D. Bacon, *Leonard Bacon, A Statesman in the Church* (New Haven, 1961), 216f.; Leonard Bacon to David Bacon, July 19, 1839, in Bacon Family Papers, Yale University Library; Bacon, *Leonard Bacon,* 162f.; Lewis Tappan to Leonard Bacon, October 4, 26, 1839, both in Bacon Family Papers, Yale University Library.

by legislative action in 1814 and had been confirmed by the state constitution of 1818. A vague foreboding among whites had been born of a recent increase in the black population and in blacks' actually voting; whites feared that blacks might enter the political process in such a way as to alter the existing distribution of power between the two parties at the polls.[50]

The pioneer agitator for Connecticut blacks' recovering the franchise was the Connecticut Anti-Slavery Society. This organization was primarily white, but its black members played a critical role in broadening its concerns. At the founding meeting in February 1838 in Hartford's city hall, Amos Beman represented Hartford and his father, Middletown. Because of threats of violence, the group had to shift its meetings to a local hotel.[51] One of this society's first official acts was to authorize the publication by its Executive Committee of a newspaper, the *Charter Oak*. It set in motion a program of questioning candidates running for governor, lieutenant governor, and state senator on a number of issues. Two of the questions focused on the civil rights of free blacks: trial by jury for alleged fugitive slaves, and the right of all citizens to petition their government. By June 1838 the Connecticut legislature had taken two encouraging steps. It repealed the "black law," passed to outlaw Prudence Crandall's or anyone else's education of out-of-state blacks. It also enacted a mandatory jury trial for those claimed as fugitive slaves; two years would pass before such would be made law in New York State. The following spring the state antislavery society, through its journal, urged petitioning the General Assembly to abolish all discriminatory practices based on race.[52]

In 1840 the statewide black organization, the Connecticut State Temperance and Moral Reform Society, included in its program a campaign for political rights. The society's 1840 meetings probably took place in Hartford's Colored Congregational Church. This church's new pastor, James Pennington, was chosen president of the gathering. Amos Beman and his brother, Leverett, delegates from New Haven and Middletown,

50. James Truslow Adams, "Disfranchisement of Negroes in New England," *American Historical Review*, XXX (1924–25), 544f.

51. The African Congregational Church's offer of its quarters for this convention had not been accepted. For the Bemans these antiabolitionist threats must have seemed a rerun of the manhandling experienced by founders of the Middletown Anti-Slavery Society four years earlier.

52. *Charter Oak*, March 1838; *Colored American*, June 16, 1838; *Charter Oak*, June 1838, April 1839.

respectively, were chosen vice-presidents. Theodore Wright and Charles Ray, who had just attended the large New York State black convention devoted to the campaign for the black vote in that state, were on hand for the Hartford meetings. On the motion of the church's deacon James Mars, the convention recommended to the black people of the state that they petition the legislature at its 1841 (spring) session "to grant us the elective franchise." Committees were set up in all the regions represented by delegates to implement the signing of petitions and their presentation to the state's lawmakers, thus following the methods used for several years in New York State.[53]

The white man who made the greatest contribution to the drive by Connecticut blacks for recovery of the franchise was Sherman Booth. He entered the state in the fall of 1840 as a volunteer agent to build up the Liberty party, and he stayed for five years on a minimal salary. During Booth's first six or eight months of recruiting for the Liberty party, he was also providing the Mendi imprisoned in New Haven with intensive tutoring in English. It was his work that enabled them to astonish a large audience in New York City after their acquittal by reading from the New Testament and singing hymns in English. During the next few years Booth showed equal zeal in his efforts to enlarge the state's Liberty party and to persuade the legislature to reenfranchise black people.[54]

New York State's black leaders continued to stay close to developments in New England. Garnet traveled to Hartford to join in the testifying for the black franchise before the state legislature in June 1841, only a few months after the Troy minister's speech to the Judiciary Committee of the New York General Assembly. Ray's *Colored American* publicized the petitioning getting under way in Connecticut.[55] By May 1843 petitions from 115 black persons had been received by that year's legislature. A year later 80 blacks from Hartford submitted similar petitions. However, each year the committee of the legislature assigned responsibility for receiving petitions denied these without submission of the question to the larger body.

In Connecticut, as in New York State, there were political developments in 1844 that seemed to enhance the chances for racial equality in voting rights. In the 1843 election for governor of Connecticut, there

53. Proceedings of meetings on September 2 and 3, 1840, in *Colored American*, September 19, 1840.

54. *Charter Oak*, June 25, 1846; *Colored American*, May 15, 22, 1841.

55. *Colored American*, June 12, 1841.

were enough Liberty party votes cast (1,872) to prevent either the Whigs or the Democrats from securing a majority. As a result, although a Democratic governor was chosen, the Whigs were able to prevent legislative approval of a constitutional revision abolishing the property requirement for white voters. In 1844 Whig Roger Baldwin was elected governor. His concern for justice for black people had been shown by his role as defending attorney for the *Amistad* defendants. Baldwin's message at the opening of the 1845 legislative assembly urged suffrage for blacks and a law to prevent Connecticut citizens from aiding in the capture of fugitive slaves. The assembly, however, gave short shrift to the black suffrage question; one representative declared that it would be as foolish to strike out the word *white* from voting requirements as to delete *male*. Baldwin did not press the matter.[56]

In June 1846 the legislature's solid wall of opposition to considering petitions for the black franchise was breached. Individual petitions by influential citizens of Hartford and elsewhere, along with the determined liberalism of the chairman of the legislature's Committee on Claims, to which the petitions that year had been forwarded, opened the way to the reading to the whole legislature of an eloquent "Remonstrance" from Sherman Booth speaking for 2,200 Liberty party voters. By a vote of 111 to 63, a resolution to strike the word *white* from the state's constitution was passed. This paved the way for final consideration in the 1847 legislature and, if approved by a two-thirds majority, submission of the matter in a referendum to the people of the state. The 1847 legislature confirmed the vote of the previous year by a vote of 142 to 68. This did not mean that over two-thirds of the state's legislators wanted blacks to have the vote but rather that many, reassured by the results of the New York State referendum of 1846, preferred to have the state's voters make the negative decision in a matter that seemed likely to antagonize some constituency whichever way they voted.[57]

Only a month before the referendum on the black vote, the Connecticut State Temperance and Moral Reform Society met. Beman, Pennington, and a member of Beman's church drew up an address to the people of Connecticut in order to urge favorable action on the vote for blacks. What these men produced was informed, of course, by similar addresses composed by such New York State leaders as Ray, Wright, and Crum-

56. Jarvis Morse, *A Neglected Period of Connecticut's History,* 201f., 315–19; *Christian Freeman,* May 16, 1844.

57. *Charter Oak,* May 21, June 11, 18, 25, July 2, 1846.

mell between 1841 and 1846. Professing not to know why Connecticut blacks had been disfranchised in the 1818 constitution, Beman and his co-authors stressed the progress made by the state's Afro-Americans over the past twenty-nine years. The level of education had risen: "We know of but a few, very few, who are not able to read and write." There had been a great increase in black property holdings, which now were worth over $300,000. The moral condition of blacks had improved with the steadily more general practice of temperance and now stood ahead of that of whites in some respects. In 1818 few blacks had practiced religion. There had been no places of public worship for blacks and no black ministers. Now there were fifteen black places of worship in the state, most of which were also the sites of sabbath schools and Bible classes. The black trio summarized the alternatives facing white voters: "Political disfranchisement tends to political, social and moral degradation, just as truly as the possession and exercise of political rights tend to elevate the political, social and moral condition of a people.—We are your fellow citizens—native born, and with you we must live and die."[58]

This address was mailed to all Connecticut newspapers, along with the request that it be printed "and thus permit us to speak for ourselves to the people of the State." The Hartford *Times* refused the request, declaring that blacks should not be treated as political equals to "the Irish, French, etc." Middletown's *Constitution,* the New Haven *Palladium* and *Morning Courier,* and the Hartford *Courant* all printed the address and endorsed the vote for blacks. The *Courant* presented a lengthy and fervent plea for ending the political inequality. Why, the writer asked, are they barred from the polls? Not because of sedition or mob action: "Among us they are orderly and quiet, characterized in general by industry and a growing intelligence. They support schools and churches. They labor steadily to advance themselves in everything that is of good report." Surely if Mexicans—an inferior race, if any is, the argument ran—are given the vote, blacks should be: "All the great truths which lie at the foundation of a free government [urge it]." What can be said against it? "Little or nothing. Significant shrugs and gestures, mysterious looks of contempt, expressions of dislike to 'niggers,' and hints about 'amalgamation' are the chief weapons employed."[59]

58. Hartford *Courant,* September 29, 1847; *Pennsylvania Freeman,* October 7, 1847.

59. Hartford *Courant,* October 1, 1847; Middletown *Constitution,* September 29, October 13, 1847; New Haven *Morning Courier,* September 21, 1847; Hartford *Courant,* September 14, 1847.

Connecticut's voters rejected opening the polls to blacks by a vote of 19,148 to 5,345. They were thus 78 percent opposed to any participation at the polls by blacks, whereas 72 percent of Empire State voters had been opposed to dropping the property qualification for the black franchise the previous year. Whereas New York City voters had been disproprotionately negative on full black enfranchisement in the New York 1846 referendum, voters from Connecticut's largest cities, Hartford and New Haven, were considerably more favorable to the vote for blacks than was the cross section of the state's population. Pennington's and Beman's reputations and the perceived contributions of their churches were undoubtedly significant factors here.

The 1847 national black convention met in the Liberty Street Presbyterian Church in Troy immediately after the Connecticut referendum. On the second evening Garnet, Douglass, Crummell, and Beman gave addresses. Beman's included emphatic comment on the Connecticut vote. According to the black reporter William Nell, Beman declared that nine-tenths of the state's Irish population had voted against black enfranchisement: "Though he [Beman] had loved Ireland, revered her great men, sympathized with her present and past afflictions, and some of her blood flowed in his veins, he could not forego administering the burning rebuke which he believed due for their recreancy to the cause of human right, and to the men who had never done harm to them." Nell, who had had ample experience with Irish racism in Boston, urged Beman and other blacks to remember the economic basis of Irish prejudice and the fact that it was proslavery Americans who had taught the Irish to abuse black people.[60]

Although Beman remained a less-militant activist than Garnet, the latter 1840s brought further radicalization for the New Haven minister also. In 1847, a few months before Garnet led the Troy Liberty Street Church out of Presbyterianism in protest against that denomination's collusion with slavery, Beman vigorously criticized the members of New York City's large (AME) Zion Church for inexcusable indifference toward their enslaved brothers. A meeting was set up in this church to raise funds toward recovering from permanent enslavement certain young men on board a Brazilian ship. Few people turned out, and not enough money was collected to pay the $13 charged by the church for holding the meeting. A major reason for the poor attendance was the failure of the

60. "Proceedings of the National Convention of Colored Citizens . . . 1847," in Bell (ed.), *Minutes of the National Negro Conventions,* 10, 14; *North Star,* December 3, 1847.

Zion pastor to read the announcement at the worship service preceding the benefit meeting. This failure may have been an intentional protest against too many appeals for contributions from various groups. The church's charging for such a meeting, said Beman, was like the Good Samaritan's asking to be paid for helping the man lying beaten on the side of the road. And was it improper to announce this emergency meeting at a worship service? Beman said, "I do not believe there is or can be any acceptable worship offered to the living God, . . . by any man, farther than he recognizes the rights, and loves the interest, and toils for the happiness, and sympathizes with the sufferings of his fellow-men." The behavior of the AME Zion church had provoked Beman to offer a definition of a true church very similar to Ray's, Garnet's and Gerrit Smith's.[61]

In September 1849 black delegates from across Connecticut gathered in Beman's New Haven Church. A comparison of the proceedings of this convention with those of the convention two years earlier, on the eve of the popular referendum on the black vote, shows a significant shift in the mood of the state's black leaders. The name under which the group came together had changed from the Connecticut State Temperance and Moral Reform Society to the Connecticut Convention of Colored Men. What New York State blacks had done in 1840, those in Connecticut came to nine years later—that is, meeting first and foremost as blacks. In the 1849 convention the first five of fifteen resolutions dealt with "the Elective Franchise as one of the most valuable and sacred rights of man." Finally, in the address to the voters of Connecticut, prepared again under the leadership of Beman, one prestigious white minister was singled out by name as a promoter of racism.

The authors of the address (Beman, the AMEZ pastor in New Haven, and a delegate from Bridgeport) cited Horace Bushnell, the leading Congregational pastor of Hartford, for embodying "the spirit of infidelity [which] . . . sometimes finds an utterance in places where reason would teach us to expect better things." To prove their point, the authors of the address quoted from a speech delivered by Bushnell in 1837 to the Phi Beta Kappa Society at Yale: "Who shall respect a people who do not respect their own blood? If it is to be seen a few ages hence that the blood of the Miltons, the Hampdens, the Hookers, and the Winthrops, has everywhere drunk of the muddy waters of the Niger, the profanation will declare itself in a people dulled in their wits, without manhood or spiritual force." Beman's address noted the influence that such "appeals and decla-

61. *Ram's Horn,* August 6, 1847.

rations . . . exert when addressed to the prejudices of men." Connecticut blacks, he went on, are denied entry to colleges and academies and are insulted with impunity by a corrupted public. When they turn in despair to Christian ministers, "instead of hearing a triumphant vindication of God's eternal truth, they are greeted with the raven cry of infidelity." Beman's publication of this statement about the Hartford minister whose prestige in that city was comparable to Leonard Bacon's in New Haven was as courageous as it was forthright. It was reminiscent of Cornish's bitter attack on the American Colonization Society, the beloved project of many of those Philadelphia and New York clergy who had ordained him. However, the greater decentralization of Congregationalism and Leonard Bacon's strong support provided Beman with more protection than Cornish had had.[62]

There was another able black Congregational minister in Connecticut in the 1840s. Former slave James Pennington had been chosen pastor of the Colored Congregational Church in Hartford in 1840 instead of Beman. He may well have been the greatest single factor in rousing Beman and other black leaders in the state to more militancy. How much time Beman and Pennington spent together cannot be known, but the state temperance society, the Union Missionary Society, and the state antislavery society often held meetings in Hartford and brought the two together. When Beman spent several weeks in Portland, Maine, in 1841 to help establsh an entirely black Congregational church in that community, his reports to the *Colored American* were in the form of letters to Pennington; this suggests that a close relationship was already established. The two men's careers offer a sharp contrast. Pennington's brilliance as a scholar, his forceful published works, and his restlessness as a fugitive slave all set him apart from Beman. The same was true of his frequent shifts in location. During the nineteen years of Beman's ministry in New Haven, Pennington labored by turn in Long Island, Hartford, Jamaica, Hartford, New York City, the British Isles, New York City, Hartford, and Long Island.

In the early 1860s Beman sent a series of acrostics to the *Weekly Anglo-African* to celebrate several of his colleagues in the ministry. The first two stanzas of the one on Pennington give a glimpse of what Beman had found impressive:

62. Foner and Walker (eds.), *Proceedings of the Black State Conventions,* II, 20–34.

Rev. J. W. C. Pennington

Justified by wisdom's high behest,
A slave no more—a man confessed—
Many have read, from the eloquent pen,
Enobling thoughts for the freedom of men.
Still upward and onward in thy way,
Which thousands admire, blessing God for the day
In which you have toiled, so nobly and true—
Like Garnet, and Douglass, and Delany, too—
Lifting the bondman from darkness and death—
Inviting him with rights—inspiring him with breath,
And sending him forward in virtue's career,
Majestic and noble, divested of fear.[63]

63. Amos Beman Scrap Book (Amos G. Beman Papers).

9. JAMES W. C. PENNINGTON: FROM SLAVE TO TEACHER, PREACHER, AND PROTESTER

Shall we not be asked in time to come, "What have your educated and privileged men done? What have they left you?"

—James W. C. Pennington, *Colored American,* June 2, 1838

James W. C. Pennington, a fugitive slave like Henry Highland Garnet, attacked the slave system on the basis of bitter personal experience and was tormented by thoughts of his own family members still at the mercy of slave owners and overseers. Of the six activist ministers discussed here, these two were evidently of pure African blood and the most conscious of physical ties with Africa. Both developed a special sense of mission to Africa and to freed Africans in the British West Indies. Behind these parallels, however, were striking differences between the experiences of Pennington and of Garnet in their youth and early adulthood. Garnet's family escaped from Maryland when he was close to nine years old. Pennington ran away by himself, leaving his whole family behind, when he was about twenty years of age. Garnet secured a sound education in New York City's African Free School, several city high schools, and the Oneida Institute. At the time of his escape, Pennington was virtually illiterate. He obtained his facility with words and his learning through informal tutoring and, above all, through teaching himself. He was justly proud of this intellectual accomplishment.

Most of what is known of Pennington's first twenty years comes from his autobiography, *The Fugitive Blacksmith; or, Events in the History of James W. C. Pennington, Pastor of a Presbyterian Church, New York, Formerly a Slave in the State of Maryland, United States.* This work was written and published in England in 1849, during the early part of a two-year stay in the British Isles. Pennington was then about forty-two years old and renewing the antislavery lecturing that he had begun in England six years earlier. Like other black lecturers in England at the time, including Henry Garnet, Samuel Ringgold Ward, and Frederick Douglass, Pennington was trying to energize British abolitionists to press the United States toward a more forthright antislavery policy. He was also painting strong pictures of American racism in the North, especially in the Christian churches of the major white denominations. His autobiography, in the slave narrative genre, dramatized episodes of cruel mistreatment of slaves and highlighted his own achievements in escaping, making his way into free territory, and learning to read and write. His description of his startlingly rapid emergence into such a command of language and control of subject matter as to be hired to teach school on Long Island served his major purpose, his crusade against southern slavery and northern racism. It also sold well—nearly six thousand copies by July 1850—and helped finance his travels.[1]

Pennington was born James Pembroke in 1807 on the eastern shore of Maryland.[2] He suffered, as so many slave children did, from parental neglect because of his mother's and father's working long hours and at a distance. He had often been hungry, was cruelly bullied by his master's sons, and was brutally whipped even in his early years by a capricious overseer. Yet Pennington seems to have had a relatively solid family life. Except for his first four years, his parents were owned by the same master and were strong forces in the development of self-pride and a clear sense of values such as truthfulness and good workmanship. Moreover, he and his older brother were very close, even when working several miles from each other. At the age of nine, James was hired out to a stonemason, six miles from home. He and his brother, who was hired out in the same town, were each living in a family where there was no other black person. At age eleven James was brought back to the home plantation to work with a skilled blacksmith. He stayed in this post for nine years and was then assigned to learn carpentry by assisting a white work-

1. The preface of the first edition contained strong testimonials to Pennington's character by Gerrit Smith and the Quaker couple who had first sheltered him in southern Pennsylvania after he had crossed over from Maryland.

2. Pennington's date of birth was given as 1809 in the document accompanying the German University of Heidelberg's award of a doctor of divinity degree to him in 1849. Since this date conflicts with several dates cited in Pennington's autobiography, we use the date of birth generally ascribed.

man in building a large barn. After six months of picking up his third trade, events involving both of his parents precipitated his running away.[3]

In the fall of 1827 on a Monday morning, Pennington's master was in a particularly bad mood, because four of his slaves were late in returning to the plantation after weekend leaves. He expressed his anger in an insulting tone to Brazil Pembroke, James's father, a scrupulously thorough and punctual workman: "The fact is, I have too many of you; my people are getting to be the most careless, lazy and worthless in the country. . . . I shall have to sell some of you and then the rest will have enough to do."[4] Brazil, protesting that he was always at work when and where he had been ordered to be, told his master that if he himself were one too many and if his master wanted to get rid of him, he would try to find a purchaser. James, telling the story over twenty years later, commented, "My father was a high-spirited man, and [felt] deeply the insult." Undoubtedly this was conveyed in his tone of voice. At any rate, his master whipped him with the "cowhide" he was carrying. After fifteen or twenty lashes administered with all his strength on Brazil's shoulders and back, his master said, "by the *** I will make you know that I am master of your tongue as well as of your time." James heard and saw the whole episode. Although shortly thereafter he was himself savagely beaten by his master without provocation, and his mother was threatened with a flogging for berating a slave informer, Pennington insisted it was his father's being whipped that had decisively changed his attitude: "I never was a *Slave* after that." Although he had found real satisfaction in his skill and aesthetic taste as a blacksmith and in working with his father at night in making straw hats and willow baskets (to secure a little extra food and clothing), all this pride was dispelled by "the family disgrace under which we were smarting."[5]

After he was beaten and his mother threatened, James decided to run away: "The man must act, or forever be a slave." Nearly 40 percent of Pennington's account of his early life was devoted to his vicissitudes between the time of leaving his home plantation and crossing into Pennsyl-

3. James W. C. Pennington, *The Fugitive Blacksmith; or, Events in the History of James W. C. Pennington, Pastor of a Presbyterian Church, New York, Formerly a Slave in the State of Maryland, United States* (3d ed. 1850; rpr. Westport, Conn., 1971), iv, xiii–xv, 1–4.

4. Pennington's own account gives the year as 1828, but the written testimonial given him by his employers thirteen months after his escape is reproduced later in his autobiography and dated October 5, 1828. *Ibid.*, 5, 50.

5. *Ibid.*, 5–11.

vania. His vivid story was guaranteed to bring alive for readers the confusion, terror, and physical misery experienced by fugitive slaves. On the third day, after traveling by night, hiding by day, and having almost nothing to eat, he took to the road in daylight and was suddenly accosted by a farmer working in his potato field. Asked for his free papers, he said he had none. Ordered to stop, he began to run. The farmer, eager for the reward for turning in a runaway, took after him. Realizing that he had brought no weapon with him, Pennington looked around for a stone and found one. Confident of his aim and his strength, he was sure he could catch his pursuer on the kneecap and disable him. However, other white men suddenly appeared, and he had no chance to use his crude weapon. Subdued by force, Pennington was grilled as to who he was and where he came from. He found himself glibly dispensing a totally fabricated account. He claimed to have been driven by a slave trader in a gang of slaves toward Georgia. He told of the trader and several slaves dying of smallpox, and the rest being released. The story bought him some time.

Pennington editorialized on his having so readily picked up a stone to maim his pursuer as well as on his so shrewdly and unhesitatingly having told a false story. His resort to lies was a betrayal of what his parents had taught him: "So far as their example was concerned, I had no habit of untruth." In retrospect he was convinced that he would indeed have become free if he had told the truth. He concluded, "See how human bloodhounds gratuitously chase, catch, and tempt [the slave] to shed blood and lie; how when he would do good, evil is thrust upon him."[6]

When his captors found a magistrate, Pennington repeated his fictitious account regarding his owner, his sale to a slave trader, and his exposure to smallpox. While he was waiting to be escorted to the magistrate's small farm to help get in the crops, he escaped once more. After two more nights and days of difficult traveling and near capture, he reached a tollgate that turned out to be in Pennsylvania. When he asked the woman who tended the gate where he could find work, she directed him to a Quaker's place three miles away. When Pennington knocked on the Wrights' door and it was opened, he saw a table spread for breakfast. William Wright's response, when this ragged and dirty black man said he was looking for work, remained engraved in the former slave's memory as a turning point in his life: "Well, come in and take thy breakfast, and get warm, and we will talk about it; thee must be cold without any

6. *Ibid.*, 20, 22, 24, 30.

coat."[7] For the next twenty years Pennington remembered these words as expressing how he himself should respond when presented with any wretchedly poor or distressed person.[8]

The decent work, friendly shelter, and food provided by Wright and his wife for the next six months were a blessing. Even more important for the long run, Pennington at the age of twenty began his book learning under the tutelage of Wright, a former schoolteacher. Pennington was an avid learner. Indeed, while working as a blacksmith in Maryland, he had studied the daybook for hours, trying to connect the written names of customers with the known sounds of those names, and the written figures of charges for particular jobs with the prices that he knew. He caught on quickly as Wright taught him reading, writing, arithmetic, and astronomy "by familiar conversations, illustrating his themes by diagrams on the slate."

The coming of spring and the increased activity of slave catchers in southern Pennsylvania forced Pennington to move on. He did so with a new surname, Pennington, which he may well have chosen because of its Quaker associations. He may have thought of Isaac Penington, a widely traveled English Quaker, or of William Penn. He later also took the middle name William in honor of his benefactor, William Wright. He settled on another Quaker couple's farm near Philadelphia. Mrs. K. was a preacher and gave Pennington his first Bible. During his seven months with the K. family, he was often left alone to manage the farm while Mrs. K. and her husband were away on preaching missions. He tried to teach himself more astronomy by drawing "rude maps of the solar system." Less than a year after almost total illiteracy, he was able to read the Bible and took pleasure in memorizing certain chapters, as well as verses of hymns. His later passion for preaching and teaching showed itself. Alone on the farm, he would go to the barn and try to speak to an imaginary audience: "My mind was constantly struggling for thoughts, and I was . . . grieved and alarmed at its barrenness; I found it gradually freed from the darkness, entailed by slavery."[9]

7. The name of this Quaker couple, which for obvious reasons was not revealed by Pennington, came out in the abolitionist W. L. Chaplin's summary of Pennington's life in a speech in Syracuse in 1851. *National Anti-Slavery Standard,* January 16, 1851.

8. Pennington, *The Fugitive Blacksmith,* 26–41. For a sketch of William Wright's efforts on behalf of fugitive slaves and another account of Pennington's stay with the Wrights, see William Still, *The Underground Railroad: A Record of Facts . . . and Advisers of the Board* (1872; rpr. Chicago, 1970), 715–20.

9. Pennington, *The Fugitive Blacksmith,* 42f., 49f.

Impatient at the slowness of learning with no teacher, Pennington left the K.'s farm; he carried a letter endorsing him as a "highly trustworthy and industrious young man." By the spring of 1829 he was settled in a good-paying job as coachman for a well-to-do Brooklyn citizen.[10] He made steady progress in his education by way of private tutoring and evening schools, and he attended a Sabbath school. As his own situation improved, he brooded over the condition of 700,000 slave children, including his own ten brothers and sisters, totally deprived of any Christian instruction. He kept asking himself what he could do for "that vast body of suffering brotherhood I have left behind." Unaccustomed as he had been to prayer, he now turned to it. In the process he became convinced that he must somehow himself get right with God if his prayers for his enslaved fellow blacks were to have weight with the Almighty. Living with the family of a Presbyterian elder, he unburdened himself to them. He was treated with sympathy and introduced the next Sunday to a distinguished guest preacher at his employer's church, Samuel Cox. Cox took an interest in Pennington and invited him to attend his Manhattan church. The young black man did so, though it meant walking three miles across the bridge. He sensed that he had been "brought to a saving acquaintance" with Christ and joined Cox's church.[11]

Continuing to ask himself what he should do to help the awesomely large body of slaves trapped in ignorance, Pennington began to focus on the wretchedness of the free blacks in New York State, many of them only recently emancipated. (Their actual mandatory freeing had not gone into effect until 1827). He heard whites who used these blacks' degradation as an argument for keeping blacks in slavery, and he thus resolved to work for the elevation of free blacks. Very soon after joining Cox's church, only two years after he was falteringly speaking to an imaginary audience in the K.'s empty barn, Pennington became a spokesman for the black community of Brooklyn. The rapidity of his emergence from illiteracy into both oral and written articulate expression of complex matters is astonishing.

At a large meeting of Brooklyn blacks in early June 1831, Pennington was one of three to give addresses criticizing the American Colonization Society. The Long Island *Star* published the text of this first recorded speech by Pennington. The talk was well-informed and forceful, though the arguments had already been made many times during fourteen years

10. Stated by W. L. Chaplin, *National Anti-Slavery Standard,* January 16, 1851.

11. *Frederick Douglass' Paper,* July 30, 1852; Pennington, *The Fugitive Blacksmith,* 53f.

of protest meetings. Pennington was chosen by this Brooklyn gathering to be its delegate at the first full-fledged national black convention, due to begin the next day in Philadelphia. Without consulting his employer, Pennington secured a substitute for his job and was absent for four days in Pennsylvania. When he returned to his post his employer, who was president of the Brooklyn ACS, had read in the Long Island paper the account of the protest meeting by Brooklyn blacks and Pennington's part in it. To Pennington's surprise his employer wanted to know whether the paper's account truly reflected black attitudes. "I have been thinking," he said, "that if the colored people for whose benefit we intend this society, do not approve of it, we had better disband." The auxiliary was dissolved. Surely Pennington was right some twenty-four years later in saying that only a "solemn sense of duty" to his race had given him the courage to compose the 1831 address and attend the Philadelphia convention, which were both strenuously opposed to his employer's organization.[12]

Pennington was again a delegate at the 1832 national convention and at those in 1833 and 1834. At these gatherings he served on committees addressing three major problems for northern blacks: white-promoted colonization, alcoholism, and disfranchisement.[13] His associations at these conventions with other black leaders and his election by them to significant responsibilities must have been immensely gratifying to Pennington. Yet he realized that little in the way of concrete improvement in the conditions of local black communities was being accomplished by all the speeches, committee reports, and resolutions. He had, however, found a way to attack one major problem, that of black ignorance.

A new school for black children, which had been built through the philanthropy of a former slave owner, opened its doors in New Town, on Long Island, about seven miles from Brooklyn. Recommended by a friend for the post of teacher in this school, Pennington applied, was examined by the school's trustees, and was hired at a salary of $200 a year. On the winter day on which school was to open, the young teacher walked the seven miles through several inches of snow to arrive at 8:30, only to find the school closed due to the storm. After sweeping out the

12. *Frederick Douglass' Paper,* April 6, 1855; Garrison, *Thoughts on African Colonization,* Pt. 2, pp. 23–28.

13. "Minutes and Proceedings of the Second Annual Convention . . . of the Free People of Color . . . 1832," pp. 3, 6–8; "Minutes and Proceedings of the Third Annual Convention . . . of the Free People of Colour . . . 1833," pp. 4, 10, 15–19; "Minutes of the Fourth Annual Convention of the Free People of Colour . . . 1834," pp. 8, 18. The minutes of these three conventions are in Bell (ed.), *Minutes of the National Negro Conventions.*

sawdust, he persuaded a black man who owned a sleigh to take him around to visit the black families in New Town. Although both the parents and the children were at first disappointed that the teacher for the new school was not white, Pennington soon secured the trust of his nine initial scholars and their parents. From his own experience he could sympathize with many of New Town's adult blacks who were only recently free from slavery. And he was intensely aware of how precious the childhood years were for getting ahead with schooling. Later he wrote, "[Slavery] robbed me of my education; the injury is irreparable. . . . The evil that besets me is a great lack of general information. . . . I can never hope now to make it up. . . . Slavery, *vile monster! thou hast hindered my usefulness, by robbing me of my early education.*"[14]

For the next dozen years, both before and after he was licensed to preach, Pennington taught in schools for black children in New Town, New Haven, and Hartford. Soon after he undertook ministry in Hartford in 1840, he sent a series of articles to the *Colored American* that drew on his years of teaching. They were models of clarity, humor, and practical wisdom. To be good at the work, wrote Pennington, a teacher must be fond of teaching and of children. Playing favorites, however, will have bad results for both the favorite and the ones discriminated against. Such partiality will undermine a teacher's hold on those pupils, as well as on parents. As for parents who are themselves ignorant, a teacher must be on the alert for rigid attitudes about how writing and arithmetic should be taught, and for readiness to start whispering campaigns against the teacher.[15]

Five of Pennington's articles dealt with parental attitudes and behavior that he defined as errors. Parents should not bring up their children as pets: "A pettish child comes to school in a fret, with back and neck crooked, eyes flashing wrath, lips chucked out, and elbow bent for battle." Parents should not send imprudent oral messages to teachers by way of the children. If such a message is demanding an exception to school rules, it encourages insubordination in the pupil, and it can easily lead the child to falsify the message or fabricate one to secure some further concession. Parents should not criticize a teacher or his methods to a child, since this fosters impudence in the pupil. Parents should not keep children out of school for days and weeks for no good reason. Parents should visit the

14. *Colored American,* August 22, 1840; Pennington, *The Fugitive Blacksmith,* 56f.
15. *Colored American,* October 24, November 7, 14, 1840.

school while it is in session; this will lift their sights about the standards expected. And parents sorely need to upgrade their ideas as to the length of time required to get a good common school education. Pennington was as distressed in 1841 as Cornish had been in 1829 by the tendency of many black parents to be proud and satisfied if their child had secured a smattering of spelling and arithmetic and a halting ability to read. The former slave recommended a minimum of seven years in school, and twelve years to be ready for college.[16]

Pennington's final recommendations were for school committees. He inveighed especially against committees' making belated or partial salary payments, or expecting teachers to persuade parents to produce the salary money: "I know not why it should ever be supposed that a school teacher can be dealt with more loosely and irresponsibly than a man of any other trade or profession. If you employ a shoemaker to make a pair of shoes, you *must pay* him." The last article from this no-nonsense teacher upbraided school committees for inadequate furnishings for school rooms: rickety seats, "patched up, . . . no-piped, broken-hearted stoves," and a miserably insufficient supply of books and slates. He concluded, "All the articles I have named are of vital importance. . . . And you may as well send a lame dog to catch a fox as to require a man to teach without them."[17]

Pennington was quite aware that his definition of a good common school education for blacks would be viewed as absurdly visionary by most black parents, many of whom were themselves close to illiteracy. With his penchant for grand organizational proposals, however, he had sketched out in earlier issues of the *Colored American* a structure that he believed would energize local communities and secure widespread backing for a radical upgrading of black educational institutions. The primary aim of this proposed structure was the opening of many more weekday schools for blacks and the establishing of a scaled-down university for black school graduates.[18] Pennington was convinced that many of the young black men and women who had gone through the New York schools were well qualified to teach in the new weekday schools. At the university level, he urged educated blacks like Theodore Wright and Peter Williams, Jr., to volunteer to give systematic instruction in the sci-

16. *Ibid.*, November 28, December 19, 1840; May 8, 1841.

17. *Ibid.*, April 10, May 8, June 26, July 17, September 4, 1841.

18. We do not know whether Pennington was familiar with the ambitious proposal for black educational institutions made by Cornish in the *Rights of All* in 1829.

ences and other subjects constituting what he called a classical education. He suggested their taking fifteen or twenty young men of New York City into a two- or three-year program, requiring eight to twelve weeks a year for lectures, which could be attended along with the young men's regular employment. Pennington was drawing on his own impressive record of self-education and school teaching. He wanted to turn able black leaders into the equivalent of night school instructors: "Shall we not be asked in time to come, 'What have your educated and privileged men done? What have they left you?'" Neither able preaching nor abolitionist activity is enough, declared Pennington: "The question turns on qualities of intellect."[19]

For all his passion for education, Pennington's primary goal after 1833 was to become a faithful Christian minister. It was after joining Samuel Cox's Presbyterian church that he had decided on the ministry as the route to maximum service of his people. On his own he began studying rhetoric, logic, and the New Testament in Greek. His respect for Cox and some association with Cornish and Wright would have inclined him toward continued affiliation with Presbyterians, but he had also come to know the Congregational minister Simeon Jocelyn. Pennington was at the 1831 national black convention when Jocelyn and William Lloyd Garrison secured the endorsement of black leaders for founding a black manual labor college in New Haven. At the next year's convention Pennington heard Jocelyn's special plea for education among blacks. In the words of the recording secretary, Jocelyn "spoke fervently and affectionately on the advantages to be derived by us, from learning temperance, industry and frugality, and seriously admonished us, to . . . particularly inculcate the early education of our children."[20]

Jocelyn was surely a man after Pennington's own heart, and vice versa. Not long after Jocelyn succumbed to increasing harassment by New Haven whites and resigned the pastorate of the first black Congregational church in the country, Pennington moved to New Haven and, though not yet licensed, assumed some of the pastoral duties at the Temple Street African Congregational Church. He also taught at a school for black children. He applied for admission into the Divinity School at Yale. He

19. Letters II, III, IV from Long Island Scribe, *Colored American,* April 19, May 3, June 2, 1838.

20. Pennington, *The Fugitive Blacksmith,* 55; "Minutes and Proceedings of the Second Annual Convention . . . of the Free People of Color . . . 1832," in Bell (ed.), *Minutes of the National Negro Conventions,* 22f.

was not accepted as a regular student but was allowed to audit lectures. Although he could not take books out of the library, he presumably did considerable reading on the premises.[21]

By the summer of 1837 Pennington was back teaching on Long Island. A few months later black people from several white churches in the New Town community gathered to consecrate a building for worship and to call Pennington to be their preacher. A member of the presbytery of New York gave an address at the consecration, but the enterprise had no denominational affiliation at first. In May 1838 Pennington's studies in New Haven, his experience as a Christian, and his sense of calling to the ministry were confirmed by ordination.[22] The next year his New Town, Long Island, church was formally organized within the Congregational denomination. Almost at once Pennington was commissioned a home missionary by the American Home Missionary Society. His quarterly reports to the society conveyed his almost limitless ambition for his "colored church"—for what it could do for individual people and for the whole community of New Town. When first organized, there were twenty-seven members. Soon the Sabbath school had thirty to forty scholars. Most of the teachers in this once-a-week school were young men and women who had received a solid education in the weekday school in which Pennington had taught.

The young pastor was convinced that the increasing vitality in his church was gradually affecting life in New Town's other five churches. In the whole area Sabbath breaking seemed on the decline and the temperance cause prospering. Moreover, the white Baptist church, long without regular ministry, was getting an excellent, experienced pastor, and the Methodist church had a large house of worship almost ready for dedication. In the midst of these promising developments on Long Island, Pennington was chosen by Hartford's black church on Talcott Street and by the city's white clergy for the pastorate of that church. With forty-seven members even in the absence of any steady ministry, this church and this city offered the former slave far wider opportunities than existed in New Town.[23]

21. Warner, *New Haven Negroes,* 83.

22. *Colored American,* August 5, October 28, 1837; *Minutes of the General Association of Connecticut . . . June, 1840* (Hartford, 1840).

23. Reports of March 29, August, November 1, 1839, January 21, 1840, from Pennington to the AHMS, and M. Badger (secretary of the AHMS) to James W. C. Pennington, February 21, 1840, all in AHMS Archives (Microfilm copy in Carter and Ripley [eds.], *BAP,* reel 2, item 247; reel 3, items 23, 40, 159, 332).

In the spring of 1840 Pennington accepted the call from Hartford's Colored Congregational Church, subsequently named the Fifth Congregational Church and still later, the Talcott Street Congregational Church. The decade of the 1840s was for Pennington, as it was for Garnet in New York State, one of solid accomplishment, including forceful criticism of northern racism. The early religious history of Hartford's blacks paralleled that of the New Haven black community. Afro-Americans fleeing the Negro pew in white churches first began worshiping by themselves in 1819 with a black minister. The following year a Sunday school for blacks only was organized under the supervision of the Hartford Sunday School Union. In 1826 blacks met with invited whites to form the African Religious Society. The group chose officers and voted to erect a house of worship; four blacks and three whites were slated for the building committee. The church was completed that year and paid for by subscription. It was seven years before this African Religious Society became a duly constituted church, and during the interim there were intense discussions as to the type of minister and worship desired. A later pastor of the Talcott Street church described the struggle: "It was a contest for intelligent preaching and helpful progressive forms of worship and work. A number were opposed to education. . . . An educated minister had no religion. Loud exhorting, singing, shouting, jumping and exaggerated emotion were extolled, without which worship was dead, no spirit, no power." The majority in the society favored the faith and order of the Congregational churches.

In 1833, at a meeting presided over by two prominent white Congregational ministers, a black Congregational church was formed. Those in the African Religious Society who came from other denominational backgrounds were given six months to withdraw and have their subscriptions refunded, if they so desired.[24] That same year a district school for black children was opened in the church building, and Amos Beman was hired to teach at it. Between 1833 and Pennington's arrival in 1840, white Congregational ministers apparently served as supply preachers, the last one being the ardent abolitionist Edward R. Tyler, formerly minister of South Congregational Church in Middletown.[25]

24. As indicated earlier, a number of Methodist-oriented former members of the African Religious Society and others were organized as an AMEZ church with Hosea Easton as pastor. Prior to the completion of their own house of worship on Elm Street, they used the Talcott Street church for services.

25. Sources for both of the preceding are "Farewell to the Talcott St. Church" (a summary of Pastor Robert F. Wheeler's historic sermon), Hartford *Courant,* March 26, 1906;

When Pennington undertook pastoral duties in Hartford in early May 1840, he was again commissioned by the American Home Missionary Society and awarded a small stipend, as had been the case in New Town. His report to the society a year later reflected vitality and growth in the church: 60 "hopeful" conversions, 34 added to the church's membership, 105 in the Sabbath school, 100 subscribers to the temperance pledge, and one young man studying for the ministry.[26]

On the morning of July 16, 1840, an ecclesiastical council of Congregational ministers and lay delegates from churches in the Hartford area met to examine Pennington as to his fitness to be formally installed as a fully accredited minister in that region. Also present were Theodore Wright, from the First Colored Presbyterian Church in New York City, and William P. Johnson, superintendent of that church's Sunday school and a traveling agent for the *Colored American*. The papers presented to the council included the Hartford Colored Congregational Church's call to Pennington and certificates of the candidate's ordination and good standing as a member of a New York Congregational association. The council examined Pennington on theology, experimental religion, and his reasons for seeking this ministerial post. William Johnson, lay delegate from Wright's church, sent the *Colored American* his impressions: "I have seen and heard many students in the first Presbytery in the city of New York, but none I am certain to equal Mr. Pennington; his answers . . . seemed to be those implanted in the soul by the Holy Spirit. . . . Mr. P. left the room whilst the council decided. They all then with one accord expressed their high satisfaction as well as astonishment." An installation service was held in the afternoon of the same day. Horace Bushnell, maligned some years later by Amos Beman for his racist views, and the Rev. J. A. Hempsted, who had been supply pastor of the church on Talcott Street for a year, gave the charge to the people.[27]

There was much strength in this church when Pennington came to be its pastor. Deacon James Mars, the church's delegate to the ordaining ecclesiastical council, had been born and brought up a slave in Connecticut until early manhood. Now fifty years old, he was an able and courageous man, a hard worker, and a fervent Christian. About the time of Pen-

---

Faith Congregational Church (UCC): Historical Sketch, 150th Anniversary, 1826–1976 (Connecticut Conference of United Church of Christ Archives, Hartford).

26. Report to the American Home Missionary Society, May 1, 1841 (Microfilm copy in Carter and Ripley [eds.], *BAP,* reel 3, item 1011).

27. *Colored American,* August 8, 1840.

nington's arrival, he had been chosen a member of the Executive Committee of the largely white Connecticut Anti-Slavery Society. Another prominent member of the Talcott Street congregation was Henry Foster, who had chaired organizational meetings of the state black temperance society.[28] Mars and Foster constituted the District School Committee, which oversaw Beman's teaching in Hartford from 1833 to 1838. And there was Ann Plato, who became a published author with Pennington's help and was an able teacher in Hartford's second district school for blacks when it opened in 1844.[29]

The Talcott Street white ministers, Hempsted and Tyler, each serving as pastor for about a year, apparently took their responsibility seriously. The 20 members in 1838 had swelled to 47 by the beginning of 1840. Under Pennington's ministry the growth was even more striking. By January 1844 there were 130 members, a peak that would not be exceeded before the Civil War.[30] Equally notable is the fact that Pennington evidently was never forced to go to the white clergy and churches of Hartford for financial rescue, as Wright was in New York City and Beman, in New Haven.

Wherein lay the strength of Pennington's ministerial leadership? Judging from the few of his sermons that were published, he made few concessions to limited vocabularies or drowsy minds. His original correctness of speech had been hard won. This correctness meant far more than mere propriety to him as a former slave and to members of his congregation, many of whom had only recently been freed from slavery in the North. Consider his description in 1849 of the painful process of mental and verbal emancipation: "It cost me two years hard labor after I fled, to unshackle my mind; it was three years before I had purged my mind of slavery's idioms; it was four years before I had thrown off the crouching aspect of slavery."[31] Pennington in Hartford, like Wright, Garnet, and Beman, was trying to raise the cultural level of his people. Correct words and sentence structure in sermons, as well as occasional classical allusions, were all part of the educational process. Moreover, the testimony of those who heard Pennington's public addresses proves that his mode of

28. *Liberator,* December 3, 1836.

29. The second district school was on Elm Street and seems to have been associated with the AMEZ church much as the first school was with the Talcott Street Congregational church.

30. Statistics of membership were published annually in *Minutes of the General Association of Connecticut . . . 1839–1858* (Hartford or New Haven, 1839–58).

31. Pennington, *The Fugitive Blacksmith,* 56.

delivery was extremely effective. The printed page of the sermon text cannot catch this dimension of his preaching.

Pennington's ministry, of course, involved much more than preaching. As a pastor he seems to have had a distinctive relationship with individuals and with his congregation as a whole. He was direct, demanding, forceful, and affectionate. The tone of his letters on teaching in a common school reflected a great deal of visiting among parents, a keen realization of how precious the opportunity for schooling was, and a mixture of caring and exasperation aroused by the counterproductive behavior of parents and the restlessness of schoolchildren. The same acute insights and loving, but stern, admonitions characterized his relations with church members.

The flavor of Pennington's pastoral relations comes through in another report from the Sunday school superintendent of the First Colored Presbyterian Church in New York City. William Johnson, attending Amos Beman's installation at the Temple Street African Congregational Church in New Haven in the fall of 1841, was particularly struck by Pennington's charge to the people. They had, in some measure, been his people between 1835 and 1837. Johnson doubted that either the Temple Street congregation or Beman had ever heard such a charge: "He [Pennington] put in his scythe, and never stopped, crooked or turned, until he got through and came down from the pulpit." He came "into the domestic circle of the church" and, fatherlike, told them how wrong it was for them to criticize their pastor for his activities outside the parish because that prevented his visiting them as often as they felt he should. Often, Pennington reminded the members of the Temple Street Church, these complainers were in debt to the church or to the pastor, a situation that made Beman's own financial situation that much more difficult. Johnson continued, "He also told them how beautiful and delightful it was to dwell together in unity. He was very solemn and affectionate, as he most always is, but sharp as a two-edged sword."[32]

When Pennington warned Beman's congregation not to complain of their pastor's "going abroad" because it took him away from parish visiting, he was surely speaking from personal experience of criticism by some members of his Long Island and Connecticut congregations of his involvement in broader causes. Almost from the beginning of his Hartford pastorate, he had shown a deep concern for the work of Christian missions overseas, especially in Africa. Indeed, Pennington later recalled

32. *Colored American*, November 20, 1841.

that in 1828 and 1829, on first coming to Long Island and pondering his responsibility to those still in slavery, he had thought of going to Africa and working on the problem at its geographic source. By 1841 he was, like Garnet, Beman, and many other activists black and white, powerfully affected by the trial of the *Amistad* crew. Whereas Lewis Tappan became engrossed in securing the legal help and the funds to enable successful defense in the courts, Pennington saw the presence of the Mendi in the United States, their acquittal, and their prospective return to Africa as a divinely intended opportunity. In late March he wrote the following to Charles Ray for publication in the *Colored American:* "I am humbly of the opinion that that signal act of Divine Providence which has, to our great joy, brought about the liberation of the citizens of Mendi . . . has brought us under solemn obligations to commence Missionary operations in Africa." Pennington hoped that the school in Farmington, Connecticut, where the Mendi were being prepared for repatriation could remain open so that other slaves, escaped or rescued from slavers in American waters, could be "taught something of civilization and Christianity before they return." Such an operation would be invaluable to "other pious young men of this country wanting to go as missionaries to Africa and needing to be taught by Africans the languages of the countries to which they were going."[33]

In early May members of the Talcott Street church and a few others interested in African missions drew up plans for a missionary convention in Hartford in mid-August. Deacon James Mars and Henry Foster were active in the proceedings. Pennington was designated chairman of a committee to expedite the proposed convention. Intending primarily to energize "colored Christians," the organizers also solicited the help of "our white friends of all evangelical denominations." A more detailed call to the August convention fleshed out the rationale for Afro-American involvement in missions to Africa in general and Mendi in particular. The needs of Africa, wrote Pennington, are incalculable. Black Americans have no missionary society. We ourselves should do something for "the land which our fathers loved as the land of their nativity." This is a time especially favorable for beginning such an enterprise. And finally, our Christian duty requires us to take seriously Jesus' own command that we go into all the world and preach the Gospel to every creature. Forty-three delegates from Massachusetts, Rhode Island, Connecticut, New York,

33. Pennington, *The Fugitive Blacksmith,* 54; letter of March 30, 1841, in *Colored American,* April 17, 1841.

and Pennsylvania attended the Hartford convention and founded the Union Missionary Society. Pennington was elected president; Amos Beman, secretary; and Theodore Wright, treasurer.[34]

The Union Missionary Society had two distinguished Afro-American forerunners. The first was the Baptist missionary to Liberia in the 1820s, Lott Cary, and the other was the Episcopalian missionary to Sierra Leone from 1831 on, Edward Jones, who had been trained at Amherst and at Andover Theological Seminary.[35]

When in the late summer of 1841 Pennington was invited to go to Mendi as a missionary, he thought the matter over with care and declined the offer. His reasons were weighty. He had been the formally installed pastor of the Talcott Street church for only a little over a year. During that time church membership had more than doubled: "The people are gaining in respectability, and we occupy the most important position in New England. Should I leave this position it would be disastrous." As a clinching argument, Pennington cited the resurgence in Hartford of black interest in settling in Liberia. Representatives of the American Colonization Society, viewed with continuing hostility and suspicion by white and black leaders such as Tappan and Wright, had recently recruited one of Pennington's own deacons. The Talcott Street pastor needed to continue to do battle with the ACS and to foster the growth of the recently formed Union Missionary Society, of which he was president.[36]

Although Pennington did not accept this call to the foreign mission field, Henry M. Wilson, a tailor and member of the Talcott Street church, and his wife did join the departing Mendi to serve as missionary teachers in West Africa. Pennington accompanied the party to New York City and, at a large send-off meeting in the Broadway Tabernacle, prayed for the departing Africans and the two black American missionaries. Two months later, Pennington and his wife deeded over to the Union Missionary Society the New Haven building lot they owned.[37]

34. *Colored American,* May 15, 1841; *Emancipator,* July 22, 1841; *Colored American,* July 3, 1841; Quarles, *Black Abolitionists,* 78f.

35. Miles Mark Fisher, "Lott Cary: The Colonizing Missionary," in David Wills and Richard Newman (eds.), *Black Apostles at Home and Abroad: Afro-Americans and the Christian Mission from the Revolution to Reconstruction* (Boston, 1982), 211–42; Hugh Hawkins, "Edward Jones, Marginal Man," in Wills and Newman (eds.), *Black Apostles at Home and Abroad,* 243–53.

36. James Pennington to the Executive Committee of the American Home Missionary Society, October 9, 1841, in AMA Archives (Microfilm copy in Carter and Ripley [eds.], *BAP,* reel 4, item 241).

37. James Pennington to A. F. Williams, November 1, 1841, James Pennington to Lewis Tappan, November 5, 1841, Promissory note of January 12, 1842, to the Union Missionary

Pennington remained president of the Union Missionary Society for several years, but his influence over its program steadily declined. From its founding, the society had grave financial problems. Reliance on black churches throughout the country for major contributions proved to be unrealistic. The organization could not do without major white contributions. Lewis Tappan, head of the Amistad Committee, had the power to start a flow of such money. A merger of the two organizations in 1842 began to solve the UMS's financial problems, but blacks lost effective control to Lewis Tappan, who held the offices of treasurer and corresponding secretary. When the UMS merged with two other mission groups in 1846 to form the American Missionary Association, Pennington's influence vis-à-vis Tappan's was further diminished.[38]

Pennington's intense interest in promoting Christianity and "civilization" in Africa, like Garnet's, illustrates the fact that activist black clergy had a sense of mission more comprehensive than the usual call to Christian ministry. Pennington's preaching and pastoral work with his Hartford people in the 1840s and his promotion of mission work in Africa were linked with a variety of other efforts aimed to uplift black people. These included school teaching again, writing for publication, and participating in ongoing protests against southern slavery and northern racism.

Although the articles Pennington sent to the *Colored American* in 1840 and 1841 on common schools were based on his experience as a teacher in New Town, they also bespoke his concern for black schooling in Hartford. This community and other towns in Connecticut had been receiving some state money since 1795 for the support of district schools, but the statewide system in the 1830s and 1840s suffered from the problems identified by Pennington in his articles: parental apathy, poorly trained and underpaid teachers, and inadequate buildings and equipment. Because school attendance was not compulsory, many children of whatever race never went to district school. For blacks the problems were even more severe. Most of the state's district schools excluded blacks. Even where black pupils were allowed to attend, they were often given humiliating treatment. Larger communities of blacks, such as in Hartford, might secure district schools of their own, but the appropriations for

---

Society, in Amistad Research Center (Microfilm in Carter and Ripley [eds.], *BAP,* reel 4, items 281, 285, 346); David O. White, "The Fugitive Blacksmith of Hartford: James W. C. Pennington" (Unpublished, longer version of what appeared under the same title in the *Connecticut Historical Society Bulletin,* XLIX [1984], 21–24).

38. R. J. M. Blackett, *Beating Against the Barriers: Biographical Essays in Nineteenth-Century Afro-American History* (Baton Rouge, 1986), 24–26.

teachers' salaries, classroom equipment, and books were far less than for white schools. Moreover, no school building was provided; classes were usually taught in black church buildings.

In 1846 Pennington formally asked Hartford's school committee to do better by the black schools. Supplies and equipment were upgraded, but no building was made available to them until 1852, four years after Pennington moved to New York City. Subjects taught in the black district schools included spelling, reading, writing, grammar, geography, and arithmetic. Pennington and his wife both taught in the North African School in the early 1840s, and a gifted member of the Talcott Street church, Ann Plato, taught in the South African School from 1845 through 1847. It can safely be assumed that the quality of the Penningtons' teaching was good. Perceptive and detailed reports from white visitors to both black schools describe the years right after the Penningtons retired from work. The teachers in the latter 1840s, all of them black, were conscientious and achieved results. Indeed, the eight years of Pennington's ministry in Hartford may well have seen the peak in the quality of the city's black district schools. By the 1850s Hartford's blacks were developing more resistance to segregated education.[39]

During his second year in Hartford, Pennington was responsible for the publication of two books, his own *Text Book of the Origin and History, Etc. Etc. of the Colored People* and a little volume of poems and essays by his protégée, Ann Plato. Both publications aimed to undercut black and white assumptions that black people were inherently inferior to whites. As Pennington himself put it, the purpose of his *Text Book* was "to unembarrass the origin" of black people and to promote "a right state of feeling on the total subject of HUMAN RIGHTS." The early part of Pennington's book followed the line of argument of previous works: disproof of the theory that blacks continued to labor under the curse on Cain and/or that on Noah's grandson Canaan; proof of the blackness of Egyptians and the glories of their culture at its height; and insistence that "the blessings of civilization" had come from Egypt to Greece, Rome, and modern Europe.[40]

39. White, "Hartford's African Schools," 47–53.

40. In these arguments Pennington may well have drawn from articles published by Cornish in *Freedom's Journal,* July 13, 20, 27, 1827, and from Hosea Easton, *A Treatise on the Intellectual Character, and Civil and Political Condition of the Colored People of the U. States; and . . . the Duty of the Church to Them* (Boston, 1837; rpr. in Dorothy Porter [ed.], *Negro Protest Pamphlets: A Compendium,* [New York, 1969]), published while Easton was still in Hartford. Also see Benjamin Quarles, "Black History's Antebellum Origins," *Proceedings of the American Antiquarian Society,* LXXXIX (1979), 95, 101ff.

Like David Walker, Pennington was responding to Thomas Jefferson's pseudoanthropological argument in support of his "suspicion . . . that the blacks . . . are inferior to the whites in the endowments both of body and mind." Remembering that Jefferson had found ways to discount the significance of brilliant individual blacks such as Benjamin Banneker, Pennington set out to prove that intellect in all human beings has been produced in the same way (by descent from the God-created Adam), has improved in the same way (for example, by growth through a common school education), and has interacted similarly with other intellects. In contrast to Jefferson's calling the universal, distinctively human faculty the *moral sense,* and in contrast to the frequent Christian practice of naming it the *soul,* Pennington called it the *mind.* In accordance with this identical makeup of mind, continued Pennington, God has established one universal moral law and one system of justice in administering that law.[41]

Pennington's showcase example of someone well known in the black community of Hartford as being intelligent, articulate, and refined was Ann Plato. By endorsing her slender volume of essays and poems and thereby helping to secure its publication and promote its sale, Ann's pastor hoped to convince Hartford's blacks of the "fallacy of that stupid theory, that *nature has done nothing* but fit us for slaves, and that art cannot unfit us for slavery." Urging his people to buy the book, Pennington assured them that her success would be their own: "As Greece had a Plato why may we not have a Platoess?"[42]

Pennington's *Text Book* concluded with an essay on American color prejudice and recommendations for checking the disease. In comparison with such earlier black attacks on racial prejudice as Cornish's, Wright's, and Easton's, Pennington's was a highly organized, rational analysis, and his anger was carefully restrained. What brought the discussion to life were the examples. Prejudice, he declared, fosters bloody riots against right-minded reformers: "What *kind* of a spirit was that which besieged our houses with brickbacks, stones and deadly weapons, broke up the Canterbury school, put a rope around Garrison's neck, burnt Pennsylvania Hall, and shot Lovejoy?" Prejudice, Pennington continued, promotes the dishonest exploiting of black people. He told of his own experience as a teacher in New Town, where he was strongly urged to tutor

41. Jefferson, *Notes on Virginia,* 143; James W. C. Pennington, *A Text Book of the Origin and History, Etc. Etc. of the Colored People* (Hartford, 1841), 52–69.

42. James W. C. Pennington, Introduction to *Essays; Including Biographies & Miscellaneous Pieces in Prose and Poetry,* by Ann Plato (Hartford, 1841), xvii–xx.

the children of a white family during the evening: "But, O! it would not do to let this be known, nor for those children to go to [my] school." And to illustrate the tendency of prejudice to engender sacrilege, Pennington cited segregated seating in churches: "Who has authorized the division of the church of God into *white* and *black* divisions?" He related episode after episode describing the humiliation he felt when he had gone to white prayer meetings or to hear Mr. Knapp, a favorite white Baptist preacher. Having long adopted the policy when attending a white church of standing in one of the aisles, he felt himself called to a more radical role: "I find that I have, as a minister of the gospel, a responsibility in the matter. I must think of it and feel it more directly than I have. And the more I do think of it the more my soul sickens. . . . There is no hope of getting right in the church so long as . . . revivals are managed strictly on the man-hating principle."[43]

The *Text Book*'s summary recommendations to blacks were three: bring biblical truths to bear on the consciences of "men hating Christians"; have only love and pity toward whites in your hearts, and pray for them; and struggle to end slavery, which is the fountainhead of prejudice.[44] As the next fifteen years unfolded, angry protest came more to the fore in Pennington's life, and patient goodwill seemed less sufficient for the battle.

Pennington's attacks on northern race prejudice continued for more than two decades after the publication of his *Text Book*. The other chief target of his protests was southern slavery. As was the case with other black leaders and with radical white abolitionists, Pennington's antislavery efforts and his aid to fugitive slaves were two sides of the same coin. Even before he left Long Island he had been solidly involved with both. Although New Town was off the major routes of the Underground Railroad, Pennington was in New York City in early September 1838 to help the newly escaped Frederick Douglass in an unforgettable way: He performed the marriage ceremony for Douglass and his Baltimore bride just before the two left for New Bedford, Massachusetts. Douglass later recalled, "I had no money with which to pay the marriage fee, but he seemed well pleased with our thanks."[45]

Less than a year later Pennington was in Newark, New Jersey, to de-

43. Pennington, *Text Book of the Origin of the Colored People,* 74–85.

44. *Ibid.*, 87–90.

45. Frederick Douglass, *Life and Times of Frederick Douglass, Written by Himself . . .* (1892; rpr. New York, 1962), 205.

liver an address in celebration of the first anniversary of the August 1 emancipation of slaves in the British West Indies. He was in powerful company, as he shared the platform with the white revival preacher Charles G. Finney and with Samuel Ringgold Ward, Henry Highland Garnet's cousin, who was emerging as one of the two or three most eloquent black antislavery orators. Pennington's speech was a solidly factual description of the remarkable transformation in a mere five years in the British West Indies of 800,000 black slaves into law-abiding freemen. And there had been no bloodshed. True to his usual scholarly bent, Pennington traced the gathering momentum of the abolition movement among the British people, its impact on a reluctant Parliament, and the political compromise granting West Indian slave owners 20 million pounds sterling as indemnity.

The main thrust of Pennington's address, as of American black celebrations of August 1 in general, was to underline the implications of British emancipation for the future of the United States: "Fellow citizens, as to the practicability of immediate emancipation, we have satisfactory evidence. The world has not seen before so successful an experiment on so large a scale. . . . This was done by a single Act, in a single day; no peace broken, no insurrection, no master's life taken." Pennington predicted that as abolitionism gathered momentum in the United States, there would be strong southern pressure for compensation for freed slaves. Such a policy might have a price tag of $1,200,000,000, and should give northerners pause. Perhaps the sheer cost would drive them to a correct view of abolition—that is, emancipation without compensation.[46]

Pennington's overall stance was both vigorously hopeful and heavy with warning. He acknowledged the power of southern slavery but reminded all Americans of "the bloody and mournful pathway of tyrants" in past history. The events in the West Indies were not only a victory for the principles of human liberty but also "evidence that these principles are in the care of God, the Judge of all the earth." Men, however, had to give body to those principles, and Pennington reminded his audience of the potential impact of a large-scale boycott of slave-grown produce by "all the great and generous powers of the earth."[47]

Within a few weeks of Pennington's arrival in Hartford in the spring of 1840, he was made a member of the Executive Committee of the newly

46. *An Address Delivered at Newark, N.J., at the First Anniversary of West Indian Emancipation, August 1, 1839* (Newark, 1839).

47. *Ibid.*

formed American and Foreign Anti-Slavery Society, the political activists' split-off from the Garrisonian American Anti-Slavery Society. Two years later he was chosen by the Connecticut Anti-Slavery Society to be the single black member of its Executive Committee.[48] In the same year, the Colored (now Fifth) Congregational Church's deacon James Mars and its pastor each took vigorous action to prevent the return of individual slaves from New England to the South.

The first case involved a slave owner named Bullock who had come to Hartford from Savannah, Georgia, to secure quality schooling for his daughter. He had brought a slave girl, Nancy, to look out for his smaller children. Mars's wife came to know the Bullocks by doing washing for them. Sometime during 1842 a party sympathetic to Nancy told Mars that she was about to be shipped back to Savannah and asked him, as an upstanding black citizen, to sign a petition for a writ of habeas corpus to bring Bullock to court. The aim was to force him to show cause for not freeing Nancy, since she had lived for two years in a state where slavery had been abolished. The writ was served on Bullock, who was put under bond to appear before the Supreme Court of Errors, which was due to sit in ten days.[49] Mars later described his own experience during those ten days: "I was frowned upon; I was blamed; . . . the house where I lived would be pulled down; I should be mobbed; and all kinds of scarecrows were talked about, and this by men of wealth and standing. I kept on about my work, not much alarmed." Two of the five judges voted to send Nancy south, and two voted to keep her. The chief judge, declaring that state law had made her free when brought into the state, broke the tie. With calm understatement Mars noted, "This made a change in the feelings of the people. I could pass along the streets in quiet."[50]

Later the same year a highly publicized case of a fugitive slave arrested and jailed in Boston prompted a sermon by Pennington that was to become one of his most widely read pieces. George Latimer had run away from Norfolk, Virginia, and had been jailed in October 1842. A mass

48. Herman E. Thomas, "An Analysis of the Life and Work of James W. C. Pennington, A Black Churchman and Abolitionist" (Ph.D. dissertation, Hartford Seminary Foundation, 1978), 237; *Charter Oak,* July, 1842.

49. Because there had been no legislation, as there had in New York State's abolition of the Nine Months Law, nor any judicial decision defining the status of slaves brought into the state temporarily, the matter was referred to Connecticut's high court.

50. *Life of James Mars, a Slave Born and Sold in Connecticut, Written by Himself* (Hartford, 1864; rpr. in *Five Black Lives: The Autobiographies of Venture Smith, James Mars, William Grimes, the Rev. G. W. Offley, James L. Smith* [Middletown, Conn., 1971]), 55f.

meeting had been held in Faneuil Hall, and the Latimer Committee was chosen to promote two mammoth petitions—one to the state and one to Congress—seeking legislation to disaffiliate Massachusetts from the practice of apprehending and jailing fugitive slaves. On Thanksgiving Day Pennington preached to his congregation the serman entitled "Covenants Involving Moral Wrong Are Not Obligatory upon Man." He had kept secret from the members of his church, and even from his wife, the fact that he was himself a fugitive slave. Only the preacher knew that his sermon spoke to his own situation as well as to Latimer's.

The text for Pennington's sermon was from Isaiah: "And your covenant with death shall be annulled, and your agreement with Hell shall not stand."[51] Pennington declared void that section of the federal Constitution requiring the turning over of an escaped slave to the person legally holding that person "to service or labor" in another state. Collusion with slave capture, declared the Talcott Street church's minister, is wrong. Such collusion not only violates the affirmation in the Declaration of Independence of freedom as the inalienable right of human beings but also violates the overall design and spirit of the Constitution itself—that is, "to form a more perfect union," "to establish justice," "to ensure domestic tranquility," and "to promote the general welfare." Pennington closed his sermon by quoting Latimer's owner, who, while waiting to take his former slave back to Virginia, said that there he would "*kill him by inches*." From February 24, 1843, into June of that year, the *Christian Freeman,* the weekly paper issued by the Connecticut Anti-Slavery Society, ran a prominent advertisement for Pennington's sermon, now available as a printed pamphlet. (It had been published in Hartford in 1842.)

In the spring of 1843 the Connecticut Anti-Slavery Society endorsed Pennington in a more substantial fashion by choosing him as its delegate to the second world antislavery convention, to be held in London in June of that year. The state society was exuberant over the worth of its representative and "the opportunity which it afford[s] of bearing our public testimony against the sinful prejudice that half enslaves the colored man at the North." When Pennington left Hartford in early May, he carried several other endorsements, one from a large meeting of blacks in Troy chaired by Garnet, one from a similar gathering in Hartford chaired by Deacon James Mars, and one from the Union Missionary Society. Finally, Pennington went as a delegate of the American Peace Society to the

51. Isa. 28:18, mistakenly identified in the published sermon as Isa. 28:8.

General Peace Convention, to be held in London shortly after the antislavery meeting. In spite of all these attestations, when the Hartford minister boarded the train in New Haven on his way to sailing from New York City, he was just another black man forced to ride in the baggage car—"a little dirty dark carriage," as he later described it.[52]

At the London antislavery convention Pennington joined a number of well-known white Americans in trying to describe, especially for English Evangelical abolitionists, the continuing strength of southern American slave power, the momentum of American abolitionism, and the virulence of northern race prejudice. A lengthy summary of Pennington's main speech was published in the London *Anti-Slavery Reporter.* It dealt primarily not with slaves but with free people of color in America, their ill-treatment, and their achievements. He did not dwell on the cruelties of American slavery, because he was not yet ready to reveal that he was a fugitive slave. Pennington instead described some of the crude phrases and ditties about Jim Crow or "the nigger" used by racist whites. He gave details on the Negro pew in white churches and declared that there was "no intercourse" between white clergy of the Presbyterian, Baptist, Congregational, and Episcopal denominations and black ministers. Finally, he cited the bar in many states against blacks' voting and their prejudicial treatment in the lower courts.

Pennington also described for the London convention the encouraging side of free blacks' life in such cities as Washington, Boston, and Cincinnati. He dwelt on black churches, schools, and libraries and proved, according to the *Anti-Slavery Reporter*'s correspondent, that Afro-Americans' conduct and desire for advancement were on a par with those of American whites. As a parting shot Pennington could not resist citing, as examples of the literature produced by the colored race, his own *Text Book of the Origin . . . of the Colored People* and *Covenants Involving Moral Wrong.*[53]

In response to Pennington's speech, a convention committee recommended sending an address to all religious bodies in the United States "earnestly and affectionately entreating them to lay aside those unlovely and unchristian prejudices which have been so long entertained." But Pennington found a more effective weapon against what angered him

52. *Christian Freeman,* May 5, 12, June 8, 1843; Davies, *American Scenes,* 268; Leeds *Mercury,* August 5, 1843 (Microfilm copy in Carter and Ripley [eds.], *BAP,* reel 4, item 624).

53. *Anti-Slavery Reporter,* June 21, 1843 (Microfilm copy in Carter and Ripley [eds.], *BAP,* reel 4, item 586).

most in his treatment by whites in Connecticut. Shortly before the world antislavery convention, on invitation from the minister of London's Surrey Chapel, he attended the chapel and shared with its minister in the distribution of the communion elements to the large congregation. The following evening, according to a report to the London *Patriot,* he delivered to the church members "a simple but scriptural and earnest address." He made clear that what he had just experienced, joining with whites "at the table of the Lord, without being the marked and despised brother," was possible in America if he went to a Roman Catholic or Unitarian church, but not in an Episcopal, Presbyterian, Methodist, Congregational, or Baptist church. There was an outpouring of sympathy from the Surrey congregants, and fervent prayer was offered that soon "this blot might be removed from the fair name of American Christians" and that their treatment of blacks might cease to violate "the very charter of their independence."[54]

Surrey Chapel's minister, seeking to show American clergy a better way, invited Pennington to preach in his place the following Sunday. The sermon was reported as having been "admirable." The text was pertinent to Pennington's situation in the United States: "Behold, I stand at the door and knock." Early in July, when the antislavery convention was over, the members of Surrey Chapel invited Pennington to a tea attended by over five hundred people. The Hartford minister was presented with an elegantly bound volume of biblical commentaries and a letter signed by the pastor, the elders, and nearly six hundred members of Surrey Chapel. The letter welcomed Pennington to England and to this church and then spelled out a long list of indignities that the signers grieved that he and other estimable blacks had suffered in America: being shut out from white ministers' pulpits; partaking of communion only "under circumstances of marked indignity"; barred, no matter what their mental capacities, from major universities; and similar exclusions "in all the [other] social and civil intercourses of life." What most astonished those at Surrey Chapel was that even the white ministers who had ordained Pennington and written letters commending him to British church people would not invite him to share a pulpit with them.[55]

Pennington spoke on many other occasions during his summer in England. His largest audience was probably the three thousand at the meeting of the British and Foreign Anti-Slavery Society in late June. Here he

54. *London Patriot,* August 3, 1843, reprinted in *Christian Freeman,* September 14, 1843.
55. *Ibid.*

focused especially on what he viewed as a reprehensible move by the English government, which had recently approved a scheme to increase emigration from Africa to the West Indies. Pennington saw this as likely to end in the virtual enslavement of the African laborers. He pleaded that Africans be left in Africa, where they were free to develop the enormously rich resources of their own continent. This concern that particularly the interior of Africa remain free of exploitation by European nations would remain with Pennington for the next fifteen years, and in this he would stand side by side with Henry Highland Garnet.[56]

The *Christian Freeman* in Hartford exuberantly reprinted the British release on Surrey Chapel's response to Pennington and his exposé of racism among American clergy. It also happily reported on the Hartford minister's having crossed the Atlantic on the homeward trip in fine style. After initially being refused a stateroom, Pennington was given a berth in a cabin also assigned to a man from Kentucky. The outraged southerner took himself off to sleep on a sofa in the forecabin. Moreover, in spite of southern whites' indignation, Pennington was allowed a regular seat at the ship's dinner table.[57]

The three months in England had been for Pennington a blessed time of being admired, applauded, and sympathized with by group after group of refined whites. He returned to Connecticut with new energy for the old battle. First he, his wife Harriet, James Mars, Henry Foster, and many other members of the Talcott Street church sent a grateful letter to the ministers, elders, and members of Surrey Chapel in London. They thanked the English congregation for its sympathy with the trials of free blacks in America. They spelled out again, and more specifically, the most flagrant cases of mistreatment: the denial of the vote to blacks in Connecticut, even in the matter of choosing a village schoolmaster, and the virtually total exclusion of Pennington from the pulpits of whites, even the pulpits of the four other Congregational churches in Hartford.[58]

Three months after Pennington's return from England, the Talcott Street church took an important step. Formally implementing the conviction of most black clergy and of many white clergy in Great Britain

56. *Anti-Slavery Reporter,* June 28, 1843 (Microfilm copy in Carter and Ripley [eds.], *BAP,* reel 4, item 592); *Christian Freeman,* August 3, 1843; *Nonconformist,* June 28, 1843, *Emancipator,* October 26, 1843, Leeds *Mercury,* August 5, 1843 (Microfilm copy of all in Carter and Ripley [eds.], *BAP,* reel 4, items 590f., 686, 624).

57. *Christian Freeman,* September 7, 1843; Blackett, *Beating Against the Barriers,* 28.

58. Letter of August 29, 1843, in *London Patriot,* October 2, 1843 (Microfilm copy in Carter and Ripley [eds.], *BAP,* reel 4, item 674).

that serious Christians, lay or clerical, had no business compromising with slaveholding, this black Congregational church banned any and every slaveholder. Such people were to be barred from its pulpit, from its communion services, and even from its pews.[59] This action by Pennington's church was not entirely symbolic. Southern slaveholders, themselves church members, often visited the North, and not a few had an interest in free black churches. One such person had gone with Lewis Tappan to worship at Theodore Wright's church in New York City.

Shortly before this edict, Pennington spoke more bluntly than ever before to white abolitionist Christians about their racist attitudes. This memorable explosion occurred at a large gathering of Connecticut abolitionist ministers and church members in Middletown. Asked to report on his trip to the London convention, Pennington said directly to these Americans what he had said in England about his treatment during his eight years in the ministry. He reluctantly concluded that he was virtually excommunicated: "I have labored hard to inform myself—I have tried to make myself useful and agreeable as a Christian—have tried to avoid everything wrong. . . . Though we [black Christians] have felt ourselves abused, we have not dared to indulge unkind feelings toward our brethren. You have helped us to build small schoolhouses and churches, or rather helped us to shoulder a debt, many times." Pennington started to check his assault, sensing that he was straying from his long-cultivated practice of Christian patience. But he went on: "I may as well speak out my convictions—it [the assistance in building black schools and churches] is done in the spirit of colonization, to get us out of the way."[60]

Even white abolitionists, Pennington insisted, as Theodore Wright had some years earlier, were infected with prejudice: "How often, in coming into a congregation like this, have I been treated with indignity. A man accidentally takes his seat by my side—he discovers that I have a dark face—he rises in contempt and leaves the slip. It is said colored people are fond of sitting together. It is such treatment as this which drives them together." Pennington went on to deplore separate black churches as a tragic necessity that meant many churches with incompetent and ill-prepared black teachers and preachers. Moreover, the necessity of manning pulpits in black churches robbed Africa of many who might have gone there as missionaries. Africa's redemption had been put back fifty years. In a final, anguished cry Pennington declared, "For years

59. Report of meeting on November 20, 1843, in *Christian Freeman*, January 11, 1844.
60. *Christian Freeman*, October 26, November 2, 1843.

I have not been able to go into the pulpit—to the communion table, or to the mercy seat, but as a complainant. Talk of peace! *There can be no peace till we are righted*. It is contrary to the law of Christian discipline, which is, *first* PURE, then *peaceable*."[61]

Pennington concluded his indictment by citing the radically different behavior of the Christians of England, Ireland, and Belgium whom he had recently met in England. He had occupied a dozen or more pulpits in or near London and had to decline invitations to as many more. He attended many "select parties among the middle classes." He traveled on railroads and went into coffeehouses. And, though he had looked hard for it, he had found no sign of color prejudice.[62]

The Middletown convention took no action in response to Pennington's rebukes, yet changes in white ministers' treatment of him did appear in the following months. The primary Congregational institution linking individual clergy with one another in meetings every month or two was the association. While Pennington was in England, the large Hartford North Association approved the formation of a new association, Hartford Central, made up of about a dozen of the old association's ministers. The able young minister of North Congregational Church, Horace Bushnell—later to be attacked by Amos Beman for his racism—was chosen moderator of Hartford Central at its first meeting. At the new association's third meeting, in early December 1843, Pennington was admitted as a member of this association "from an Association in New York."[63]

At association meetings there was discussion of topics of professional interest to those present. Not infrequently one of the members would present a skeleton of a sermon, a more or less detailed outline of a sermon he had preached or planned to preach on a given text. At the meeting at which Pennington was received into the association, he and two others were deputed to present skeletons of sermons at the next meeting, to be held February 6, 1844, in West Avon, not far from Hartford. As arranged, Pennington presented his sermon outline. Even more important, on the following Sunday Pennington preached in the Farmington Congregational Church at the invitation of the Rev. Noah Porter, D.D., who preached the same Sunday at the Talcott Street church. Porter had been

61. *Christian Freeman,* November 2, 1843.

62. *Ibid.*

63. Congregational Church, "Records of the Hartford Central Association . . ." (Connecticut Conference of the United Church of Christ Archives, Hartford).

the president of the Middletown antislavery convention the previous October, at which Pennington berated white churches for having virtually excommunicated him and his fellows. By the following September Pennington could report to his distinguished British abolitionist correspondent Thomas Clarkson that he had exchanged pulpits with ten or twelve white ministers at their invitation.[64]

Hungry as Pennington was for ministerial fellowship, he did not find it in any substantial sense with Hartford's white clergy. He attended no meetings of the Central Association between early February 1844 and the end of the year. He attended three meetings in 1845. Much has been made of his being chosen moderator of one of these meetings. Actually, at this meeting all but four ministers were absent, including the moderator. Pennington was chosen to preside. He opened the meeting with prayer, and soon thereafter the little group adjourned. By contrast, Pennington's visits with black ministers in other cities were meat and drink to him. Consider, for instance, his week-long visit with Henry Garnet in Troy. There he explored the black community and assessed its property ownership, its two churches (Garnet's and an AMEZ church), Garnet's weekday school, and the black Young Men's Association Reading Room. He especially enjoyed living with Garnet's family and having long talks with Garnet himself. "From time immemorial," Pennington wrote, "educated men have sought and prized conversation with each other."[65]

Pennington's week in Troy was part of a larger pattern. He visited the sizable black communities in nearby Schenectady and Albany, where he attended a large antislavery convention and renewed his friendships with Lewis Tappan, Joshua Leavitt, and Gerrit Smith. He returned to Hartford by way of the black communities in Pittsfield, Lenox, and Springfield, Massachusetts. And he urged other black ministers to broaden their views by breaking away from local parish duties to visit other communities.[66]

Pennington viewed his own role as distinctive among American black

64. *Christian Freeman,* February 15, 1844; James Pennington to Thomas Clarkson, A.L.S. in Anthony Family Collection, Henry E. Huntington Library, San Marino, Calif. (Microfilm copy in Carter and Ripley [eds.], *BAP,* reel 4, item 922). One of the white ministers who preached at Talcott Street described it as "a decent congregation," and one of the members of a white church where Pennington preached commented that the congregation had "survived" the shock. White, unpublished version of "The Fugitive Blacksmith of Hartford," 9f.

65. James Pennington to the sub-editor of his own *Clarksonian,* December 14, 1844, in Amos Beman Scrap Book (Amos G. Beman Papers).

66. James Pennington to Thomas Clarkson, December 14, 1844, in Carter and Ripley (eds.), *BAP,* reel 4, item 966.

clergy. In 1843 in England he had been the only clerical spokesman for free blacks in America, and now, after his return to the United States, he aimed likewise to speak for them. In early November 1843 he had published a sample issue of the *Clarksonian,* hoping that its semimonthly appearance might replace the *Colored American.* Named after the grand old man of British abolitionism, this paper was warmly endorsed by Hartford's *Christian Freeman.* However, the journal never secured a solid footing in spite of substantial contributions by Beman and Garnet. After about a year of irregular appearances the *Clarksonian* ceased publication, underlining again how distinctive the *Colored American* had been in its vigorous and regular weekly appearances for almost five years.

By 1845 Pennington was growing restless. James Polk's election to the presidency the previous fall seemed to be tilting the balance toward the annexation of Texas. The Whig defeat in New York State meant a setback in the campaign for the reenfranchisement of New York blacks. Liberty party strength in Connecticut continued to hover at only two thousand votes, which were hardly enough to secure the franchise for blacks in that state. Indeed, there was a movement afoot in the Connecticut legislature to exempt blacks from property taxes, thus removing leverage for the black vote based on the principle of "no taxation without representation." Pennington had editorialized against this proposed law.[67] On the personal front, perhaps because of close association with the college graduate Henry Garnet and extensive conversation with educated Englishmen in 1843, Pennington was chafing at his own lack of higher education. His verbal agility and distinct success as a preacher and public speaker in America and England did not prevent his continuing frustration over that great lack of general knowledge, which he would identify in his autobiography as the fearful cost of enslavement that had lasted into his adult years.

Pennington was anxious as well as restless. He had recurring nightmares about being discovered and recaptured by his former owner. Although he had kept his fugitive slave status a secret from everyone in Connecticut, he had written in 1844 of his Maryland origins to his British Quaker friend Joseph Sturge. The London-based *Anti-Slavery Reporter* published the information, not realizing that it might inform James Tilghman, Pennington's owner, as to James Pembroke's present whereabouts. About this time Pennington learned from an Underground Railroad passenger that Tilghman had fallen upon hard times and was about to sell

67. *Northern Star* and *Clarksonian,* reprinted in *Christian Freeman,* August 1, 1844.

those members of the Pembroke family whom he still owned. Pennington shared his secret with John Hooker, a Farmington lawyer, and deputed Hooker to approach Tilghman about the possibility of purchasing Pennington and his parents. Tilghman wrote back demanding $550 for the 1827 runaway but making no mention of the parents, perhaps because neither was any longer on his plantation. In the meantime Pennington had sold his precious collection of four hundred books to secure some of the funds needed to make these purchases. However, he was unwilling to complete any transaction that did not include his parents, and negotiations broke down. A definite possibility remained, however, that Tilghman would send a slave catcher to Hartford.[68]

In August 1845, Pennington formally requested of his church a two-year leave of absence without pay, to start November 1. His official reason was "to spend two years in classical studies." His church members granted his request. On November 2 he preached "A Two Years' Absence, or a Farewell Sermon . . ." (published later that year in Hartford). Before his final Sunday, Pennington addressed to his people a letter giving in more detail his reasons for taking this leave. For the first time, he divulged to his church the fact that he was a fugitive slave. Now he could explain that his first objective was "to relieve [himself] from that increasingly unhappy situation." For practical reasons he did not say where he intended to be in the near future. He was assured by loyal parishioners that he need not fear recapture in Hartford. He replied that he knew that if he wanted to buy himself, he could secure $1,000 within the city limits in twenty-four hours. And if he wanted physical protection, he said, he "could raise ten thousand of the truest hearted and hardest handed men in Connecticut." However, he did not see himself as suited for the role of George Latimer in Boston. After the furor referred to earlier, Latimer's owner had accepted $400 for the man's release.

Pennington's second objective, he told his congregation, was higher education. He believed that colleges were now more open to black entrants than when he had escaped from slavery. He said. "I am still a young man. Our part of this nation is yet in its elements, to be moulded. *And the last half of the present century will be our great moral battle day.* I GO TO PREPARE FOR THAT."[69]

68. Pennington, *The Fugitive Blacksmith,* 61–64; John Hooker, *Some Reminiscences of a Long Life* (Hartford, 1899), 39f.; Blackett, *Beating Against the Barriers,* 32.

69. James W. C. Pennington, *A Two Years' Absence, or a Farewell Sermon, Preached in the Fifth Congregational Church by J. W. C. Pennington, November 2d, 1845* (Hartford, 1845), 3–8.

The core of Pennington's farewell sermon was the testimony of a biblical Christian who had been a slave and was constantly encountering white Christians who defended slavery by noting that it was an accepted part of Hebrew and early Christian society. "Is the word of God silent on this . . . greatest of . . . curses?" he asked. "I, for one, desire to know. My repentance, my faith, my hope, my love, and my perseverance all . . . turn upon this point. . . . If the word of God does sanction slavery, I want another book, another repentance, another faith, and another hope!" Pennington did not leave this question hanging. He insisted that "slavery is condemned by the general tenor and scope of the New Testament," which does not sanction cruelty or the imprisonment, starvation, or torture of other human beings. At the end of his sermon Pennington addressed self-avowed Christians involved in slave owning: "O do let the past days of your bloody doings suffice; slacken your hands, let us go that we may make friendship, and do a little for the glory of God before the day of account comes with us both."[70]

A warm letter that Pennington received from the Hartford Central Association testified that he was a member of the association in good standing and affectionately recommended him "to the sympathy and fellowship of the people of God, wherever Providence shall cast his lot." However, these white ministers never really fought the moral travesty that so agonized Pennington. The only time the association considered slavery in its meetings between 1843 and 1845 was at this final gathering before Pennington's departure. A presentation was made on the compatibility between slaveholding and membership in a Christian church. The matter was discussed at length, but no vote on the question was taken.[71]

In hardly any respect did Pennington's leave of absence work out as he had hoped. He secured neither college education nor his freedom. The Oneida Institute, where Beman had spent one year and Garnet four, had been harassed out of existence the previous year because of the radical abolitionism of its president, Beriah Green, and because of its practice of regularly admitting black students. Pennington considered applying to Dartmouth College on the basis of the favorable experience there of the young black man Augustus Washington, who had been hired to take Pennington's place as teacher of the North African School. Although financial pressures had forced Washington to abandon college, he testified

70. *Ibid.*, 22–38.

71. Congregational Church, "Records of the Hartford Central Association . . ." (Connecticut Conference of the United Church of Christ Archives, Hartford).

that he had experienced no prejudice against him on the part of the Dartmouth faculty or students, or of residents of the village of Hanover, New Hampshire.[72]

Before Pennington sent his application to Dartmouth, however, he saw a recent letter from the president of the college to the governor of Vermont on the college's policy in admitting blacks. Resolved to follow the Christian policy of accepting a few, the president was nevertheless nervous about taking in more black students. Of the three whom the college had admitted, one (Thomas Paul) had graduated with honor, and the other two (one of whom was Washington) had failed "from fickleness, inconstancy and unmorality": "We doubt the fitness of Africans, in their present state of civilization, for the grave and considerate pursuit of students. . . . Now and then there may be a successful instance. But they will need cultivation as a people for centuries, before many of them will hold their way with long civilized and Christian Saxons, if, indeed, that is ever to be expected, which I doubt." Pennington saw the odds stacked against him by prejudice if he should apply and be accepted at the New Hampshire college. Already in his late thirties and with limited time available, he doubted the wisdom of undertaking the mission of proving false the negative expectations of Dartmouth's president. After all, wrote the black minister to a sympathetic white friend in Connecticut, "I am the third generation from native 'Mandingo,' with a little touch of the royal blood of that tribe of Africans."[73]

Instead of going to Dartmouth, Pennington sailed to Jamaica as a representative of the Union Missionary Society. So fearful was he of recapture as a fugitive slave that he shared his plans only with officers of the society. Neither his wife nor his close friends in Hartford knew where he was going. That Pennington's fears were not unwarranted is suggested by Frederick Douglass's experience. When he was in the British Isles from 1845 to 1847, his owner and other slaveholders publicly threatened to apprehend him when he returned to the United States.[74]

During some seven months in Jamaica, Pennington was especially useful to British missionaries to the recently freed slaves on the island, indigenous black leaders, and American missionaries at various rural sta-

72. Augustus Washington to Theodore Wright (his former pastor), from Hartford, January 15, 1846, in Amos Beman Scrap Book (Amos G. Beman Papers), I, 60f.

73. *Christian Freeman,* December 18, 1845.

74. Lewis Tappan to James Pennington, June 16, 1846, A.L.S. in Lewis Tappan Papers (Microfilm copy in Carter and Ripley [eds.], *BAP,* reel 5, item 242); *Charter Oak,* May 21, 1846 (reprint of article in *Liberator*).

tions. West Indian black leaders were avid for help from the United States in setting up training programs for black teachers and ministers.[75]

Pennington hoped that by publicizing his dilemma as an escaped slave, as well as by undertaking his evangelical and educational mission in Jamaica, he could secure the additional funds needed to purchase his own and his parents' freedom. Donations were made for his mission work and his personal needs. It later became evident, however, that he had failed to keep a record of how much had been given by whom for what purpose, both during his time in Jamaica and during his later travels in Great Britain. This carelessness was a major factor in his getting the reputation with white abolitionists, especially Lewis Tappan, of not being trustworthy. However, such lack of scrupulous bookkeeping by overseas fund-raisers, both black and white, was not that unusual.

Pennington's work in Jamaica was cut short by the death of his wife, Harriet, in early June 1846. As soon as word reached him, he returned to the United States. Notwithstanding, he followed through with his two-year leave from his church and spent much of the following sixteen months in "classical studies," as he had told his congregation he would. He abandoned the idea of formal instruction and pursued his work on his own, perhaps with some suggestions from fellow clergy.[76]

Pennington was also intensely involved in furthering slave escapes. He wrote to a British friend, "I keep here one of the prominent depots of the great Underground R.R." He reported that he was receiving an average of two fugitives a day. On a recent Thursday morning his doorbell had rung at six o'clock, and four "fine sturdy men" came into his sitting room with a letter from the corresponding secretary of the New York Vigilance Committee. They were part of a lot of twenty-five who had recently arrived in New York City. Two days later Pennington received a father, a mother, and five children, the oldest a seventeen-year-old daughter. Some of these fugitives settled near Hartford. Others were sent into Massachusetts and on to Canada: "It requires much care and labor to make them comfortable as they generally come to us destitute." Penning-

75. James Pennington to *Union Missionary,* from Kingston, February 10, 12, 1846, both in *Union Missionary,* May, June, 1846 (Microfilm copy in Carter and Ripley [eds.], *BAP,* reel 5, items 216, 235).

76. James Pennington to Mr. Soul (an associate of John Scoble, secretary of the British and Foreign Anti-Slavery Society), November 17, 1847, A.L.S. in Rhodes House, Department of Manuscripts, Oxford, England, Mss. British Empire C159/194 (Microfilm copy in Carter and Ripley [eds.], *BAP,* reel 4, item 296).

ton exulted in this stream of escapees, seeing it as a safety valve: "I know from experience, that those spirits that fly, if they could not do that would do worse. Desperation would seize upon the mass."[77]

The slaves especially on Pennington's mind were his parents and siblings. It is known that his brother Stephen escaped to New York a decade later, but otherwise knowledge of the family's circumstances is sketchy. The Hartford minister's part in their movements after the Tilghman slaveholdings were dispersed remains obscure. Three of Pennington's brothers were sold nearby. His mother and a sister were sold to Missouri. Pennington's sister and father escaped to Canada. Still another brother made his way, as Pennington had, to freedom in Pennsylvania. Pennington was later accused of having secured contributions in Jamaica to buy his parents' freedom but never confirming the use of those funds for their advertised purpose. Some of his vagueness had been prompted by prudence: "The means I had acquired by the contributions of kind friends to redeem myself, I laid by, in case the worst should come; and that designed for the purchase of my parents, I used in another kind of operation, as the result of which, my father and two brothers are now in Canada."[78]

After the death of Theodore Wright in March 1847, the First Colored Presbyterian Church of New York City offered its pastorate to Pennington. He declined, feeling an obligation to return to the Talcott Street church, now renamed the Fifth Congregational, in November 1847 because of an understanding between him and his congregation when he was given his two-year leave. The New York church renewed its invitation, and by the spring of 1848 he accepted the post. He was dismissed by the Hartford Central Association and received into New York's Third Presbytery. A farewell tribute to Pennington by Hartford's black teacher Augustus Washington was as much the stereotypical definition of a black activist minister committed to the elevation of his people as it was an actual description of Pennington: "He has ever secured the confidence and respect of the whole community, and has had one of the most orderly, respectable and intelligent audiences that I ever knew. He is a sound theologian, a good self-made scholar, and a gentleman; aside from pastoral duties, actively engaged, heart and hand in temperance, education,

77. *Ibid.*

78. Blackett, *Beating Against the Barriers,* 32; Pennington, *The Fugitive Blacksmith,* 63.

anti-slavery, and all the reforms that tend to improve, refine and elevate society."[79]

Within a month of Pennington's accepting the pastorate of the First Colored Presbyterian Church in New York City, the church building at Frankfort and William streets was sold. The prospective widening of William Street would mean assessments of some $2,400 on the church in the near future. But more important was the fact that a large part of the congregation now lived "in the upper part of the city at a great distance from the present location of the church." The Third Presbytery's committee on the First Colored Presbyterian Church, consulting with that church's trustees and session, sold the downtown building for $14,175. Not long afterward a new church was purchased on Prince Street, north of Canal Street, and in January 1849, at the request of Pennington's congregation, the Third Presbytery approved a name change from the First Colored to the Prince Street Presbyterian.[80]

In moving to New York City, Pennington was undertaking ministry in the largest black Presbyterian church in the country. At the end of Wright's last full year of ministry, it had 413 members. During Pennington's first year, over 40 more members were added. At first glance the move seems now as it must have seemed to Pennington: a shift to a more prestigious position where his abilities and ambition to better himself and serve his people would have wider scope. His new church had more than three times as many members as the one on Talcott Street. Those members included numerous men and women of substance; people of some means; and people who were conspicuous for their services to the black community as Sunday school teachers, contributors of time and money to the vigilance committee, or supporters of black schools, cultural societies, and newspapers. Finally, as has been shown, this church was again and again the place chosen for large gatherings of the city's black people of whatever denomination to protest the colonization movement, to promote support for fugitives, and to deliver antislavery manifestos.

In spite of the promising aspects of the move, however, the shift had a fateful aspect. For five years Pennington had been publicly attacking white denominations for their refusal categorically to disavow slavery and slave owners. However, he was moving from ministry in a denomi-

79. Washington's encomium had appeared first in the *Ram's Horn* and was reprinted in the *North Star,* April 7, 1848. (Pennington had warmly supported Douglass' journal from the time of its birth in 1847.)

80. Minutes of the Third Presbytery of New York, April 5, 1848; January 3, 8, 1849.

nation largely confined to the North, with few members who were actual slave owners, to one that was powerfully represented in southern states. That the First Colored Presbyterian Church belonged to the New School Third Presbytery did not negate the fact that most Presbyterian ministers, like Methodists, hesitated to say flatly that a slave owner could not be a conscientious Christian. Even if the ministers were not slave owners themselves, they had too many clerical associates, if not friends, whose congregations included seemingly upstanding church members who did own slaves.

The fatefulness of Pennington's move is highlighted by the fact that Garnet was leading his Liberty Street Presbyterian Church in Troy out of Presbyterianism just as Pennington was becoming pastor of the most conspicuous black church in the denomination. It is not known whether the two had talked over these matters. The final irony unfolded eight years later, when Pennington, after years of being maligned by certain white and black abolitionists for remaining a minister in a denomination so conspicuously in collusion with the slave system, resigned his Prince Street pastorate. His successor would be none other than Garnet.

Another storm signal was thrown up in the spring of 1848: personal criticism by Lewis Tappan and eventually by other white abolitionists close to him. How justified this criticism was remains unclear to this day. As has been described, Tappan and Pennington worked together closely in the Union Missionary Society, as well as the executive committees of the American Missionary Association and the American and Foreign Anti-Slavery Society. With the AFASS they both stood foursquare behind the Liberty party as late as the summer of 1848. It was only natural, then, that when Pennington found himself in financial difficulty in 1844, undoubtedly stretched to the limit by the needs of fugitive slaves, he asked Tappan for a short-term loan. Tappan had no funds with which to respond. Roughly eighteen months later, at the time of Pennington's return from Jamaica, Tappan's letter of condolence over the death of Harriet Pennington was largely devoted to passing on someone else's criticism of Pennington on two scores: for having written from England in 1843 that he was about to receive an honorary degree, which was never awarded, and for going off to Jamaica in late 1845 without telling his congregation or wife of his destination.[81] (As indicated earlier, there had been valid reasons for this secretiveness.)

81. The story had been circulated, with no clear evidence that Pennington had had anything to do with it, that he was receiving a doctor of divinity degree from a Surry

Tappan's strongest warning to date was sent in March 1848. Although Pennington had just arrived in New York City and would not leave for England for over a year, he was already planning his return to the British Isles. Tappan was exasperated by Pennington's vagueness in defining the purpose of the trip. He described Pennington's movements in going to Jamaica as surreptitious and said they were equally so now in speaking of going "for the objects as usual." Was it not the case, asked Tappan, that Pennington intended to raise needed funds in England? "If so, dear brother," Tappan wrote, "is it not best to open the subject to your friends & co-laborers here that, in their correspondence with English friends, they may speak of you and your plans unambiguously?"[82] White Evangelical philanthropists such as Tappan could raise money more easily in the United States in the 1840s and 1850s than could blacks. This fact tended to twist Tappan's relationship with Pennington into the same pattern evident in white presbyteries' and Congregational associations' control over, as well as support of, black clergy.

Pennington did not make his second trip to England until the late spring of 1849, and it is doubtful that Tappan ever received the clearly defined statement of intent he asked for. Pennington apparently went for a number of reasons: to attend the World Peace Conference in Paris in the summer of 1849, to intensify British criticism of American slavery and promote the Free Produce Movement, to escape the increasing threat of recapture that was hanging over the heads of well-known and aggressive fugitive slaves, and to raise money for several causes. He stayed in the British Isles for two years, being joined there by Garnet in 1850.

The 1850s were to be a difficult and demanding time for Afro-American leaders. Pennington, Garnet, and Beman all faced trauma in their family lives and serious criticisms from some of their parishioners. For blacks all over the North, political developments were discouraging until the last years of the decade. Congressional legislation facilitated the recovery of fugitive slaves by their owners and opened western territories to the slave system. In New York and Connecticut renewed statewide efforts to se-

University. When Pennington returned to Hartford and heard this rumor, he wrote the *Christian Freeman* to indicate that the story was false—indeed, that there was no Surry University (*Christian Freeman,* August 10, 31, 1843). This paper was still refuting the false report a year later.

82. Lewis Tappan to James Pennington, March 25, 1848, in Lewis Tappan Papers (Microfilm copy in Carter and Ripley [eds.], *BAP,* reel 5, item 603).

cure the vote for all adult black males failed. However, the growing sectional polarization in the country offered discerning blacks glimpses of a crisis that might bring an end to American slavery. Within the personal and racial setbacks of these years, Pennington would see clearly and state memorably the special destiny of Afro-Americans.

10. STRUGGLES, DEFEATS, AND FRESH TASKS IN THE EARLY 1850s

The 1850s was a decade to try the souls of Afro-American activists—bitterly so for the ones who were former slaves. To be sure, early in the decade James Pennington was remarkably sanguine about his own situation. He wrote Harriet Beecher Stowe in 1852: "My European tour was certainly useful, because there the trial was fair and honorable. . . . I got what was due to man. . . . I put myself into the harness, and wrought manfully in the first pulpits, and the platforms, in peace congresses, conventions . . . etc.; and in these exercises that rusty old iron came out of my soul, and went 'clean away.'" Pennington was confident that he had finally won out over feelings of being inferior because he was black. Within a few years, however, victory turned into defeat in his personal life. His reputation was besmirched, and he lost his church. Yet by the end of the decade he was able to make the following optimistic statement in an article in the *Anglo-American Magazine:* "To anyone who looks at the course of events in the history of the colored people in this country for the last twenty or thirty years, it will be obvious that every attempt of our oppressors to swallow us up, has ended in their defeat."[1] What an astonishing affirmation of Afro-American triumph over American racism! A careful look at the efforts, the setbacks, and the resilience of activ-

1. James Pennington to Harriet Beecher Stowe, November 30, 1852, in Stowe, *A Key to Uncle Tom's Cabin; . . . Corroborative Statements Verify the Truth of the Work* (Boston, 1853), 51f.; James W. C. Pennington, "The Self-Redeeming Power of the Colored Races of the World," *Anglo-African Magazine,* I (1859), 316.

ist black clergy during these ten years helps in evaluating Pennington's brave statement in 1859.

In the 1850s two pieces of national legislation and a Supreme Court decision all strengthened the position of slave owners and southern political leaders. The Fugitive Slave Act of 1850, as already noted, facilitated slave owners' recovery of runaway slaves in the northern states. The Kansas-Nebraska Act of 1854 repealed the Missouri Compromise and opened the way for the expansion of slave owning into the western territories. And the Dred Scott decision by the United States Supreme Court in 1857 declared that Scott, as a Negro, could not be a citizen of the United States and therefore could not sue in a federal court. Moreover, in spite of major efforts toward constitutional revision in states where blacks were wholly or partially disfranchised, only Rhode Island retreated from its exclusionary clause. Indeed, the dislike of free blacks by many whites with substantial exposure to them in large urban centers such as New York City seemed to have remained as intense as ever.[2]

In claiming the defeat of the blacks' oppressors, Pennington was referring to something more fundamental than the racism evident in Congress and among northern white voters. He was paying tribute to the stubborn determination of Afro-Americans, whether enslaved or ostensibly free, to shape their own destinies in America. The very passage of the 1850 Fugitive Slave Act had been in reaction to the growing tide of slave escapes. But the primary proof cited by Pennington in his 1859 article had to do with free blacks in Maryland, the state where he had been born and raised to adulthood. In 1831 the Maryland legislature had forbidden the freeing of slaves unless they were sent out of the state. It had also supported the American Colonization Society in its program of draining off "troublesome" free blacks by transporting them to Liberia. However, these blacks, by and large, had refused to emigrate. A slaveholders' convention held in Baltimore in 1859 had taken a very different position than the legislature of 1831. It had strenuously protested against current proposals to remove free blacks from the state. The slaveholders declared that such Afro-Americans, now numbering over eighty thousand, were indispensable to the state's agriculture, industry, and urban white households. Rank-and-file American free blacks' insistence on remaining Americans had, at the fundamental level of economic contribution, been validated. Pennington read the Maryland story as a parable in support of his,

2. Field, *Politics of Race,* chap. 4.

Garnet's, Beman's, and Ray's efforts to lead their fellow blacks toward claiming their full rights as Americans.

The Civil War and the Emancipation Proclamation might seem to validate Pennington's interpretation, yet the subsequent century and a quarter would make appallingly clear how tenacious was the destructive energy of American racism. And the course of Pennington's own life after the triumphant trip abroad referred to in his letter to Harriet Beecher Stowe would make bitterly evident that the "rusty old iron" had not, after all, come "clean away" from his soul.

Pennington's, Beman's, Ray's, and Garnet's ministries and efforts toward the elevation of their fellow Afro-Americans took many forms during the 1850s. Much of what they did was an extension of earlier labors. They continued to proclaim the fundamental release and assurance available in the Christian "good news," and they highlighted the special contributions of black churches. They fought against slavery and focused particularly on help for fugitive slaves. And they continued the struggle for civil rights. Each leveled a distinctive challenge against a particular pattern of injustice based on race. Pennington challenged Jim Crow arrangements on New York City's street railways. Beman led a renewed campaign by Connecticut blacks for equality at the polls. Ray, serving as president of the New York Society for the Promotion of Education Among Colored Children, won substantial improvement in New York City's school facilities for black children. Garnet, appalled by the unemployment and underemployment of American blacks, tried to open new opportunities for achievement and Christian service by American blacks in Africa. For all four, pastoral and sociopolitical callings remained intertwined. To express and strengthen what they viewed as their peculiar collective mission, they renewed and expanded the Association of Colored Ministers of Presbyterian and Congregational Churches in the United States. By the end of the decade this body had a score of members.

Philip S. Foner, in the third volume of his *History of Black Americans,* devoted nearly 40 percent of his treatment of the 1850s to the Fugitive Slave Act and blacks' resistance against it. It was here that blacks won their most visible victories against slavery during that decade.[3] The roles of Pennington and Garnet in this life-and-death struggle were more dramatic than those of Beman and Ray. As former slaves, Pennington and

3. Philip S. Foner, *From the Compromise of 1850 to the End of the Civil War* (Westport, 1983), 3–108. Vol. III of Foner, *History of Black Americans;* Pease and Pease, *They Who Would Be Free,* 283f.

Garnet were personally at risk of being kidnapped or arrested, and they could speak about the evils of enslavement with more authority. Both left the United States to carry on their antislavery crusades in the British Isles—Garnet on the eve of the passage of the Fugitive Slave Act and Pennington over a year earlier.

Pennington had a variety of reasons, over and above personal safety, for returning to the British Isles when he took leave of his New York pastorate in 1849. He went with a mandate from the American and Foreign Anti-Slavery Society to undercut growing British support for the American Colonization Society. He hoped to rouse again those receptive congregations and audiences that he had found in 1843 and to reenlist them in the crusade against slavery in the American South and against racism in the American North. Finally, he had in mind specific financial needs likely to awaken British generosity: his own church's outstanding indebtedness for its building on Prince Street, the perennial urgent claims of the New York Vigilance Committee, and his personal need for funds to secure, at long last, his own emancipation.

During his first months in England, Pennington wrote the story of his early life. By July 1850 nearly six thousand copies had been sold. *The Fugitive Blacksmith,* like the *Narrative of the Life of Frederick Douglass, A Slave,* aimed above all to make clear the suffering and brutal destructiveness inherent in the slave system. Each account highlighted the irrepressible urge to learn to read in a man brought up almost totally deprived of schooling. But Pennington's volume had an explicitly Christian emphasis not present in Douglass's. Pennington stressed God's providence: "My object in writing this tract . . . has been to shew the reader the hand of God with a slave." In an appendix that reproduced a letter he had written five years earlier to his still-enslaved parents and siblings, he affirmed the simple belief that God had foreordained slavery. However, he was left with a difficult question that would soon force him to more complex explanations: "God is never straitened. . . . Could he not have made this great and wealthy nation without making its riches to consist in our blood, bones and souls? And could he not also have given the gospel to us without making us slaves?" His final counsel to fellow slaves urged against vengeful anger against slaveholders: "The only harm I wish to slaveholders is, that they may be speedily delivered from the guilt of a sin, which, if not repented of, must bring down the judgment of Almighty God upon their heads."[4]

4. Pennington, *The Fugitive Blacksmith,* 56, 57, 76f. When directly addressing his

Pennington spent the fall of 1849 in northern England; there he preached and lectured on slavery, war, and intemperance. By the end of the year he was in Edinburgh, and there he tried to refute once and for all the slaveholders' contention that the New Testament endorsed slave owning. Slavery was, he declared, a "system of theft," clearly included in First Timothy's condemnation of man stealing. Moreover, the primary biblical justification of slavery referred to by both southern and northern clergy and laity, Paul's letter to Philemon, depended, Pennington insisted, on a gross misreading. The man whom Paul had urged in that letter to return to his master was no slave, but was instead a free man formerly working in the household of Philemon. In light of these understandings of biblical material, Pennington recommended that American Christian churches having slave owners as members expel these people (perhaps as many as twenty thousand) as "so much dead-weight, so many stumbling blocks in the way of the sincere Christian."[5]

While Pennington was in Edinburgh, word reached the British press that an extraordinary honor had come to him. On December 19 the University of Heidelberg had awarded him an honorary doctor of divinity degree. A member of the Heidelberg theological faculty, Friedrich Carové, had met Pennington at the 1843 General Anti-Slavery Convention in London. Carové had been immensely impressed by the black American's addresses and remarks at this convention. Before returning to the United States from his 1843 trip abroad, Pennington had asked Carové to recommend him for the honorary doctorate. The dean of the theological faculty, in urging the awarding of the degree, acknowledged that it was generally given only in recognition of "scientific achievements," of which there was no evidence in this case; here there was only "the unusually speedy and fortunate development of the intellectual abilities of a man who, until his 20th year was a slave and a laborer and who was driven by burning desire for education and qualification for the office of preacher." The degree was granted with no significant opposition.[6]

"owner" in 1844, Pennington had been fiercely blunt in spelling out the man's brutal sins, but he ended by affirming that if Tilghman would truly repent, Christ's atoning blood could reconcile him to God—and to Pennington. *Ibid.*, 82f.

5. *Christian News,* January 3, 1850; *Nonconformist,* January 2, 1850 (Microfilm copy in Carter and Ripley [eds.], *BAP,* reel 6, items 333, 332).

6. *British Banner,* January 9, 1850 (Microfilm copy in Carter and Ripley [eds.], *BAP,* reel 6, item 338); Herman E. Thomas, "Life and Work of Pennington," App. I, 315f., 327f., 330–39. The conversations between Carové and Pennington in 1843 regarding the possible awarding of an honorary doctorate help illuminate where the false rumor had arisen back in

Pennington was quite aware of the tricky nature of the degree-granting phenomenon. On the eve of his departure for Jamaica in 1845, he had sent a letter to the Hartford *Christian Freeman* to ask why American colleges were awarding doctor of divinity degrees to British abolitionists but not to homegrown ones. What is not clear is whether Pennington remembered the bitter scorn with which Samuel Cornish had editorialized in the *Colored American* on churchmen like Willbur Fisk, president of Wesleyan University, who had been awarded a doctor of divinity degree, in Cornish's view, as a reward for supporting the American Colonization Society and for trying to suppress abolitionism within the Methodist church. Since the University of Heidelberg's theological faculty was Evangelical, since both the American and Foreign Anti-Slavery Society and the British and Foreign Anti-Slavery Society had Evangelical clergy and lay people in seats of power, and since Pennington had just taken a pastorate in a denomination known for its slave-owning membership, it was easy for anticlerical abolitionists to assume that this black minister had been rewarded for some compromise with slave power or with racism comparable to Fisk's several years earlier.[7]

In February 1850 Pennington moved on to Glasgow, where he delivered the most ambitious of all his addresses that have survived. Perhaps inspired by his own recent recognition by the University of Heidelberg, his attack on slavery was here set in the context of a panoramic review of Afro-American achievement. He depicted the epic struggle during the past centuries in America between the descendants of Japheth (the English) and the descendants of Ham (the Africans) carried on in the process of enslavement, survival, and liberation. Of all enslaved peoples down through history, Pennington reminded his audience, only Jews and Negroes had survived, and that had been according to the plan of God. Equally remarkable was the fact that enslaved Afro-Americans were increasing in numbers, in spite of their life spans being shortened by brutal treatment. Most of all, Pennington stressed the struggle of the mind of the enslaved against the mind of the enslaver, which was at every turn trying to subjugate the inborn thinking faculty of his human property. Concrete proof of African mental vitality was the "tide of exits from the

---

the United States that Pennington had been given the degree that year. Indeed, it seems quite possible that Pennington had written someone in America on the basis of overly sanguine expectations. If so, there had been some justification for Lewis Tappan's throwing the matter in Pennington's face in 1846, upon the latter's return from Jamaica.

7. *Christian Freeman,* November 6, 1845; *Colored American,* June 2, 1838.

slave states," perhaps thirty thousand in the previous fifteen years. Citing the herculean efforts of planters to recover runaways, in both the South and the North, Pennington exuberated, "In this great work of self-emancipation, the slave evinces all the great elements of mind out-scheming mind, iron will, penetrating judgment, quick invention, profound insight of human nature, power of endurance, physical and moral courage, and practical knowledge of heavenly bodies."[8]

The second half of the Glasgow lecture documented the barriers overcome by free blacks and the progress won in "popular education, agriculture, commerce, mechanic arts and Christianity." Under Christianity, Pennington emphasized the powerful role being played by independent black churches in America. He also pointed out the vigorous reinforcement of white racism by the American Colonization Society over the previous three decades, and he mentioned the unprecedented mob actions that had tried to convince blacks that they did not belong in America. But his final message showed hope for the black cause. He spoke with euphoria of the elimination of Jim Crow carriages from railroads, of the abolition of the black code in Ohio and Connecticut, of the passage by free states of laws to protect fugitive slaves, and of the opening of colleges to young blacks.[9] Pennington cited the success stories of seven black men as being emblematic of the progress of the race in the United States. They included David Ruggles, water-cure practitioner; James McCune Smith, a doctor trained in medicine in Glasgow who had a large practice among blacks and whites in New York City; Charles Reason, a recently appointed college professor at New York Central College; Rev. Samuel Ringgold Ward, pastor of a white church; Rev. Henry Highland Garnet; an unnammed black minister (Pennington himself) invited to exchange pulpits with distinguished white clergy in Farmington and Hartford, Connecticut; and Frederick Douglass.[10]

Against this backdrop of general and individual Afro-American achievement, Pennington testified to God's role in the past and future of his race. Declaring that blacks had practiced more faithfully than any other people "the true Christian law of *moral power* . . . the law of *for-*

8. James W. C. Pennington, *A Lecture Delivered Before the Glasgow Young Men's Christian Association; and Also Before the St. George's Biblical, Literary and Scientific Institute, London* (Edinburgh, 1850), 1–10.

9. Mabee lists six colleges in New York State that were believed to have accepted black students between 1830 and 1860. Oberlin in Ohio also admitted blacks. Mabee, *Black Education in New York State*, 165f.

10. Pennington, *Lecture Before the Glasgow Young Men's Christian Association*, 11–19.

giveness and endurance of wrong," he declared that God's moral government never had permitted and never would permit to be crushed a minority with justice on its side and adhering to this Christian moral law. "On this grand basis the coloured people of America are safe for their future destiny," he said. "The American oppressor may destroy himself; but destroy the coloured man he never can."[11]

Most of Pennington's preaching and lecturing between February and midsummer 1850 was done in Scotland and in the London area. In August he attended the World Peace Conference in Frankfurt, Germany, along with Henry Highland Garnet, who was newly arrived from the United States. Upon their return to England the two traveled across northern England and Scotland and lectured against American slavery and the Fugitive Slave Act, and for the Free Produce Movement, sometimes together and sometimes apart. Pennington's long-standing interest in promoting the use of free-labor produce had been sharpened by his association with Quaker Joseph Sturge during Pennington's 1843 visit to England and by correspondence thereafter.

Garnet had left the United States in the summer of 1850 in a quite different mood from Pennington's at the time of his departure over a year earlier. Pennington, as has been noted, had taken leave from his church. Garnet, having publicly severed the Presbyterian ties of Troy's Liberty Street Presbyterian Church, and having founded a nonsectarian black community church in western New York State, seemed to have burned most of his ecclesiastical bridges behind him.[12] His official reason for crossing the Atlantic, as noted earlier, was to become the paid agent of the Free Produce movement in Great Britain. Through that movement, he hoped to strike a major blow against American slavery.

Not unrelated to the Free Produce cause was Garnet's developing a more favorable view of selective emigration of blacks out of the United States. Such emigration, whether to the West Indies or to Africa, could swell the free-labor force in warm climes and produce goods to compete with those sent to market by slave owners. Garnet's emigrationism also included a concern for Christian missions in Africa. In this he was at one with the long-standing commitment of Pennington, Wright, and Beman as expressed in the founding of the Union Missionary Society in 1841.

11. *Ibid.*, 20.

12. In actuality, the Troy Presbytery did not drop Garnet's name from its rolls until 1857, when he requested his dismission in order to join New York's Third Presbytery.

Garnet's support of emigration was also linked with the conviction, forcefully stated for years by Cornish, Wright, Ray, and Garnet himself, that urban blacks in America would be better off, materially and morally, if they would move to a rural area and start earning a living from the soil.[13] Finally, Garnet's interest in free blacks' moving away from the United States reflected his own disillusionment with the country.

Although some of Garnet's language after his arrival in Great Britain suggested he wanted to leave the United States for good, his disgust with the country had been, and would remain, paradoxically combined with pride at being an American. An address to the Female Benevolent Society of Troy in 1848 had included a hopeful vision of blacks' future destiny as Afro-Americans. Like Pennington, Garnet had sketched the glories of earlier African cultures, the tragic pilfering of the continent by the slave trade, and the remarkable story of the survival and increase of blacks in America in spite of brutal exploitation and repression by whites. Rejecting the utopian futility of the plan to colonize all American blacks in Africa, he had declared, "We are now colonized. We are planted here. . . . It is too late to make a successful attempt to separate the black and white people in the New World. They love one another too much. . . . *This western world is destined to be filled with a mixed race.*" However, he had also affirmed the glorious future of blacks as such. "The star of our hope is slowly and steadily arising above the horizon. . . . This race shall come forth and re-occupy their station of renown." Finally, he had switched back to a pledge of allegiance to the United States: "America is my home, my country, and I have no other. . . . I love every inch of soil which my feet pressed in their youth, and I mourn because the accursed shade of slavery rests upon it. I love my country's flag, and I hope that soon it will be cleansed of its stains, and be hailed by all nations as the emblem of freedom and independence."[14]

A year later, in a careful letter to his cousin Samuel Ringgold Ward, Garnet admitted that he had grown more favorable toward colonization in Liberia. This did not mean that he had turned his back on the long and often discouraging struggle of American blacks for enfranchisement and other rights, but that he now viewed Liberia as having a future role bene-

13. For example, see "Proceedings of the National Convention of Colored People, . . . Troy, N.Y., . . . October 1847," in Bell (ed.), *Minutes of the National Negro Conventions,* 13.

14. Henry Highland Garnet, *The Past and Present Condition, and the Destiny, of the Colored Race: A Discourse Delivered at the Fifteenth Anniversary, of the Female Benevolent Society of Troy N.Y., Feb. 14, 1848* (Troy, N.Y., 1848), 6–9, 11–15, 24–29.

ficial to Africa. Like Paul Cuffe some forty years earlier, he saw the success of this republic as helping to destroy the slave trade "by turning the attention of the black [African] traders to some other and honorable business." He looked hopefully toward Liberia's developing solid commercial and political ties with European countries, and he believed that this development could do much "to create respect for our race throughout the civilized world."[15] Garnet endorsed colonization "in any part of the United States, Mexico or California, or in the West Indies or Africa, wherever it promises freedom and enfranchisement." Especially Garnet urged any black sincerely convinced "that he can never grow to the stature of a man in this country . . . to go . . . immediately. If he remains here, he will contaminate . . . every one of his brethren over whom he has any influence." At the moment, Garnet added, he personally was not so pessimistic. Nevertheless, his mind was open toward Africa as never before: "There is work enough for me here, and if I were in Africa there would be work for me also there."[16]

Garnet's recommending voluntary emigration by American blacks meant a sharpening of controversy between him and Frederick Douglass. Their differences of conviction and their rivalry were substantial and, although there were times of rapprochement, would last through the 1850s. As discussed earlier, Douglass's was the initial and eloquent voice in opposition to Garnet's "Address to the Slaves," delivered to the 1843 national black convention in Buffalo. To be sure, two years after the Buffalo confrontation Douglass had given Garnet a remarkable tribute. In a major address in Ireland, the former, whose father was a white slave owner, had declared, "It has been said that it is none but those persons who have a mixture of European blood who distinguish themselves. This is not true. I know that the most intellectual and moral colored man that is now in our country is a man in whose veins no European blood courses—'tis the Rev. Mr. Garret [Garnet]."[17] There were, however, deep springs of antagonism between the two men. One of these was their

15. Joel Schor makes a convincing case for Garnet's being an influential forerunner of the shift by a number of black leaders in the 1850s toward a more favorable view of emigration—to Africa and elsewhere. Garnet's role in this shift paralleled his having led the way in the early 1840s toward a more positive view of civil disobedience, as well as of slave violence if need be. Schor, *Henry Highland Garnet,* 110, 150.

16. Henry Garnet to Samuel Ringgold Ward, from Geneva, February 10, 1849, in Douglass' *North Star,* March 2, 1849, reprinted from Ward's *Impartial Citizen.*

17. John W. Blassingame (ed.), *The Frederick Douglass Papers,* Vol. I of Ser. 1 (New Haven, 1979), 69.

differing views of the black church. The second was personal and political rivalry.

Early in 1848, only a few months after Douglass had launched the *North Star,* he had written at length urging the abandoning of religious institutions based on racial distinctions. Black churches, he declared, were "negro pews on a higher scale, . . . a mere counterpart of colonization"; they were injurious to the best interests of blacks and a violation of the basic equality of human beings. Challenging white ministers to be as interested in the salvation of the souls of blacks as they were in those of whites, he insisted, "a white minister is as good as a black one for us." With remarkable optimism, he urged blacks to abandon their separate churches and return to the white churches they had left: "With the light which sixteen years' agitation has thrown on the subject, the examples of Europe, and the word of God in their hands, the churches would not dare exclude us from the house of prayer, or proscribe us when once admitted. Come, brethren, let us be men, equal men—Christians and equal Christians."[18]

Douglass did praise the founders of independent black churches, saying they had struck a blow for religious liberty. He felt, though, that black churches' coming out of white churches should have been a temporary phase. The continuation of black churches, and the black schools often associated with them, encouraged segregation everywhere—in theaters and on railroads and steamboats, as well as in churches and schools. In addition to promoting segregation and thereby strengthening white assumptions of black inferiority, religious separation condemned most black churches to inferior leadership. Douglass' words were harsh: "With few exceptions, colored ministers have not the mental qualifications to instruct and improve their congregations; . . . they retard the intellectual progress of the people." He bemoaned the fact that some of the most popular black preachers in the country could not even write their own names. Such ministers often denounced "letter-learning" as destructive of the spirit that gives life. Douglass also deplored the expense of separate churches and ministry in small black communities. He cited a case in which a dozen black washerwomen and as many black male day laborers had to try to raise two hundred or three hundred dollars a year to support a black minister and his family.[19] Douglass's criticism must have struck

18. *North Star,* February 25, March 3, 1848.
19. *Ibid.,* March 10, 1848.

sympathetic chords in many of the better-educated black clergy of his time, including Garnet. However, Douglass's recommended solution denied the validity of Garnet's and others' careers as ministers of black churches committed to furthering the learning, especially the biblical learning, of their members. And there was little hard evidence to support Douglass's optimism about the reintegration of the races in white churches.

Hostility between Douglass and Garnet flared anew when Douglass learned that Garnet was going to England to lecture for the Free Produce Movement. Douglass felt professionally threatened, fearing the loss of the loyal following he had built up in England during his visit from 1845 to 1847. Contributions from those supporters had helped him launch his weekly newspaper soon after his return to the United States, and the continuation of that support was important for the journal's future. By highlighting Garnet's dependence on violence and suggesting Garnet's personal instability, Douglass hoped to prevent his rival's securing a widespread British following. Garnet responded in kind. He spoke of Douglass's having once been a preacher in the AMEZ denomination. "But he deserted them," Garnet said, "and now derides and ridicules them. Being matchless in mimicry, and unrivalled in buffoonery, he amuses scoffers and infidels by imitating their religious exercises." Garnet saved his most bitter words for Douglass's commitment to nonviolence. Having known the cruelty and licentiousness of the slave system, Douglass, according to Garnet, now said it would be wrong "to smite the incarnate devil that would, by violence, dishonor your daughter." In such a man's veins, taunted Garnet, "there runs no blood—no! not even clear water." Whatever black fugitive "advocates such trash, he is either a coward, a hypocrite, a fool, or a knave."[20]

Garnet sailed for England in August 1850, taking his five-year-old daughter, Mary, with him but leaving his wife and two small sons in Geneva, New York. He promised to send money back to Julia Garnet but also arranged with Gerrit Smith that, in case of financial emergency, the Peterboro radical would help the Garnet family. Henry Richardson,

20. This charge overlooked the fact that Douglass had, in June 1849 in Boston, before a packed hall, said he would welcome news of a devastating slave uprising in the South (Quarles, *Black Abolitionists*, 228). *Impartial Citizen*, August 8, 1849 (Microfilm copy in Carter and Ripley [eds.], *BAP*, reel 6, item 78); *North Star*, September 7, 1849; also see Joel Schor's useful article, "The Rivalry Between Frederick Douglass and Henry Highland Garnet," *Journal of Negro History*, LXIV (1979), 30–38.

Quaker Free Produce leader and peace advocate, and his wife Anna took Garnet and little Mary into their home in Newcastle-upon-Tyne in northern England.[21]

Garnet began a feverish schedule of antislavery/Free Produce meetings in Methodist and Baptist chapels, Friends' meetinghouses, town halls, and private homes in northern England. By mid-October he could report eight flourishing Free Labor associations formed, all linked with the Ladies' New Castle Anti-Slavery Society. There was a logic in working especially through women's antislavery societies, for in most households it was the women who were the primary buyers of food and clothing. Garnet urged women to reject all slave-grown articles and predicted, with an optimism that proved unwarranted, that if they did so, shopkeepers would start stocking free-labor produce, for reasons of self-interest if not of altruism.[22]

As the months went by, Garnet dwelt upon another theme in his addresses. He attacked certain distinguished white ministers in America for giving aid and comfort to slaveholders. Dr. Gardiner Spring, veteran New York City Presbyterian clergyman, had said that if by one prayer he could emancipate all the slaves, he would dare not breathe it. Rev. Moses Stuart, professor of sacred literature at Andover Theological Seminary, had used his biblical learning to prove that nothing in the Scriptures declared slaveholding and Christianity inherently incompatible. And Dr. Samuel Cox had endorsed the Fugitive Slave Act.[23]

Garnet's was one of the major addresses at the annual meeting of the British and Foreign Anti-Slavery Society in London in May 1851. As Pennington had done in Glasgow, Garnet spoke of the notable accomplishments of free blacks in America. A reporter paraphrased, "He trusted the energies of the black race; their motto was Onward! Upward! . . . They were rising and increasing in influence. Go to the churches and witness it there." Garnet also paid vivid tribute to Africa as his original home, thus foreshadowing his ardent involvement in the late 1850s in the African Civilization Society. The finale of Garnet's address to this prestigious gathering of British abolitionists was a discussion of the Free

21. A handwritten account in the possession of Charlotte Mebane, Mary Garnet's granddaughter.

22. *Non-Slaveholder,* November, 1850 (Microfilm copy in Carter and Ripley [eds.], *BAP,* reel 6, item 658); Report on a meeting held November 6, 1850, in *Anti-Slavery Reporter,* January 1, 1851 (Microfilm copy in Carter and Ripley [eds.], *BAP,* reel 6, item 722).

23. *Patriot,* May 10, 1851; *Anti-Slavery Reporter,* June 2, 1851 (Microfilm copy in Carter and Ripley [eds.], *BAP,* reel 6, item 963).

Produce Movement's moral appeal and economic vision. He pleaded with his hearers to boycott slave-grown produce and urged England to invest capital in producing sugar, cotton, and tobacco with free labor in Africa.[24]

Some six weeks after Garnet had addressed the British and Foreign Anti-Slavery Society, the rest of his family joined him in England. Julia Garnet had had a bitterly difficult time. Money mailed to her by her husband in December had still not reached her in mid-February, and she had had to turn to Gerrit Smith for assistance. The Garnets' two sons had been very sick, and one of them had died. Garnet had been full of anxiety but incapable of helping. Shortly before his wife and son docked in London, he wrote Smith, "She (my dear wife) has born her trials most nobly, and truly her heroism in times of severe trials has added to the love I cherish for her, unfeigned veneration." If his wife and son would only land safely, he said, his "cup of earthly happiness" would be full. Julia Garnet and her son did land safely, and with them Stella Weims, a young fugitive slave who had found shelter with the Garnets in Geneva, New York, before Henry had left for England. These three were warmly welcomed into the Richardsons' home. Reunited with his family and revived by the openness of British society, Garnet wrote Gerrit Smith, "Unless Providence bids me otherwise, I never mean to reside in [America] again."[25]

By early 1851 the Prince Street Presbyterian Church in New York City was growing restive over its pastor's long absence. However, if Pennington should return, still a fugitive slave, his situation would be even more dangerous than when he had left the United States before the passage of the Fugitive Slave Act. Some of his friends in Scotland contacted John Hooker, the Connecticut lawyer, asking him to negotiate with the administrator of Pennington's owner's estate in Maryland. Berwickshire supporters of the American black minister organized local committees and began raising funds. By the time word came back from Connecticut that Pennington's freedom could be purchased for $150, Berwickshire had raised nearly twice that amount. The purchase money was forwarded to Hooker, and the balance was given to Pennington for his and his wife's

24. *London Patriot,* May 22, 1851 (Microfilm copy in Carter and Ripley [eds.], *BAP,* reel 6, item 942). Garnet's boyhood friend Alexander Crummell, currently studying at Cambridge, was present on this occasion.

25. *Anti-Slavery Reporter,* January 1, 1851 (Microfilm copy in Carter and Ripley [eds.], *BAP,* reel 6, item 722); Julia Garnet to Gerrit Smith, February 2, 1851, Henry Garnet to Gerrit Smith, July 7, 1851, both in Gerrit Smith Papers.

return to New York City. They left Scotland for the United States in the early summer of 1851.[26]

Garnet stayed in the British Isles for nearly eighteen months more before sailing with his family to Jamaica, where he would serve several years as a missionary for the United Presbyterian Church of Scotland. In over two years in the British Isles, Pennington and Garnet had drawn large and enthusiastic crowds. By their efforts the British Free Produce Movement gained considerable strength, although it was destined never to become a major political or economic force in the international antislavery crusade. The two black ministers also crystallized their audiences' condemnation of American slavery, of American churches temporizing with that system, and especially of the United States government's passage and efforts at enforcement of the Fugitive Slave Act. Finally, Garnet and Pennington seem to have succeeded in their fund-raising. Much was contributed toward their travel and living expenses. In 1853 the New York Vigilance Committee reported that between January 1851 and March 1853 it had received over $3,000 from Great Britain.[27] Lastly, enough was raised by Pennington to retire the Prince Street Church's debt.

Accompanying these successes, however, was substantial hostility that had developed against Pennington and Garnet both in England and Scotland. At the center of the antagonism were British abolitionists committed to William Lloyd Garrison and the Garrisonian movement as expressed in the American Anti-Slavery Society. British Garrisonians, like their American counterparts, opposed the Free Produce Movement as a futile distraction from the established methods of promoting radical abolitionism. Even more basic, however, was their fundamental distrust of mainstream American Protestant churches and their clergy. The anticlericalism that had been present in the American Anti-Slavery Society in 1840, at the time of the breakaway of the American and Foreign Anti-Slavery Society, with its substantial black ministerial contingent, permeated British Garrisonian attitudes toward the British and Foreign Anti-Slavery Society in 1850. Accordingly, Pennington and Garnet were suspect as ministers and as protégés of the British Society.[28]

British Garrisonian antagonism focused particularly on Pennington

26. Blackett, *Beating Against the Barriers,* 52f.

27. Schor concluded that the winning of the crowds to American black lecturers' points of view during the 1850s "in no small way influenced British foreign policy after the firing on Fort Sumter in 1861" (Schor, *Henry Highland Garnet,* 120). *Report of the New York Vigilance Committee* (New York, 1853).

28. Blackett, *Building an Antislavery Wall,* chap. 4, is a richly specific account of the role of American black visitors in the British abolitionist movement of the early 1850s.

and was nourished by such American warnings as that of Wendell Phillips in a letter to an Englishwoman, Elizabeth Pease: "Pennington is with you just what he was here, self-seeking, trimming and utterly unreliable."[29] By the spring of 1851 a British Garrisonian was declaring that Pennington had shown his unreliability by questionable financial transactions. The specific accusations against him were two. First, he was raising money for his own ransom under false pretenses; in his autobiography he had written that he had secured funds for this purpose in Jamaica in 1846.[30] Second, Pennington was continuing to solicit contributions toward discharging the Prince Street Church's indebtedness long after he had secured the amount needed. Try as his opponents would, however, they were not able to prove financial duplicity on Pennington's part.[31]

The chief reason for Pennington's having been especially singled out for bitter accusations was that he was firmly ensconced in a prestigious Presbyterian pastorate at a time when both Garrisonians and many free-floating British abolitionists had become bitter over orthodox American denominations continuing to condone, or even to excuse, slave owning among their southern members. That Pennington had been awarded a doctor of divinity degree by an Evangelical theological faculty in Heidelberg—in no small measure on the basis of recommendations by white New York City clergymen, and perhaps also through special representations of the British and Foreign Anti-Slavery Society—made him all the more suspect. A hostile article in the American Garrisonian *Anti-Slavery Standard* in June 1851 augured ill for Pennington's return to America. Along with giving news of John Hooker's having effected this famous fugitive's emancipation, the article noted that Pennington had lost the confidence of many antislavery people in Great Britain because of his hostility against the American Anti-Slavery Society and because his financial transactions had cast doubt on his integrity.[32]

While Pennington and Garnet were in Great Britain, Ray and Beman, acutely conscious of the absence of these co-workers, did all they could to

29. Wendell Phillips to Elizabeth Pease, February 19, 1850, in Pease and Pease, *They Who Would Be Free,* 78.

30. In January 1851, in a prepared statement to the Glasglow Emancipation Society, Pennington stated that funds raised in Jamaica had been insufficient to buy his freedom (Blackett, *Building an Antislavery Wall,* 131). Other evidence suggests that when the effort to secure the release of his parents along with himself failed, the money was spent on other aid to fugitive relatives.

31. Blackett, *Building an Antislavery Wall,* 127–34.

32. *Anti-Slavery Standard,* June 19, 1851.

help other fugitives to a safe destination. During the 1840s Ray had been the authorized fund-raiser for New York City's vigilance committee and then for the state committee founded in 1847. In 1849 he and the two others on the state committee's executive board broadcast a plea for funds. Noting the increase of runaways and the arrival of over four hundred in New York City during the previous fifteen months, the board pleaded, "In the care of so many helpless strangers, you can understand how a constant and inexorable demand has been made upon our anxieties, our labors and our funds."[33]

The passage of the 1850 Fugitive Slave Act made New York City an even more dangerous place for former slaves. Indeed, the city's black population declined almost 15 percent between 1850 and 1855, yet runaways kept streaming through. Ray and his family were again and again hosts in their own home to individuals and groups seeking food, shelter, and safety. One summer morning fourteen fugitives entered Ray's home in one party. A young woman stayed with the family for three weeks and a young man, for six weeks. Ray evidently lived near New York City's Mutual Relief Hall, which was said to have a secret room that ran the whole length of the building.[34] Although Ray had one of the larger black property holdings in New York City (probably through the holdings of his second wife), what he could spare, and more, was exhausted time and time again.[35] Often he would turn to Gerrit Smith, who had been so impressed by the 1849 state vigilance committee's constitution that he had sent $500. A typical request from Ray begged Smith in 1856 to provide the $800 needed to snatch from enslavement in Virginia the twenty-one-year-old daughter of a woman whom Congressman Smith had helped redeem earlier that same year. Ray ended his letter, "I have had so many of these cases . . . that I not only have used myself up, but my friends [also]."[36]

In February 1850 Ray joined AMEZ bishop Christopher Rush, the Tappans, and S. S. Jocelyn in a circular letter to "each friend of Liberty in

33. Quarles, *Black Abolitionists,* 154; Freeman, "The Free Negro in New York City," 90ff.; Ray and Ray, *Sketch of Charles B. Ray,* 32–34.

34. Ray and Ray, *Sketch of Charles B. Ray,* 45f., Freeman, "The Free Negro in New York City," 279.

35. According to a listing of residents in New York City who paid heavy taxes on real estate and personal property in 1856–57, Ray owned $3,000 worth of real estate; James McCune Smith, $7,700; and George Downing $6,800. Ray's annual income from this was probably under $200. Freeman, "The Free Negro in New York City," 279.

36. Gerrit Smith to Charles Ray and the other two vigilance committee Executive Board members, March 14, 1849, Ray to Smith, April 29, 1856, both in Gerrit Smith Papers.

the United States." It was sent to newspapers across the country, as well as to abolitionists, urging the resumption of massive petitioning to Congress to protest the drift of federal policy. In particular, the authors singled out "the cruel and arbitrary manner in which alleged fugitives from slavery are seized and carried away." They also pressed for the abolition of slavery in the District of Columbia and the prohibition of slavery in the new territories.[37] The following summer, shortly before the final passage of the Fugitive Slave Act, the New York State vigilance committee called a convention in Cazenovia, New York, for those who had run away from slavery and those "resolved to stand by them." Roughly two thousand gathered. Ray, as secretary of the state committee, was chosen as vice-president, and Frederick Douglass chaired the occasion. Money was raised for the defense of a man imprisoned in Washington for aiding armed slave runaways.[38] A moving letter was drawn up from fugitive slaves to their brothers in the South; it reported on the conditions in the North and Canada and urged slaves to secure weapons, to steal fast horses and money, and to make their way, if possible, to New York State, "the safest place to steer for."[39]

About a year after this meeting of former slaves in Cazenovia, a state convention of blacks gathered in Albany. The Fugitive Slave Act was prominent on the agenda. Amos Beman attended. Although he was from out of state, he was made an official delegate and was chosen vice-president and chairman of the three-man Committee on the Fugitive Slave Act. This trio's report forcefully declared that black citizens of New York saw their own liberties "fearfully endangered" by the new federal law. Affirming their "tender sympathy with our brethren who escape from slavery," they declared the Fugitive Slave Act to be a gross violation of the Bible, of the Declaration of Independence, and of the federal Constitution.[40] It may well have been Beman who included in this report the story of an earlier glorious episode in New Haven's history, when it had secreted from their pursuers the English judges who had handed down the

37. *National-Era Supplement,* February, 1850 (Microfilm copy in Carter and Ripley [eds.], *BAP,* reel 6, item 425).

38. William L. Chaplin was indicted in the District of Columbia and in Maryland for assault with intent to murder and for assisting slaves to escape. Gerrit Smith was treasurer of the Chaplin fund and himself contributed $10,000 to the movement that secured Chaplin's freedom.

39. Foner and Walker (eds.), *Proceedings of the Black State Conventions,* I, 43–50.

40. The biblical texts quoted were "Thou shalt not deliver unto his master the servant which is escaped from his master unto thee" (Deut. 23:15) and "All things whatsoever you

verdict of death for King Charles I.[41] Calling upon whites to aid them, the convention delegates unanimously adopted the committee's report, ending with three resolutions: "Revolved, that the fugitive slave law is the law of tyrants. Resolved, that disobedience to tyrants is obedience to God. Resolved, that we will obey God."[42]

For all of Beman's deep concern over the impact of the Fugitive Slave Act, and the shelter he and his church gave runaways coming through New Haven, it was Ray and Pennington (after his return from Great Britain) who labored in a nerve center of assistance to fugitive slaves. In September 1852 Ray was the president of New York City's vigilance committee, for which both Garnet and Pennington had been raising funds in the British Isles. That month Ray wrote Garnet details about the whereabouts of the original family of Garnet's adopted daughter, Stella Weims. Weims's father, a free man, had been frantically trying to raise money to purchase from their owner Stella's mother and Stella's seven younger siblings. The owner had promised to sell John Weims his family members on easy terms, but this owner had died, and his heirs had sold the Weimses to a slave trader for $3,300, a sum far beyond anything Weims could raise. It looked as though the best he could do was to redeem his wife and youngest child (priced at $900) and let the other children—five boys and two girls (one aged sixteen and strikingly beautiful)—be sold. By mid-October Garnet, by now appointed for missionary service in Jamaica and due to leave Scotland with his family shortly, released the Weims story to the British press. He announced that his host, Henry Richardson, had agreed to be treasurer of a fund to be forwarded to Ray for purchase of all the Weimses. Garnet added to the eloquent appeal of the case by reporting that his adopted daughter was so overwhelmed with grief that he feared she would lose her reason. Editors of the *Anti-Slavery Reporter,* the *Christian News,* the *Nonconformist,* and other English papers joined in a whirlwind fund-raising campaign, though at least one disapproved of paying slave owners to free their slaves. As a result $5,000 was raised and forwarded to Ray, who had managed to keep track even of

---

would that men should do to you, do ye so to them" (Matt. 7:12). The following was quoted from the Declaration of Independence: "All men are endowed by their Creator with certain inalienable rights; among these are life, *liberty,* and the pursuit of happiness." From the Constitution, the right of every person in the United States to a trial by jury in a court, as well as the privilege of habeas corpus, was cited.

41. The fugitive judges were Goff, Whalley, and Dixwell, after whom New Haven eventually named three of its major streets.

42. Foner and Walker (eds.), *Proceedings of the Black State Conventions,* I. 55f., 58, 72f.

the family members sold south to Alabama. Even after the money was in hand, shrewd maneuvering by Ray with a Washington, D.C., trader and an Alabama slave owner, as well as one escape in disguise, was required before the family were all free. Ray's daughters were so proud of his achievements in this case that after his death they devoted ten pages of their pamphlet biography of their father to the freeing of the Weimses.[43]

Pennington had resumed heavy involvement in the fugitive slave effort as soon as he had returned to the United States. He joined Ray and others in speaking at a series of meetings that defended and raised money for those arrested after the Christiana riot. A group of blacks and a white man had resisted a Maryland slave owner who was trying to recapture four escaped slaves in southern Pennsylvania, and the owner had been killed. At gatherings promoting aid for the Christiana defendants, both Pennington and Ray strongly endorsed resorting to violence, if need be, to prevent the recapture of slaves. When the defendants were acquitted by a Philadelphia jury, Pennington sent an exuberant account to Great Britain. A year later he had another success story for the *Scottish Press*. He and others acting for the vigilance committee had used the writ of habeas corpus to bring before a superior court judge eight slaves brought temporarily into New York City by a Virginia slaveholder. After the owner defended at length his property rights, the judge had declared the eight free. The trustees of the Prince Street church had given them a public reception, which was attended by Ray and Cornish, as well as Pennington. The Prince Street pastor was by this time remarried, and his wife, a native of Hartford, had accompanied the eight former slaves to that city and had turned them over to the care of John Hooker, Pennington's lawyer friend. Four months later Pennington was seeking a contribution from John Jay, the prominent New York liberal, to help out this same group of former slaves, now in Canada but still destitute.[44]

43. Charles Ray to Henry Garnet, September 27, 1852, in *Anti-Slavery Reporter,* December 1, 1852 (Microfilm copy in Carter and Ripley [eds.], *BAP,* reel 7, item 844); Henry Garnet to *Anti-Slavery Reporter,* October 16, 1852, in *ibid.;* Editorial comments in *ibid.; Christian News,* November 11, 1852 (Microfilm copy in Carter and Ripley [eds.], *BAP,* reel 7, item 825); *Nonconformist,* November 7, 1852 (Microfilm copy in Carter and Ripley [eds.], *BAP,* reel 7, item 827); Ray and Ray, *Sketch of Charles B. Ray,* 36–45. Anna Richardson wondered whether the recent publication of Harriet Beecher Stowe's *Uncle Tom's Cabin* was in part responsible for the surge of interest in the case of the Weims family. Ray and Ray, *Sketch of Charles B. Ray,* 43.

44. James Pennington to *Scottish Press,* December 12, 1851, in *Christian News,* December 12, 1851 (Microfilm copy in Carter and Ripley [eds.], *BAP,* reel 7, item 222); James Pennington to *Christian News,* November 20, 1852, in *Christian News,* December 16, 1852 (Microfilm copy in Carter and Ripley [eds.], *BAP,* reel 7, item 866); James Pennington to Hor-

Pennington's most excruciating experience in trying to help fugitives involved his own brother and nephews. In the spring of 1854 he received a letter from William Still, intrepid agent of the Underground Railroad in Philadelphia, stating that the black minister's brother Stephen Pembroke and that man's two sons were on their way to New York City, having escaped from their Maryland owners. The owners, however, helped by professional slave catchers, were hot on the heels of the Pembrokes, found out where they were sleeping their first night in New York City, and sent police with a warrant to break into the place of refuge and recapture them. Early the next morning the fugitives were examined by a magistrate, certified as runaways, and sent back to Maryland with their owners. Pennington, given false information as to the time of the hearing, had neither an opportunity to secure counsel for his brother and nephews nor a chance himself to testify. The Philadelphia and New York City vigilance committees had remarkably good records in getting their passengers to safe territory. Commentators have therefore tended to blame Pennington for letting his guard down and allowing the recapture. Since the vigilance committee's arrangements for newly arrived runaways involved a number of parties, and no detailed account of the planning for that first night has survived, it is difficult to pinpoint the blame. William Still, shocked by the recapture, attributed it to Pennington's tumultuous feelings at being reunited with his brother after twenty-five years—"enough to incapacitate the Doctor for the time being, for cool thought as to how he should best guard against the enemy."

Within a few days Pennington received a desperate letter from Stephen in Sharpsburg, Maryland; he was about to be sold to a slave driver. Pennington wrote to Stephen's owner and indicated a willingness to pay the $600 he understood to be his brother's current valuation. Told that the price was $1,000, Pennington agreed to that. Then $375 more was added for expenses. Pennington agreed to the whole—about two years' worth of his annual salary—and secured his brother's release, but his nephews were sold to slave drivers. Starting from nothing to pay off his indebtedness and to help his brother get established was to be a major burden for Pennington for years.[45]

ace Greeley and Mr. Harned, November 27, 1852, A.L.S. at Columbia University, New York (Microfilm copy in Carter and Ripley [eds.], *BAP,* reel 7, item 839); James Pennington to John Jay, March 2, 1853, A.L.S. in Jay Family Papers, Columbia University, New York (Microfilm copy in Carter and Ripley [eds.], *BAP,* reel 8, item 150).

45. Sources for both of the preceding paragraphs are James Pennington to William Still, May 24, 1854, in Still, *The Underground Railroad,* 170–73; *National Anti-Slavery Standard,*

It was in assistance to fugitive slaves that free blacks won their most dramatic victories in the northern United States in the 1850s. However, it was important for black morale before the Civil War and for subsequent Afro-American history that the struggles to secure the right to vote, the right to equal treatment on common carriers, and the right to good, non-segregated education for the young were continued during this decade. Along with laymen such as Frederick Douglass, James McCune Smith, William Nell, and Thomas Downing, the ministers Pennington, Beman, and Ray continued to make crucial contributions on the civil rights front in New York and New England. They did so along with meeting demanding day-to-day responsibilities as pastors of congregations. Indeed, the role of prominent minister of an influential black church was for Pennington and Beman a major factor in their political leverage in the black community, as would be more dramatically the case a century later with Adam Clayton Powell, Jr., pastor of the large Abyssinian Baptist Church in New York City. It was, accordingly, doubly tragic that within five years of his return from England to New York City, Pennington lost the confidence of his Prince Street congregation and found himself forced to resign his pastorate.

Many factors indicated a bright future for Pennington when he returned to New York City in 1851. As he had after his trip to England in 1843, he now had come back to his American pastorate buoyed by months of easy association with prominent British clergymen and by the enthusiastic responses of English and Scottish people who had listened to his speeches and sermons. Moreover, he had returned to his New York parish a free man and the bearer of an honorary doctor's degree. He had seemed ready to take on Theodore Wright's role as honored pastor of the largest black Presbyterian church in the country, and as one of the statesmen of New York City's black community. But it did not work out that way.

In early October 1851 Pennington attended the Third Presbytery meeting for the first time in over two and a half years. He was heartily congratulated on his recent emancipation and warmly welcomed back to

June 3, 1854; *Pennsylvania Freeman,* June 8, 1854 (Microfilm copy in Carter and Ripley [eds.], *BAP,* reel 8, item 862); *Rhode Island Freeman,* July 7, 1854 (Microfilm copy in Carter and Ripley [eds.], BAP, reel 8, item 912); *Anti-Slavery Reporter,* September 1, 1854 (Microfilm copy in Carter and Ripley [eds.], *BAP,* reel 9, item 58). For Stephen Pembroke's own vivid description of his fifty years as a slave and of his escape and recapture, see John W. Blassingame (ed.), *Slave Testimony: Two Centuries of Letters, Speeches, Interviews and Autobiographies* (Baton Rouge, 1977), 167, 169.

his "field of labor."[46] Within a year he could be encouraged by what was happening in his church. Although membership had lost ground during his absence, it was back up to 446 in 1852 and stayed between 450 and 470 during the remaining four years of his pastorate. From the time of his return late in 1851 to September 1, 1855, he received a $700-per-year salary (a handsome figure for a black minister at that time). The elders and trustees of the church consistently produced $500, and the remaining $200 was provided by the American Home Missionary Society, which enthusiastically renewed his commission year by year.

Strengths in the church emerge from the quarterly reports that Pennington submitted. On an average, over a dozen new members were joining each year. Many nonmembers attended services, and the congregation often totaled about seven hundred. Pennington took his pastoral duties very seriously. He usually preached twice each Sunday, lectured once during the week, and visited each weekday among the sick and destitute black people in various parts of the city, as well as in Hoboken, New Jersey, and Brooklyn, Williamsburgh, and New Town, New York. Finally, church members seemed to be financially responsible. Over and above contributing enough to pay the agreed-upon pastor's salary, they met periodic levies by the city and, their pastor proudly reported, gave significant sums to aid a struggling church in Hoboken, to help redeem enslaved friends or relatives of church members, to maintain the Colored Orphan Asylum, and to support a variety of denominational or interdenominational missionary efforts. To be sure, there were recurrent shortfalls in the church's income. Although Pennington had raised enough money in Great Britain to retire the Prince Street church's debt at that time, a substantial new deficit had been incurred in 1852 in the process of modernizing the interior of the church and introducing gas. Yet there was nothing unusual about a black Presbyterian church being in debt, and nothing to raise basic questions about Pennington's ministry.[47]

During 1853, the second full year of Pennington's ministry after his return from England, he seemed to be moving from strength to strength. In mid-March a heartwarming occasion was staged at the Prince Street

46. Minutes of the Third Presbytery, October 6, 1851 (MS at Presbyterian Historical Association, Philadelphia).

47. Pennington's reports to the American Home Missionary Society, February 4, August 2, November 1, 1852, February 14, May 2, August, November 1, 1853, August, December 1, 1854; March 2, June 1, September 24, 1855, all in AHMS Archives (Microfilm copy in Carter and Ripley [eds.], *BAP,* reel 7, items 399, 686, 813; reel 8, items 128, 237, 389; reel 1, item 340; reel 8, item 996; reel 9, items 7, 252, 464, 678, 845).

church by the ladies of the church and several of Pennington's close clerical friends. A handsome pulpit gown and a fine black suit had been ordered from Edinburgh, Scotland. After a Scottish-style tea the gown was presented by Amos Freeman (now pastor of Brooklyn's Siloam Presbyterian Church) before a large gathering, including quite a number of white men and women. Freeman and Charles Ray gave speeches of tribute, and appropriate resolutions were passed, including reference to the honorary degree that had prompted the gift of the gown.[48]

Also in 1853, the Third Presbytery of New York chose Pennington to be its moderator. As was the custom, he was asked to preach to the members of the presbytery at the end of his term of office. His sermon urged the importance of taking the Christian message to the poor and pressed the Third Presbytery to do something for the lower wards of Manhattan. New churches must be put up to replace the twenty-two that had been vacated and destroyed in the previous decade and a half as middle- and upper-class people had moved to upper Manhattan. The continuing heavy flow of immigrants into the older wards, Pennington insisted, made such a program all the more important.

Toward the end of his sermon Pennington turned to the slavery question. "No member of this Presbytery," he declared, "has felt more keenly the uncomfortableness of his position than I have, in regard to our general body on the subject of slavery." He noted the common opinion that American Presbyterians owned eighty thousand slaves. His recommendations, however, were mild. He spoke against the use of the Bible to justify slavery, urged taking the Bible to slaves, and commended the antislavery example of the United Presbyterians in Scotland. His final words expressed confidence in the working of the Presbyterian system in an astonishingly optimistic statement: "I rejoice to know that our church is the friend of progressive opinion, and the time will soon come when she will be as united on this subject [slavery] as she is on those of missions, temperance, Sabbath, . . . etc."[49]

It is not difficult to understand why Pennington, having been officially honored by the Third Presbytery, was powerless to deliver to its members the kind of angry denunciatory statements on the church's implication in slavery and racism that had come from his lips in Great Britain and Connecticut. There was also another important fact of which

48. *New York Evangelist,* March 17, 1853.

49. *Christian Zeal: A Sermon Preached Before the Third Presbytery of New York, in Thirteenth St. Presbyterian Church, July 3rd, 1853* (New York, 1854).

Pennington was probably aware. The New School General Assembly of 1853, meeting just prior to Pennington's preaching to his presbytery, had seemed at last to be moving off dead center on the slavery issue. During the 1840s it had received numerous memorials from presbyteries and synods, especially in the Midwest and in western New York State, that demanded that the General Assembly act to rid the national church of slave owning among its members. The assembly's established policy had been to rule that disciplining members for slave owning was a matter for the local judicatories (sessions and presbyteries).

In 1853, however, the General Assembly, holding eleven petitions urging action, recommended that presbyteries in the South look into, and report about, how much slave owning there was among church members in their jurisdictions. It would, to be sure, be four more years before the General Assembly would decide that it could, constitutionally, discipline individual slave owners, a decision that would drive twenty-one of the southern presbyteries and six synods to secede from the New School General Assembly.[50] In 1853 Pennington could not forsee the details, but he could sense a growing polarization among New School Presbyterians that gave some promise of ending, for his branch of the Presbyterian church, that collusion with slavery that he and other radical abolitionists, black and white, had so categorically denounced. For many abolitionists with little sympathy for the organized church, however, Pennington's acceptance of the moderatorship had been a compromise with corruption for the sake of personal honor.

In September 1854 the chronically abusive Garrisonian Parker Pillsbury wrote the Glasgow *Sentinel* a long letter, which was reprinted in the *National Anti-Slavery Standard,* a Garrisonian paper. Pillsbury raked up the old criticisms of "coloured ministers" for their sectarian abuse of Garrisonians. However, his primary target was Pennington (whom he did not know personally): "He is a member, a minister and a doctor of Divinity in one of the most pro-slavery, slave-breeding, slaveholding and slavehunting churches in the United States." Pillsbury cited a recent meeting of Pennington's presbytery as having adopted, at the request of a Virginia presbytery, a resolution to suppress all discussion of the slavery question in the presbytery and in the General Assembly. Pennington, Pillsbury charged, had concurred in the resolution. Pennington responded to these and similar charges in four letters to the *Frederick Douglass' Paper.* His pri-

50. Nichols and Nichols, *Presbyterianism in New York State,* 158f.; Howard, "Anti-Slavery Movement," 153, 156, 181–86, 193–200, 206, 210, 218–20.

mary line of defense was that twenty years of experience as a slave had taught him more about the evils of slavery than any white man could know. He attacked superficially argued efforts to drive him out of the Presbyterian church as suppression of the "rights of private judgment and conscience": "I have yet to learn that the mere profession of abolitionism gives any white man a right to take me by the coat button and lead me whithersoever he will." Pennington also flatly denied that he had ever endorsed his presbytery's resolution to suppress the discussion of slavery in that body or in the General Assembly.[51]

In spite of all the spirit in these rebuttals, there had been signs, even before Pillsbury's abusive letter had appeared, that Pennington's personal life was coming unraveled. In early 1854 Lewis Tappan, sometimes inclined to exaggerate in making moral judgments, had recorded in his diary that Pennington had become a "confirmed drunkard, has used his friends wrongfully, is greatly in debt, is neglecting his parishioners, and contriving . . . to obtain money under false pretenses." A couple of months later the Third Presbytery appointed a committee to confer with Pennington, at his own request, "in relation to his personal affairs." The conferring had to do with rumors about his obtaining money by untrue statements. The committee reported back to the presbytery that Pennington's description of the transactions connected with the purchase of his freedom "had been completely satisfactory." Lewis Tappan, however, was not satisfied. In the summer of 1855 he pressed Pennington to refund substantial amounts to Jamaican donors—money, he said, "not required for the purpose for which it was given." This Pennington could not do. When his lawyer's negotiations with his owner had fallen through, the money was evidently used in other efforts to gain freedom for family members.[52]

By late 1855 the session of the Prince Street Church was struggling with other ministerial shortcomings. It wrote the presbytery that it was "aggrieved at certain conduct on the part of [its] pastor." It needed help. Early the next year Pennington appeared before the presbytery "in relation to certain rumors." After listening to him, the body concluded that "the confession made by Dr. Pennington, his expression of penitence,

51. *National Anti-Slavery Standard,* October 28, 1854; *Liberator,* January 5, 1855; *Frederick Douglass' Paper,* February 23, April 6, May 4, 11, 1855.

52. Tappan's diary entry for February 13, 1854, cited by Wyatt-Brown, *Lewis Tappan,* 306*n*12; Lewis Tappan to James Pennington, July 26, 28, 1855, A.L.S.'s in Lewis Tappan Papers (Microfilm copy in Carter and Ripley [eds.], *BAP,* reel 9, items 750, 765).

and his professed purpose carefully to guard against a repetition of the acknowledged offence, are satisfactory." Although the minutes were vague throughout as to the nature of the offense, it can only be concluded that the transgression was the occasional or regular consumption of alcohol. At any rate, the presbytery heartily forgave its distinguished and distinctive member for the past and "commend[ed] him for the future to the grace of the Great Shepherd & Bishop of Souls." Pennington asked that his pastoral connection with the Prince Street Church be dissolved so that he might accept a call from his old church in Hartford. The Prince Street Church and the Third Presbytery acquiesced.[53]

Pennington had been found wanting in that steady strength that the older members of this New York church remembered in Theodore Wright. For a session that expected every member of the church to "take the pledge," it was bound to be a jolt to find out that their pastor, who had been an ardent promoter of temperance for twenty-five years, had become a drinking man, to whatever degree. Yet the church's criticism of its minister was softened in some measure by its knowledge of the extreme strains under which he had been laboring for two years. The escape and recapture of his brother had increased Pennington's already severe financial problems, to say nothing of the emotional toll. And his debts had grown in the summer and fall of 1855 because of legal expenses incurred by his defying the Sixth Avenue Railroad's Jim Crow regulations and his suing the railroad. The eight years in the New York City pastorate had brought striking accomplishments but had ended in a major personal defeat.

For Amos Beman, as well as for Pennington, the 1850s brought valiant efforts, bitter loss, and the resignation from his pastorate. It has been noted that in the early 1850s Beman was intensely involved in aid to fugitive slaves and in protest against the Fugitive Slave Act. By 1854 he was leading another campaign for black enfranchisement comparable to the one eight years earlier.

In the spring of 1854 the Connecticut legislature again voted a review of the constitutional provision excluding blacks from the polls. A few months later a convention was held in Middletown for the state's black leaders. They chose Amos Beman's father, who had been pastor of Middletown's first black church, as their president. The younger Beman de-

53. Minutes of the Third Presbytery, April 4, 24, 1854; July 2, December 10, 1855; January 14, 28, February 25, 1856.

livered the primary address; he sketched the past, present, and future of the colored people of Connecticut for a full seventy-five minutes. He drew especially on the story of the community he knew best, contrasting the life of New Haven blacks in 1854 with what it had been fifty years earlier. Then no blacks had owned their own homes. There had been no black church building and no school for black children. Now, in a black community of about a thousand, some $200,000 worth of real estate was owned over and above bank and railroad stocks. There were seven black churches, four Methodist, and one each Congregational, Episcopal, and Baptist. And four schools for blacks were full and prospering. American Colonization Society propaganda about the decline in the spirit of the state's blacks was so false as to be absurd. Granted there were intemperate, immoral, and uneducated blacks, but this was so among every people. Beman concluded his address "with a soul stirring appeal to those around him to 'be up and doing with a heart for any fate.'" A white reporter for the Hartford *Republican* who wrote an extended account of these meetings was astonished by Beman's tour de force: "Such rich strains of eloquence as we never before heard from the lips of any man, white or colored, in this State—such as Samuel R. Ward and Frederick Douglass might equal but not excel."[54]

Within the general subject of the progress of blacks in Connecticut, it was their education that received special attention at this convention. Ebenezer Bassett, head of one of New Haven's public grammar schools and soon to become principal of the excellent Institute of Colored Youth in Philadelphia, was chairman of the convention's Education Committee. He expanded on Beman's remarks about the development of black schools. Back in 1837, on the eve of Beman's arrival in the city, after six hours of talk, some of it harsh, the New Haven government had voted $80 for salaries for two black teachers for the following year. No provision had been made for a schoolhouse, so "benevolent citizens" had provided two miserable shacks. Eighty pupils had attended. By contrast, in 1854 there were "four colored schools in fine and teeming operation, in as many commodious school houses, conducted on the graded system, with . . . 190 pupils." Three female teachers each received $200 a year and a male teacher, $500. Blacks who could not read and write, Bassett declared, were as few as those who could do so thirty years earlier. He praised the

54. Foner and Walker (eds.), *Proceedings of the Black State Conventions,* II, 35–37; Report by Normal in Hartford *Republican,* October 3, 1854 (Amos Beman Scrap Book [Amos G. Beman Papers], III).

New Haven Board of Education. Although he disliked separate black schools and churches, he considered them necessary evils for the time being.[55]

When it came to passing resolutions, this 1854 black convention had praise for steps taken by the recent state legislature: the passage of one law designed to suppress intemperance and of another aimed at protecting black people's liberty in Connecticut (in the face of the 1850 federal Fugitive Slave Act). The gathering also celebrated the recent vote by the House of Representatives, including representatives of all political parties, that recommended reconsideration of the constitutional ban against voting by blacks. The convention's harshest resolution was one censuring Connecticut blacks "who are recreant to the cause of equal rights, and by their acts and indifference, are not only degrading themselves and us with them, but their children and our children."[56]

In April of 1855, some six weeks before the state legislature would confirm or reject their actions of the preceding year on the franchise, black men from over the state gathered once more, this time in the Colored, now named Fifth, Congregational Church in Hartford. All of the resolutions passed by this body focused on the forthcoming legislative decision on sending the black franchise question to a popular referendum, as had been done in 1847. Black political activists were encouraged the next month. The new governor of the state was William T. Minor, who had run on the Know-Nothing, or American (antiforeigner), party ticket. In his opening speech to the senators and representatives, Governor Minor strongly recommended that both legislative bodies confirm the action by the House the previous year endorsing referral to the people of a constitutional amendment extending the vote to blacks, but also limiting it to those who could read. "The legislature ought not to prevent," he declared, "final action by the people." If those to be given the vote "are in the main moral and industrious, and qualified to act understandingly, . . . it is difficult to understand why this, the highest right of a freeman, should not be conferred upon them."[57]

On May 23 the Senate approved by more than the required two-thirds vote the proposed amendment opening the vote to blacks and restricting it to those who could read. The House had a lengthy debate on the matter

55. Amos Beman Scrap Book (Amos G. Beman Papers), II, 115.

56. *Ibid.*

57. *Frederick Douglass' Paper,* May 4, 1855; *Journal of the House of Representatives of the State of Connecticut, May Session, 1855* (Hartford, 1855), 16–18.

on May 31. Those favoring black enfranchisement appealed to the established principle of no taxation without representation; they stressed that the blacks involved were native born, had helped Americans gain their freedom from Great Britain, and knew the nation's institutions. Other states (Rhode Island, for example) had given the vote to blacks without disastrous results. "The wonder was not that the colored population was degraded, but that under their depressing circumstances, they had risen so high in the scale of intelligence," one proponent of black enfranchisement said. Simple justice required giving blacks this political right. Since Connecticut was opposed to American slavery, "we should show slaveholders that a black is a *man,* capable of exercising all the functions of a man."[58] One supporter added that giving blacks the franchise did not necessitate abolishing prejudicial feelings against them.

Those opposed to the enfranchisement of blacks were led by Joseph Maddox, a Kentuckian by birth. He declared that "there was a feeling of aversion to the colored race, implanted by nature in man (*white man*); there were no sympathies in common between the two races; it [the proposed amendment] was taking a viper into our bosoms." Worthy whites who could not read would have to give way to a "nigger" who could. It would be an abomination. Blacks, Maddox continued, had not been injured in the United States. Indeed, their condition had been improved by their being brought from Africa. "God had set his seal of distinction upon the race, and had designed that they should be sent here into slavery. [Here there was laughter.] Gentlemen might laugh, but their laughter did not controvert the facts."[59]

Maddox and his allies had the last laugh. The House took two votes, but each time the amendment failed by a narrow margin to receive the necessary two-thirds' support (the votes were 132 for and 79 against, and 135 for and 74 against). It was, as to be expected, the Democrats who defeated the measure.[60] Those supporting the amendment, however, would not give up. One of them had an idea that he hoped would persuade the House to reconsider, and this time to approve, the amendment. He proposed that Amos Beman challenge Joseph Maddox to a debate in the Assembly Hall on the enfranchisement question. Beman agreed to the proposal and wrote Maddox a letter of challenge. The House voted the

58. Amos Beman's grandfather, when freed from slavery, had taken the new name Beman ("Be a man").

59. Hartford *Courant,* June 1, 1855.

60. *Journal of the House of Representatives, May 1855,* 153ff.

use of its hall for this purpose and chose three of its members, two of them ministers, to umpire the occasion. The Hartford and New Haven newspapers gave the prospective event much publicity. The New Haven *Journal and Courier* ventured the opinion that "the Reverend gentleman is the smartest man of the two." However, Maddox disappeared from view and never replied to the letter of challenge. Beman spent most of one day trying to locate the Kentuckian in Hartford without success.[61]

In the fall election the proposed amendment that all voters be required to be able to read was passed, although over ten thousand voted against it. Beman bitterly noted that evidently, for many thousands, an illiterate white was a more valuable elector than a literate black. He said, "The color of the skin is [of] serious, solemn moment, the darkness and ignorance of the mind and the degradation of the morals are of no consequence." Although over two-thirds of the state's senators and nearly 65 percent of its representatives had voted to submit the question of the black franchise to a popular vote, Beman could well have felt that his seventeen years of labor in New Haven, along with the striking efforts of his father, Hosea Easton, and James Pennington, had had little effect on rank-and-file racial prejudice in Connecticut.

Franchise campaigns by blacks and liberal whites in New York during the latter 1850s brought little more success than had the efforts in Connecticut. However, during those years equal suffrage became a more substantial political issue among whites than it had ever been before in the state. In 1854 the American, or Know-Nothing, party, which expressed established Americans' resentment against recent immigrants, was born. Another bloc of voters emerged, strongly opposed to the Kansas-Nebraska Act. A third group was pressing the temperance issue. When the Republican party appeared on the New York political scene in 1855, it drew support from members of these blocs and fashioned a coalition against the Democrats. The Republicans, along with their anti-slavery and anti-immigrant orientation, tended to favor equal suffrage for blacks, who were, after all, native born. By 1860, when the question would again be submitted to the state's citizens in a referendum, there would be stronger Republican voter support for equal suffrage than had been evident among Whigs in 1846.[62]

61. Hartford *Courant,* June 7, 13, 1855; New Haven *Journal and Courier,* June 9, 1855; *Journal of the House of Representatives, May 1855,* 195, 225; Amos Beman Scrap Book (Amos G. Beman Papers); Amos Beman to Gerrit Smith, June 20, 1855, in Gerrit Smith Papers.

62. Field, *Politics of Race,* 86f.

In the summer of 1855 Ray, James McCune Smith, and Pennington headed a list of forty black New Yorkers calling for a state convention, as black leaders in 1840 had done. The present time seemed favorable for pressing blacks' claims on the state government. "There is," the call declared, "a sacred obligation resting upon the colored citizens of this State, to give the ear of our Legislature no rest till every legal and political disability, with all its depressing and degrading tendencies, shall be swept from the Empire State." At least four black ministers were among the signatories: Pennington, Ray, Jermain Loguen (AMEZ pastor in Syracuse), and Jonathan Gibbs (a Dartmouth graduate and student at Princeton Theological Seminary who was just beginning his pastorate in the Liberty Street Presbyterian Church in Troy). (Garnet would not return from his missionary work in Jamaica until the following year). The convention designated five lecturers on the suffrage issue for five regions. Among these Loguen was to be responsible for fourteen counties in upper New York State and Ray, resuming his work of the late 1830s and early 1840s, was to cover New York City, Long Island, and Staten Island. The chief action of the convention was the founding of the New York State Suffrage Association with Frederick Douglass, who had given the keynote address, as its president.[63] This association and its local branches, during the next five years, used the instruments forged in the 1840s: convention resolutions and open letters to the citizenry, petition drives, and lobbying directed at key legislators.

In 1856 and 1857 the New York legislature approved a referendum to the people of the state on equal suffrage, as it had in 1846, but actually submitting the matter to the people in the fall was prevented by a technicality. A referendum did take place in the fall of 1860, preceded by six months of herculean activities by black suffrage associations. Pennington was one of several who served from May to November as paid agents of the state association. Traveling as lecturers, they also raised money for the campaign. Although blacks were especially urged to contribute and prove themselves politically self-reliant, it turned out that a few whites gave the lion's share to make possible the distribution of tracts and sample ballots. Heavy white contributors included Gerrit Smith, Wendell Phillips, and Brandhurst Schiefflen, scion of a family successful in the drug business. James McCune Smith, who orchestrated the drive, had been

63. *Frederick Douglass' Paper,* July 20, 1855; Foner and Walker (eds.), *Proceedings of the Black State Conventions,* I, 88–98.

appalled in 1846 by "that terrible majority" that had voted down black enfranchisement. For him it had spelled "a hate deeper than I had imagined." Accordingly, workers in the 1860 campaign were warned to avoid the term "Negro enfranchisement" and to stress the general elimination of the "property qualification."[64] The anxiety that prompted this strategy proved to be justified by the prereferendum politicking. Democrats did not now have, as they had had in 1846, substantial support in upstate prosuffrage areas. More and more dependent on immigrants, they felt free to exploit fear of blacks, dislike of them, or both by violent attacks on that race and the amendment proposing to broaden its power at the polls. Republican strategists were accordingly driven to avoid the race issue in such areas as eastern New York, where support was essential and where there was opposition to blacks' being given equal rights.

The equal suffrage amendment was defeated, 345,791 voting against it and 197,889 for it. The 63.3 percent of the voters in opposition were 8.8 percent fewer than the percentage in 1846, surely a significant shift. But what caused the shift is harder to define. The Republican party had fashioned a more coherent rationale for political justice for blacks than had the Whigs fourteen years earlier. Another new, though related, element in 1860 was the increase in sectional feeling in the North against the South, which included more widespread antislavery feeling and, by association, some increase in opposition to discrimination against free blacks. What part the efforts of black leaders had in this shift in white attitudes is impossible to determine with any precision. The final fact was that though Democrats lost the state election, they had succeeded in promoting racism and again burying equal suffrage for blacks. They could take some credit for the fact that in New York County, home of the largest concentration of black people, over 86 percent of the voters still opposed black suffrage.[65]

A demogogic heating up of racist feelings in New York State occurred primarily on the eve of important elections, but the whites' belief that black people were inferior was confirmed every day in New York City by Jim Crow regulations on its street railways or omnibus lines. Generally

64. Freeman, "The Free Negro in New York City," 149–51; Pease and Pease, *They Who Would Be Free,* 186f.

65. Field, *Politics of Race,* chap. 4; also see Freeman, "The Free Negro in New York City," 143–45, 149–51. Freeman gives blacks more credit for the better showing on the black vote in 1860 than does Field. Says Freeman, "The free Negro community had reached a level of sophistication and maturity far beyond the talk and posing of two decades earlier."

blacks were allowed to stand on platforms on the front of cars, and infrequent omnibuses were run for blacks only. In May 1855, some two months before Pennington was to join other black leaders, as just described, in a call for a convention to press once more for equal rights at the polls, he had launched a direct action campaign against discriminatory practices on New York City's public carriers. The result would be the founding of the New York City Legal Rights Association. By 1855 a considerable tradition of protest against humiliating treatment on common carriers had developed. Noted earlier were Garnet's refusals, in 1841 and 1848, to shift his seat to a railroad car designated for Negroes. And David Ruggles and Frederick Douglass were acknowledged as forerunners in these protests. The most systematic effort had been in Massachusetts, and by the late 1840s most of that state's railroads had been desegregated. In New York City prior to 1854, protest had been episodic. George Downing, Sr., celebrated oyster vendor, had initiated black noncompliance in December 1840 on the Harlem Railroad. After boarding a car to go downtown, Downing had sat down inside. When ordered to get out, he had refused. The conductor and driver had beaten and kicked him brutally in the process of ejecting him. Downing had sued the two for assault and battery. They had been acquitted by a court of sessions jury on the grounds that a reasonable regulation excluding black people from the cars had been made and advertised by the railroad company, and that no undue force had been used in ejecting Downing.[66]

In 1852, less than a year after his return to New York City from the British Isles, Pennington had had a letter published in the New York *Evangelist,* outlining the hardships imposed on him as a pastor by being rejected by omnibus drivers. Noting that his parish extended from Hoboken, New Jersey, to Brooklyn and Williamsburgh, New York, and from Pearl Street to Sixty-fifth Street, he described the specific problems of a particular day and concluded, "It is a hard case that a man should be compelled, in the public service, to walk ounce after ounce of his heart's best blood out of him every day, and not be allowed to avail himself of the public conveyances designed to save time, health and life."[67] A couple of months later Pennington had written a delightfully humorous letter to

66. Mabee, *Black Freedom,* 112–26; *National Anti-Slavery Standard,* February 18, 1841; also see the outraged editorial by Charles Ray in *Colored American,* February 20, 1841. Finding little hope for justice for black people in New York City courts, Ray had concluded, "We advise our people to keep out of legal trials."

67. The *Evangelist* article was reprinted by the New York *Times,* September 25, 1852, with sympathetic endorsement of Pennington's protest. The *Maryland Colonization Journal,*

the New York *Times* telling of a black Baptist minister's uneventful ride uptown with no objection from a busload of whites.[68]

In 1854 a young black organist, Elizabeth Jennings, the daughter of a dentist, picked up where George Downing had left off fourteen years earlier. Using the Third Avenue line to get to the Congregational church where she regularly played, she was ordered out of the first car into the second, a crowded one reserved for blacks. She refused to move. The conductor offered to consult the white passengers as to their willingness to have her stay. She rejected this solution as humiliating and was thrown off the car. Climbing back on, she was again thrown off and seriously injured. Suing the car line for damages, she eventually won a favorable state supreme court decision awarding her $225.[69]

Encouraged by Jennings's successful suit, early in May 1855 Pennington urged his Prince Street congregation to tell their friends coming into the city for the anniversary meetings that blacks could no longer be excluded from the city's public carriers. He said that only "the utmost tameness" and "impious cowardice" would now prevent black men and women from claiming "the privilege of common transit" through the streets of New York City. Pennington also sent a notice of this new policy to Douglass's paper, saying to blacks, "You can take the conveyances at any of the Ferries or stopping places. Ask no questions but get in and have your five cents ready to pay. Don't let them frighten you with words; the law is right, and so is the public sentiment." If, urged Pennington, any driver or conductor laid a finger on anyone, he should have the railroad employee arrested or report the case to James McCune Smith, T. L. Jennings (Elizabeth's father), or Pennington for complaint to the mayor.[70]

Public carrier policy, however, had not become color-blind. Some of the city's black people did follow Pennington's advice, upon occasion boarding a car and, when unmolested, getting off it to test the next one. Suits were brought, with varying results. Pennington followed his own counsel. When he boarded and entered car number 22 of the Sixth Avenue Railroad in the latter part of May, the conductor refused to take his fare and kept asking him to get off or go to the front platform of the car.

October, 1852, reprinted it as proof that Pennington and his people should go back to Africa, and the ACS's *African Repository,* March, 1853, reprinted the *Maryland Colonization Journal* piece.

68. New York *Times,* November 10, 1852.

69. Pease and Pease, *They Who Would Be Free,* 167.

70. Article from the New York *Tribune,* reprinted in *Frederick Douglass' Paper,* May 18, 1855; *Frederick Douglass' Paper,* May 11, 1855.

He refused both options and, in spite of strenuous resistance, was ejected by force. With the backing of the New York City Legal Rights Association, founded three weeks after he was forced off the Sixth Avenue car, Pennington sued the railroad for assault and battery, claiming $1,000 in damages. Frederick Douglass exploded in angry sympathy: "Boasting and ranting about Freedom and Equality, the American people, as a whole, are the most inconsistent, and the most tyrannical people, the sunlight ever revealed to the gaze of men or of devils. Caste is the god the nation delights to honor. Caste is in their preaching, their singing, and their praying. . . . This spirit follows us by day and night. . . . It goes with us to the market, to the workshop, to the polls, to the church, to the cars, to the graveyard. . . . Thank God! it cannot go beyond the tomb.—It can enter neither Heaven nor Hell."[71]

The case was finally tried before a jury over eighteen months later. Pennington's lawyer began by describing his client as a respectable man who "moves in good society and is deemed by the religious world as a fit person to teach others." He was, moreover, a city taxpayer. The lawyer tried to disarm the jury by repeating deprecatory remarks Pennington had made when he had first sought legal counsel: "Mr. Tallmadge, I know the prejudice which the people of this country have against our color. We do not claim, however, to be their equals. We do not expect to be invited to sit at their tables or to share their beds. But I have yet to learn that I cannot pass from one part of the country to another in your rail cars and steamboats." The jury decided for the defending railroad, declaring that excluding blacks from all cars but those designated for their use was a reasonable regulation necessary to keep the white patronage that would be driven away by indiscriminate service to both races.[72]

Although Pennington lost the battle, it was part of a general campaign coordinated by the Legal Rights Association that did accomplish some gains in the latter 1850s. The association raised enough money to prosecute a number of cases, and a female branch was organized in 1856. By 1859 a major campaign was under way in Philadelphia. And by early 1860 Henry Garnet, Pennington's successor as pastor of the Prince Street Presbyterian Church (now renamed the Shiloh Presbyterian Church), had resumed his crusade of the 1840s. At a meeting of the New York City Legal Rights Association Garnet recalled the earlier success of protests against Jim Crow practices on railroads in New England. Only recently he had

71. New York *Times*, May 26, 1855; *Frederick Douglass' Paper*, June 8, 1855.

72. New York *Times*, December 18, 20, 1856.

exercised his rights on the Fourth Avenue cars. He was reported as telling his audience that "after detaining the cars until patience had become exhausted, he was suffered to ride." He advised against unnecessary violence, "but when convenience called upon us to ride, be firm." In May 1860 Pennington told blacks coming to the city for anniversary meetings that the First, Second, Third, perhaps the Fourth, and surely the Eighth and Ninth Avenue lines would carry all "respectable" passengers.[73]

The single area of social improvement, other than the abolition of slavery and help for fugitive slaves, to which black activist clergy devoted the most energy between 1830 and 1861 was education. All Christian ministry—Catholic as well as Protestant, and white as well as black—involved a large element of education. In particular, the Sunday schools operated by many Protestant churches taught reading—especially reading of the Bible—to large numbers of working adults who had never had schooling. Black ministers, faced with widespread educational deprivation, had a special passion for founding schools, which often gathered in their churches and often were taught by themselves.

The quality of schooling available to blacks differed hugely from state to state and from city to city. Black education, as has been noted, suffered by comparison with white in two primary ways. Far less public money was spent per pupil on school buildings, teachers' salaries, and classroom materials. And in many, many communities only elementary education was provided for black children. For the vast majority of northern blacks right up to the Civil War, high school education was unavailable, to say nothing of college. Although some communities, like Portland, Maine, accepted blacks and whites alike in their schools, in the great majority segregated schooling was the pattern. Often black parents preferred this, knowing how racist persecution militated against learning where schools were open. Quality private education was rarely available to blacks.

However, progress in black schooling, sometimes striking, did take place in a number of northern communities during the three decades before the Civil War. Earlier chapters have described some of the contribu-

73. Philip S. Foner, *Essays in Afro-American History* (Philadelphia, 1978), chaps. 3, 4; *Weekly Anglo-African*, October 1, 1859; March 24, 1860; Pease and Pease, *They Who Would Be Free*, 167f.; *Weekly Anglo-African*, March 3, 1860; Freeman, "The Free Negro in New York City," 108, 110. In the course of the 1863 Draft Riots, this desegregation policy would be reversed and would not be restored until after the Civil War. Freeman, "The Free Negro in New York City," 111f.

tions of Cornish and Wright to black education in New York City; of Garnet in Troy and Geneva, New York; of Pennington on Long Island, in New Haven, and in Hartford; and of Beman in Hartford and New Haven. By 1859 the excellent high school in Hartford had opened its doors to qualified blacks; Beman and Pennington had paved the way for that development. Most dramatic were the black boycotts against segregated schools; these boycotts won open admission for blacks in the 1840s and 1850s in a number of communities, including Nantucket, Salem, and Boston, Massachusetts; Newport, Rhode Island; and Rochester, New York. Leaders in the prolonged struggles in Rochester, Boston, and Newport, respectively, were Frederick Douglass, journalist and author William Nell, and hotelier Thomas Downing.[74]

The most highly organized black effort before the Civil War to improve the quality of schooling for blacks in a large city occurred in New York City. Charles Ray was central in the enterprise. He had three daughters borne by his second wife, Charlotte Augusta Burroughs, whom he had married in 1840. He thus had personal reasons for concern over the kind of education available to black children in New York City—reasons similar to Cornish's on the same subject twenty years earlier. The New York Society for the Promotion of Education Among Colored Children came into being in 1847 through black initiative, when Protestant-Catholic controversy caused a decline in Public School Society funds. Ray, whose church was small but who was very widely known and respected among New York City blacks, was one of the founders of the society and its president for some fifteen years. The charter for this new organization authorized the allocation to it of public funds for the founding and staffing of new elementary schools for blacks, if the opening of such was authorized by the New York City Board of Education. The board of trustees of the Society for the Promotion of Education Among Colored Children was to consist of twenty-one persons, all black. Although city officials were made ex officio members and the board of education kept general supervisory responsibility, the actual management of the schools was to be in the hands of the society. Among those who brought about this society and who were on its first board of trustees were Samuel Cornish, Charles Ray, Alexander Crummell, George Downing, James

74. Mabee, *Black Freedom,* chap. 11; Foner and Walker (eds.), *Proceedings of the Black State Conventions,* 36f.; Amos Beman Scrap Book (Amos G. Beman Papers), II, 133; Warner, *New Haven Negroes,* 73ff.; J[ames] T. H[olly], "The Colored Public Schools of New Haven," *Weekly Anglo-African,* April 28, 1860.

McCune Smith, and Philip Bell. From 1851 to at least 1865, Ray was president of the organization. The society's most significant achievements were three: (1) the founding and operation of two new elementary schools for black children; (2) the awarding each year of prizes to children in all the black schools for good attendance records and excellence in scholarship; and (3) in 1857 a thorough review of the whole system of black shools, along with recommendations to the board of education for changes that, astonishingly enough, were taken seriously.[75] Between 1848 and 1852 the enrollment in the schools run by Ray's society rose from 652 to 975. The Public School Society thought so highly of these black-managed schools that it seriously considered transferring all black schools in the city to the jurisdiction of private black society.

Late in 1857 Ray, as president of the society, presented a detailed description and evaluation of common schools for blacks to the commissioner charged by the governor of New York with evaluating all of the city's common schools. Ray pointed out that the number of whites going to schools was about 40 times the number of black attenders. However, expenditures on sites and school buildings for whites had been, since the founding of the board of education, 1,600 times greater than those for blacks. The report provided detailed and often dismal descriptions of the nine schools for blacks in operation. In one case it spoke of "much difficulty and confusion" because of the lack of classrooms. In another it described the rooms as "dark and cheerless" and without adequate facilities. In a third case there was always four feet of water in the cellar. And in a fourth case the school was located in "a most degraded neighborhood, full of filth and vice." Ray contrasted these schools with "the splendid, almost palatial edifices, with manifold comforts, conveniences and elegancies" available to whites. "It is evident," he concluded, "that the colored children are painfully neglected and positively degraded." In spite of these discouragements, however, roughly 38 percent of blacks between the ages of four and seventeen were attending school, as compared with some 29 percent of whites of those ages. Moreover, New York City's superintendent of schools, attending a general examination of colored pupils the previous summer, had declared their reading and spelling equal to

75. Mabee, *Black Education in New York State,* 63ff.; Freeman, "The Free Negro in New York City," 352ff. Distinguished blacks such as James McCune Smith and Henry Highland Garnet were brought in to test the students, and the award ceremony, in one of the black churches, was a festive occasion replete with music and speeches. Freeman, "The Free Negro in New York City," 354ff.

those of pupils in any of the city's schools. Ray's recommendation was to desegregate the schools, as Boston had just done. If this was not done, the commissioners should recommend to the state legislature a mandate to the board of education "to erect at least two well appointed modern grammar schools for colored children . . . in respectable localities." Ray's clinching argument was that blacks were paying city taxes comparable to those paid by whites. He pointed out that "they who pay taxes for schools and school-houses should be provided with schools and school-houses."[76]

Within a year and a half the board of education mandated substantial improvements, though not all that Ray had asked for. It tore down the forty-year-old Mulberry Street School (a primary school and separate grammar schools for boys and girls). This had been the best-attended and best-taught of all the city's black schools, but its space had been abysmally inadequate. In place of the old building, the board committed itself to build "a new and elegant structure replete with all the modern furniture and equipments." The board moved another school building from a vice section to "one of the finest locations in the fifth ward." Finally, the board allocated a large sum to remodel the Laurens Street School (primary and grammar).[77]

When Ray's dramatic role in assisting such fugitive slaves as Stella Weims's family and his remarkable accomplishments as president of the New York Society for the Promotion of Education Among Colored Children are highlighted, it is easily forgotten that throughout the 1850s and well into the 1860s he was first and foremost a Christian minister. However, his pastoral and his public service were interwoven to a degree unique among the six activists this book has been considering. Ray's own words, spoken in the mid-1860s to someone close to him, put it best.

> More than twenty years ago, with the advice of friends, I entered upon this work to reach, first, the outcast portions of the people seldom reached with the Gospel and the means, motives, and blessings of a higher material, moral, and spiritual life. I have not, however, as well I could not, confined my labors exclusively to this class, but have been led to labor with and interest a better

76. "Communication from the New York Society for the Promotion of Education Among Colored Children, to the . . . Commissioners for Examination into the Condition of Common Schools in the City and County of New York [December 28, 1857]," *Anglo-African,* I (1859), 222–24.

77. Footnote to the "Communication" (*ibid.*) written in the summer of 1859.

class with me in the same work. Thus I have gone through more than twenty years of my more vigorous life, caring less, in fact, for my own interest than for the interest and spiritual welfare of others.

My work has not been, exclusively, a religious work; my public position has necessarily brought to me every form of claim and work peculiar to a poor and somewhat dependent people, and my advice and aid have been sought; my sympathies have consequently led me to give such counsel and aid as I could, often quite a tax on my time and energies. I have no disposition to sit idly by when there is so much Christian work within reach and pressing upon one's hands to do. Christian work is rest for me, it is refreshing; to look and not to do is not rest.[78]

78. Ray and Ray, *Sketch of Charles B. Ray,* 16f.

11. DEFEATS, FRESH TASKS, AND VISIONS OF A NEW DAY IN THE LATE 1850s

The efforts of Charles Ray, Amos Beman, and James W. C. Pennington during the 1850s to help fugitive slaves and to secure equality for blacks at the polls, on public transport, and in school systems were a continuation of efforts during the preceding decades. And this civil rights struggle, despite all the brave hopes of the Civil War and Reconstruction period, would be a continuing necessity in America for the ensuing century and more.

During the 1850s, especially in the latter part of the decade, there were three other developments of crucial importance for Afro-Americans. First, there was a widening of concern among black leaders, lay and clerical, for the restoration and expansion of relations between Afro-Americans and Africans. In part this was an urge to develop a sound African colonization program—that is, one managed by black people and drawing free blacks who really wanted to migrate, as contrasted with the program of the American Colonization Society. In part this deepened concern for Africa was an urge to share Christianity with the lands from which the African ancestors of American blacks had come. Henry Highland Garnet, prominent in the founding of the African Civilization Society in 1858, became the energetic and controversial president of this organization. Its aim was to combine sound colonization with substantial economic and religious contributions to parts of West Africa. Interrupted by war in West Africa and by civil war and its aftermath in the United

States, Garnet would turn again to this sense of mission near the end of his life.

The second development in the 1850s with great import for the post-bellum period was the increasing involvement of the American Missionary Association in support of American free black communities' efforts at self-improvement. Amos Beman, for some years a recipient of annual grants from the AMA, was hired in 1859 to work full-time as the AMA's roving visitor to black communities in New England, New York, and New Jersey. In accepting this commission, Beman was expanding, and on a salaried basis, a long-time practice of visiting black churches at a distance from New Haven. The AMA staff member to whom Beman would report was Simeon Jocelyn, his forerunner in ministry to the black Congregational church in New Haven. During and after the Civil War the AMA would shift its work with Afro-Americans from northern free blacks to freedmen in the South. There, over the next decades, it would found more than five hundred schools and colleges and spend more money, in so doing, than the federal Freedmen's Bureau.[1]

The third accelerating development during the 1850s was one that would affect all who lived in the United States but that had special import for black Americans: the growing sectional polarization over the slavery issue. This chapter will describe how the events of 1859, and John Brown's Harpers Ferry raid in particular, were understood by Pennington, Garnet, Beman, and Ray as the prelude to a costly struggle, but also to a potentially glorious new day.

Although Garnet did not reach Africa until 1881, he had had a missionary concern in that direction at least as far back as the summer of 1841, when the *Amistad* Mendi had returned to their homeland. His work in western New York State in the latter 1840s had been that of a home missionary; his efforts paralleled those of Ray among the unchurched poor in New York City. After lecturing for the Free Produce Movement in England from 1850 to 1852, Garnet had accepted appointment by the United Presbyterian Church of Scotland to be its first black missionary to Jamaica. He, Julia Garnet, their daughter (Mary), their adopted daughter (Stella Weims), and their young son left Great Britain in December 1852. On the voyage tragedy struck the family again. The Garnets' second son died, and Garnet's first task upon landing at Kingston was to conduct the burial service. His mission parish was over one hundred

1. Clara M. DeBoer, "Blacks and the American Missionary Association," in Barbara B. Zikmund (ed.), *Hidden Histories in the United Church of Christ* (New York, 1984), 81–94.

miles west of Kingston. The population was dense and made up mostly of recently freed slaves. After six weeks the number attending Sunday service had risen from an initial one hundred to nearly four hundred. During the week there were prayer meetings and classes for religious instruction. A weekday school associated with the church was taught by a young black man, his work presumably overseen by Garnet. Julia Garnet opened a school for females, teaching them reading, sewing, and deportment.

A few months later Garnet wrote friends in Newcastle, England, "We are at last *at home*." He described his and Julia's comfortable home and beautiful three acres as not unlike a country parsonage in northern England: "As I am the only black man in this vicinity in the position of a minister, they look upon me as a prodigy, and, strange to say, they call me 'buckra' (white), which is certainly a singular title to give *me*."[2]

In the summer of 1855, some two and a half years after arrival in Jamaica, the physical health of the Garnet family disintegrated. Henry Garnet was stricken with a bilious fever that lasted intermittently for over eight months. At the time he fell ill, Garnet was in correspondence with the United Presbyterian Church of Scotland about the possibility of a transfer to a mission post in Africa. The "redemption of Africa" had appealed to white and black American ministers alike as an especially worthy cause since the latter 1700s. The distinguished white theologian and Newport, Rhode Island, Congregational minister, Samuel Hopkins, had arranged for two blacks in his congregation to be trained at Princeton for Christian service in Africa. Hopkins saw this project as a small atonement for the incalculable sin of the American slave trade and slave ownership. The American Revolution put an end to this mission enterprise, but in 1820 Daniel Coker, an able African Methodist Episcopal minister, set sail for Sierra Leone with help from the American Colonization Society. The next year Lott Cary, a black Baptist minister from Richmond, Virginia, took a shipload of black colonists to Liberia and remained to found several Baptist churches and, in spite of his harsh criticism of the ACS, to accept appointment as vice-governor of the colony.[3]

2. Schor, *Henry Highland Garnet,* 125; A commercial contact in Kingston (to whom the AMA had recommended Garnet) to William Jackson (president of the American Missionary Association), December 20, 1852, in AMA Archives, no. 81163; Excerpts from Henry Garnet to Mrs. S. J. Davis, February 8, 1853, in *American Missionary,* April 1853 (Microfilm copy in Carter and Ripley [eds.], *BAP,* reel 8, item 125); *Inquirer,* April 23, 1853 (Microfilm copy in Carter and Ripley [eds.], *BAP,* reel 8, item 228).

3. Schor, *Henry Highland Garnet,* 113*n*58; Wilmore, *Black Religion and Black Radicalism,* 104–106.

Garnet was familiar with the substantial accomplishments of Coker and Cary. More influential, however, was the example of Garnet's boyhood friend Alexander Crummell, who had been thwarted in his career as a black Episcopal priest in America. Crummell had graduated from Queen's College, University of Cambridge, and had gone to Liberia as a missionary of the Episcopal church in 1853, shortly after Garnet had left England for Jamaica. The severe illness that struck the Garnet family in 1855, however, forced cancellation of plans for missionary service in Africa. Julia Garnet, who had come to New England to arrange for the education of the children—especially Mary, age eleven, who would graduate from the Hopedale female seminary near Boston in 1863—came down with the fever soon after arrival in the United States. Stella Weims, who stayed with Garnet in Jamaica, contracted the disease and died of it. By early March 1856 Garnet had been granted sick leave by the Scottish Presbyterians and had come back to the United States, hoping to return to Jamaica in six or eight months. But such a return was not to be. Writing Gerrit Smith in late March, his mood was very different than it had been in the summer of 1850: "Everything looks very pleasant in my dear native land—old faces, as familiar voices, are indeed cheering. The kind welcome too of my valued friend Douglass is gratifying in the extreme. . . . I give him my heart and hand in the good cause."[4] Absence had made Douglass and Garnet fonder of each other, but also Douglass was acutely aware of how much Garnet's re-dedication to the freedom struggle in the United States could mean both for the antislavery cause and for the struggle for free blacks' civil rights.

Although still in a debilitated condition, Garnet was asked by the members of the Prince Street Presbyterian Church, now without a pastor, to start preaching for them. He did so at once as a city missionary.[5]

Garnet also quickly resumed the antislavery lecturing to which he had devoted so much time in the 1840s. He sensed promising developments in the United States in spite of several years of proslavery legislation and the prospect of Kansas being admitted to the Union with a stipulation excluding blacks. He found antislavery feeling in the North more intense than when he had left. The North, he said, was like a coward forced into a corner. It would soon really fight back, "and when a coward does fight

4. Schor, *Henry Highland Garnet,* 129f.; Henry Garnet to Gerrit Smith, from Boston, March 25, 1856, in Gerrit Smith Papers.

5. Henry Garnet to S. S. Jocelyn, March 4, 1857, in AMA Archives, no. 83325.

he is always dangerous." He predicted a devastating civil war growing out of recent bloody events in Kansas, in which John Brown had engineered a brutal retaliation against bullying proslavery settlers.[6]

After Massachusetts senator Charles Sumner was beaten senseless in the Senate chamber following a vituperative speech attacking South Carolina senator Andrew Butler, Garnet was involved in a number of rallies protesting the violence. During the summer and early fall of 1856, the New York minister was delivering addresses in Philadelphia and upper New York State. Often he shared the platform with Douglass, the two of them again pressing for equal suffrage for blacks. Although both men were much drawn to the Radical Abolition party, as the national election drew near they came out strongly for the Republicans because of their evident commitment to halting the expansion of slave territory.[7]

In September 1856, somewhat more than six months after Pennington had resigned from the Prince Street pastorate, Garnet was invited to become the permanent minister of the church. Although he seemed to agonize over whether to accept the post or to return to Jamaica, he was too much involved once more in the many-sided struggle in the United States to leave it. And his specifically Christian sense of mission to free black people in his home country had been reborn. He spelled it out to Gerrit Smith: "Of all places in the world I think this land needs the labors of black men. My people (your people) are perishing for lack of knowledge—and I believe they will give me their ears as readily as any other." Garnet saw his calling clearly: "I desire to be a Missionary of Liberty and the Gospel to my people in this land, if it be God's will." However, he had two firm stipulations. First, he wanted to be able to work without financial distractions and asked Smith to help make up an annual salary of $1,000, of which one-half could be secured from the Prince Street Presbyterian Church and part of the rest, from Lewis Tappan and the American Missionary Association. Second, Garnet insisted he would not "re-connect myself with the pro-slavery Church." Evidently Garnet's financial requirements were met. The development of the clearer-cut antislavery stand within New School Presbyterianism, which has been noted,

6. Henry Garnet to a staff member at the AMA, May 5, 1856, in AMA Archives, no. 82922; New York *Daily Tribune,* May 7, 1856, cited by Schor, *Henry Highland Garnet,* 148*n*23.

7. Schor, *Henry Highland Garnet,* 141–44; Henry Garnet to Gerrit Smith, July 9, 1856, in Gerrit Smith Papers.

further allayed Garnet's anxiety on this score and opened the way to his accepting this influential pastorate and the income which he and his family desperately needed.[8]

Early in 1857 Garnet reported to the AMA on the developments during the year since he had begun work as a city missionary at the Prince Street Presbyterian Church, now renamed the Shiloh Presbyterian Church. There had been a striking reinvigoration. A year earlier the Sunday congregation had numbered 150 to 200. Now there were morning, afternoon, and evening sessions drawing 150, 500 to 600, and 300 people, respectively. Eleven had joined the church at the last communion (six weeks earlier), and forty-eight were now candidates, most of them young people. Soon after Garnet submitted this report, there was a remarkable revival in the church. One day, March 29, 1857, would be remembered for a long time. Attendance had been 150 at a preparatory prayer meeting at 5:00 A.M. There had been a large turnout for the regular morning service. The afternoon service attracted "the largest congregation of colored persons that ever was convened in New York for a religious purpose." The 1,200 seats were filled; more people packed the aisles, pulpit stairs, vestibules, and front steps; and many more were unable to find any access. Garnet was assisted by William Patton, a prominent white Presbyterian minister, and Elymas Rogers, pastor of the Plane Street (African) Presbyterian Church in Newark. When those prepared to join the church were called forward, sixty-eight responded.[9]

From 1856 to 1860 Garnet was commissioned by either the American Missionary Association or the American Home Missionary Society and was given a stipend of $250 to $300 a year to augment the salary paid him by Shiloh.[10] By the spring of 1859 the church was meeting current expenses, doing repairs, and starting payments on an $800 organ recently purchased. Evening worship was attended by 1,000 to 1,100 people, and for the first time in the history of the black community in New York City, the largest black congregation was Presbyterian. Beneath these positive developments, however, trouble was brewing. As Garnet had made plain in 1856, he felt that he needed and deserved a salary of $1,000 a

8. Henry Garnet to Gerrit Smith, October 3, 1856, January 8, 1857, both in Gerrit Smith Papers.

9. Henry Garnet's report to Simeon Jocelyn, March 4, 1857, Garnet's report to an undesignated party at the AMA, April 10, 1857, both in AMA Archives, nos. 83325, 83356.

10. Howard, "Anti-Slavery Movement," 237. Garnet, denied an AMA commission from 1857 to 1859, accepted one for those years from the AHMS.

year. At no time had Shiloh paid him more than $750, and in September 1859 his salary was reduced to $500. He wrote the Third Presbytery to request that his resignation be implemented. His old friends in the American Missionary Association stepped in and recommissioned him with a stipend, specifying that he work especially with the black schools of New York City. They made this commission contingent, however, on Shiloh's providing him a salary of $625 a year. After some balking, the church agreed to this sum and paid it through the ensuing year.[11]

There were at least two other areas of contention between Garnet and some of his members: the strict moral discipline imposed by the session under Garnet's supervision, and the controversial social and political causes outside the church with which Garnet allied himself. Shiloh's session started regular meetings, with Garnet as moderator and secretary, in November 1857. His minutes over the next three years are a priceless record of a big city, largely middle-class black church's struggle to keep its membership faithful to the covenant they had entered into in joining the church. Garnet's standards and methods were essentially those he had applied as pastor of Troy's Liberty Street Presbyterian Church some fifteen years earlier. The problems he dealt with were, by and large, the same ones most Protestant ministers, black and white, North and South, were facing, with greater and lesser urgency: violation of the sexual code, intemperance, slander, and systematic absence from church services.[12]

Resentment against Garnet came to be concentrated in the church's board of trustees, which during Garnet's pastorate was evidently made up entirely of blacks belonging to the church. Their hostility seems to have had a number of sources besides the strictness with which the moral behavior of church members was supervised: (1) the refusal of the session

11. Henry Garnet's reports to the AHMS, March 1, June 1, September 1, November 30, 1858, March 1, June 1, September 13, 1859, Garnet's letter of resignation, February 28, 1860, M. Badger to Henry Garnet, September 21, 1858, all in Carter and Ripley (eds.), *BAP,* reel 11, items 171, 236, 340, 372, 429, 630, 776; reel 12, items 35, 522; Henry Garnet to Simeon Jocelyn, September 14, 1859, in AMA Archives, no. 84310; Henry Garnet to Third Presbytery of New York, November 28, 1859, at Presbyterian Historical Association; Henry Garnet to S. S. Jocelyn, October 4, 1860, in AMA Archives, no. 84939.

12. Minutes of the Session of Shiloh Church, New York, January 20, February 4, 11, April 15, September 22, 30, October 11, November 17, 1858; January 20, 30, March 14, April 16, June 20, 1859; September 3, 19, December 5, 1860; February 3, 1861 (Presbyterian Historical Association, Philadelphia). For parallel discipline cases in white Presbyterian churches in the South, see W. D. Blanks, "Corrective Church Discipline in the Presbyterian Churches of the Nineteenth Century South," *Journal of Presbyterian History,* XLIV (1966), 89–105.

to allow the trustees to rent out the church for such secular purposes as a concert of nonsacred music; (2) Garnet's habit of making personal, and sometimes censorious, allusions to officers or members of the church from the pulpit; (3) his insistence on having a salary well above what the trustees saw as affordable; and (4) his devotion of time, energy, and sometimes the church building to causes of which the trustees disapproved. Morale in the church would reach a new low in July 1861, when the trustees would lock up the church just before a Sunday evening service and disappear with the key. By the following summer the Third Presbytery was weighing whether or not to approve Garnet's resignation in protest against harassment by the trustees. The presbytery's conclusion was that the fault lay with both sides, but the measure of reconciliation effected was enough to allow for Garnet's remaining in the pastorate until 1864.[13]

For the purposes of this analysis, the most important of these charges against Garnet was the last one. The cause to which Garnet was devoting much time between 1858 and 1861 that aroused antagonism among not a few members of the Shiloh Presbyterian Church was the African Civilization Society. Founded in 1858 with Garnet as its president, this society won considerable support from both whites and blacks during the next three years. It aimed to start a settlement in the Niger Valley, where established tribal government seemed to be hospitable, vacant land available, and the climate more healthful than on the coast. The goal was threefold: (1) agricultural and commercial development centered on the growing of cotton; (2) Christian evangelization; and (3) the shaping of a new social and political order blessed with technology but not cursed with the materialism that had been fueling the European imperialistic exploitation of Africa.

Most of the major figures in the founding of the African Civilization Society were white. However, from the white promoters' point of view, as well as Garnet's, he was the appropriate person to be president. He was of undiluted African ancestry. He had been proudly outspoken about his African origins, at least from his early twenties. In a major address in 1848 in Troy, he had dwelt at length on Africa's past and future. He had reveled in the advanced culture of Egypt, whose people, as attested to by

13. Minutes of the Session of Shiloh Presbyterian Church, July 14, 1861; *Weekly Anglo-African*, January 11, 1862; Report of the Committee from the Third Presbytery on the Shiloh Church, June 1862, Minutes of the Session of Shiloh Presbyterian Church, 1848–70. Evidently, during Garnet's pastorate the Shiloh Presbyterian Church's board of trustees was made up entirely of blacks belonging to the church.

the famous Greek historian Herodotus, were black and woolly haired. In a reversal of emphasis from the recurrent appeal by blacks to the Exodus as the paradigm of liberation of the oppressed, Garnet had said of the Egyptians, "They became masters of the East, and the lords of the Hebrews. No arm less powerful than Jehovah's could pluck the children of Abraham from their hands." Garnet went on to praise the Hebrew king Solomon for flouting the laws of his nation in order to take as his favorite concubine the black daughter of a pharaoh: "To her honor and praise he composed that beautiful poem called the Canticles, or Solomon's Song." Finally, following the path of African Methodist bishop Richard Allen and African Baptist missionary Lott Cary, Garnet spoke of the mysterious role of Ethiopia as one of the few nations whose destiny was spoken of in prophecy. He cited Psalm 68:31, "Princes shall come out of Egypt, and Ethiopia shall soon stretch out her hands unto God." Thus Garnet early on supported Ethiopianism which would be a central element in the pan-Africanism of Alexander Crummell and of Henry McNeil Turner, the radical black nationalist AME bishop.[14]

In other respects Garnet seemed an ideal president for the African Civilization Society. He had a well-deserved reputation among both American blacks and white abolitionists for eloquent anger over the abomination of slavery. He had also himself been susceptible to the logic of the idea that blacks should emigrate out of the United States in order to lead more productive lives elsewhere. When Garnet had gone to England in 1850 to promote the Free Produce Movement, both he and Pennington had become more deeply drawn toward the mission of Christian evangelism in Africa. However, they had not, as did many American supporters of African missions, stress the benighted state of African culture. They had seen a Christian mission as representing religious progress and as optimally linked with the development of African agricultural and commercial life. And such development could weaken American slavery by challenging American trade in slave-grown cotton.

With such a background, Garnet seemed in 1858 the natural choice to organize a movement among American blacks to support a nonimperialistic transmission of the best in American culture to hospitable regions of West Africa. During Garnet's five-year absence in Great Britain and Jamaica, a few black leaders in America had won more of a hearing among their people for possible settlement in Africa. In 1852 Martin Delany had

14. Garnet, *The Condition and Destiny of the Colored Race,* 6–11.

published a persuasive book, *The Condition, Elevation, Emigration, and Destiny of the Colored People of the United States*. It was in the tradition of Pennington's 1841 *Text Book of the Origin and History . . . of the Colored People* and of Garnet's 1848 *Past and Present Condition, and the Destiny, of the Colored Race.* Delany's book included a proud litany highlighting Afro-American businessmen and professional men and women. It was in the mode of Cornish's and Ray's publicizing news of successful black enterprise. However, the final quarter of Delany's book drew pessimistic conclusions regarding the present and future possibilities for free blacks in the United States a decade after the collapse of the *Colored American*. After a somber review of twenty years of black and radical white efforts to elevate free American blacks, Delany came to the grim conclusion that they had little more freedom than did slaves. Migration to a land of their own was clearly the answer. Although Delany's message was unpopular among abolitionists, who continued to fight for black liberation within the United States, his emigrationism and black nationalism were important elements in Afro-American thought during the 1850s and thereafter.

Equally important were Delany's views on Christianity and Afro-Americans. He claimed that one of the great weaknesses of American blacks was that they were too religious, too inclined to attribute their present oppressed condition to past sins and to recommend prayer as the most effective road to deliverance. Delany, like the activists whose lives this work has been following, insisted that blacks, whether enslaved or free, had to help themselves. At the same time, however, he insisted on the contributions that Christianity could bring to Africa, if and only if the missionaries were black.[15]

In August 1854, some eighteen months before Garnet's return to the United States from Jamaica, the National Emigration Convention had been held in Cleveland. Delany had been primarily responsible for the convention's report, which favored emigration to Central America, South America, and the West Indies. Although the proposed investigation of sites for possible settlement included the Niger Valley, Delany downplayed West Africa because of the influence of the American Colonization Society and its offspring, Liberia, in that region. In the discussion among black leaders before, during, and after the Cleveland convention, an influ-

15. Martin R. Delany, *The Condition, Elevation, Emigration, and Destiny of the Colored People of the United States* (1852; rpr. New York, 1968), 36–48, 92–133, 159–90; Wilmore, *Black Religion and Black Radicalism*, 110f., 120f.; St. Clair Drake, *The Redemption of Africa and Black Religion* (Chicago, 1970), 48–57.

ential group took a generally antiemigration position. Frederick Douglass, James Pennington, James McCune Smith, and George Downing stoutly maintained the thirty-year-old anticolonization platform, insisting that the race problem could and should be solved by blacks' staying in the United States.[16]

By the time Garnet came back to the United States in early 1856, there was considerable momentum behind the movement for black emigration to some area in the Western Hemisphere, and also hardened positions among black leaders who opposed all emigration. During 1857 and 1858 new developments drew the attention of many American blacks back to Africa as a site that offered scope for American blacks' abilities and promise for the emergence of a distinctive black culture. These same developments seemed to offer Garnet, through the African Civilization Society, an opportunity to continue to fight American slavery through the Free Produce Movement and to Christianize Africa, even though he himself had decided to stay in America. A primary agent in these new perspectives was a white Baptist minister, Thomas Jefferson Bowen, who had been sent to the Niger Valley in 1848 and had established a mission in Abeokuta. He had returned to the United States about the time Garnet had come back from Jamaica. Bowen had gone on the lecture circuit, providing his audiences with much factual information about the Yoruba people with whom he had worked. He emphasized the advanced culture in Yoruba communities, including methods of agriculture and of weaving, dyeing, and cloth making. He also insisted on the importance for the future of the region of American blacks' settling there. He was said to have declared, "If colonized by civilized blacks from America, it [the area] would soon command the trade of all central Africa." Bowen saw a black middle class as essential to steady advancement and to a permanent Christian movement in this part of West Africa.

Garnet, on the basis of his knowledge of British textile companies' interest in cotton growing by free labor in West Africa, endorsed Bowen's proposals. In August 1858, at a meeting of blacks in New York City, Garnet announced the program of the African Civilization Society. For the next three years he spent much energy trying to gain support for this new organization. Often his task was to answer the criticism that this society, like the American Colonization Society, was proposing to siphon off American black leadership to Africa. Garnet had indeed projected the

16. Foner, *History of Black Americans*, III, 139–49.

emigration to West Africa of as many as several thousand enterprising American blacks with Christian commitment. To heighten black suspicion of the new enterprise, it was being funded in no small measure by the American Colonization Society and by some of that organization's well-to-do supporters.[17]

Easily misunderstood and misrepresented as Garnet's intentions were, they were fundamentally different from those of the American Colonization Society. The African Civilization Society did not seek support by denigrating blacks in America or by belittling the achievements of black leaders. Moreover, its vision of the new nation to be developed in Africa was not a white colonial vision but a genuinely African and Afro-American one. In sharp contrast to American black Liberians' tendency to look with contempt on the native African population, Garnet seems to have viewed Yoruba culture with respect. He was, indeed, prepared to accept African legal codes and African governors for the proposed settlement in the Niger Valley. Glorying in earlier African states and in his own African origin, he hoped for a nation with a flourishing economy and a flag that he could respect. Whites could not achieve these results, and Garnet declared that God was calling on blacks to join in this enterprise "and found a nation of which the colored American could be proud." By the summer of 1859, after much hostile criticism, he put the goal of the African Civilization Society even more strongly: "to establish a grand center of Negro nationality, from which shall flow streams of commercial, intellectual and political power which shall make colored people respected everywhere."[18]

Early and strong black supporters of the African Civilization Society included John T. Raymond, who had been the pastor of black Baptist churches in Boston and New York City; J. Sella Martin, young minister at Boston's Joy Street Baptist Church; and Henry M. Wilson, pastor of the Seventh Avenue (formerly Immanuel) Presbyterian Church in New York City. The great majority of black social and political activists, however, opposed the program of the new society. Prominent among these were Frederick Douglass, James McCune Smith, William Wells Brown, George Downing, and, in his customary quiet way, Charles Ray. The

17. The sources for the preceding two paragraphs are Richard MacMaster, "Henry Highland Garnet and the African Civilization Society," *Journal of Presbyterian History,* XLVIII (1970), 91–112; Schor, *Henry Highland Garnet,* 153–57.

18. Schor, *Henry Highland Garnet,* 156–61; New York *Tribune,* August 11, 1858; *Weekly Anglo-African,* September 10, 1859.

primary lines of argument were familiar ones. Colonization enterprises in Africa robbed the American struggle of needed brains and spirit and threatened Africa with further imperialistic exploitation.

James Pennington, by this time back in his pastorate in New Town, Long Island, needed more time to come to a firm stand against Garnet. Pennington had come to know and respect a number of Englishmen active in the development of Sierra Leone. And he, as has been noted, had a long-standing missionary interest in both the West Indies and Africa. As early as 1850 he had written the American Missionary Association from Great Britain to urge that efforts at evangelization in Africa should be in the interior, not on the coast, where European commercial interests tended to dominate. Pennington was deeply concerned about the fact that Great Britain and France were both "currently engrossing Africa" with little concern for the evangelization of the native people. Two years later he wrote Frederick Douglass that even in Africa black people could not escape whites: "The Saxon is there! The real landstealing, unscrupulous, overreaching Saxon is even in Africa, and is pushing his way into the interior." When the African Civilization Society's program was first publicized, Pennington had endorsed its objectives. It seemed to offer a grand alternative to previous instances where European colonists had captured kings and annexed territories and populations. However, at the same time that Garnet came to depend more and more on white American Colonization Society supporters to make his beleaguered case at tempestuous public meetings, Pennington became convinced that the African Civilization Society's vision of a melding of truly African and western Christian values was a mirage. He called on Garnet to disband the society.[19]

In addition to formidable opposition to the program of the African Civilization Society among black leaders, Garnet met sharp criticism among some influential members of his own church. One can sympathize with their position. Promotion of the African Civilization Society consumed much of Garnet's time and emotional energy from 1858 to 1861. It became a substitute for his previous involvement in national politics, including his campaigning for the Liberty party in the early 1840s and for the Republican party from 1856 to the summer of 1858.

The most vocal among Garnet's critics at Shiloh were on the church's

19. James Pennington to George Whipple of the AMA, February 20, 1850, James Pennington to the editor of the *American Missionary,* [August, 1853], both in AMA Archives; *Frederick Douglass' Paper,* April 22, 1852; *Weekly Anglo-African,* September 3, 1859; March 3, 31, 1860; Blackett, *Beating Against the Barriers,* 74f.

board of trustees. They resented the church's having been the scene of more than one heated debate over selective emigration to Africa or, as Garnet had started to urge by early 1861, to Haiti. (James Redpath, head of the Haitian Emigration Bureau, had appointed Garnet as an agent for New York City.) The trustees' dismay and anger were communicated to the Third Presbytery in July 1861, after they had locked church members out of a Sunday evening service: "We have deemed it nessary to close the Church in order to protect her peace and prosperity. . . . Sabaths have been invaded by church meetings held by the Pastor of the church but under Protest by representative men of the *church* wich at the time exciting debate and ugly feelings have been exhibited quiet and inoffensive members have been *annoyed*."[20]

Along with advocacy of the African Civilization Society, Garnet continued to devote himself to those missions in New York City and New York State to which, he had told Gerrit Smith in 1856, he felt himself powerfully called. Like Pennington and Ray, Garnet was constantly appalled by the living conditions of many of his people in Manhattan. Indeed, his home on Laurens Street was in the midst of black degradation. In receiving a commission as city missionary from the AMA early in 1860, he was formally turning to the constituency with whom Ray had been working for fifteen years. Reporting to Jocelyn in June of that year, Garnet expressed shock at "the limited provision . . . made for the spiritual wants of the poor." Four years of experience in the city had convinced him that a great many died each year "without Christian instructions and the consolations of the gospel." And black people in their youth badly needed "more ample provision for their moral and intellectual culture." As a contribution in this direction, Garnet had founded and been publicizing for some time an Anglo-African reading room on Prince Street. Discouraged at its lack of appeal, he was closing it down at a substantial personal loss.[21]

The AMA also assigned Garnet a more encouraging task: to visit the city's public schools for colored children. He found that these had, indeed, been vastly improved as the result of Ray's presidency of the New York Society for the Promotion of Education Among Colored Children. On the political front Garnet remained involved, though not a prime mover, in the efforts during the summer of 1860 to prepare for the fall

20. James Boyd to the Third Presbytery, July 8, 1861, A.L.S. at Presbyterian Historical Association, Philadelphia.

21. Henry Garnet to S. S. Jocelyn, June 1, 1860, in AMA Archives.

referendum on the black franchise. Finally, trustee hostility at the Shiloh Presbyterian Church should not cloud the fact that by and large Garnet's ministry in that church had been effective. Although the membership had fallen from 475 to 400 during the early months of his activity in the African Civilization Society, it had risen again to 460 by early 1860.[22]

Amos Beman, in contrast to Pennington and Garnet, continued ministry in the same community throughout the 1840s and the greater part of the 1850s. Like Garnet, Beman suffered bitter bereavement because of deaths in his family in the mid-1850s. As Pennington's ministry in New York City had come to a dismal close in 1856, so the momentum of Beman's pastorate in New Haven slowed markedly in 1856 and 1857, leading to his resignation, perhaps under pressure from his congregation. And like Garnet, in the closing years of the decade Beman focused his energies on a cause broader than that of the local parish.

Having twice weighed a move to a Presbyterian pastorate in Philadelphia in the 1840s, Beman was again responding to a Presbyterian overture in 1855. The trustees and elders of the Fifteenth Street Presbyterian Church of Washington, D.C., invited him to visit them. He spent two weeks in Washington, preaching and getting acquainted with the congregation. The response was enthusiastic. The church, about the size of that in New Haven, offered Beman a post. Although it gave promise of more financial stability than what the Temple Street African Congregational Church had provided, Beman declined the position. He shrank from the move to a strange southern city and was reluctant to uproot his wife and four children, who had been periodically afflicted with severe illness.[23]

Early in 1856, recognizing the progressive sectional polarization over the slavery issue, discouraged by the failure to secure the franchise for Connecticut blacks, and sensing that he had done what he could to stir New Haven blacks toward self-elevation, Beman became an itinerant preacher and lecturer against slavery and for the uplift of free blacks. (He did not give up his New Haven church, but he was sitting more loosely in the position.) Although he could not electrify an audience as did Garnet, Pennington, and Douglass, Beman was an immensely popular

22. *Ibid.*

23. Amos Beman's reports of February 27, 1854, March 22, 1855, to the AHMS, both in AHMS Archives; Amos Beman to S. S. Jocelyn, November 20, 1855, April 2, 1854, both in AMA Archives.

speaker in demand among whites and blacks, and especially so with the increasing intensity of abolitionist sentiments after the passage of the Kansas-Nebraska Bill.[24] He kept a careful log of his lecture tours. In January 1856 he traveled 1,500 miles to Buffalo and northward. He preached or lectured almost every evening for over three weeks and then succumbed to a spell of illness. In April, May, and June he took two trips to New York and New Jersey and one to Long Island.

In July, returning from a three-thousand-mile swing that included Illinois and southern Canada, Beman reached home to find his family all laid low by typhoid fever. His 16-year-old son, Amos, died in early August, and his wife, Mary, succumbed three weeks later. His eldest daughter, Fannie, and a younger daughter and son went to live with relatives in Farmington. Fannie's health declined slowly but steadily, and she died in early February 1857. Beman, hurrying back from Buffalo, preached to his Temple Street congregation two days after her death and saw her buried the next day. He wrote in his journal, "I am alone." On a Saturday some two weeks later, he was at Garnet's home in New York City. He spent the evening with Garnet in his study and then went to work on four sermons he was scheduled to preach, including two for Garnet's congregation and one for Ray's. Before leaving New York City he visited the enfeebled Cornish in Brooklyn and spent an evening with his longtime friend Amos Freeman. Ten days later he was back in New York City preaching for Freeman at Brooklyn's Siloam Presbyterian Church, attending a prayer meeting at Henry Ward Beecher's church, and going to the funeral of Garnet's sister. The warm support by friends and the testimonies inherent in his own preaching had helped him through this especially desolate time. Not long after his daughter's death, Beman resumed the lecture circuit, logging about five thousand miles and speaking about two hundred times during 1857. He estimated that he had also written about three hundred letters that year.[25]

Late in 1857 Beman was corresponding with the Abyssinian Congregational Church (also named the Sumner Street Church and the Fourth Congregational Church) in Portland, Maine, where he had served as an interim minister in the early 1840s. The church wanted him back. Early

24. Warner, "Amos Gerry Beman," 216. That Beman was chosen president of the national black convention in 1843 and in 1855 and that his written pieces were so often published in *Frederick Douglass' Paper* and the *Weekly Anglo-African* suggest wide respect among his peers for his poise in public meetings and his powers of expression.

25. Amos Beman Scrap Book, 1856–57 (Amos G. Beman Papers), III.

in 1858 he accepted its call and resigned the pastorate of the Temple Street Church. A few months later he married Eliza Kennedy, of New Haven. A white woman who had been brought up in England, she was a few years younger than Beman. Her first husband had died. She had a grown son at sea and two younger daughters living at home. There has been much speculation as to why Beman took the radical step of embarking on an interracial marriage and why he left New Haven for the comparatively small black community in Portland. The marriage evidently roused considerable hostility in the black communities in New Haven and Portland. Was this marriage an act of defiance against the whites of New Haven, who had never accepted Beman as an equal despite all his abilities and gentility? Or was it a "failure in the sphere of the personal and social," a too-literal belief in "the Christian ideal of the brotherhood of all men under God?"[26] A more likely explanation than either of these seems to be that Beman and Eliza Kennedy had come to care a great deal for each other, that each of them had two children in need of a second parent, and that they could not foresee all the practical problems that the marriage would cause. Certainly the frequent references to his new wife in Beman's many letters written before her death of cancer in 1864 suggest a rich and devoted companionship.[27]

Why did Beman resign his New Haven pastorate? A later pastor at the Temple Street Church claimed that Beman had left New Haven because his congregation had been alienated by his plans to marry across the color line. A contemporary of Beman's, however, denied this allegation, saying that for Beman to marry a white woman was "not at all unnatural as he was nearly white himself." Beman had, this source claimed, "resigned of his own accord." Beman's frenetic traveling during 1856 and 1857 indicates that he was deeply restless. There was no hint of criticism in the tributes paid to him by the two New Haven newspapers and by the white ministers meeting to authorize his departure. Reports from New Haven to the *Weekly Anglo-African* in 1859, however, make clear that resentment among at least a few influential parishioners had been substantial. All credit is due to the newly married couple, for they kept their home in

26. Amos Beman to S. S. Jocelyn, June 2, 1858, in AMA Archives; Warner, "Amos Gerry Beman," 220.

27. It is instructive to compare Beman's interracial marriage in 1858 with the marriage in 1853 of William G. Allen, an Afro-American faculty member at New York Central College, to a white student. After a secret ceremony and a forced resignation from the faculty, he and his wife had gone to live in England. Sernett, *Abolition's Axe,* 60f.

New Haven, returned there to live after about two years, and seem largely to have overcome the ill will.[28] Two factors unrelated to hostility over his marriage may well have drawn Beman to Portland. First, the Maine city had a good public school system that, in contrast to New Haven schools, was entirely open to blacks. Beman's son, Charles Torrey, now about thirteen years old, went with his father and attended school in that system. Second, Beman's health, taxed by two years of strenuous travel and by the jolting losses of his first wife and two of his children, may well have prompted him to seek work in a smaller and less demanding community.

The chief practical problem in the move to Portland, where neither the black church nor the white churches had as strong an economic base as they did in New Haven, was how Beman could secure the $500-a-year salary that he had found to be essential. The Abyssinian Congregational Church guaranteed him $200 a year and endorsed his request for another $200 annually from the American Home Missionary Society. Finding himself beset by special expenses in moving and furnishing a new home, he asked Simeon Jocelyn, staff member of the American Missionary Association and a close personal friend, for an emergency grant from the AMA. It was sent to him, but more was needed, because his Portland parishioners had withdrawn the customary individual contributions toward household needs (furniture, carpet, and so forth) when they discovered that the new bride was white. As a result, Beman had to ask that the emergency donation from the AMA be made a regular grant of $25 a quarter. The deacons of his church endorsed this request, and it was approved. Jocelyn and Beman agreed that in return for the AMA grant, Beman would publicize the association's program, and particularly its mission among the Mendi, which had been of special importance to Beman from the time of the *Amistad* crew's trial, acquittal, conversion to Christianity, and return to Africa.

About four hundred blacks lived in Portland. After a year in the city, Beman reported that he had visited over ninety of the one hundred black families. The Abyssinian Congregational Church had tripled in size. Sixteen young ladies were in Beman's Bible class. He had held several tem-

28. Amos Beman to the Temple Street congregation, January 3, 1858, in Amos Beman Scrap Book (Amos G. Beman Papers); Warner, "Amos Gerry Beman," 217f.; New Haven *Daily Palladium*, January 19, 1858; New Haven *Journal and Courier*, January 19, 1858; Record of the New Haven Ecclesiastical Council Meeting of January 11, 1858, approving Beman's release and describing him as "an able and faithful minister of the gospel," in Amos Beman Scrap Book (Amos G. Beman Papers); *Weekly Anglo-African*, November 26, December 26, 31, 1859.

perance meetings, presumably for any blacks in the city, and 109 people had taken the pledge of total abstinence.[29]

By the end of June 1859, after eighteen successful months in the Portland pastorate, Beman resigned the post to take a full-time position with the American Missionary Association. The new post offered him a more widely influential role than did the Portland pastorate—or, indeed, the one in New Haven. Beman had himself formulated this new mission and convinced Jocelyn and other AMA personnel of its potential value. He was to be a missionary especially charged with visiting black churches in New England, New York, and New Jersey; inspiring them to more vigorous life; and presenting to them and to nearby white churches the claims of the mission and temperance causes. In particular, Beman was to increase church people's support for the American Missionary Association and its projects in the North, the South, the West Indies, and Africa. Beman had persuasively sketched to Jocelyn and Lewis Tappan his strengths for the work. He was already known to many blacks of all denominations in the proposed region. When speaking in country towns and villages, for each black contacted he would reach ten whites. He pointed out, "What an increase of men—and means may flow into the American Missionary Association if . . . the free people of this land . . . are enlightened and their sympathies rightly directed by suitable agencies among them." Beman's vision of his prospective task was vintage evangelicalism, breathtaking (or frightening) in its idealistic terminology: "I desire now to go to the great work of my life—if *God so wills* and I think, by his Providence I have in some humble degree been fitted—disciplined, and prepared for it. I hope with my twenty years of experience to do much good—with my tongue—and my pen. . . . For God and Humanity I desire to live toil and die."[30]

In fact, almost from the start of his pastorate in New Haven, Beman, like Theodore Wright, had been deeply interested in the development of younger black Congregational and Presbyterian churches, as well as in the careers of their pastors. He had been a major force in the growth of the Abyssinian Congregational Church in Portland in the early 1840s. Likewise, he assisted in the organization in 1846 of the Second Congrega-

29. Letters to the AMA, most addressed to S. S. Jocelyn, April 6, June 2, 14, 21, August 11, September 21, December 3, 13, 1858, March 26, 1859, [?] to the AHMS, February 28, 1859, all in AMA Archives; Report of March 1, 1859 (Newspaper clipping in Amos Beman Scrap Book [Amos G. Beman Papers], II, 123).

30. Amos Beman to Simeon Jocelyn, March 26, June 25 and 27, 1859, in AMA Archives.

tional Church in Pittsfield, Massachusetts. Over the next several years Beman frequently took the lengthy trip from New Haven to western Massachusetts to preach to this young congregation. Also, he chaired the committee that arranged fellow Oneida student Jacob Prime's ordination in Geneva, New York, in 1849, and he preached at the service of dedication of Prime's Presbyterian church in Buffalo in 1857, even though his daughter was lying desperately ill in Farmington, Connecticut. Beman remained a close friend of another Oneida schoolmate, Amos Freeman. Having assisted at Freeman's installation as pastor of the black Congregational church in Portland, Maine, he joined Pennington for Freeman's installation eleven years later at the Siloam Presbyterian Church in Brooklyn. Finally, in 1855 Beman joined Charles Ray and Amos Freeman for the ordination of the first pastor of the First Colored Congregational Church in Greenport, Long Island, which Beman had helped organize two years earlier.[31] This earlier concern for the fate of other black Congregational and Presbyterian churches and their pastors was highly relevant to the proposed new work with the AMA.

The Executive Committee of the AMA responded favorably to Beman's proposal but wanted to clear up one matter. Would he be making "Political Speeches"? He reassured them that "the Hope of my people is in the Gospel of our Lord Jesus Christ—in a personal Faith and obedience to him." In late July Jocelyn relayed to Beman his commission "to devote your time with, and for the true elevation, spiritual, moral, educational, social and Civil of the People of Color." He was to promote temperance, antislavery, schools, Sabbath schools, and Bible classes. He was to visit homes and encourage parents in "the religious and industrious training of children." He was to gain the confidence of Evangelical churches, black and white, keeping "a truly catholic spirit toward all Christian people." And he was to be paid $250 for six months, if the funds were available.[32]

Beman's primary news outlet during his year with the AMA was Thomas Hamilton's *Weekly Anglo-African*. The emergence in 1859 of two

31. See Amos Beman Scrap Book (Amos G. Beman Papers), II, for the 1846 organization of the Pittsfield church, Prime's ordination, the dedication of his church, Freeman's installation, and the founding of the Greenport church; Dennis Dickerson, "Reverend Samuel Harrison: A Nineteenth Century Black Clergyman," in Wills and Newman (eds.), *Black Apostles at Home and Abroad*, 147–60; see *Frederick Douglass' Paper*, August 3, 1855, for the ordination in Greenport.

32. Amos Beman to Simeon Jocelyn, March 26, June 25, 27, July 9, 18, 1859, all in AMA Archives; Jocelyn to Beman, July 23, 1859, in Amos Beman Scrap Book (Amos G. Beman Papers), III.

new periodicals, ably edited by Hamilton, had made clear that Afro-American activism was still much alive and articulate. A monthly, the *Anglo-African,* appeared in January and the *Weekly Anglo-African,* in July. Because they were published in New York City and financed by the black community, they came nearer to replicating the function and spirit of the *Colored American* than had Frederick Douglass' weekly, for all its indispensable contributions over the previous dozen years. Also important to Pennington, Ray, and Beman was the fact that Hamilton, whose father had been one of the founders of the original AME Zion church in New York City, was convinced of the important role of the black church and its ministers.[33]

In August 1859 the *Weekly Anglo-African* announced that Beman, long the "gifted pastor" of the black Congregational church in New Haven, was entering the missionary field under the AMA. Editor Hamilton requested that black people in the communities Beman was to visit give careful attention to his message.[34] Whether formally agreed upon or not, Beman saw it as part of his mission to promote the circulation of the *Weekly Anglo-African* wherever he went, much as Charles Ray had done for the *Colored American* roughly twenty years earlier.

The first four months on the road seemed to match Beman's and the AMA's expectations. He first visited three communities on eastern Long Island: Greenport, Shinnecock, and Sag Harbor. His report on the Sag Harbor community of approximately two hundred blacks illustrates his concerns and methods. An AMEZ church had been founded here twenty years earlier. Its present pastor was also in charge of an AMEZ church in Greenport. No one in the community was subscribing to either an antislavery or a temperance newspaper. Many of the men worked as whalers and came back addicted to "destructive habits" after long voyages. When Beman left, however, he was hopeful for the future. Parents seemed roused to "a deeper and a wiser interest in their children." The young people were planning a public meeting at which they would recite Charles Langston's "eloquent and masterly argument" before the court in Ohio trying the case of the Oberlin-Wellington fugitive slave rescuers. And at one of Beman's public meetings those present had donated the money to

33. Penelope L. Bullock, *The Afro-American Periodical Press, 1838–1909* (Baton Rouge, 1981), 55–63.

34. *Weekly Anglo-African,* August 27, 1859. The *American Missionary,* the monthly publication of the AMA, also announced Beman's appointment and frequently ran lengthy accounts by him of his work.

subscribe to the *Weekly Anglo-African* for their AMEZ pastor and to the AMA's *American Missionary* for his wife.[35]

In the latter part of September, after several days in Brooklyn at a gathering of black Presbyterian and Congregational ministers, Beman went to Newark and Morristown, New Jersey. The *Anglo-African*'s regular reporter from Newark was jubilant about Beman's "Improvement of the Colored People," his address to a large public meeting. As Pennington and Garnet had done in America and the British Isles, Beman stressed American blacks' great achievements in spite of a long history of oppression. He spoke of churches, Sabbath schools, and day schools that had produced scientists, doctors, lawyers, and teachers—famous women as well as men. He pointed out that "thirty years ago such a state of things did not exist." He reminded his audience that there were four million Afro-Americans. "He would," said the reporter, "have it *stamped indelibly* on every *soul,* that we belong to a mighty people, we are identified with the four millions, and must use all [our] energies." The most personally rewarding aspect of the Newark visit was the chance for Beman to renew his long-time friendship with Elymas Rogers, pastor of the Plane Street (African) Presbyterian Church since 1846. Beman and Rogers had known each other in Hartford in the mid-1830s, when Beman was teaching school in that city and Rogers was a member of the African Congregational Church. Rogers had attended Gerrit Smith's school for black youth and spent four years at the Oneida Institute after Beman was there. Beman preached three times on one Sunday to Rogers's congregation.[36]

On his way back from New Jersey to Maine, Beman stopped in Hartford for several days. Here, where the Union Missionary Society, forerunner of the AMA, had been founded in the Colored Congregational Church in 1841, Beman spoke in detail of the AMA-supported mission station in Mendi and of its origin in the conversion of the *Amistad* captives while they were forcibly detained in Connecticut. When he arrived home in Portland in early October, he had been away for six weeks. He stayed in Maine for the next month, visiting Bangor and other communities and sending in reports each week to the *Weekly Anglo-African*. Two items in these reports show how important to the moderate Beman, at this stage, the most radical black and white voices had become. In describing the benefits gained from small gatherings to hear edifying material read aloud, he recalled one such group that had sat through the whole night

35. *Weekly Anglo-African,* September 3, 17, 24, 1859.
36. *Weekly Anglo-African,* October 1, 1859; Sernett, *Abolition's Axe,* 58f.

listening to David Walker's "Appeal to the Colored People of America [*sic*]" (probably the reading group Beman had known as a young man in Middletown). "Would that that book," wrote Beman, "could be read by every person in these United States. Its pages thunder—its paragraphs blaze." He urged all to get the edition published recently by Garnet, which included Garnet's own address to American slaves. While Beman was in Bangor, John Brown led his men into Harpers Ferry. After his capture Beman wrote editor Thomas Hamilton; he urged all proslavery people to listen to Brown, in chains, speaking to a reporter: "I claim to be here in carrying out a measure I believe perfectly justifiable, and not to act the part of an incendiary or ruffian, but to aid those suffering great wrong. . . . You may dispose of me very easily. I am nearly disposed of now; but this question is still to be settled—this negro question I mean."[37]

In November Henry Garnet wrote the *Weekly Anglo-African* that his Oneida classmate Beman had been in New York City for a week, "laboring with great acceptance" in the Shiloh Presbyterian Church. After his work in Garnet's parish, Beman again visited Rogers's church in Newark and then came north to New Haven. Here he lectured on three successive nights to large audiences in Zion's Church (AME Zion). The Temple Street African Congregational Church had been invited to be Beman's host, but two or three diehards on the committee responsible for building use had declined the offer. On Christmas afternoon, however, he did preach to an enthusiastic congregation at his former church. The *Weekly Anglo-African*'s New Haven reporter, "Observer," wrote to Hamilton of Beman: "Whatsoever reputation and honor the colored people of New Haven have abroad, he stands first and foremost as the maker of that reputation. He and his departed sire have not only prominently identified New Haven but the whole State of Connecticut and all New England with the national councils of our people for the last quarter of a century." "Observer" went on to declare that Beman's Christmas sermon seemed to have erased among some of his former parishioners the ill will that had played a part in his leaving.[38]

The prospects for the Beman family at the beginning of 1860 seemed good. The work for the American Missionary Association was going well. Previous hostility in the Temple Street parish against the interracial marriage was dying down. And Mrs. Beman and the children hoped

37. *Frederick Douglass' Paper,* October 13, 1854; *Weekly Anglo-African,* October 22, 29, November 5, 12, 1859.

38. *Weekly Anglo-African,* November 26, December 3, 26, 31, 1859.

soon to be able to move back to the New Haven home, which had been rented for the previous eighteen months. The year 1860, however, brought serious reverses. For over six weeks in February and March, Beman was seriously ill with a large lupus growth on his neck (a tubercular and ulcerous skin condition that ate at the flesh). Weakened by surgery and successive cauterizations, he was, for the most part, confined to his room at the home of a friend. He was deeply apologetic to Jocelyn for not being able to work and offered to give up one month's salary ($30). To complicate matters further, Beman had now incurred fresh expenses in connection with his family's moving from Portland back to New Haven. Once more, however, he was able to borrow from a man who had helped him out financially again and again over the years—Deacon Townsend, cashier of the New Haven bank, who had had a special interest in abolitionism and in the New Haven black community. Through the spring and early summer Beman regained his momentum in effective visits to Providence, Rhode Island; Danbury and New London, Connecticut; and New Bedford, Massachusetts.

At a regional conference of the AMEZ church and at a Bethel (AME) conference, both meeting in New Haven, Beman spoke about the work of the AMA in Africa. At the latter gathering, Bishop Daniel Payne was so fascinated by Beman's address on the AMA that he proposed that Beman become a lecturer for six months among black Methodist churches in New England, where he would tell the story of AMA work in Africa. Beman was at first inclined to accept, given AMA approval, but by July he had decided to stay in his present agency. He pressed Jocelyn for a renewal of his commission and gave a detailed summation of his work during the previous year: the miles traveled, the sermons and lectures given on missions and the elevation of American blacks, and the informal talks to Sunday schools on the importance of education and on the evils of addiction to alcohol and tobacco.

The AMA delayed month after month in extending Beman's commission. Not only did this mean no salary but also that the black minister could not accept invitations to preach and lecture, since he did not know when and how his responsibilities with the association would be resumed. Financial survival again depended on "Brother Townsend." By December it finally became clear that the AMA had major hesitations. Prominent white clergy in Portland who were central in the oversight of the Maine Missionary Society had accused Beman of dishonesty while he was pastor in Portland. He had, for over a year, received a $200 annual grant from this society and at the same time $100 a year from the AMA, without telling either of the other's support. It was indeed a standing rule with both the American Home Missionary Society (of which the Maine society was an auxiliary) and the AMA that a minister should receive a grant from only one such organization at a time. Both Jocelyn and Beman were familiar with this regulation. Since AMA and AHMS staff in New York City had frequent contact, Jocelyn probably knew of the grant from the AHMS auxiliary. In all likelihood he and Beman considered the latter's case special enough to warrant an exception. However, Lewis Tappan, AMA treasurer and always a stickler for exact and full accounting, took the complaint of the Maine Missionary Society very seriously. Moreover, Tappan had been exasperated by Beman's failure to send in regular monthly reports of contributions to the AMA received during his travels. To make matters worse, a rumor circulated in Portland that Beman had physically mistreated his wife, whose screams at night had brought a crowd around the Beman home. Beman insisted that all he had done was forcibly restrain her when she was in a disturbed state following the death of a sailor son in the West Indies and of both her parents in New York City. Quite apart from these criticisms and rumors, the AMA Executive Committee's needs for missionaries far exceeded its funds, as usual. As it delayed month after month making a decision on Beman's commission, he wrote staff member George Whipple, "Never in my life was I in such a trying situation, no money—no employment and sad and low spirit to the last degree."[39]

By early 1861 Beman knew that his agency with the AMA was ended. For the next several years, maintaining his residence in New Haven, he pieced together a minimal income by lecturing, supply preaching, and serving for two years as pastor of the small Presbyterian/Congregational church in Greenport, Long Island. Here Eliza Kennedy Beman died in 1864.[40]

Pennington, Garnet, Beman, and Ray had been scattered geographically in the earlier 1850s, but by the latter years of the decade, with Garnet and

39. Amos Beman to George Whipple, December 12, 1860 (Microfilm copy in Carter and Ripley [eds.], *BAP,* reel 13, item 31).

40. For the whole of Beman's dealings with the American Missionary Association after his becoming their agent, see his letters, mostly to Simeon Jocelyn, July 29, [*ca.* October 1], October 3, 7, 28, 1859, February 7, 14, 28, March 10, May 1, 7, 22, 23, May [?], July 19, 24, 26, 27, 28, August 1, 3, 6, 24, October 25, November 17, 26, December 1, 3, 5, 12, 1860, January 7, March 21, 1861, all in AMA Archives; see also a lengthy memorandum, evi-

Ray in New York City, Pennington on Long Island, and Beman coming to the New York area now and then in his travels for the AMA, they saw more of each other. From 1856 through 1859 they formalized their sense of a common and distinctive vocation in annual meetings of the Evangelical Association of Colored Ministers of Congregational and Presbyterian Churches.[41] In 1856 the group gathered at the Shiloh Presbyterian Church, where Garnet was now pastor. Elymas Rogers chaired the sessions. In 1857 the association met at the Central Presbyterian Church in Philadelphia, with Amos Freeman as moderator. The meetings in 1858 were scheduled for the Talcott Street Congregational church in Hartford. In 1859 the group gathered in Brooklyn at Amos Freeman's Siloam Presbyterian Church, with Amos Beman presiding. By this time there were twenty-seven black churches belonging to the Congregational or Presbyterian denominations, though the pulpits of nine were vacant.[42] Of the twenty black ministers belonging to these denominations, thirteen were present at the association meetings in Brooklyn.[43] Churches currently without a pastor in Reading, Pennsylvania, and Hartford were represented by an elder and deacon, respectively. Jermain Loguen,

dently from someone at the AMA to someone in the Maine Missionary Society, dated December 1860 and in a hand other than either Lewis Tappan's or Simeon Jocelyn's, in AMA Archives.

41. Pennington had hosted a meeting of this group in 1851, shortly after his return from Great Britain. They had sent out to all black Presbyterian and Congregational churches a questionnaire seeking basic data on church and Sunday school membership, mission and temperance work, and the impact of the Fugitive Slave Act on the church. There is a copy of questionnaire, Pennington Papers, Moorland-Spingarn Research Center, Howard University, Washington, D.C.

42. The churches listed by Amos Beman as being without ministers were those in Portland, Maine; Hartford and New Haven, Connecticut; Shinnecock and Troy, New York; Princeton, New Jersey; and Reading, Pennsylvania (Amos Beman to S. S. Jocelyn, October 5, 1859, AMA Archives, no. 47724). There were also two struggling churches in Philadelphia, the First African Presbyterian and the Second (African) Presbyterian, or Saint Mary Street Presbyterian, both of which had sought Beman's services but were now without pastors (Catto, *A Semicentenary Discourse,* 110).

43. The following list of clergy was sent by Amos Beman to Simeon Jocelyn shortly after the meetings of the Evangelical Association of Colored Ministers: Charles Gardiner (Harrisburg); Jonathan Gibbs (Central Presbyterian Church, Philadelphia); H. R. Revels (Baltimore); James Pennington (Newtown, Long Island); James Carter (Greenport, Long Island); Elymas Rogers (Newark); Charles Ray, Henry Garnet, and Henry Wilson (Bethesda Congregational, Shiloh Presbyterian, and Seventh Avenue Presbyterian churches in New York City, respectively); Jacob Prime, Amos Freeman, George Levere, and James Gloucester (Brooklyn); Benjamin Lynch (Newport, Rhode Island); Jacob Rhodes (Newark); William Catto (Washington, D.C.); Daniel Devere (Elizabethtown, New Jersey); Amos Beman; Samuel Harrison (Pittsfield, Massachusetts); and Ennaus Adams (Buffalo).

AMEZ pastor and president of the Underground Railroad in the Syracuse region, also attended. The choice of Beman as president was appropriate, since the goals of his black community visitation under the AMA and the themes of his sermons and lectures closely corresponded with the aims of the whole body of black Presbyterian and Congregational churches. As if to confirm this fact, the white Congregational minister Simeon Jocelyn, staff member of the AMA, was present by invitation—the only white man in the group.

These sessions of the association lasted over five days and were held in succession at the Siloam Presbyterian Church and at New York City's Shiloh Presbyterian and Seventh Avenue Presbyterian churches. The program included a sermon, addresses, prayer services, and extensive discussion of the pressing tasks to which they were all urgently called—above all, "the best means to be employed for ameliorating the condition of their people." There were reports on black progress in various parts of the country. To implement its goals the association made plans for a fund to help destitute black churches and to employ someone to do precisely what Beman was doing under the AMA, "to travel from place to place to inquire into the condition of the people, and bring to bear upon them such influences as may tend to the promotion of their interests, socially and religiously." (These ministers' hope for this independent black program was evidently never realized.) Garnet's address was especially eloquent. He berated white clergy in America for continuing to support slavery. He reminded blacks that the heavier the burden of wrong laid on them by oppressors, the closer they should draw to God. And he concluded, in the words of a reporter, "with a soul stirring peroration, thanking the God of liberty for the signs of the times, and the omens of not distant triumph." The import of the five days of meetings was summed up in concluding remarks by Garnet, since Beman had had to leave early to fulfill speaking engagements. Garnet bade the group an affectionate farewell, urged its members to be more loving toward one another, and charged them "to work more earnestly for their own and [the race's] elevation."[44]

Less than a month after these sessions of the Evangelical Association of Colored Ministers, John Brown led his armed force of thirteen whites and five blacks into Harpers Ferry on the night of October 16 and captured the arsenal. Taken prisoner within two days, he had been tried and

44. *Weekly Anglo-African*, September 24, 1859.

convicted of murder, criminal conspiracy, and treason against Virginia by October 31. He was hanged on December 2. It is difficult to overestimate the depth of emotional response of black people, both leaders and rank and file, to the raid and to Brown's execution. Brown originally had envisioned what was virtually a large-scale expansion of the work of the Underground Railroad—a mass exodus of slaves from plantations of the upper South to his mountain fastness and thence to freedom in the North or Canada. By the summer of 1859, however, he saw the raid as, in Frederick Douglass's words, "striking a blow which should instantly rouse the country." During his last two years of planning he had asked both Douglass and Garnet to join him. He had come to Garnet's home and laid out his plans to him in 1857, a year after the bloodshed in the Kansas territory. Garnet's response had been as follows: "Sir, the time has not come yet for the success of such a movement. Our people in the South are not sufficiently apprised of their rights, and of the sympathy that exists on the part of the North for them. Our people in the North are not prepared to assist in such a movement in consequence of the prejudice that shuts them out from both the means and the intelligence necessary. The breach between the North and the South has not yet become wide enough." Brown had replied, "Mr. Garnet, let us ask God about it." Kneeling, he had poured out his prayer with such a depth of religious feeling and "intense interest . . . in the emancipation of mankind," that Garnet later said that "never in his life had he been so moved by a prayer."[45] To refuse to join Brown, sensible as it was, must have been especially difficult for Garnet in light of his own "Address to the Slaves," delivered in 1843 and published in 1848.

Within a week of Brown's capture in Harpers Ferry, Pennington, as pastor of the Second Colored Presbyterian Church in Newtown, Long Island, sent a column on Brown to the *Weekly Anglo-African*. He declared that history would vindicate the memory of Brown, who was ahead of his age, though regarded as "imprudent, unfortunate, or conscientiously wrong." He urged all black ministers to have the moral courage to bring the trial and probable execution of Brown "squarely and openly before the people." He concluded, "Pray for old John Brown of Osawatomie!

45. Reported by J. Sella Martin, black pastor of the Joy Street Baptist Church in Boston (and a former slave), in a speech reproduced in the *Liberator,* December 9, 1859. For Douglass's account of John Brown's effort to recruit him and his refusal to go, out of "discretion or . . . cowardice," see Douglass, *Life and Times of Frederick Douglass,* 316–20.

That he may be delivered or die, like a man, and that his blood may be sanctified to the cause of freedom."[46]

In early November Garnet led three prayer meetings for Brown at Shiloh, and there were dozens of similar occasions in other black churches throughout November. On the evening of December 1 in the AMEZ church in New Haven, Beman chaired a mass meeting of blacks that was held to pray for Brown being executed "for his heroic and praiseworthy efforts for the oppressed slaves in the South." On the day of Brown's execution a general antislavery meeting for New York City blacks was held at Shiloh, and Garnet presided. Ray prayed "with much feeling and fervency that the sacrifice of this dear old friend of freedom may mark the downfall of this sinful system of bondage." Beman read a verse from Psalm 86 and two from Acts describing the faith that had sustained the early Christian martyr Stephen when he was being stoned to death. Garnet gave the central eulogy, concluding, "Farewell, brave old man! God be with thee. Steal forth from the scaffold into the chariot of fire which awaits thee. . . . Hero-martyr, farewell!" On December 2 and thereafter, many occasions were staged specifically to raise money for John Brown's family. Julia Garnet set up the New York Liberty Fund for this purpose and at one time in the spring of 1860 took in $60.[47]

During the year after John Brown's execution, it must have seemed to activist black clergy all the more important to press on in the antislavery, civil rights, and educational causes to which they had given so much during the previous decades. For Pennington, Garnet, and Ray, ministry in the Newtown, Shiloh, and Bethesda churches was, if anything, more relevant than ever before, for the "God of Liberty" seemed about to break into history in a wondrous and devastating way. The pull toward Africa remained strong for Garnet, but war broke out in the land of the Yoruba in May 1860 and had grown more bitter and destructive by the end of the year. Meanwhile, Elymas Rogers, Garnet's and Beman's personal friend, had decided to leave his fourteen-year pastorate in Newark and to go out, at his own expense, to seek a suitable location in Africa for a mission station under the auspices of the American Missionary Associa-

46. Letter from James Pennington, October 25, 1859, in *Weekly Anglo-African*, November 5, 1859.

47. Freeman, "The Free Negro in New York City," 211; *Weekly Anglo-African*, December 10, 17, 1859; see Ofari, "*Let Your Motto Be Resistance*," 186f., for the full text of Garnet's eulogy; Freeman, "The Free Negro in New York City," 212.

tion. (The African Civilization Society was without funds though still very much alive.) Reaching Sierra Leone in early December 1860, Rogers moved slowly southward along the coast, seeking a site suitable for a missionary station and colony. His death on shipboard in late January 1861, before reaching Lagos, was a bitter personal blow to all his devoted friends in America. It was also another setback for what the African Civilization Society had been working toward. Meanwhile, Amos Beman, with no pastorate of his own, saw in emigration possible employment and a cause to give himself to, as had Garnet. Beman applied to James Redpath for an agency promoting emigration to Haiti, but Redpath already had several agents engaged and had no funds to add to his staff.[48]

Another disappointment, especially for black leaders in New York State, came on the home front in the fall of 1860. The referendum on the enfranchisement of blacks, as has been seen, resulted in a solid refusal to end the property requirement for black voters. Pennington, Ray, James McCune Smith, and Douglass had been especially active in this campaign to rouse white voters to a sense of justice. For them and all black leaders this seemed strong further evidence that the dispelling of racial prejudice in America was occurring with glacial slowness, if at all.

Many black people in the United States, however, and especially activist ministers, had a presentiment that apocalyptic changes were in the offing. Early in January 1861 Ray, Garnet, AMEZ bishop Christopher Rush, African Baptist minister John Raymond, and clergy and laymen from other black churches in New York City and Brooklyn called the Christian Union Convention to gather in the Shiloh Presbyterian Church. The aim was to institute among black Christians throughout the United States a day of fasting and prayer "to Almighty God for his interposition in our behalf in these times of trial and peril." Raymond was chosen president of the gathering, Ray a vice-president, and Garnet a secretary. During the two days of the gathering, Garnet and Ray were among those who gave addresses. The resolutions, adopted unanimously, recognized the imminence of civil war and saw it as the natural result of the violation of God's law, "especially in the oppression of the weak and defenceless." Acknowledging that "the most dreadful forebodings fill every mind," but believing that God was "a kind Heavenly Father who taketh no plea-

48. *American Missionary,* April, May, 1861; MacMaster, "Henry Highland Garnet," 276f; James Redpath to Amos Beman, March 25, 1861, A.L.S. in Carter and Ripley (eds.), *BAP,* reel 13, item 430. Even Frederick Douglass was supporting emigration to Haiti by January 1861.

sure in punishing the innocent with the guilty," the convention recommended to Christians throughout "the free States" a day of prayer that "God would avert the judgments about to fall on this guilty nation . . . and cause righteousness and truth to prevail." The body urged blacks to pray that God give them, "a poor, despised, . . . scattered and pealed people," a unified trust in "the strong arm of Almighty power" in whatever ordeal they might undergo.[49]

Exactly three months after the Christian Union Convention and three days after the firing on Fort Sumter, a very different kind of gathering of New York City blacks occurred. As if to make crystal clear how much Garnet's vigor, deep faith, and fighting spirit had meant to them and how little they sensed that he had abandoned America for Africa, his supporters at the Shiloh Presbyterian Church and throughout New York City held a mammoth testimonial dinner for him in the (AME) Zion's Church, the largest black church building in the city. There was music by the church's choir. Scripture was read by John Peterson, veteran and able black grammar school principal. There was an address by a layman, the presentation of a silver service, an address by a black minister, the singing of "How Beauteous Are Their Feet" by the choir, the presentation of a china dinner service to Julia Garnet, an address by the wife of the longtime Sunday school superintendent, the presentation of a gold-headed cane by the Independent Order of Brothers and Sisters of Love and Charity, the presentation of a replica of Joshua's trumpet by Baptist minister John Raymond and all the other clergy present, the presentation of a framed scroll signed by "twenty-five young ladies and twenty-five young gentlemen," and a closing address. Why all of this? It was declared to be a "testimonial of respect [from] the people of New York, in consideration of the faithful and self-sacrificing adherence of the Rev. Henry Highland Garnet, to the cause of truth and Universal Freedom for a period of twenty-five years." Garnet's words of thanks defined his motto as including "Unconditional Emancipation; . . . African Civilization; Haytian Emigration; God and Negro Nationality." And Alexander Crummell, back from Liberia on a promotional visit, praised Garnet for respecting Africa and Africans.[50]

49. *Weekly Anglo-African,* February 2, 1861.

50. "Order of Exercises" published in advance of this event, *Weekly Anglo-African,* April 6, 1861; *Weekly Anglo-African,* April 27, 1861; Pasternak, "Rise Now and Fly to Arms," 171f. Pasternak's description of this dinner as being staged by Garnet's "friends at the African Civilization Society" is too narrow.

By the time of this testimonial dinner Garnet alone of the surviving four of the black activists to whom this work is devoted was pastor of a strong and influential church. However, Pennington and Ray, based in small Newtown and New York City churches, and Beman, supply preaching in and out from New Haven, continued to be powerful presences in their local communities and at general black conclaves in New York City. Many hundreds would gladly have paid tribute also at some suitable occasion to each of these three for their having shown "faithful and self-sacrificing adherence . . . to the cause of truth and Universal Freedom" over many years.

12. THE CLOSING YEARS

Before drawing conclusions as to the significance of the antebellum careers of Samuel Cornish, Theodore Wright, Charles Ray, Henry Highland Garnet, James W. C. Pennington, and Amos Beman, brief sketches of the later lives of those who survived Wright are in order. After Cornish had resigned his post with the *Colored American,* he never again had a position of influence comparable to his editorships. However, there were periods of effective ministry and ongoing usefulness as a black elder statesman on numerous antislavery, educational, and missionary boards.

Early in 1840 Cornish began a salvage operation for the Colored Presbyterian Church of Newark; the church had been shattered by the recent departure of its minister and over thirty of its congregation, who were bound for settlement in Trinidad. Commissioned by the American Missionary Association, Cornish reported that after six months the Sunday school had a hundred regular attenders, and Newark's white churches were supplying it with able teachers. The congregation, however, were mostly working people, and in Newark, hard hit by a depression, many blacks were unemployed. It was a difficult assignment for the aristocratic Cornish, but he stayed with it for upwards of two and a half years and laid the groundwork, as he had at New York City's First Colored Presbyterian Church twenty years earlier, for what would become a vigorous church. Here in Newark Elymas Rogers would minister quietly and effectively during the later 1840s and the 1850s.[1]

1. Reports from Cornish to the American Home Missionary Society, July 15, 1840, January 12, 1841, April 11, 1842, all in AHMS Archives.

Cornish left Newark in 1845, after the death of his wife, and returned to live in an upper ward of New York City, where he had kept property. Here he ministered to black people "attached by profession and preference to the Presbyterian denomination" but living too far north on Manhattan conveniently to attend the First Colored Presbyterian Church. In the summer of 1846 the Immanuel Presbyterian Church was founded with eight members who had been in regular standing at other Presbyterian churches. The little congregation worshiped in a rented temperance hall. When Cornish resigned from this post in 1851, there were 56 members. Immanuel's subsequent pastor, Henry M. Wilson, though never formally installed by the presbytery, was a conscientious leader whose efforts must have been largely responsible for the church's growth to 139 members by 1860. (The church's name was changed to the Seventh Avenue Presbyterian Church in 1856.)[2]

Having turned away from the black separatist state conventions of the early 1840s, and having conscientiously opposed third party politics, Cornish's muted activism in the 1840s and 1850s was primarily expressed in biracial efforts. He was on the Executive Committee of the American and Foreign Anti-Slavery Society at its founding in 1840 and again for six years after he returned to New York from Newark. He was one of the founders of the American Missionary Association in 1846, was on its Executive Committee from 1846 to 1855, and was a vice-president of the organization from 1848 to his death in 1858. From 1850 on Cornish would occasionally emerge from retirement to speak at a mass meeting to protest the Fugitive Slave Act of 1850 or to continue his longstanding crusade against the American Colonization Society. And he would, from time to time, attend gatherings of the association of Black Presbyterian and Congregational clergy. However, his health was frail, and his spirit was further depressed by his daughter's falling ill in 1851 and dying insane in 1855. At Cornish's funeral in November 1858, the white minister George Potts, who had overseen his education for the ministry in Philadelphia, preached the funeral sermon. For all of the withdrawal from radical activism and the debilitation of the last quarter of Cornish's life, Potts's words accurately recognized the seminal role he had played earlier: "This excellent brother . . . was among the foremost of those who have . . . labored for the improvement, and the temporal and spiritual welfare of the colored man." In Cornish's will it was his

2. "Session Book of Immanuel Presbyterian Church" (Presbyterian Historical Association, Philadelphia); Murray, *Presbyterians and the Negro,* 37.

former associate editor Charles Ray who, along with Potts, was named executor.[3]

Ray, Garnet, Pennington, and Beman were all prominent at certain times and in certain places during the Civil War. As had been his wont for nearly twenty years, Ray went quietly about his work as pastor of the Bethesda Congregational Church and as supporter of concerned outreach to sufferers beyond the bounds of his parish. He was, for example, president of the long-lived New York African Society for Mutual Relief and chaired the celebration of its fifty-second anniversary on an evening in March 1862.[4] He also continued to watch with care and pride the education and development of his three daughters. Of most of this no written record survives. At one ghastly time, during and after the deadly anti-black mob actions in the draft riots in New York City in 1863, he was, as will be described, again center stage.

Garnet continued his feuding with Frederick Douglass, James McCune Smith, and George Downing over the African Civilization Society even after its program had been primarily redirected toward aid to freedmen. But periodically these four, recognized by many whites as well as blacks as primary voices for northern blacks, spoke from the same platform with substantially the same message.

It was noted earlier that in March 1861, after the political situation in West Africa had deteriorated, Garnet accepted a post as New York City agent for the Haitian Emigration Bureau. Martin Delany, Frederick Douglass, and James McCune Smith attacked him for working for a white man. Smith taunted him, "How come, Mr. Garnet, your position always changes when you are offered a handsome salary?" Garnet replied, "My father on the plantation taught me never to fight with a skunk."[5] Stung by these accusations, Garnet severed all connection with Delany and his efforts to develop a settlement in Nigeria for American blacks. When the British responded to renewed intertribal warfare by

3. Pease and Pease, *Bound with Them in Chains,* 158f.; *Dictionary of American Negro Biography,* 134f.; *Anti-Slavery Reporter,* January 1, 1850; January 1, 1852 (Microfilm copy in Carter and Ripley [eds.], *BAP,* reel 6, item 329; reel 7, item 311); *National Anti-Slavery Standard,* October 10, 1850; October 30, 1851; Christian, "Samuel Cornish," 6, App. (on Cornish's will); *American Missionary,* December, 1858, p. 298.

4. *Weekly Anglo-African,* April 12, 1862 (Microfilm copy in Carter and Ripley [eds.], *BAP,* reel 14, item 237).

5. *Weekly Anglo-African,* January, 1861, cited by Pasternak, "Rise Now and Fly to Arms," 168.

taking over Lagos, Garnet decided to visit England again, his aim to interest British merchants in financing what the African Civilization Society had been promoting for three years, a free-labor cotton-growing settlement in West Africa. Garnet had a second aim, as he had had when he had gone in 1850: to stimulate British action against American slavery, which now meant taking a stand against the Confederacy. In securing his passport, Garnet insisted that it register that he was a black man as well as that he was a United States citizen. Secretary of State William Seward yielded the point, and Garnet reveled in having, for all practical purposes, negated the Dred Scott decision. However, once he arrived in England, Garnet's trip was a disappointment. In some three months he roused little mercantile interest in investing money in war-torn West Africa.[6]

Pennington's efforts during the Civil War were more clearly focused on the American scene than were Garnet's. The single issue for him was the ending of slavery. Military defeat of the Confederate army seemed essential to achieve that goal, and blacks should insist on having a vigorous share in the fighting. The hiatus in Pennington's public activity after his resignation from the Prince Street Presbyterian Church was clearly in the past. He spoke at the mass celebration of West Indian emancipation on August 1, 1861. To the *Weekly Anglo-African* he wrote, "Mark my words, gentlemen, we cannot get out of this terrible scrape, without in some way helping to decide the contest; we are on the eve of the grand heroic age of the race, when the last vestige of African slavery shall be wiped out." He circulated a petition to Congress to end southern slavery immediately as a first and necessary step toward permanent peace. He also addressed a large gathering at the Zion Baptist Church in New York City "with great ability, as the Doctor is ever wont to do," urging his listeners not to let white prejudice, which thus far had barred their enlistment in the Union army, quench "the fiery ardor of their patriotism."[7]

Following Garnet's example, Pennington secured a passport and took

6. Pasternak, "Rise Now and Fly to Arms," 168–70; *Anti-Slavery Reporter,* October 1, 1861; *Weekly Anglo-African,* November 11, 1861; Pasternak, "Rise Now and Fly to Arms," 175f.

7. *Weekly Anglo-African,* August 10, 17, October 5, 1861. Blackett sees the Draft Riots of 1863 as the event that caused Pennington "to abandon his cherished principles of 'moral power,' that ability to suffer oppression peacefully while working diligently to ensure its cessation" (Blackett, *Beating Against the Barriers,* 80). Actually, Pennington had been shifting his position over a period of ten years, as evident in his defense of the Christiana rioters and his encouragement of black enlistment as soon as possible. What the Draft Riots did was to prove that the battlefront was sometimes in the streets of northern cities.

ship for Great Britain in October 1861. His message for English audiences was a simpler version of the autobiographical accounts and the blistering attacks on southern slavery that he had delivered from 1849 to 1851. In the introduction to a slave biography that he published in Liverpool, he opposed Garnet's continuing promotion of Afro-American settlement in West Africa, affirming his belief that Africans in the United States were to become free, "remain where they are, and eventually occupy the lands which they have watered with their sweat and tears." Although Pennington's speeches were consistent with his message of a decade earlier, there is no indication that his presence in Great Britain in 1861 and 1862 had any more impact than Garnet's on the Britons' support of the Union cause as against the Confederacy. Pennington's visit ended disastrously in June 1862, when he was arrested in Liverpool for attempted theft of a three-shilling book from a secondhand bookstore. His explanation to the magistrate—that he had intended to pay for the book but had put it in his pocket while looking at others and then forgotten it—did not prove convincing, and he was given a sentence of one month at hard labor.[8]

Once Garnet was back in the United States, early in 1862, with hopes for "Christian colonization" in West Africa dashed, he joined forces with Delany, J. M. Smith, Douglass, and Beman in trying to get the national administration to declare unambiguously that the aim of the war was to end slavery, as well as to get both federal and state governments to allow black enlistments. The old animosities seemed to have melted away. At a gathering of several thousand at the Cooper Institute in May 1862 to celebrate the federal government's freeing slaves in the District of Columbia, Garnet shared the platform with George Downing and Smith, as well as with Ray. Garnet, Downing, and Smith spoke, in that order, praising President Abraham Lincoln but deprecating the colonization clause in the emancipation legislation and warning the president that slavery at large must be ended forthwith. There were more mammoth celebrations by blacks and white abolitionists when, in September 1862, Lincoln issued a preliminary overall emancipation edict giving the southern rebels until January 1, 1863, to return to the Union or have their slaves freed by fed-

8. Report of a speech by Pennington, in Manchester *Examiner,* February 20, 1862, reprinted in *Weekly Anglo-African,* March 15, 1862; James W. C. Pennington, *A Narrative of Events of the Life of J. H. Banks, an Escaped Slave, from the Cotton State, Alabama, in America, Written, with Introduction, by J. W. C. Pennington, D.D.* (Liverpool, 1861), 5 (Microfilm copy in Carter and Ripley [eds.], *BAP,* reel 13, items 111–157); Blackett, *Beating Against the Barriers,* 79f.

eral mandate. Lincoln, however, having anticipated northern white opposition to mass emancipation, had previously secured token black support for announcing a plan to settle freed slaves in Central America, thus defusing white antagonism. Douglass had rejected Lincoln's proposal with scorn, but Garnet had defended it as realistic: "Neither the North, the West, nor the East will receive them [the freed slaves]. Nay—even colored people do not want them here. They all say, white and black—'these Southern negroes if they come here *will reduce the price of labor and take the bread out of our mouths.*' Let the government give them a territory and arm and defend them until they can fully defend themselves, and thus hundreds of thousands of men will be saved." The old antagonisms between Garnet and antiemigrationists flared up again. Victory went to the latter. In the face of massive black opposition, Lincoln dropped the plan.[9]

The Emancipation Proclamation of New Year's Day 1863 permitted blacks to serve in the Union army, though in segregated units under white officers and with lower pay than white troops. The governor of Massachusetts promptly set in motion a program to recruit black soldiers. Garnet, along with Douglass, William Wells Brown, and Delany, were deputed to persuade blacks to enlist. Garnet composed eloquent slogans for posters (for example, Rather Die Freemen Than Live As Slaves . . . Rise Now and Fly to Arms), but he and the others won few volunteers. Even a mass meeting in April at the Shiloh Presbyterian Church, at which Douglass and Pennington urged enlistments in the Fifty-fourth Massachusetts Volunteers, evoked little response.[10] Part of the problem was the opposition of New York's governor to raising black troops in the state. A petition by prominent whites and Garnet to Lincoln to override this opposition was unsuccessful. Not until near the end of the year, long after the devastating losses at Gettysburg, did Secretary of War Edwin Stanton agree to oversee the recruitment and training of blacks in New York State. With Garnet's and Douglass's help 2,300 had soon enlisted. The preceding summer the ghastly violence of the Draft Riots had broken out against blacks in the streets of New York City and was ended only when the secretary of war released federal forces to quell the mayhem. The terrifying helplessness of blacks during those days may

9. *Liberator,* May 23, 1862, *Pacific Appeal,* October 11, 1862 (Microfilm copy in Carter and Ripley [eds.], *BAP,* reel 14, items 321, 543); Foner, *History of Black Americans,* III, 342f.

10. *Liberator,* May 22, 1863 (Microfilm copy in Carter and Ripley [eds.], *BAP,* reel 14, item 868).

have affected Stanton's eventual decision, as well as having accelerated black enlistments.[11]

During the first two years of the Civil War, Beman had been speaking out on the same issues as those exercising Garnet and Pennington. Although based in Connecticut, Beman traveled as far afield as Alexandria, Virginia. All the evidence indicates that he had recovered much of his earlier vigor and effectiveness after his brief time of unemployment and personal depression.

In New Haven as in New York City there was a mammoth meeting in late April 1862 to celebrate federal action ending slavery in the District of Columbia. The meeting of whites and blacks in Temple Hall was called by a reporter "probably the largest and most spirited meeting ever held in the State of Connecticut." Beman was chosen presiding officer and introduced several distinguished speakers. These were all white men, including Beman's longtime white advisor and advocate, Leonard Bacon. Those men singled out in a resolution honoring "philanthropic Christian statesmen" were, understandably enough, also white (that is, members of the United States Senate and House). Another resolution stressed free blacks' new responsibility to impart to recently freed slaves industry, domestic economy, temperance, and moral and mental education. This was a tall order indeed, but Beman would take it very seriously.[12]

For most of the year following this New Haven meeting, Beman was again sending in reports to the *Weekly Anglo-African* similar to those he had submitted while commissioned by the American Missionary Association. In June 1862 in Middletown, he worshiped at the Cross Street AME Zion Church, now blessed by the ministry of a worthy successor to his father. He also spent an hour in the dormitory room of a black Wesleyan student from Brooklyn who was due to graduate soon. Back in New Haven Beman went to the meetings of the General Association of Connecticut which represented all the Congregational churches of the state. By mid-July he was in Washington, D.C., attending the sixteenth anniversary of the Sabbath School Union, the black counterpart of the American Sunday School Union. What Beman saw of the contrabands (slaves who had escaped to, or had been brought within, the Union lines)

11. Pasternak, "Rise Now and Fly to Arms," 187–96. To his sorrow Garnet was turned down for a chaplaincy in the Union army because of his amputated leg. He did serve as chaplain for three black regiments during their training on Rikers Island, but as a civilian.

12. Amos Beman Scrap Book (Amos G. Beman Papers), II, 37, 140.

had a profound effect on him. These confused and penniless people, he wrote, gave terrible evidence of the human price of slavery. An immense job lay ahead for northern blacks and whites, enough to tax the resources of the benevolent for years.[13]

It may well have been that Beman had gone to Washington because of the Fifteenth Street Presbyterian Church's continuing interest in calling him to be their pastor. Benjamin Tanner had been their effective minister for two years but had transferred to the AME denomination and now was in charge of three churches in the Washington area. Beman visited him and was much impressed by the mature discussion in an adult Bible class and by the schools Tanner had organized. Tanner's shift of affiliation was a great loss to Presbyterians. He would become an able editor (of the AME journal the *Christian Recorder*), author, and educational leader—indeed, a worthy colleague of Daniel Payne.[14]

Back in Connecticut in October, Beman spoke in Hartford of the desperate poverty of the contrabands, "the Lord's poor." Both the Talcott Street Congregational Church, where Amos Freeman was now pastor, and the Pearl Street Methodist Zion Church responded with a will and were soon packing donated clothing into twelve barrels for shipment to Washington. Beman could not resist giving a brief homily on black progress in Hartford. Previous generations' efforts at "elevating the colored people" had not been in vain. The comfortable income and social refinement of many black families proved that "industry and frugality is rewarded." Similar efforts, this time to help the freedmen, were made the following spring under the direction of Beman and the black ministers of Episcopal, AME, and AMEZ churches in New Haven.[15]

In New Haven, as in so many other cities, the Emancipation Proclamation of January 1, 1863, prompted a massive public celebration; hundreds or even thousands were unable to get into the Temple Hall where it was held. This time Beman was truly the central figure, opening the meeting with prayer and later giving a scholarly speech on the history of slavery that commanded the respectful attention of the audience. And it was Beman who composed the resolutions that were presented, affirm-

13. Reports to the *Weekly Anglo-African* dated June 4, 20, July 17, August 1, 1862.

14. *Ibid.*, September 6, 1862.

15. *Ibid.*, October 25, 1862; Hartford *Courant*, November 10, 1862; *Morning Journal and Courier*, May 31, 1863 (Clipping in Amos Beman Scrap Book [Amos G. Beman Papers], II, 35).

ing "the glorious developments of Divine Providence" and the new responsibilities resting upon blacks brought up free.[16]

During the late winter and spring of 1863, Beman returned to Newport, Rhode Island, which he had visited for the American Missionary Association three years earlier. One of his reports from this city included high praise of George Downing, who had led the long and successful campaign to desegregate the public schools of Newport. The final report urged massive enlistment of Afro-Americans in black infantry, artillery, and cavalry regiments. Beman was in step with the mass meeting at the Shiloh Presbyterian Church, at which Douglass and Pennington had spoken. Let young blacks study military tactics and great military campaigns, urged Beman. Let them read William C. Nell's *Colored Patriots of the American Revolution with Sketches of Several Distinguished Colored Persons . . .*, David Walker's *Appeal . . . to the Colored Citizens of the World,* and Garnet's *Address to the Slaves.* Let them also read about such black heroes in the Civil War as Robert Smalls and William Tillman, who had seized Confederate vessels and/or piloted them into Union hands. These men had shown that the blood of Denmark Vesey, Nat Turner, Joseph Cinqué, and Toussaint L'Ouverture was not extinct. Finally, Beman urged that Pennington and Jermain Loguen be hired to recruit blacks for the Union army.[17]

Beman was delighted when the black Twenty-ninth Connecticut Regiment was organized. Visiting it in 1864 he "felt a glow of honest pride and joy which never filled [my] heart before." The pride was amplified because his son, Charles Torrey Beman, now some eighteen years of age, had enlisted in the Fifth Massachusetts Cavalry, which saw heavy action in the early summer of 1864.[18]

During the last two years of the war Beman was, as has already been noted, minister of the small black Congregational church and teacher in the day school for blacks in Greenport, Long Island (the Jamaica area). Although the need here was less desperate than among the freedmen, it was enough to engulf a conscientious pastor-teacher. Most adults could not read the Bible, let alone write. Even fewer knew simple arithmetic.

16. New Haven *Palladium,* January 13, 1863; Amos Beman Scrap Book (Amos G. Beman Papers), II, 76, 91.

17. Reports to the *Weekly Anglo-African* dated February 16, 27, March 6, 24, May 2, 1863.

18. Clippings in Amos Beman Scrap Book (Amos G. Beman Papers), including an extract from Charles Torrey to his father, June 20, 1864 (letter written after intense fighting).

The sort of positive religious, moral, and cultural influences that black churches in Hartford and New Haven, especially Pennington's and Beman's churches, had provided had no steady presence among blacks in Jamaica and many other Long Island communities. The situation cried out for home missionaries, and for some two years, in one small town, Beman was that missionary, as Charles Ray had been for many years in New York City.[19]

Beman entirely escaped the fierce mob actions against blacks in urban centers in 1862 and 1863. Resentment had smoldered among white factory workers and stevedores against blacks' being hired in a time of job scarcity. Bitterness grew with the Emancipation Proclamation and exploded with the enactment in March 1863 of a comprehensive conscription law to supplement enlistments and provide the Union army with desperately needed manpower. Draftees with $300 could buy exemption.

The result was the Draft Riots. The explosion in New York City occurred in mid-July 1863, two days after the drawing of names for the draft. Stevedores stayed home from work and joined crowds of other angry whites in rioting that lasted for five days and more. The Colored Orphan Asylum, on Fifth Avenue between Forty-third and Forty-fourth streets, was burned to the ground. The 130 black children were saved only by the intervention of firemen. The Colored Seamen's Home was rifled, the owner-director barely saving his own and his family's lives by hiding on the roof. The Shiloh Church was sacked but not destroyed. Some of the rioters knew Henry Garnet well enough to remember that his home was on Thirtieth Street. Shouting his name, they rushed down the street. His daughter, Mary, had had the forethought to rip his nameplate from the door, and the mob passed by. Wooden shacks housing low-income blacks were burned. Tenement buildings were stormed, and men, women, and even babies were brutally slaughtered. Blacks were hanged on trees and lampposts. Some five thousand escaped to police stations and to swamps and woods on the outskirts of the city. Only when the secretary of war released eleven regiments to check the rioting was it stopped. From thirty to one hundred blacks had been killed, and one thousand families had lost all they owned.[20]

19. Amos Beman to Reverend P. D. Oakey, August 4, 1865, S. S. Jocelyn to Amos Beman, July 28, 1865, both in Amos Beman Scrap Book (Amos G. Beman Papers), III.

20. "Incidents of the Riot," in *Report of the Committee of Merchants for the Relief of Colored People Suffering from Late Riots in the City of New York* (New York, 1863), 14–27; Smith,

Charles Ray was less well known to angry whites than Garnet, so he was able to provide his house as a refuge and hospital for many who had been hurt. Before the violence was entirely quelled, New York's white merchants, appalled by what had occurred, set up a committee to organize relief for the blacks who had suffered the most. Over $40,000 and some two thousand pieces of clothing were collected from many hundreds of donors from as far afield as Vermont. Ray, Garnet, and two other black ministers visited about three thousand black families to discover the extent of their need and thus expedite the flow of appropriate relief. Nearly thirteen thousand people were aided.[21]

Pennington had been out of the city when the riot began, having gone to Poughkeepsie in mid-June to take a teaching position under that city's board of education. He had left his family in New York City at the residence on West Twenty-sixth Street, where they had lived with seven other black families for several years. After closing his school for vacation, Pennington, unaware of the riot, came back to the city just as the violence was subsiding. When he had almost reached his home, he was set upon by a number of whites with stones and brickbats and the shout "kill the d——d nigger." Thinking it unwise to seek shelter in his own residence or nearby stores, he hurried north and east several blocks. He later recalled, "At every step death and desolation stared me in the face. I had a number of narrow escapes. I believe that had I shown any signs of fear or cowardice, I should have been set upon and killed." Pennington took a boat back to Poughkeepsie, eventually finding out that his wife and other women in the same tenement building had not been hurt, though grievously harried by a mob outside that was waiting for the return of "absent marked victims [males]."[22]

Garnet's and Pennington's subsequent statements about the riot were made, understandably, from quite different angles of vision. Garnet, Ray, and others who had distributed relief to the stricken families composed a powerful letter of gratitude to the merchants who had, they declared, responded to the injured and bereaved blacks as true Good Samaritans. They wrote, "You obeyed the noblest dictates of the human heart, and by

"Sketch of Garnet," in *A Memorial Discourse by . . . Garnet,* 58f.; Headley, *The Great Riots of New York,* chaps. 10–20; Foner, *History of Black Americans,* III, 392–401.

21. *Report of the Committee of Merchants,* 7–13, 39–48.

22. Pennington's account of July 20, 1863, "Six Hours' Walk over the Blood-Stained Pavements of New York," *National Principia,* July 30, 1863 (Microfilm copy in Carter and Ripley [eds.], *BAP,* reel 14, item 983).

your generous moral courage you rolled back the tide of violence that had well nigh swept us away."[23] For Garnet, however, the Draft Riots in New York City and elsewhere had frightening implications for the growing number of slaves being freed in the South. Southern resentment against free blacks had fueled antiblack violence in the North and would do so in the South. All the more reason, therefore, to revitalize the African Civilization Society and its implementation of voluntary emigration. In late November 1863 Garnet and other members of the society's board of directors sent a lengthy missive to President Abraham Lincoln, evidently responding to a request by Lincoln for advice. At this juncture these black leaders and the president were still hoping for large-scale freeing of slaves by southern owners, short of total military defeat and perhaps with federal compensation. Garnet and his associates refused to give clear-cut advice but recognized the government's care of freedmen as an awesome responsibility. And they saw "danger to the white race and their republican institutions, because of the presence of a disfranchised and distinct class of laborers in the heart of the Republic." Reviving Delany's recommendations made over a decade earlier, they urged the establishment of an independent state where the majority of the freed would want to go—probably "to the American tropics; but not a few will go to Africa." Finally, Garnet and his colleagues asked Lincoln to allocate $5,000 to the African Civilization Society from the monies appropriated "for emigration purposes."[24]

Approximately six weeks after the New York City riot Pennington produced a lengthy analysis of its causes and the lessons to be learned from it. He blamed the violence on forces at work in the North since the beginning of the Civil War: Catholic immigrant resentment of Protestants, the old antiblack spirit of colonization, and southern rebel attitudes transplanted to the banks of the Hudson. The conclusions to be drawn, Pennington declared, were clear. Let blacks learn to use weapons in self-defense, which is "the first law of nature." Let the able-bodied enlist in the Union army "with the distinct understanding that WE ARE TO HAVE ALL OUR RIGHTS AS MEN AND AS CITIZENS"—the right to jobs, to wages, to

23. "An Address to the . . . Merchants for the Relief of Colored People . . . Presented by Colored Ministers and Laymen, August 22, 1863," in *Report of the Committee of Merchants*, 32–34.

24. George W. Levere, Henry Garnet, and others to Abraham Lincoln, November 25, 1863, A.L.S. copy in Records of the Secretary of the Interior Relating to the Suppression of the African Slave Trade and Negro Colonization, National Archives (Microfilm copy in Carter and Ripley [eds.], *BAP*, reel 15, item 62).

the support of families, to the education of children, and to the support of chosen religious institutions. Let blacks rise up again against the spirit of colonization that advised against protesting "the colored car" (Jim Crow) system. Finally, let the northern black Congregational and Presbyterian churches quickly rally and follow the example of AMEZ and AME churches in supplying ministers and teachers for the freedmen in the South.[25]

Pennington acted on his own advice and went South to work with freedmen. Late in 1864 he requested that the Third Presbytery of New York recommend him to the Missouri Conference of the AME church. In the fall of 1865 he put his plan into action, going to New Orleans, where he was ordained by the Missouri Conference gathered there. His preaching and teaching post was Natchez, Mississippi. From this location he sent a detailed report to the *Weekly Anglo-African* on the progress of Reconstruction. Buoyed up by the presence of a black regiment and by a circular letter from Major General Oliver O. Howard, commissioner of the Freedmen's Bureau, he was laboring to combat the bullying and misinforming of ignorant freedmen by their former owners. He spent much time explaining to the newly freed their rights of lease or purchase of land, of freedom of speech, and of testifying in the courts.

By early 1867 Pennington was back in New England serving the black Congregational church in Portland, Maine. Some two and a half years later, suffering from ill health and eager to resume work "in the great cause of education and Christian Reconstruction," he was back in the South, this time in Jacksonville, Florida, on an appointment from the Presbyterian Committee of Missions for Freedmen. Here he founded a small Presbyterian church and school and struggled against poverty, as he had done for most of the preceding fifteen years. A year later, in October 1870, Pennington died, far from family and most of his friends. His death, however, did not go unrecognized. An obituary notice in the New Haven *Palladium* recalled his ministry in Hartford thirty years earlier: "He was then of erect bearing, had a fine intelligent countenance, black as ebony. He was received as a brother by, and attended weekly ministerial

25. Lecture given on August 24, 1863, in Poughkeepsie, printed in *National Principia,* January 7, 14, 1864 (Microfilm copy in Carter and Ripley [eds.], *BAP,* reel 15, items 192, 205). Within a few days of the ending of the New York City riots, Pennington was urging the raising of money to combat in the courts the retrogression, after the violence, in the practices of New York City's common carriers. *National Principia,* August 4, 13, 1863 (Microfilm copy in Carter and Ripley [eds.], *BAP,* reel 14, items 996, 1008).

meetings with, Drs. Hawes, Bushnell, and Daggett, and was highly respected by them and by all the churches for attainments as a scholar, and his real worth and piety as a minister."[26]

Amos Beman's concern for freedmen, which had been sparked by his visit to Washington, D.C., in 1862, has been described. During his pastoral work on Long Island from 1863 to 1865, he became an active supporter of the African Civilization Society, which by this time had transferred its primary efforts from voluntary colonization to work among the freedmen. Because, as Pennington had stated, the AME and AMEZ churches had more resources for this enterprise during the Civil War than did black Congregationalist and Presbyterian churches, Beman was drawn back toward the AMEZ denomination, in which he had been raised. At African Civilization Society meetings in AME and AME Zion churches in New York City in December 1863, it was Beman who presented a resolution affirming that this society's work for the colored race and for the world was based in the Gospel, as well as resolutions urging the adding of five thousand members a year to the society's rolls.[27] During Beman's brief postwar pastorate in the Mount Zion Congregational Church in Cleveland and during two subsequent years of home mission work among the freedmen in Tennessee, William Howard Day's AMEZ journal, *Zion's Standard and Weekly Review,* reported on his doings.[28]

Beman's work in the South, begun in September 1866, was sponsored by the Presbyterian Home Missions Committee (white). His salary for twelve months was to be $600, of which the northern committee would supply $200 and the Presbyterian churches and black people in the vicinity of Greenville, Tennessee, would provide the rest. The task was immense—so many old former slaves and parentless children, and such a sea of ignorance. After six months Beman could report that there was in Greenville a Sabbath school of some eighty people, of every age. However, they were teaching themselves, because no white person, no elder or minister, would think of teaching them; and their progress was very

26. *Weekly Anglo-African,* December 23, 1865 (Microfilm copy in Carter and Ripley [eds.], *BAP,* reel 16, item 560); James Pennington to Gerrit Smith, September 17, 1869, in Gerrit Smith Papers; Blackett, *Beating Against the Barriers,* 80–82; Amos Beman Scrap Book (Amos G. Beman Papers), II, 94.

27. Report by Philo, December 28, 1863, in *Christian Recorder,* undated clipping in Amos Beman Scrap Book (Amos G. Beman Papers), II, 39.

28. *Zion's Standard and Weekly Review,* August 6, 1866; September 5, 1867; February 5, 1868.

slow. Drunkenness was common, though not as prevalent as among whites. Old masters were bitter toward their former slaves. Perhaps worst of all, in Beman's eyes, was that "they know nothing of the history of their race in this land, nothing of the condition of the colored people of the north or of the West Indies or of Africa." Revealing the conscious goal of his own life, Beman wrote, "They need precept illustrated in 'living epistles'—they need to see those of them, 'bone of their bone, flesh of their flesh' who have been elevated and improved." They need to know about the Garnets, Crummells, Theodore Wrights, Elymas Rogerses, Cornishes, and Gloucesters. And Beman added to his black honor roll Frederick Douglass; Charles Remond; William Wells Brown; Martin Delany; the educators Ebenezer Bassett, John Peterson, and Sarah Douglass (for years the head of a superior secondary school for blacks in Philadelphia); and the abolitionist poet and lecturer Frances Watkins Harper. Hearing of these persons and of northern black improvement over the previous thirty years (the period of Beman's own ministry), "they will thank God and take courage, and march forward from victory to victory."[29]

There was no practical way of implementing Beman's vision, but he did his best for two years. He won the plaudits of the Republican congressman from Tennessee for "preaching and lecturing . . . with signal success." Word of his work drew some financial support from as far away as Chicago and Niagara Falls. And after nearly a year of labor, Beman joined in a grand celebration in Green County to raise money to complete the building of a schoolhouse for black children. On a visit back in the North in September 1867, Beman attended a border state convention in Baltimore as a delegate from Tennessee. Settling in New Haven once more, he shared the platform with William Lloyd Garrison at an 1870 celebration by the black community of the Emancipation Proclamation, issued seven years earlier. He was kept informed by United States senator Charles Sumner of progress in Washington toward federal approval of the Fifteenth Amendment, which would, at long last, open the polls to Connecticut blacks. In recognition of Beman's labors for his people in the state, the Connecticut Senate invited him to serve as chaplain for a session in 1872. He was married again in 1871, this time to a black woman. Between 1870 and 1872 he served as supply pastor for the black Congregational church in Pittsfield, which he had helped found some twenty

29. Amos Beman to Reverend George Whipple (staff member of the Presbyterian Home Missions Committee), from Greenville, Tenn., February 25, 1867, reprinted in "Documents," *Journal of Negro History* XXII (1937), 222–26.

years earlier. Beman died in 1874 at the age of sixty-two. As one of his biographers put it, Beman had lived in a difficult time. Much had been asked of him as an educated Afro-American, and he had responded to the very best of his ability.[30]

From the time of Garnet's (and others') letter of late 1863 to President Abraham Lincoln on the possible colonization of freedmen in Central America to the early months of 1869, when Ulysses S. Grant was beginning his administration, Garnet stayed close to developments in Washington. Because of these interests, and because of continued bickering with the trustees of the Shiloh Presbyterian Church, in April 1864 Garnet accepted a call from the Fifteenth Street Presbyterian Church in the nation's capital.[31] Garnet was present in the gallery of the House of Representatives in late January 1865 when that body voted on ratification of the Thirteenth Amendment, to guarantee that courts or future administrations not overturn Lincoln's Emancipation Proclamation. Garnet joined other blacks and whites in an explosion of cheering from the gallery when the two-thirds majority was secured. A few days later William Henry Channing, the chaplain of the House, having secured the approval of Lincoln and his cabinet, invited Garnet to preach a sermon on February 12 in the House to celebrate the amendment's passage. With the backing of the Fifteenth Street Presbyterian Church's choir, Garnet spoke for over an hour to a crowd of blacks and whites that filled the main floor and the gallery. His text was Matthew 23:4, "For they [Scribes and Pharisees] bind heavy burdens, and grievous to be borne, and lay them on men's shoulders, but they themselves will not move them with one of their fingers." His message offered America little reason for self-congratulation but stressed instead the vast unfinished task:

> It is often asked when and where will the demands of the reformers of this and coming ages end? It is a fair question, and I will answer.
>
> When all unjust and heavy burdens shall be removed from every man in the land. When all invidious and proscriptive distinctions shall be blotted out from our laws, whether they be constitutional, statute, or municipal laws.

30. Amos Beman Scrap Book (Amos G. Beman Papers); Warner, "Amos Gerry Beman," 219–21; Robert Harris, "Amos Beman: A Moral Leader in Nineteenth Century America" (November, 1972).

31. Minutes of a Meeting of the Members and Pewholders of the Shiloh Presbyterian Church, April 10, 1864 (MS at Presbyterian Historical Association, Philadelphia). These minutes, written by the moderating elder, recalled Garnet's eight years as pastor as a time of successful and faithful ministry.

> When emancipation shall be followed by enfranchisement, and all men holding allegiance to the government shall enjoy every right of American citizenship. . . . When there shall be no more class-legislation, and no more trouble concerning the black man and his rights, than there is in regard to other American citizens. When, in every respect, he shall be equal before the law, and shall be left to make his own way in the social walks of life.[32]

The following summer the American Home Missionary Society, which had made grants to Garnet in the latter 1850s to supplement the salary provided by the Shiloh Presbyterian Church, again commissioned Garnet. This time his mission was to travel through the "South and South Western States" for several months as the "Exploring Agent among Freedmen" for the AHMS.[33] Garnet went on this trip with a second responsibility: to serve as short-term editor of, and reporter for, the *Weekly Anglo-African*. He and Julia Garnet first visited the plantation in Kent County, Maryland, where he had lived his first years. From there they traveled to Richmond, a city in ruins. Here Garnet found black men being beaten up by Union soldiers, said to be mostly Irish. Only a garrison of black soldiers and continued federal surveillance, he declared, could protect the rights of southern freedmen. After two months of travel as far west as Missouri, Garnet returned to his Washington pastorate and to relief and educational efforts for freedmen in the nation's capital. In the summer of 1866 he and Douglass attended the Republican national convention as honorary delegates, were asked to speak on the question of black suffrage, and were dismayed to have the issue shelved. In the fall of 1867 Garnet and Douglass, hearing that Mary Todd Lincoln was in financial extremity, raised funds to help her. In gratitude she gave Garnet one of Lincoln's walking canes.

A year later Garnet resigned his Washington pastorate and accepted the presidency of Avery College in Pittsburgh. Financed by a bequest from a successful cotton merchant and conductor on the Underground Railroad, the college had an all-black staff, faculty, and student body. While in this post, Garnet kept in touch with congressional debate on the Fifteenth Amendment, which would provide a federal guarantee of black suffrage throughout the United States. Douglass called a national con-

32. Garnet, *A Memorial Discourse by . . . Garnet,* 69–91; William J. Wilson's description of the occasion in Smith, "Sketch of Garnet," in *A Memorial Discourse,* 65–67; Pasternak, "Rise Now and Fly to Arms," 205–208.

33. Presbyterian Church, U.S.A., Minutes of Sessions, Fifteenth Street Presbyterian Church, Washington, D.C., July 5, 1865 (Moorland-Spingarn Research Center, Box 34-1, Folder 1, p. 151).

vention of blacks to meet in Washington in January 1869. Garnet attended and aroused general antagonism by proposing the former president of Liberia as an honorary delegate. However, when a committee was chosen to wait upon President-elect Grant on the black suffrage issue, Garnet was there. With him were Douglass, George Downing, and Robert Purvis, well-to-do Philadelphia black activist and author of the *Appeal of Forty Thousand Citizens,* the Pennsylvania blacks' 1838 appeal for the franchise. Grant responded favorably, and following ratification by the required number of states, the right for which black leaders had struggled so hard for over thirty years was given the federal Constitution's guarantee.[34]

Garnet was neither particularly successful nor happy in the position of college president. Taking a huge cut in salary (Avery had paid him $1,400 a year), he returned in 1870 to the Shiloh Presbyterian Church. It had greatly deteriorated during his six years of absence, it lacked a steady ministry, and many of its members had moved uptown. Garnet requested financial help from the American Missionary Association but was turned down because of "past irregularities."[35] Far more of a blow than this was the death in March 1871 of Julia, his devoted wife of thirty years. Writing Gerrit Smith nearly two years later, he was still mourning "as much as ever, the loss of my gentle, sweet-tempered, and God-loving Julia." Garnet's daughter, Mary, "a good child, and a sterling woman," had two daughters and was living in New Jersey. His son, Henry, talented but as yet "unconverted to Christ," was teaching in South Carolina, his mother's home state.[36] In financial extremity, Garnet asked for Smith's help and promptly received $20. There were also broader matters that Garnet was commending to Smith's attention: agitation among Cubans in New York City, supported by some blacks, for United States annexation of Cuba and the emancipation of its slaves. On this issue, as well as that of the franchise, Garnet had been to see President Grant, and for this cause Smith sent him $200.[37]

The remaining nine years of Garnet's life were largely a period of declining involvement in any broad efforts to improve the lot of black Americans. And the church on Prince Street saw its numbers decline still further as cast-iron factories and warehouses were steadily being built in

34. Pasternak, "Rise Now and Fly to Arms," 218–37.

35. *Ibid,* 242f.

36. Henry Garnet to Gerrit Smith, January 27, 1873, in Gerrit Smith Papers.

37. Henry Garnet to Gerrit Smith, February 1, 20, 1873, both in Gerrit Smith Papers; Pasternak, "Rise Now and Fly to Arms," 246–48.

the area. At last, in 1878, the prominent Republican politician and editor Thurlow Weed gave the money needed to provide the Shiloh Church with a new home uptown (on Twenty-sixth Street). That same year Garnet married the assertive and self-confident black feminist and educator Sarah Thompson. As more and more black students were being admitted into white schools in New York City, black schools were being closed and black teachers' employment terminated. In 1879 the city's board of education threatened to close one of the three remaining black schools. (Sarah Thompson Garnet was principal of one of them.) A public meeting was called, and five hundred blacks attended. Henry Garnet presented a series of resolutions, one applauding the opening of formerly white schools to blacks and another urging the board of education to keep the present black schools open as long as the number of pupils warranted continuation. Finally, he urged black parents to get their children to these three schools in order to keep them open. The school board, for the time being, dropped its plan to close one of the schools.[38]

Garnet's marriage to Sarah Thompson lasted only a year. His daughter was also having trouble with her marriage. She asked her father to expedite her appointment by the Ladies Board of Missions of the Presbyterian Church for work in Africa. Garnet enthusiastically carried out her request, and she left for Liberia in the fall of 1880. The following summer President Garfield, persuaded by Thurlow Weed, appointed Garnet United States minister and counsel general to Liberia. Garnet joyfully accepted, preached his last sermon to the Shiloh congregation on November 6, 1881, and arrived in Monrovia two weeks later. Not strong when he left the United States, Garnet found himself quickly in the grip of tropical fevers similar to those he had contracted in Jamaica twenty-five years earlier. He died on Lincoln's birthday in 1882 and was buried, as he had wished, on African soil.

Of the many tributes to Garnet delivered shortly after his death, the most perceptive—and extravagant—was that of Alexander Crummell, who had been deprived of the satisfactions and spared the vexations of working closely with him over the years.

Charles Ray would die in 1886, having had a longer life by over a decade than any of the other activists whose careers this work has been considering. He continued to reside in New York City. Reveling in the ratifica-

38. Mabee, *Black Education in New York State,* 208–10.

tion of the Fifteenth Amendment, he noted that it gave body to the ideal of equality formulated at the beginning of the Revolution, just as the Civil War had given body to the ideal of freedom for which that earlier war had been fought.[39] In the 1870s, in his late sixties, Ray was still trying to help beleaguered fellow blacks. He wrote his longtime friend Gerrit Smith of his efforts to establish a program to provide employment in New York City for southern freedmen trained as domestics and wanting to come north. Unemployed or miserably underpaid where they were, they would, Ray was sure, be in demand in New York City.[40]

Ray took great pride in the accomplishments of the three surviving daughters born to him and his second wife, Charlotte. By 1870 his daughter Charlotte was on the verge of becoming the first woman to graduate from the Howard University Law School. It had been desperately hard for Ray to secure the funds for her training. His many friends, ready to contribute to other causes, were "not in accord with *this calling for women*." Knowing Gerrit Smith's views on women's rights, Ray wrote him to ask for $100. Charlotte Ray did graduate two years later and was shortly thereafter the first woman to be admitted to the bar of the Supreme Court of the District of Columbia. A second daughter, Florence, evidently received some legal training, and the third, Henrietta, was trained in the School of Pedagogy of New York University.[41]

By 1884 two of these women were teaching in New York City schools but were in danger of losing their jobs because the city's board of education was about to close its two remaining black schools. As in 1879 concerned blacks in the city organized a protest. This time they attempted a flanking movement. They petitioned the state legislature to continue the two black schools, requiring them to accept whites also and to keep the present black teachers until they were "removed for cause." The Senate and Assembly passed a bill to this effect, but Governor Grover Cleveland was known to oppose integrated schools. A delegation of four blacks carrying the New York City blacks' petition waited on Cleveland. The group's leader was an immensely popular AME preacher, William Derrick, who was also chairman of New York State's chief black Republican organization. The other three in the embassy were the threatened schools' principals, Sarah Thompson Garnet and Charles Reason, and the seventy-six-year-old Charles Ray. These four stressed the injustice of de-

39. Ray and Ray, *Sketch of Charles B. Ray*, 52.

40. Charles Ray to Gerrit Smith, August 22, 1870, in Gerrit Smith Papers.

41. Charles Ray to Gerrit Smith, August 2, 1870, in Gerrit Smith Papers.

stroying the color line for pupils but refusing to apply the principle to teachers. Ray testified that the petitions brought by the group had been signed by some of New York's best citizens. And Derrick made a passionate appeal. Cleveland signed the bill, and the schools remained open for another decade, though their staffs suffered a variety of harassments.[42]

Ray died in the summer of 1886. That he had been chosen two years earlier to be one of those making representation to Governor Cleveland in the interests of New York City's black educators was clear evidence of the esteem still accorded him by the city's black leaders. In Daniel Payne's autobiography, published two years after Ray's death, Ray was lovingly remembered as well educated, modest, and refined—indeed, a "sainted man." Payne especially celebrated Ray's daughters, who had been given a "sound and wholesome education" at home and in the public schools and who were now so usefully involved in the training of children. The chief tribute to Ray, however, was a fact-filled and admiring biography written by his daughters Florence and Henrietta and published the year after his death.[43]

42. *Ibid.;* New York *Globe,* May 3, 10, 1884, summarized and quoted in Mabee, *Black Education in New York State,* 217–19, 321*n*11.

43. Payne, *Recollections of Seventy Years,* 48; Ray and Ray, *Sketch of Charles B. Ray.*

CONCLUSION

This has been a story of stultifying racism in the United States, of Afro-American refusal to accept it, and of the energetic hopefulness of a Christian ministry that, though thwarted again and again, would not be finally discouraged. Religion had been central in the Afro-American freedom movement down to the 1830s, and remained of critical importance thereafter. The black people's sense of the undeniable worth of their own lives and of one another's was nourished in the relationships of lovers, of parents and children, of devoted friends, and of the local black community, southern or northern, slave or free. The assurance, joy, and hopefulness born of these elemental experiences survived in many, no matter how brutalized or demeaned they were by slavery or northern racism. Reinforcing these relationships and sometimes transcending them was the experience of being caught up in the awesome, empowering, and loving vitality of the Spirit. Slave preachers knew this Spirit well, as did free black preachers. Rank-and-file slaves and free black people, led by the preacher, or in their own singing and praying, experienced the Spirit as an undeniable liberation.

Ministers of the early independent black Methodist and Baptist churches and then those of the black Presbyterian, Congregational, and Episcopal churches were possessed by a biblical faith that envisioned social liberation. With imagination and daring, these ministers led in the creation of new institutions to implement that liberation, whether African mutual aid societies or freedom journals or vigilance committees. In the press of radical reform activities, the religious faith remained controlling. What energized these clergy was knowing that they were struggling toward the way things were meant to be in a world still mysteriously controlled by God.

The emphasis on social liberation so crucial in Richard Allen's founding of the Bethel African Methodist Episcopal Church and in Absalom Jones's founding of Saint Thomas' African Episcopal Church came into its own in the 1830s and 1840s in the efforts of black leaders, both clerical and lay. This work has focused on the roles of six Presbyterian and Congregational ministers in this freedom movement. It has done so because of the distinctiveness of their innovations and their persistence. They were distinctive as compared with the nearly twenty other black Presbyterian and Congregational clergymen serving independent black churches by 1860. And they were distinctive vis-à-vis the great bulk of black clergy in African Methodist, African Baptist, and African Episcopal churches. In another sense, however, the six activists described in this book were merely conspicuous embodiments of the longings and achievements, defeats and anger, confusion and faith present in the lives of all Afro-American ministers.

Activist black clergy had good reason to become driven men. Intolerable systems of enslavement and caste oppression indeed had to be ended, and these men's leverage for accomplishing basic change often seemed very slight. That God would eventually destroy the forces of evil was as much a mandate to his chosen spokesmen to declare war on these forces now as it was an assurance about the final end. As if this prophetic task were not enough, the claims of parish ministry were endlessly demanding: preaching soundly and compellingly, often twice a week; giving support to those nearly overwhelmed by poverty, grief, or the debilitation of grave illness; and admonishing those who treated one another shabbily, along with those who chafed at what seemed to them puritanical disciplines imposed by church membership. The pastor's chief support in the midst of these demands lay in his sense of a close and sustaining relationship with his Lord and Maker. However, he also depended heavily on other human beings: on his family, on the members of his church, and on his clerical colleagues committed to the same dual calling of ministry and social reform.

The most unreliable of these supports was the minister's own church members. The able and faithful preacher inspired and energized his congregation, but he often seemed to be expecting too much. The same was true of his personal counseling. The parishioner frequently found new insight and vitality as a result of his minister's work, and admiration and deep loyalty could be the result. Not infrequently, however, resentment was roused because too much seemed to be demanded or too severe a judgment seemed to be imposed on what were termed worldly enjoyments or ethically questionable practices. Elite activist clergy like Cornish, Wright, and the others labored under another burden. The tradition of full-time ministry in the Presbyterian and Congregational denominations precluded taking other employment to piece together an adequate income. This was often a costly privilege and made the minister especially dependent on the trustees of the church. Frequently the only recourse left to a financially beset pastor was to threaten to resign unless a promised salary was actually paid. In light of all these pressures it is not so much remarkable that Cornish's, Garnet's, and Pennington's pastorates were many and often brief as that Wright's, Ray's, and Beman's were so lengthy and stable.

Granted these dimensions in the pastorates of these six men, two concluding questions cry out for answers. What was the impact of these men on blacks and whites in their time? And what was their significance for subsequent American history?

It is clear that a large part of the black population of the North was fundamentally uninterested in the moral and social reforms into which these six poured so much energy. Many blacks in New York City never read *Freedom's Journal* or the *Colored American,* let alone took seriously the exhortations of Cornish and other black ministers to stop spending money on liquor, gambling, and flashy clothes, and instead to devote it to the support of black churches, schools, and newspapers. Further weakening the appeal of activist clergy for many black people was the visionary and grandiose character of some of their proposals. Cornish's and Pennington's projected networks of black schools, colleges, and apprenticeship programs were theoretically desirable but unrealistic. The same can be said of the proposal establishing a National Council of the Colored People adopted by the 1853 national black convention, of which Pennington was president and Amos Beman, Frederick Douglass, and William Nell were vice-presidents.

Elite black clergy, however, did have a major impact on contemporary Afro-Americans. Their influence can be usefully viewed in the context of black leadership at large during the 1840s and 1850s. In the generally sound concluding chapter of the solid book *They Who Would Be Free,* the

Peases discuss the quality of leadership provided by black abolitionists in the antebellum North. They acknowledge that such leaders "wrenched modest improvements from a reluctant society," but they emphasize "the problems of being leaders without followers," of being an early form of the black bourgeoisie with a gap separating them from the masses. These problems, the Peases continue, were accentuated by bitter feuding among prominent black leaders, not a few of whom were prima donnas. Judged by its unity as to goals or its efficiency of organization, black abolitionism was a failure, declare the Peases. The primary cause of the failure was black economic and political powerlessness: "Only here does one find a coherent explanation of why a struggle for freedom, equality, personal dignity, and group identity was futile in a society whose dominant group avowedly espoused the values these goals embraced."[1]

Valid as most of this analysis is, to label this struggle futile is off the mark. Assessing the work of a specific type of antebellum black leader, the activist clergyman like those whose lives this work has followed, leads to a different and sounder conclusion. Along with massive black indifference and the recurrence of clerical proposals that were long on desirability and short on practicality, there is evidence of substantial success in leadership. Periodically in some cases, and consistently in others, these six men were effective leaders in their own pastorates. Moreover, on the social reform front, the imagination and assurance that prompted the founding of black newspapers, schools, and petition drives gained the interested support, at least for a time, of thousands of northern blacks. By 1860 the parishes of the more than twenty black Presbyterian and Congregational ministers included many hundreds of people. These church members, along with a great many in black Baptist and Methodist churches, were being urged with a measure of success toward an active struggle for equal rights as part of Christian discipleship. Some clues have survived as to the feelings of their black contemporaries for these clerical leaders. There were published characterizations of them. On some occasions they won triumphant accolades. And there were other manifestations of the hold that some of these men gained over rank-and-file blacks in their communities. These evidences of positive response by black constituencies to their activist clerical leaders need to be placed alongside the political failures of particular antebellum civil rights efforts.

In the latter years of the nineteenth century, the celebration of promi-

1. Pease and Pease, *They Who Would Be Free,* 284, 288, 291–97.

nent black achievers that had been initiated in the pages of *Freedom's Journal* and the *Colored American* and had been amplified in dozens of fugitive slave narratives emerged as a wider literary genre. For instance, in 1863 and 1874 William W. Brown's two volumes of biographical vignettes of notable blacks appeared.[2] These included discerning and positive portraits of Pennington, Ray, and Garnet.

Brown, along with making a general statement about Pennington's zealous and effective labors for the educational, social, and religious advancement of his race, stressed his intellectual achievement. He was "a good student, a ripe scholar, and deeply versed in theology." Brown had heard him preach in Paris at a worship service for American and English delegates to the Peace Congress: "His sermon . . . was an elegant production, . . . and created upon the minds of all a more elevated idea of the Negro."[3]

When he came to speak of Ray, Brown showed sensitivity to the strengths and contributions of a man who had never been one to seek or be given the headlines. Brown described him as "well educated, . . . a terse and vigorous writer, an able and eloquent speaker," and a man well informed on contemporary affairs. He noted Ray's omnipresence and indispensability at the many state and national conventions of the 1840s. As editor of the *Colored American,* Ray had shown "signal ability." The journal had always been faithful to the cause of the slave in the South and "the elevation of the black man everywhere." As to physical appearance, "Dr. Ray [was] of small stature, neat and wiry build, in race standing about half-way between the African and the Anglo-Saxon." (Brown was under the impression that Ray had been awarded a doctor of divinity degree, although no other evidence confirms this.) Ray was polished in manner, and his sermons given before white congregations always left a good impression of the black race. Brown's concluding evaluation of Ray was high praise indeed, even considering the generally laudatory tone of these sketches: "Blameless in his family relations, guided by the highest moral rectitude, a true friend to everything that . . . better[s] the moral, social, religious and political condition of man, Dr. Ray may be looked upon as one of the foremost of the leading men of his race."[4]

2. William Wells Brown, *The Black Man, His Antecedents, His Genius, and His Achievements* (New York, 1863), and *The Rising Son; or, The Antecedents and Advancement of the Colored Race* (Boston, 1874).

3. Brown, *The Rising Son*, 462.

4. *Ibid.*, 472f.

Although Pennington's striking accomplishments and Ray's ability, commitment, and integrity were warmly acknowledged, it was Garnet who received the most extended, and even fulsome, tribute from fellow Afro-Americans. In Brown's earlier book, published during the Civil War, the biography of Garnet followed that of Denmark Vesey, the organizer of the massive slave conspiracy in the Charleston area in 1822. Brown stressed Garnet's princely African ancestry and his skill and power as an orator, especially when excoriating the original enslavement of Africans and the continuing brutal exploitation of their offspring: "Mr. Garnet is unadulterated in race, tall and commanding in appearance, [with] an eye that looks through you, and a clear ringing voice."[5]

Detailed lives of Garnet by James McCune Smith and Alexander Crummell, though euphoric, give further insight into the impact of Garnet on black contemporaries. After Garnet had preached in the hall of Congress in 1865, Smith was asked by the elders and trustees of the Fifteenth Street (African) Presbyterian Church to prepare a "sketch of the life of our pastor." The result was a fact-filled fifty-page biography that was published along with the text of the sermon Garnet had delivered on that memorable February 12. Smith had known Garnet for a quarter of a century. They had worked closely in the campaign for the restoration of the franchise to blacks, but they had fallen out bitterly over Garnet's promotion of the African Civilization Society. Smith, however, rose to this request. His recital reached its climax in an account of Garnet's sermon before Congress. It is notable, however, that the words used to capture the impact of Garnet on his audience that day were almost the same as those used by reporters on earlier occasions when Wright, Ray, Pennington, or Beman were addressing whites: "Men who went to the house to hear a colored man, came away having heard a MAN in the highest and fullest sense . . . and they were amazed."[6]

Smith, trained as a physician, had often written and spoken on phrenology and the comparative physiology of the races. Smith himself was described by William W. Brown as "rather more Anglo-Saxon than African," but he reveled in Garnet's being "an African of pure lineage, with

5. Brown, *The Black Man,* 149–51. In Brown's later book, sketches of slave revolt leaders were missing, and the biography of Garnet was briefer and the praise more measured. Brown, *The Rising Son,* 457–59.

6. Smith, "Sketch of Garnet," in *A Memorial Discourse by . . . Garnet,* 67. Smith, who had evidently not been present for this occasion, was quoting from an account by William J. Wilson, who had often written for *Frederick Douglass' Paper* and the *Weekly Anglo-African* using the name Ethiop.

no admixture of Saxon blood as the source of his unquestionable talent and genius." What most fascinated Smith, however, was the similarity of Garnet's features to those of distinguished Anglo-Saxons. Garnet had the "well developed, nearly perpendicular forehead, the long mobile eyebrow, overhanging eyes that prominent themselves, . . . luxuriant lids, a large nose . . . under muscular control, yet hooked, . . . a wide but well cut mouth with the thin compressed lips which indicate high determination, and a fighting chin." Smith noted that some would describe these as "all white features," but they would be wrong: "They were the features which God has stamped upon the leaders of mankind in all ages and nations." Against this background, Smith's concluding tribute was to Garnet as a leader of blacks: "So earnest, so zealous, so true, so constantly on the watch-tower, ready to sound the first alarm, ready to receive or ward off or strike the first blow, we have come to look upon him as our natural, our appointed leader."[7]

At the time of Garnet's death in Liberia, Alexander Crummell, his boyhood friend and longtime Episcopal missionary in West Africa, published a eulogy of enduring value to those trying to understand Garnet's nature and significance. Crummell's descriptions of the Garnet family and of young Henry's vicissitudes before being ordained a Presbyterian minister have already been presented. Crummell also brought alive the complex makeup of the mature Garnet as no one else had done. The man being mourned had been a basically amiable person, whether in a social gathering or on the lecture platform. He had been fun loving and also "almost womanly in temper and affectionateness." When indignant over some wrong or tyranny, however, or when publicly opposed, "he was a very lion in debate, and nothing could stand before him." Crummell saw Garnet as one of the four great black abolitionist orators of the 1840s, the others being Charles Remond, Frederick Douglass, and Garnet's cousin Samuel Ringgold Ward. Crummell described Garnet as "more restrained and less fiery and monotonous than Remond; not so ponderous as Douglass; inferior in cast-iron logic to Ward; there was a salience, a variety, . . . and above all a brilliancy and glowing fire in our friend's eloquence which gave him his special and peculiar place."[8]

Crummell's compact summary of Garnet's public life cited first his having been a lifelong Presbyterian minister and pastor. He also de-

7. Smith, "Sketch of Garnet," in *A Memorial Discourse by . . . Garnet,* 54, 67f.

8. Crummell, *Africa and America,* 272, 288, 291f.

scribed Garnet as an antislavery orator, an active friend of fugitive slaves, an agent for Gerrit Smith's program of land grants to New York blacks, a temperance lecturer, a delegate to Europe for peace and freedom, a missionary to Jamaica, a promoter of African Civilization, and a leader in the Liberty party and then the Republican party.[9]

There are also clues as to how whole communities of black people felt about several of these activist black ministers. There can be little doubt that apart from the ups and downs of black parishioners' support of their pastors, rank-and-file Afro-Americans in a given community were proud of the learning, the poise, the eloquence, and the reputation of their activist clergy. Accounts by black reporters of major addresses given by Pennington and Beman catch some of this admiration of blacks at large for their men of distinction. In the summer of 1852 members of Brooklyn's Siloam Presbyterian Church and their guests gathered for the installation of Amos Freeman, recently called to this pastorate after a decade in Portland, Maine. Several white Presbyterian ministers, including the famous, and notorious, Samuel Cox, participated in the service. Cox gave the charge to the black pastor. According to the reporter for *Frederick Douglass' Paper,* Cox was eager to make up for recent offenses against blacks (such as strong support of the 1850 Fugitive Slave Act), and he delivered a superb and appropriate exhortation. The next speaker was Pennington. The reporter called his "one of the most splendid discourses that [it] has ever been my fortune to listen to." Cox, well aware that he had been bested where he considered himself incomparable, "turned alternately red, purple and white." The reporter described Cox: "For the first time he had been distanced in the popular race—he had not fully counted on his man. . . . Our present and destined position in this country, as defined by Dr. Pennington, so unlike anything [Cox] had ever heard before; . . . so clear, yet to him so startling and so new, yet so convincing that the old Dr. was fairly routed horse and foot." As Pennington continued his address, "his voice deepened and mellowed into indescribable sublimity, till at last theme and speaker alone retained places in our thoughts, and like the setting summer's sun, they ended, shedding a golden hue over all."[10]

Similar pride was evident in the words, cited earlier, of the *Weekly Anglo-African*'s New Haven correspondent reporting on Amos Beman's lectures in that city in 1859. These addresses, given on three successive

9. *Ibid.*
10. Report by Ethiop, in *Frederick Douglass' Paper,* July 30, 1852.

nights to large audiences in the commodious Zion's Church, were, as usual, broad in scope, packed with facts, and delivered with great force. Beman, declared the reporter, had been the "first and foremost . . . maker of . . . [the] reputation and honor the colored people of New Haven have abroad." And Beman and his father had, for a quarter of a century, been the foremost representatives of Connecticut blacks and, indeed, of New England blacks in national Afro-American conventions.[11]

In addition to pride in the learning, eloquence, and reputation of their noted ministers, black people often felt grateful affection toward them. The pride and the affection were both evident in the turnout for Theodore Wright's funeral in 1847 and for the testimonial dinner honoring Garnet in 1861.

It has often been noted that one of the problems for antebellum black leaders was the distance between them and black people at large, many of whom had had very little education. This distance clearly existed for Cornish and probably was a problem for Garnet as well. It was less of a factor for Wright and Beman, both of whom spent roughly two decades in a single pastorate. Least of all did distance from black people at large obtain for Ray, who lived and worked in New York City for fifty-three years. In his case black people of every class and condition learned early that he would respond appropriately to their needs or concerns. Widespread trust and gratitude were blended with respect for him among the hundreds he had helped, both those within his congregation and many, many others.

When Ray resigned from formal citywide missionary responsibilities, he commented, "Having been so long engaged in this general work, and become so well known, it will be impossible for me to get out of it, if I really wanted to." True to his prediction, some six years later he was again sending an annual report as city missionary. It was shortly after the devastating draft riots. Ray had finished his work with Garnet on the Relief Committee interviewing black families and assessing their eligibility for a share of the funds donated by New York City merchants. However, the task was barely begun: "None know, excepting those who have witnessed it, the extent of the suffering among them, from the loss of their goods and clothing. I have consequently been sought by many of them through the winter, for advice in relation to their claims, and to render them assistance or secure aid for them, all of which I was happy to do, as

11. *Weekly Anglo-African*, November 26, 1859.

best I could. This I have felt to be proper missionary work, and I have reason to know that good has been the result."[12]

It is even more difficult to assess the impact of black leaders on whites than on their own people. It is well documented that the speeches and sermons of activist black Presbyterian and Congregational ministers immensely impressed the whites who heard them at meetings of abolitionists and of blacks at their state conventions; on occasions of public protest against the American Colonization Society or the Fugitive Slave Act; and when Garnet spoke in Congressional Hall or Beman in Temple Hall in New Haven. The same held for some state legislators exposed to Garnet's and Beman's lobbying efforts and for white reporters who sent in to their papers accounts of these ministers' speeches on a variety of subjects in many different communities. There is also ample documentation of the reactions of whites in England and Scotland to the logic and eloquence of many of the Afro-American lecturers in their countries, including Pennington and Garnet. However, it is impossible to say how many whites were won over to a fundamentally different view of race by their association with elite blacks, or what difference such changes in attitude made in subsequent white community behavior toward black people.

Over and above the impact of activist clergy on Afro-Americans and on whites in their own time was the fact that their careers created or helped shape institutions of ongoing importance. One of these was a primarily white organization that was to make a remarkable contribution to the education and church life of freedmen and their descendants in the South during the latter nineteenth and the twentieth centuries. Pennington had presided over the founding in 1841 of the Union Missionary Society, which a few years later became a major element in the newly formed American Missionary Association. Among the twelve men who constituted the first board of the AMA were Wright, Pennington, and Ray. In subsequent years Cornish, Garnet, and Amos Freeman also served as officers. Equally important was the fact that during the fifteen years between the founding of the AMA and the Civil War, Cornish, Ray, Garnet, Beman, and Pennington applied to the AMA for commissions and received them along with financial aid for their respective pastorates. The dozens of quarterly or annual reports submitted by these men on their

12. DeBoer, "The Role of Afro-Americans in the AMA," I, 192; Ray and Ray, *Sketch of Charles B. Ray*, 51.

work in black Congregational and Presbyterian parishes offered a liberal education for white AMA board members, making clear the gifts, ambitions, and frustrations of these black ministers. This educational process was facilitated by Simeon Jocelyn, a central figure in the original formation of the Temple Street African Congregational Church in New Haven and a staff member for the AMA during the antebellum years. This prewar AMA experience was a direct preparation for the huge task that manifested itself after the war. Indeed, antebellum black ministers working in struggling black communities of the North were forerunners of the postbellum AMA missionaries, white or black, sent to the South during Reconstruction.

Recent writing by the American church historian Ralph Luker has placed the work of the American Missionary Association at the center of post-Reconstruction white Protestant concern over the condition of southern blacks. Luker takes issue with the traditional definition of the American Social Gospel as a response in the 1880s and thereafter by a few Protestant ministers (for example, Washington Gladden, Josiah Strong, and Walter Rauschenbusch) to the urban-industrial crisis in the North. The origins of the Social Gospel, according to Luker, lay in the antebellum voluntary associations promoting home missions. "The social gospel itself," he writes, "is less an abstract quest for social justice than it is the proclamation of those religious beliefs and values which can serve to hold the social together." Using this new definition of the Social Gospel, Luker partially exonerates the latter nineteenth-century white movement for social justice from the accusations of blindness to racial oppression that numerous historians writing in the 1960s and 1970s had made against it. The American Missionary Association is the model Luker used to show how extensive was the mission by northern Protestants to southern relief and education. Nearly a third of the total contribution of benevolent agencies in the North (including the Freedmen's Bureau) to education and relief in the South came from the AMA. And a major portion of this assistance was initially provided by white teachers and ministers for the benefit of former slaves.[13]

Most important for the long run was the founding of southern black Presbyterian and Congregational churches whose pastors were black and the launching of over five hundred schools and colleges for blacks, often in the face of extreme white hostility. The quality of the AMA's educa-

13. Ralph E. Luker, "The Social Gospel and the Failure of Racial Reform, 1877–1898," *Church History*, XLVI (1977), 80–85.

tional contribution is clear if it is remembered that the association played a major role in the development of such institutions as Howard University, Berea College, Hampton Institute, Atlanta University, Fisk University, Straight (later Dillard) University, and Tougaloo and Talladega colleges.

From the latter nineteenth century on, AMA and denominational Presbyterian missionaries had done their work so well that the main strength of American black Presbyterianism—its churches, schools, and colleges—lay in the South. However, the condescending paternalism of many white missionaries and educators remained a heavy burden for black ministers and teachers. Somewhat the same contribution was made by the AMA to the development of southern black Congregationalism, though that denomination never developed the strength of Presbyterianism among either southern whites or freedmen.[14]

The primary contribution of Cornish, Wright, Ray, Garnet, Beman, and Pennington to subsequent American history was, however, not by way of even such remarkably broad-minded institutions as the American Missionary Association. The chief permanent significance of these activists lay in their melding of religious life and social protest. As was noted early in this work, Cornish's editorials so interwove religious affirmation and secular reformism as to distinguish them from most white ministerial journalism. Black activist ministers in later generations, whatever their denomination, have shared in this tradition by seeing the promotion of community welfare and the struggle against social injustice—both within the church and in society at large—as being an inextricable part of gospel ministry.

A vivid example of continuity between the attitudes and work of the six ministers whose story this book has been telling and later developments lies in the black caucus within primarily white denominations. The meetings of black Presbyterian and Congregational ministers in the 1850s have been described. The questionnaire sent out by Pennington, Beman, and Elymas Rogers in 1851 to a score or so of black Presbyterian and Congregational churches aimed "to collect facts and statistics in relation to the interests and usefulness of colored Presbyterian and Congregational churches in America." Along with questions on church ac-

14. Clara DeBoer, "Blacks and the American Missionary Association," in Zikmund (ed.), *Hidden Histories in the United Church of Christ,* 81–94; Wilmore, *Black and Presbyterian,* 68f.; Jesse Barber, *Climbing Jacob's Ladder: Story of the Work of the Presbyterian Church U.S.A. Among the Negroes* (New York, 1952), 31–45; J. Taylor Stanley, *A History of Black Congregational Christian Churches of the South* (New York, 1978), 26–57.

tivities and the numbers involved were questions about the impact on these congregations of the Fugitive Slave Act and the current colonization/emigration agitation.[15] By 1856 there were, as has been noted, annual meetings of the Evangelical Association of Colored Ministers of Congregational and Presbyterian Churches, which lay representatives also attended. The agenda centered in worship, encouraged the sharing of problems, and provided powerful mutual support for men often beset by their demanding vocation. The meetings also sounded the theme of Cornish's and Ray's editorials and of Wright's, Ray's, and Pennington's earlier speeches to abolitionists on the heinous racism in white churches and among white clergy. A presupposition of these association meetings was that political activism was not an optional but a mandatory element in Christian discipleship. Ray's quiet but forceful chiding in 1841 of some AME ministers and Garnet's angry rebuke of black churches too cautious to host aggressively antislavery gatherings had been earlier expressions of this presupposition.

A rebirth of those antebellum meetings of black Presbyterian and Congregational clergy occurred after Reconstruction in the founding in 1893 of the Afro-American Presbyterian Council. This council offered black Presbyterian clergy the mutual support and inspiration that was unavailable in the theoretically integrated presbyteries and synods of the northern church. Prominent among the founders of this council was Francis Grimké, nephew of Theodore Weld's wife and for more than four decades pastor of the Fifteenth Street Presbyterian Church, where Garnet had ministered. In 1909 Grimké would join William E. B. Du Bois in the founding of the National Association for the Advancement of Colored People (NAACP). Grimké had long been a bitter critic of racial discrimination within the Presbyterian church, having experienced the same kind of social humiliation as had Cornish and Wright many years earlier in New York City. When invited by his presbytery to join in a drive to evangelize blacks, he refused because of the whites' failure at many presbytery meetings to provide hospitality for blacks.[16]

A decade after the founding of the Afro-American Presbyterian Council, Grimké led it in a campaign in northern presbyteries and the General

15. A copy of this questionnaire is in Moorland-Spingarn Research Center, Howard University, Washington, D.C., in Presbyterian Church, U.S.A., Minutes of Sessions and other records of the Fifteenth Street Presbyterian Church, Washington, D.C.

16. Francis Grimké's father was a South Carolina planter, brother of Angelina Grimké Weld, and his mother was one of his father's slaves.

Assembly to oppose the proposed union of northern Presbyterians with southern Cumberland Presbyterians. The latter had refused in their presbytery meetings to integrate delegates from black Cumberland Presbyterian churches within their boundaries and would consider union with the northern Presbyterians only if allowed to continue their policy of racial segregation. The Afro-American Presbyterian Council failed to prevent this union of northern and southern Presbyterians, but under the name of Council of the North and West, it became in reality a black jurisdiction within the white church.[17]

This black council disbanded in 1957 in the wake of the 1954 Supreme Court decision banning the "separate but equal" basis for public schools. In 1968 a new organization emerged, Black Presbyterians United (BPU). In the words of an early BPU pamphlet, "the walls of segregation seemed as impregnable as ever, and there was little evidence that the church's practice was beginning to correspond with professions." Working within the denominational structure from its inception, the BPU had a leverage never known by previous black Presbyterians. As a bloc at the General Assembly, it played a role comparable with the Black Caucus in the United States Congress. In the words of Robert L. Washington, pastor of the Elizabeth Avenue Weequahic Church in Newark and former BPU member at large in the northeastern states, the aim of Black Presbyterians United was to keep this church honest, to root out the racism that still exists in the denomination and, for instance, prevents the placing of blacks in an "Avenue Church" (Fifth Avenue, Madison Avenue, and so forth) in New York City.

Careful plans were recently made for a more broadly influential and independent black entity within the Presbyterian Church (USA). Black Presbyterians United became the National Black Presbyterian Caucus (NBPC) in January 1988. Those designing this new caucus spoke for over 65,000 communicants in 450 black congregations and for many thousands in predominantly white or racially diverse congregations. The planners for the NBPC have said,

> Against the back-drop of many and varied forms of racial oppression, it should come as no surprise that Black Presbyterians have maintained caucus-like organizations since the 1850s. . . . We're still in the same business, after 180 years of Black Presbyterianism, of contending against our church's heresy of white racism, of making another new start in the same old struggle, of re-

17. Wilmore, *Black and Presbyterian*, 69ff.; Murray, *Presbyterians and the Negro*, 184f.

> lying still on the moral and spiritual resources of our Black religious heritage. That's the way it's been, now is, and likely will be in the foreseeable future—if we want to be equal partners in the mission of the Presbyterian Church.[18]

In listing proposed programs the planners for the National Black Presbyterian Caucus, place education in the black heritage first. This would include "lifting up our rich heritage from the Nile Valley civilizations in Africa, correcting racist perspectives about the contributions of Africa to world culture . . . and reinterpreting the experience of Black people in America." Also prominent among the programs envisaged is an effective blending of the mind and the emotions in the life of the congregation: "We can help Black Presbyterians develop a balanced spirituality which embraces both a tough mind and a tender heart. That is, we can embody the cold formality associated with Presbyterian structures and the warm, affirming, affectionate and relational approach of Black communities." Finally, the National Black Presbyterian Caucus will increase support for black colleges and other black institutions of education. The NBPC design of mission, referring to the present crisis in inner-city schools, declares, "Black Presbyterians have a strong track record in providing quality educational opportunities for the Black community. The challenges of the present school situation calls us to a new level of action."[19]

Appropriately enough, the president of Black Presbyterians United during this period of transition to a stronger and more independent caucus was Lenton Gunn, Jr., pastor of Saint James Presbyterian Church in Harlem. Founded in 1895, this is the oldest extant black Presbyterian church in Manhattan. It can be considered the successor to the First Colored Presbyterian Church, later the Prince Street Presbyterian Church, and still later the Shiloh Presbyterian Church, which has been so prominent in this story. Cornish, Wright, Pennington, and Garnet would surely approve of the Saint James's nonprofit housing corporation and other programs for minority empowerment.

Within Congregationalism also, a tradition of black social activism has kept alive the struggle for racial justice in which Ray, Beman, and Pennington had been early inspiring leaders. Because the proportion of the nation's white Congregational churches in the South in the nineteenth century was far smaller than that of white Presbyterians, support for such

18. *National Black Presbyterian Caucus Mission Design, April 1987* (N.p., n.d.), 3.
19. *Ibid.*, 5, 7.

blatant racist practices as segregation was weaker or more subtle during the postbellum years among Congregationalists than among Presbyterians. However, there was an ongoing need for a Congregational witness for racial justice, and it issued in a series of programs and publications.

Congregationalists having merged with Evangelical and Reformed churches in 1957, the denominational descendants of Leonard Bacon, Simeon Jocelyn, Amos Beman, and Charles Ray now belong to the United Church of Christ (UCC). Within the national and state structure of the UCC there is a Church and Society Department devoted to social action and, within that department, a Peace and Justice Committee and a Minority Empowerment Committee. Although blacks are in positions of major responsibility at both the national and state levels in the Church and Society Department and on the Peace and Justice and the Minority Empowerment committees, black ministers and laypeople in the UCC, like black Presbyterians, have seen the need for a black caucus. United Black Christians is the UCC parallel of Black Presbyterians United, with about 2,500 members representing about 70,000 communicants.

It is in part a tribute to Amos Beman that the Temple Street African Congregational Church, relocated and renamed the Dixwell Avenue Congregational Church in the late 1800s, has remained a vigorous church with continuing programs seeking equity for blacks and other minorities. The church's present activities include a housing development corporation, a corporation to assist black businesses through loans, and the Black Consensus, a political action group organized to promote voter registration and participation. The Dixwell Avenue pastor, Edwin Edmonds, has, like Beman, had a long pastorate (close to thirty years). He is active on the state United Church of Christ Minority Empowerment Committee.

Much in American life has changed over the century since the death of Charles Ray. However, the career and death of Martin Luther King, Jr., and the ongoing labors and discouragements of thousands of black ministers in the whole range of denominations make very clear that the racist attitudes and actions against which Cornish and Wright, Ray and Garnet, and Beman and Pennington struggled have their counterparts in the America and the American church of today. It is equally clear that Afro-American clergy remain a powerful force claiming and proclaiming freedom while remaining rooted in their distinctive religious heritage.

It seems appropriate to conclude with a few of the historical and theological ruminations of those antebellum activist ministers. They take the long view, and for those responsive to their sort of language, their affirmations are still powerful. Educated black ministers and laypeople were bound to wrestle with the biblical theme of God's ultimacy as creator and ruling power in history, as well as with the theme of the Hebrew people's and early Christians' special sufferings, special strengths, and future hopes. Such educated Afro-Americans had also assimilated much from the Protestant theology of whites. In this theology divine sovereignty, human answerability, and divine redemption were elaborated in myriad ways. One that had powerful clout for racists and imperialists, but also for oppressed peoples, was the concept of divine providence. Providence could mean the foresight and care of God for his creatures or it could be used to explain an important public or private event or to validate a particular social structure. The theme of providential design was one that fascinated and profoundly perplexed many nineteenth century Afro-American ministers. Cornish, Wright, Garnet, Beman, and Pennington were all trained in Presbyterian theology. Their statements on God's involvement with Afro-Americans, past and future, were rich strands woven by black thinkers in the tapestry depicting the meanings of providential design.[20]

Granted that there were differences depending upon the year and the speaker or writer, certain themes reappeared in clerical activists' statements about God, Afro-Americans, and history. Afro-Americans, they declared, are in some sense God's chosen ones. There has been a divine intention latent in the sufferings of black people that depends for its working out upon the attitudes and efforts of blacks. A great work of liberation, to be wrought by God and man, is at hand. Afro-Americans must be ready to play their divinely intended roles as bearers of light and truth.

As early as 1840 Garnet was singling out blacks as notably supportive of true religion. Such religion, which rejects collusion with slavery, was in Garnet's mind the salt that had kept the country from moral decay and divine rejection. The spirit of Christianity intends good for man, and its God "most assuredly forgets not the petitions of his chosen [black] people." A decade later Pennington saw the survival and growth in numbers of Afro-American slaves not only as a tribute to African vitality but

20. The distinguished sociologist St. Clair Drake has been at work for years on providential design, and specifically on the significance of the "Redemption of Africa" in the thought of Afro-Americans.

also as a sign of God's intention for these people. They were God's chosen because they had stayed closer to the Christian principles of forgiveness than others. By 1859 Pennington was putting survival ahead of forgiveness, but he still saw Afro-Americans as a distinctive people, unique in their powers of endurance and in their capacity for hope. Black Americans had a remarkable "self-redeeming capacity."[21]

Black leaders wrestled again and again with the difficulties of reconciling belief in a good and sovereign God and the undeniable fact of Afro-Americans' having been subjected to extensive, excruciating, and ongoing suffering. It is notable that activist black clergy did not explain the suffering of black people as punishment for sin. Rather, it was a hidden sign of having been chosen, though these ministers made no reference to Isaiah's portrayal of someone or some group as the Suffering Servant of the Lord nor to the Crucifixion of Christ. In 1848 Garnet made the following brief and sanguine comment: "Many things that were intended as evil for us, will result, I trust, in good." When Wright and Ray looked the awful facts of black suffering in the face, their statement, cited earlier, was both more agonizing in its implied bewilderment and more specific in its affirmation:

> The good God, when He suffered the first swarth man to be inveigled, entrapped, and stolen from Africa, when He suffered untold thousands of such, to perish in the agony of the way to the sea coast, . . . when He meted out the cruel sufferings of the sugar and rice plantations, when He gave us the better [*sic*] fate of Tantalus, in this land of Christian light and Christian glory—He overruled the evil intentions of men for the benefit of mankind, by placing us in the midst of the path of progress, that we might work out the great problems of human equality.[22]

By the late 1850s Garnet and Pennington were agreed that their people's plight in the United States was miserable and their prospect bleak if viewed from a merely human angle. Garnet pressed harder for an escape route for some Afro-Americans by way of the African Civilization Society. However, in this time of confusion both he and Pennington strongly affirmed the invasive power of a sovereign God. To his fellow black Pres-

21. Ofari, "*Let Your Motto Be Resistance*," 130f; Pennington, *Lecture Before the Glasgow Young Men's Christian Association*, 18–20; *Anglo-African*, I (1859), 314f.

22. Garnet, *Past and Present Condition*, 27; Theodore S. Wright, Charles B. Ray, and James McCune Smith, *An Address to the Three Thousand Colored Citizens of New York Who Are the Owners of One Hundred and Twenty Thousand Acres of Land in the State of New York, Given to Them by Gerrit Smith, Esq. of Peterboro, September 1, 1846* (New York, 1846), 18.

byterian and Congregational ministers in 1859, Garnet spoke of God as the God of liberty, as he had so often before. This time, however, he read the signs of the times as omens of an imminent triumphant liberation. Pennington had reached the same conclusion: "The cries and groans of murdered victims long since have filled the courts of heaven, . . . and God will surely soon visit the earth." The day of the American tyrant was almost over and the year of jubilee close by. In this time of fearful and wonderful possibilities, Amos Beman unabashedly appropriated a favorite image of early Puritan leaders in New England to affirm the special role and responsibility of Afro-Americans: "The colored race is an element of power in the earth, 'like a city set upon a hill it cannot be hid.' Thanks to our friends—and to our foes—and to the providence of God."[23]

Men like Beman, Pennington, and Garnet, however, knew that this was too simple a view of what it meant to be chosen of God. There was ample evidence in the history of New England and of Afro-Americans to prove that those given a special role cannot be counted on to possess political power, wealth, or prestige without being corrupted. In the middle 1850s Pennington had seen both his influential pastorate and his personal reputation dissolve through addiction to drink. Garnet had become embittered against his well-to-do colleagues Dr. James McCune Smith and Reverend John Gloucester when he found them improving their valuable New York City properties with sizable lily-white construction crews. Yet they had vehemently attacked Garnet for appealing to employment barriers based on race as a reason to promote emigration.

The final word of these six black activist ministers was not that all Afro-Americans are truly God's elect but that those having the true spirit of Christianity are such. The metaphors of human failure and achievement were universal—applicable to all humanity of whatever nation, race, or religion. Garnet had likened true religion to salt and sunlight and declared that it was universe-wide and desiring good for all human beings.[24] Pennington also affirmed the fundamental impartiality of divine Providence with an impersonal metaphor: "On the wheel of Providence has ever been a dangerous place for tyrants to play their pranks, while to those who act in concert with God, the higher they ascend on its great circle the safer is their position.[25]

23. "The Great Conflict Requires Great Faith," *Anglo-African*, I (1859), 337, 343–5. A few months later Pennington spoke of 500,000 free blacks and 4 million slaves as "strong because driven to God." *Weekly Anglo-African*, April 18, 1860.

24. Ofari, "*Let Your Motto Be Resistance*," 130f. Jesus had himself used the metaphors of salt, light, and a city on a hill. Matt. 5:13–15.

25. *Anglo-African*, I (1859), 345.

BIBLIOGRAPHY

PRIMARY SOURCES

Manuscripts

Amistad Research Center, Tulane University, New Orleans
American Home Missionary Society Archives.
American Missionary Association Archives.

Beinecke Rare Book and Manuscript Library, Yale University, New Haven, Collection of American Literature
Johnson, James Weldon. Collection.
Beman, Amos G. Papers.

Connecticut Conference of the United Church of Christ Archives, Hartford
Congregational Church. Records.
"New Haven East Consociation Records, 1731–1893." Vol. XV.
"Records of the Hartford Central Association . . ."
"Votes and Proceedings of the North Association of Hartford County." Vol. II.

Franklin Trask Library, Special Collections, Andover Newton Theological School, Newton Centre, Mass.
Bacon, Leonard. Letters.

George Arents Research Library for Special Collections, Syracuse University, Syracuse, N.Y.
Smith, Gerrit. Papers.

Houghton Library, Harvard University, Cambridge, Mass.

Cornish, Samuel, Theodore Wright, Henry Sipkins, and Thomas Van R[e]ns[se]laer. "Address in Commemoration of the Great Jubilee of the First of August 1834."

Library of Congress, Manuscripts Division, Washington, D.C.

Black History Collection.

Tappan, Lewis. Papers.

Middlesex Historical Association, Middletown, Conn.

Baldwin, Jesse. Collection.

Moorland-Spingarn Research Center, Howard University, Washington, D.C.

Pennington, James W. C. Papers from various collections.

Presbyterian Church, U.S.A., Minutes of Sessions and other church records of the Fifteenth Street Presbyterian Church, Washington, D.C.

National Archives, Washington, D.C.

Records of the Secretary of the Interior Relating to the Suppression of the Slave Trade and Negro Colonization.

Letter from George W. Levere, Henry Garnet, and others to Abraham Lincoln, November 25, 1863.

Presbyterian Historical Association, Philadelphia

Records of the Presbyterian Church, U.S.A.

"A General Report of the Session of Shiloh Presbyterian Church from April 1st, 1853 to July 12th 1856 & Made in Compliance with the Direction of the Moderator of 3rd Presbytery."

Minutes of the New York Presbytery.

Minutes of the Philadelphia Presbytery.

Minutes of the Second and Third Presbyteries of Philadelphia.

Minutes of the Session of Liberty Street Presbyterian Church, Troy, N.Y., 1840–1921.

Minutes of the Session of Shiloh Presbyterian Church, New York, N.Y., 1848–70.

Minutes of the Third Presbytery of New York City, 1831–70.

"Session Book of Immanuel Presbyterian Church," New York, N.Y.

Rhodes House, Department of Manuscripts, Oxford, England

A.L.S. from James Pennington to Mr. Soul, November 17, 1847.

Schomburg Center for Research in Black Culture, New York Public Library, Astor, Lenox and Tilden Foundations, New York

A.L.S. from Henry Highland Garnet to Alexander Crummell, May 13, 1837.

Wesleyan University Archives, Middletown, Conn.
Fisk, Willbur. Papers.
Minutes of the Joint Board of Trustees and Visitors of Wesleyan University, 1830–68.
Yale University Library, Manuscripts and Archives, New Haven
Bacon Family. Papers.

NOTE: Microfilm copies of many of the manuscripts used in this work are provided in George E. Carter and C. Peter Ripley (eds.), *Black Abolitionist Papers, 1830–1865* (17 reels; Sanford, N.C., 1981).

Newspapers and Periodicals

American Missionary, 1853–61.
Anglo-African, 1859–60.
Charter Oak, 1838–48.
Christian Freeman, 1843–45.
Colored American, 1837–41.
Emancipator, 1836–38.
Freedom's Journal, 1827–29.
Liberator, 1831–65.
National Anti-Slavery Standard, 1840–65.
North Star/Frederick Douglass' Paper, 1848–60.
Rights of All, 1829.
Weekly Advocate, 1827.
Weekly Anglo-African, 1859–63.

Other Published Contemporary Materials

Alexander, Archibald. *A History of Colonization on the Western Coast of Africa.* Philadelphia, 1846.

Alexander, James W. *The Life of Archibald Alexander, D.D., L.L.D.* Philadelphia, 1857.

Allen, Richard. *The Life Experience and Gospel Labors of the Rt. Rev. Richard Allen. . . .* New York, 1960.

American Anti-Slavery Society. *First Annual Report.* New York, 1834.

———. *Sixth Annual Report.* New York, 1839.

Andrews, Charles C. *The History of the New-York African Free-Schools. . . .* 1830; rpr. New York, 1969.

Appeal of Forty Thousand Citizens, Threatened with Disfranchisement, to the People of Pennsylvania, 1838. Philadelphia, 1838.

Aptheker, Herbert, ed. *The Correspondence of W. E. B. Du Bois.* Vol. I of 3 vols. Amherst, Mass., 1973.

———, ed. *A Documentary History of the Negro People in the United States.* Vol. I of 2 vols. New York, 1964.

Armistead, Wilson. *A Tribute for the Negro: Being a Vindication of the Moral, Intellectual, and Religious Capabilities of the Coloured Portion of Mankind. . . .* Manchester, England, 1848.

Asher, Jeremiah. *An Autobiography, with . . . Some Account of the History of the Meeting Street Baptist Church, Providence, R.I., and of the Shiloh Baptist Church, Philadelphia, Pa.* Philadelphia, 1862.

[Barnard, Henry]. *History of Schools for the Colored Population.* New York, 1969. Reprinted from *Special Report on the Improvement of Public Schools in the District of Columbia* (1871).

Barnes, Gilbert H., and Dwight L. Dumond, eds. *Letters of Theodore Dwight Weld, Angelina Grimké Weld, and Sarah Grimké.* Gloucester, Mass., 1965.

Bell, Howard H., ed. *Minutes of the Proceedings of the National Negro Conventions, 1830–1864.* New York, 1969.

Birney, James G. *The American Churches the Bulwarks of American Slavery.* 2d ed. Newburyport, Mass., 1842.

Bishop, William G., and William H. Attree, eds. *Report of the Debates and Proceedings of the Convention for the Revision of the Constitution of the State of New York.* Albany, 1846.

Blassingame, John W., ed. *The Frederick Douglass Papers.* Vols. I, II of Ser. 1. New Haven, 1979, 1982.

———, ed. *Slave Testimony: Two Centuries of Letters, Speeches, Interviews, and Autobiographies.* Baton Rouge, 1977.

Bourne, George. *The Book and Slavery Irreconcilable.* Philadelphia, 1815.

Brown, William Wells. *The Black Man, His Antecedents, His Genius, and His Achievements.* New York, 1863.

———. *The Rising Son; or, The Antecedents and Advancement of the Colored Race.* Boston, 1874.

Carter, George E., and C. Peter Ripley, eds. *Black Abolitionist Papers, 1830–1865.* 17 reels of microfilm. Sanford, N.C., 1981.

———. *Black Abolitionist Papers, 1830–1865: A Guide to the Microfilm Edition.* Sanford, N.C., 1981.

Catalogue of the Officers and Students in the Oneida Institute. Whitesborough, N.Y., 1836.

Catalogue of the Trustees, Faculty and Students of the Oneida Institute. Whitesborough, N.Y., 1837.

Catto, William T. *A Semi-Centenary Discourse, Delivered in the First Af-*

rican Presbyterian Church, Philadelphia, on the Fourth Sabbath of May, 1857: With a History of the Church from Its First Organization: Including a Brief Notice of Rev. John Gloucester, Its First Pastor. Philadelphia, 1857.

Congregational Church. *Minutes of the General Association of Ct. . . . , 1839–1858.* Published annually in Hartford or New Haven.

Constitution of the American Anti-Slavery Society: With the Declaration of the National Anti-Slavery Convention at Philadelphia, December, 1833. New York, 1838.

Cornish, Samuel E., and Theodore S. Wright. *The Colonization Scheme Considered, in Its Rejection by the Colored People—In Its Tendency to Uphold Caste—In Its Unfitness for Christianizing and Civilizing the Aborigines of Africa, and for Putting a Stop to the African Slave Trade.* Newark, 1840.

Croswell, A., and R. Sutton. *Debates and Proceedings in the New York State Convention for the Revision of the Constitution.* Albany, 1846.

Crummell, Alexander. *Eulogium on Henry Highland Garnet, . . . May 4, 1882.* Springfield, Mass., 1891. Also pub. in Alex Crummell. *Africa and America: Addresses and Discourses.* 1891; rpr. Miami, 1969.

Davies, Ebenezer. *American Scenes and Christian Slavery: A Recent Tour of Four Thousand Miles in the United States.* London, 1849.

Debate on "Modern Abolitionism" in the General Conference of the Methodist Episcopal Church, Held in Cincinnati, May 1836. Cincinnati, 1836.

Delany, Martin. The *Condition, Elevation, Emigration and Destiny of the Colored People of the United States.* 1852; rpr. New York, 1968.

Douglass, Frederick. *Life and Times of Frederick Douglass, Written by Himself. . . .* 1892; rpr. New York, 1962.

Du Bois, W. E. B. *The Philadelphia Negro: A Social Study.* New York, 1967.

———. *The Souls of Black Folk: Essays and Sketches.* New York, 1969.

Dumond, Dwight L., ed. *Letters of James Gillespie Birney, 1831–1857.* 2 vols. New York, 1938.

Easton, Hosea. *A Treatise on the Intellectual Character, and Civil and Political Condition of the Colored People of the U. States; and . . . the Duty of the Church to Them.* Boston, 1837; rpr. in Dorothy Porter, ed. *Negro Protest Pamphlets: A Compendium.* New York, 1969.

Eighth Annual Report of the City Missionary to the Destitute Colored Population. New York, 1852.

Faith Congregational Church (UCC) [formerly the Talcott Street Congregational Church]. *Historical Sketch, 150th Anniversary, 1826–1976.* Hartford, n.d.

Fisk, Willbur. *Substance of an Address Delivered Before the Middletown Colonization Society at their Annual Meeting, July 4, 1835.* Middletown, Conn., 1835.

Five Black Lives: The Autobiographies of Venture Smith, James Mars, William Grimes, the Rev. G. W. Offley, James L. Smith. Introduction by Arna Bontemps. Middletown, Conn., 1971.

Foner, Philip S., and George E. Walker, eds. *Proceedings of the Black State Conventions, 1840–1865.* 2 vols, Philadelphia, 1979–80.

Garnet, Henry Highland. *An Address to the Slaves of the United States of America.* 1848; rpr. New York, 1968.

———. *A Memorial Discourse; by Rev. Henry Highland Garnet, Delivered in the Hall of the House of Representatives, Washington City, D.C. on Sabbath, February 12, 1865.* Philadelphia, 1865.

———. *The Past and the Present Condition, and the Destiny, of the Colored Race: A Discourse Delivered at the Fifteenth Anniversary, of the Female Benevolent Society of Troy N.Y. Feb. 14, 1848.* Troy, N.Y., 1848.

Garrison, William Lloyd. *Thoughts on African Colonization.* 1832; rpr. New York, 1968.

Hooker, John. *Some Reminiscences of a Long Life.* Hartford, 1899.

Jay, William. *An Inquiry into the Character and Tendency of the American Colonization and American Anti-Slavery Societies.* 3d ed. New York, 1835.

Jefferson, Thomas. *Notes on the State of Virginia.* Edited by William Peden. New York, 1972.

Journal of the House of Representatives of the State of Connecticut, May Session, 1855. Hartford, 1855.

The Journal of the Stated Preacher to the Hospital and Almshouse, in the City of New York, 1811. New York, 1812.

Loguen, J. W. *The Rev. J. W. Loguen, as a Slave and as a Freeman: A Narrative of Real Life.* 1859; rpr. New York, 1968.

Matlack, Lucius. *The Life of Rev. Orange Scott.* New York, 1851.

Merrill, Walter M., and Louis Ruchames, eds. *The Letters of William Lloyd Garrison.* 6 vols. Cambridge, Mass., 1971–81.

Minutes and Sermon of the Second [Black] Presbyterian and Congregational Convention, . . . Philadelphia, on the 28th Day of October 1858 [1857]. New York, 1858.

Minutes of the Convention of [Black] Ministers, of the Presbyterian and Congregational Churches, in the United States of America, Held October 22, 1856. New York, 1856.

Minutes of the General Association of Connecticut . . . 1839–1858. Hartford or New Haven, 1839–58. Published annually.

National Black Presbyterian Caucus. *National Black Presbyterian Caucus Mission Design, April 1987.* N.p., n.d.

Nell, William C. *The Colored Patriots of the American Revolution with Sketches of Several Distinguished Colored Persons. . . .* 1855; rpr. New York, 1968.

New York Committee of Vigilance. *Fifth Annual Report . . .* 1842. New York, 1842.

———. *First Annual Report . . . 1837.* New York, 1837.

Payne, Daniel A. *History of the African Methodist Episcopal Church.* 1891; rpr. New York, 1969.

———. *Recollections of Seventy Years.* 1888; rpr. New York, 1969.

Pennington, James W. C. *An Address Delivered at Hartford, Conn., on the First of August, 1856.* Hartford, 1856.

———. *An Address Delivered at Newark, N.J., at the First Anniversary of West Indian Emancipation, August 1, 1839.* Newark, 1839.

———. *Christian Zeal. A Sermon Preached Before the Third Presbytery of New York, in Thirteenth Presbyterian Church, July 3rd, 1853.* New York, 1854.

———. *Covenants Involving Moral Wrong Are Not Obligatory upon Man: A Sermon Delivered in the Fifth Congregational Church, Hartford, on Thanksgiving Day . . . 1842.* Hartford, 1842.

———. *The Fugitive Blacksmith; or, Events in the History of James W. C. Pennington, Pastor of a Presbyterian Church, New York, Formerly a Slave in the State of Maryland, United States.* 3d ed. 1850; rpr. Westport, Conn., 1971.

———. Introduction to *Essays; Including Biographies & Miscellaneous Pieces in Prose and Poetry,* by Ann Plato. Hartford, 1841.

———. *A Lecture Delivered Before the Glasgow Young Men's Christian Association: And Also Before the St. George's Biblical, Literary and Scientific Institute, London. . . .* Edinburgh, 1850.

———. *A Narrative of Events of the Life of J H. Banks, an Escaped Slave, from the Cotton State, Alabama, in America, written with introduction, by J. W. C. Pennington, D.D.* Liverpool, 1861.

———. *The Reasonableness of the Abolition of Slavery at the South, a Legitimate Inference from the Success of British Emancipation: An Address Delivered at Hartford, Connecticut on the First of August 1856.* Hartford, 1856.

———. *A Text Book of the Origin and History, Etc. Etc. of the Colored People.* Hartford, 1841.

———. *A Two Years' Absence, or a Farewell Sermon, Preached in the Fifth*

Congregational Church by J. W. C. Pennington, November 2d, 1845. Hartford, 1845.

Porter, Dorothy, ed. *Early Negro Writing, 1760–1837*. Boston, 1971.

———, ed. *Negro Protest Pamphlets: A Compendium*. New York, 1969.

Presbyterian Church, U.S.A. *General Assembly Minutes*. Philadelphia, 1830–60. (After the schism in 1837, these were Old School assemblies. Minutes of the New School assemblies, held every year except 1841, 1842, 1844, 1845, 1847, and 1848, were published in New York City.)

The Present State and Condition of the Free People of Color, of the City of Philadelphia and Adjoining Districts, As Exhibited by the Report of the Committee of the Pennsylvania Society for Promoting the Abolition of Slavery. Philadelphia, 1838.

Proceedings of the Fourth New England Anti-Slavery Convention . . . May 30, 31, and June 1 and 2, 1837. Boston, 1837.

Proceedings of New England Anti-Slavery Society, May 24–26, 1836. Boston, 1836.

Ray, F. T., and H. C. Ray. *Sketch of the Life of Rev. Charles B. Ray*. New York, 1887.

The Report of the Board of Trustees of the Second African Presbyterian Church [Philadelphia], for the Year 1842. N.p., n.d.

Report of the Committee of Merchants for the Relief of Colored People, Suffering from the Late Riots in the City of New York. New York, 1863.

Ripley, C. Peter, ed. *The British Isles, 1830–1865*. Chapel Hill, N.C. 1985. Vol. I of Jeffrey S. Rossbach, assoc. ed., *The Black Abolitionist Papers*. 4 vols. projected.

The Second Journal of the Stated Preacher to the Hospital and Almshouse, in the City of New York, 1813. Philadelphia, 1815.

Simmons, William J. *Men of Mark: Eminent, Progressive and Rising*. 1887; rpr. New York, 1968.

A Sketch of the Condition and Prospects of the Oneida Institute, by the Board of Instructors and Government. Utica, N.Y., 1834.

Smith, James McCune. "Sketch of the Life and Labors of Rev. Henry Highland Garnet." In *A Memorial Discourse, by Rev. Henry Highland Garnet . . . February 12, 1865*. Philadelphia, 1865.

A Statistical Inquiry into the Condition of the People of Colour of the City and Districts of Philadelphia. Philadelphia, 1849.

Still, William. *The Underground Railroad: A Record of Facts . . . and Advisers of the Board*. 1872; rpr. Chicago, 1970.

Stowe, Harriet Beecher. *A Key to Uncle Tom's Cabin: Facts and Documents upon Which the Story Is Founded, Together with Corroborative Statements Verifying the Truth of the Work*. Boston, 1853.

Tappan, Lewis. *The Life of Arthur Tappan*. New York, 1870.

Walker, David. *Appeal . . . to the Coloured Citizens of the World, but in Particular . . . Those of the United States of America . . . 1829*. 1830; rpr. in Herbert Aptheker, ed. *"One Continual Cry": David Walker's Appeal . . . Its Setting and Its Meaning*. New York, 1965.

Walker's Appeal, with a Brief Sketch of His Life, by Henry Highland Garnet, and Also Garnet's Address to the Slaves of the United States of America. 1848; rpr. New York, 1969.

Ward, Samuel Ringgold. *Autobiography of a Fugitive Slave: His Anti-Slavery Labours in the United States, Canada & England*. London, 1855.

Weld, Theodore. *The Bible Against Slavery*. 1864; rpr. Detroit, 1970.

Williams, George W. *History of the Negro Race in America, 1619–1880*. 2 vols. combined in one. 1883; rpr. New York, 1968.

Williams, Peter. *A Discourse Delivered in St. Philip's Church for the Benefit of the Coloured Community of Wilberforce, in Upper Canada, on the Fourth of July, 1830*. New York, 1830.

Woodson, Carter G. *Negro Orators and Their Orations*. New York, 1925.

———, ed. *The Mind of the Negro as Reflected in Letters Written During the Crisis, 1800–1860*. 1926; rpr. New York, 1969.

———, ed. *The Works of Francis James Grimké*. Vol. I of 4 vols. Washington, D.C., 1942.

Wright, Theodore S. *A Pastoral Letter, Addressed to the Colored Presbyterian Church, in the City of New York, June 20th, 1832*. New York, 1832.

Wright, Theodore S., Charles B. Ray, and James McCune Smith. *An Address to the Three Thousand Colored Citizens of New York Who Are the Owners of One Hundred and Twenty Thousand Acres of Land in the State of New York, Given to Them by Gerrit Smith, Esq. of Peterboro, September 1, 1846*. New York, 1846.

SECONDARY SOURCES

Books

Abzug, Robert H. *Passionate Liberator: Theodore Dwight Weld and the Dilemma of Reform*. New York, 1980.

Adams, Alice. *The Neglected Period of Anti-Slavery in America, 1808–1831*. Boston, 1908.

Aptheker, Herbert. *The Negro in the Abolitionist Movement.* New York, 1941.

Bacon, Leonard. *Contributions to the Ecclesiastical History of Connecticut.* 1861; rpr. Hartford, Conn., 1973.

Bacon, Theodore D. *Leonard Bacon, a Statesman in the Church.* New Haven, 1961.

Barber, Jesse B. *Climbing Jacob's Ladder: Story of the Work of the Presbyterian Church U.S.A. Among the Negroes.* New York, 1952.

Bardolph, Richard. *The Negro Vanguard.* New York, 1961.

Barnes, Gilbert H. *The Antislavery Impulse, 1830–1844.* Gloucester, Mass., 1957.

Bell, Howard Holman. *A Survey of the Negro Convention Movement, 1830–1861.* New York, 1969.

Benson, Lee. *The Concept of Jacksonian Democracy.* New York, 1964.

Blackett, R. J. M. *Beating Against the Barriers: Biographical Essays in Nineteenth-Century Afro-American History.* Baton Rouge, 1986.

———. *Building an Antislavery Wall: Black Americans in the Atlantic Abolitionist Movement, 1830–1860.* Baton Rouge, 1983.

Bloch, Herman D. *The Circle of Discrimination: An Economic and Social Study of the Black Man in New York.* New York, 1959.

Bracey, John H., Jr., August Meier, and Elliott Rudwick, eds. *Blacks in the Abolitionist Movement.* Belmont, Calif., 1971.

Bradley, David H., Sr. *A History of the A.M.E. Zion Church: Pt. I, 1796–1872.* Nashville, 1956.

Bucke, Emory S., ed. *The History of American Methodism.* 3 vols. Nashville, 1964.

Bullock, Penelope. *The Afro-American Periodical Press, 1838–1909.* Baton Rouge, 1981.

Burkett, Randall K. *Black Redemption: Churchmen Speak for the Garvey Movement.* Philadelphia, 1978.

Clark, Dennis. *The Irish in Philadelphia: Ten Generations of Urban Experience.* Philadelphia, 1973.

Coan, Josephus R. *Daniel Alexander Payne, Christian Educator.* Philadelphia, 1935.

Cone, James H. *God of the Oppressed.* New York, 1975.

Cottrol, Robert J. *The Afro-Yankees: Providence's Black Community in the Antebellum Era.* Westport, Conn., 1982.

Curry, Leonard P. *The Free Black in Urban America, 1800–1850: The Shadow of the Dream.* Chicago, 1981.

Dann, Martin E. *The Black Press, 1827–1890: The Quest for National Identity*. New York, 1971.

Dean, David M. *Defender of the Race: James Theodore Holly, Black Nationalist Bishop*. Boston, 1979.

Dedication of the Black Press Archives and Gallery of Distinguished Newspaper Publishers on the Occasion of the Sesquicentenary of the Founding of the Black Press in the United States. Washington, D.C., 1977.

Dick, Robert. *Black Protest: Issues and Tactics*. Westport, Conn., 1974.

Drake, St. Clair. *The Redemption of Africa and Black Religion*. Chicago, 1970.

Duberman, Martin, ed. *The Antislavery Vanguard: New Essays on the Abolitionists*. Princeton, 1965.

Dumond, Dwight L. *Antislavery: The Crusade for Freedom in America*. Ann Arbor, 1961.

Ernst, Robert. *Immigrant Life in New York City, 1825–1863*. New York, 1949.

Faith Congregational Church (UCC): Historical Sketch, 150th Anniversary, 1826–1976. Hartford, [1976].

Feldberg, Michael. *The Philadelphia Riots of 1844: A Study of Ethnic Conflict*. Westport, Conn., 1975.

Field, Phyllis F. *The Politics of Race in New York*. Ithaca, 1982.

Filler, Louis. *The Crusade Against Slavery, 1830–1860*. New York, 1960.

Foner, Philip S. *Essays in Afro-American History*. Philadelphia, 1978.

———. *History of Black Americans*. 3 vols. Westport, Conn., 1975–83.

Fordham, Monroe. *Major Themes in Northern Black Religious Thought, 1800–1860*. Hicksville, N.Y., 1975.

Foster, Charles I. *An Errand of Mercy: The Evangelical United Front, 1790–1837*. Chapel Hill, N.C., 1960.

Fox, Dixon Ryan. *The Decline of Aristocracy in the Politics of New York*. New York, 1919.

Fox, Early Lee. *The American Colonization Society, 1817–1840*. Baltimore, 1919.

Franklin, John Hope. *From Slavery to Freedom: A History of American Negroes*. New York, 1952.

Franklin, Vincent F. *The Education of Black Philadelphia: The Social and Educational History of a Minority Community, 1900–1950*. Philadelphia, 1979.

Fredrickson, George M. *The Black Image in the White Mind: The Debate on Afro-American Character and Destiny, 1817–1914*. New York, 1971.

Friedman, Lawrence J. *Gregarious Saints: Self and Community in American Abolitionism, 1830–1870*. Cambridge, England, 1982.

Fuller, Edmund. *Prudence Crandall: An Incident of Racism in Nineteenth-Century Connecticut*. Middletown, Conn., 1971.

Gara, Larry. *The Liberty Line: The Legend of the Underground Railroad*. Lexington, Ky., 1961.

George, Carol V. R. *Segregated Sabbaths: Richard Allen and the Rise of Independent Black Churches, 1760–1840*. London, 1973.

Gettleman, Marvin E. *The Dorr Rebellion: A Study in American Radicalism, 1833–1849*. New York, 1973.

Griffin, Clifford S. *Their Brother's Keepers: Moral Stewardship in the United States, 1800–1865*. New Brunswick, N.J., 1960.

Harding, Vincent. *There Is A River: The Black Struggle for Freedom in America*. New York, 1981.

Harlow, Ralph V. *Gerrit Smith, Philanthropist and Reformer*. New York, 1939.

Harris, Sheldon H. *Paul Cuffe: Black America and the African Return*. New York, 1972.

Haynes, George E. *The Negro and Work in New York City: A Study in Economic Progress*. New York, 1912.

Headley, Joel T., *The Great Riots of New York, 1712–1873*. 1873; rpr. Indianapolis, 1970.

Hershberg, Theodore, ed. *Philadelphia: Work, Space, Family and Group Experience in the Nineteenth Century: Essays Towards an Interdisciplinary History of the City*. Oxford, England, 1981.

Horsman, Reginald. *Race and Manifest Destiny: The Origins of American Racial Anglo-Saxonism*. Cambridge, Mass., 1981.

Horton, James Oliver, and Lois E. Horton. *Black Bostonians: Family Life and Community Struggle in the Antebellum North*. New York, 1979.

Isely, Jeter Allen. *Horace Greeley and the Republican Party, 1853–1861*. Princeton, 1947.

Jacobs, Donald M., ed. *Antebellum Black Newspapers: Indices to New York "Freedom's Journal" (1827–1829), "The Rights of All" (1829), "The Weekly Advocate" (1837), and "The Colored American" (1837–1841)*. Westport, Conn., 1976.

Jordan, Winthrop D. *White over Black: American Attitudes Toward the Negro, 1550–1812*. Baltimore, 1969.

Kaestle, Carl F. *The Evolution of an Urban School System*. Cambridge, Mass., 1973.

Laurie, Bruce. *Working People of Philadelphia*. Philadelphia, 1980.

Litwack, Leon F. *North of Slavery: The Negro in the Free States, 1790–1860*. Chicago, 1965.

Logan, Rayford W., and Michael Winston, eds. *Dictionary of American Negro Biography*. New York, 1982.

Loggins, Vernon. *The Negro Author: His Development in America to 1900*. Port Washington, N.Y., 1964.

Lovell, John. *Black Song: The Forge and the Flame: The Story of How the Afro-American Spiritual Was Hammered Out*. New York, 1972.

Mabee, Carleton. *Black Education in New York State: From Colonial to Modern Times*. Syracuse, 1979.

———. *Black Freedom: The Nonviolent Abolitionists from 1830 Through the Civil War.* New York, 1970.

Martin, Waldo E., Jr. *The Mind of Frederick Douglass*. Chapel Hill, N.C., 1984.

Mathews, Donald G. *Religion in the Old South*. Chicago, 1977.

———. *Slavery and Methodism: A Chapter in American Morality*. Princeton, 1965.

McKivigan, John R. *The War Against Proslavery Religion: Abolitionism and the Northern Churches, 1830–1865*. Ithaca, 1984.

McPherson, James M. *The Negro's Civil War: How American Negroes Felt and Acted During the War for the Union*. New York, 1965.

Mead, Arthur R. *The Development of Free Schools in the United States, as Illustrated by Connecticut and Michigan*. New York, 1918.

Merideth, Robert. *The Politics of the Universe: Edward Beecher, Abolition and Orthodoxy*. Nashville, 1968.

Miller, Floyd J. *The Search for a Black Nationality: Black Emigration and Colonization, 1787–1863*. Urbana, Ill. 1975.

Mohl, Raymond A. *Poverty in New York, 1783–1825*. New York, 1971.

Morris, Thomas D. *Free Men All: The Personal Liberty Laws of the North, 1780–1861*. Baltimore, 1974.

Morse, Jarvis M. *A Neglected Period of Connecticut's History, 1818–1850*. New Haven, 1933.

Moses, Wilson J. *The Golden Age of Black Nationalism, 1850–1925*. Hamden, Conn., 1978.

Muraskin, William A. *Middle Class Blacks in a White Society: Prince Hall Free-Masonry in America*. Berkeley, 1975.

Murray, Andrew E. *Presbyterians and the Negro—A History*. Philadelphia, 1966.

Newman, Richard. *Lemuel Haynes: A Bio-Bibliography*. New York, 1984.

Nichols, James Hastings. *Democracy and the Churches*. Philadelphia, 1951.

Nichols, Robert Hastings. *Presbyterianism in New York State: A History of the Synod and Its Predecessors*. Edited and completed by James Hastings Nichols. Philadelphia, 1963.

Oates, Stephen. *To Purge This Land with Blood: A Biography of John Brown*. New York, 1970.

Ofari, Earl. *"Let Your Motto Be Resistance": The Life and Thought of Henry Highland Garnet*. Boston, 1972.

Ottley, Roi, and William J. Weatherby. *The Negro in New York: An Informal Social History, 1626–1940*. New York, 1967.

Pease, Jane H., and William H. Pease. *Bound with Them in Chains: A Biographical History of the Antislavery Movement*. Westport, Conn., 1972.

———. *They Who Would Be Free: Blacks' Search for Freedom, 1830–1861*. New York, 1974.

Pease, William H., and Jane H. Pease. *Black Utopia: Negro Communal Experiments in America*. Madison, Wis., 1972.

Penn, I. Garland. *The Afro-American Press and Its Editors*. 1891; rpr. New York, 1969.

Perry, Lewis, and Michael Fellman, eds. *Antislavery Reconsidered: New Perspectives on the Abolitionists*. Baton Rouge, 1979.

Quarles, Benjamin. *Black Abolitionists*. London, 1969.

———. *Frederick Douglass*. 1948; rpr. New York, 1968.

Raboteau, Albert P. *Slave Religion: The "Invisible Institution" in the Antebellum South*. New York, 1978.

Richards, Leonard L. *"Gentlemen of Property and Standing": Anti-Abolition Mobs in Jacksonian America*. London, 1971.

Richardson, Harry. *Dark Salvation*. Garden City, N.Y., 1976.

Rose, James W., and Barbara W. Brown. *Tapestry: A Living History of the Black Family in Southern Connecticut*. New London, Conn., 1979.

Schor, Joel. *Henry Highland Garnet: A Voice of Black Radicalism in the Nineteenth Century*. Westport, Conn., 1977.

Sernett, Milton. *Abolition's Axe: Beriah Green, Oneida Institute and the Black Freedom Struggle*. Syracuse, 1986.

———. *Black Religion and American Evangelicalism: White Protestants, Plantation Missions and the Flowering of Negro Christianity, 1787–1865*. Metuchen, N.J., 1975.

Sewell, Richard H. *Ballots for Freedom: Antislavery Politics in the United States, 1837–1860*. New York, 1980.

Sherman, David. *History of the Wesleyan Academy, at Wilbraham, Massachusetts, 1817–1890.* Boston, 1893.

Siebert, Wilbur H. *The Underground Railroad from Slavery to Freedom.* 1898; rpr. New York, 1968.

Singleton, George A. *The Romance of African Methodism.* New York, 1952.

Slotkin, Richard. *The Fatal Environment: The Myth of the Frontier in the Age of Industrialization, 1800–1890.* New York, 1985.

Smith, H. Shelton. *In His Image, But . . . : Racism in Southern Religion, 1780–1910.* Durham, N.C., 1972.

Sorin, Gerald. *Abolitionism: A New Perspective.* New York, [1972].

———. *The New York Abolitionists: A Case Study of Political Radicalism.* Westport, Conn., 1971.

Stanley, A. Knighton. *The Children Is Crying: Congregationalism Among Black People.* New York, 1979.

Stanley, J. Taylor. *A History of Black Congregational Christian Churches of the South.* New York, 1978.

Staudenraus, P. J. *The African Colonization Movement, 1816–1865.* New York, 1961.

Strout, Cushing. *The New Heavens and New Earth: Political Religion in America.* New York, 1975.

Sweet, Leonard I. *Black Images of America, 1784–1870.* New York, 1976.

Thomas, Benjamin P. *Theodore Weld: Crusader for Freedom.* New Brunswick, N.J., 1950.

Thomas, John L. *The Liberator: William Lloyd Garrison, A Biography.* Boston, 1963.

Turner, Edward R. *The Negro in Pennsylvania: Slavery—Servitude—Freedom, 1639–1861.* 1911; rpr. New York, 1969.

Van Deusen, Glyndon G. *William Henry Seward.* New York, 1967.

Wade, Harold, Jr. *Black Men of Amherst.* Amherst, Mass., 1976.

Walker, Clarence E. *A Rock in a Weary Land: The African Methodist Episcopal Church During the Civil War and Reconstruction.* Baton Rouge, 1982.

Walls, William J. *The African Methodist Episcopal Zion Church: Reality of the Black Church.* Charlotte, N.C., 1974.

Walters, Ronald G. *The Antislavery Appeal: American Abolitionism After 1830.* Baltimore, 1976.

Walzer, Michael. *The Revolution of the Saints: A Study in the Origins of Radical Politics.* New York, 1970.

Warner, Robert A. *New Haven Negroes: A Social History.* 1940; rpr. New York, 1969.

Washington, James M. *Frustrated Fellowship: The Black Baptist Quest for Social Power.* Macon, Ga., 1986.

Williams, Loretta J. *Black Freemasonry and Middle-Class Realities.* Columbia, Mo., 1980.

Williamson, Chilton. *American Suffrage: From Property to Democracy, 1760–1860.* Princeton, 1960.

Wills, David W., and Richard Newman, eds. *Black Apostles at Home and Abroad: Afro-Americans and the Christian Mission from the Revolution to Reconstruction.* Boston, 1982.

Wilmore, Gayraud S. *Black and Presbyterian: The Heritage and the Hope.* Philadelphia, 1983.

———. *Black Religion and Black Radicalism: An Interpretation of the Religious History of Afro-American People.* 2d ed. Maryknoll, N.Y., 1983.

Wilmore, Gayraud S., and James H. Cone, eds. *Black Theology: A Documentary History, 1966–1979.* Maryknoll, N.Y., 1979.

Wolseley, Roland E. *The Black Press, U.S.A.* Ames, Iowa, 1971.

Woodson, Carter G. *The Education of the Negro Prior to 1861.* 1919; rpr. New York, 1968.

———. *The History of the Negro Church.* 3d ed. Washington, D.C., 1972.

Wright, Richard R., Jr. *The Negro in Pennsylvania: A Study in Economic History.* 1912; rpr. New York, 1969.

Wyatt-Brown, Bertram. *Lewis Tappan and the Evangelical War Against Slavery.* Cleveland, 1969.

Young, Henry J. *Major Black Religious Leaders, 1755–1940.* Nashville, 1977.

Zikmund, Barbara B., ed. *Hidden Histories in the United Church of Christ.* New York, 1984.

Zilversmit, Arthur. *The First Emancipation: The Abolition of Slavery in the North.* Chicago, 1967.

Articles

Adams, James T. "Disfranchisement of Negroes in New England." *American Historical Review,* XXX (1924–25), 543–47.

Banner, Lois. "Religious Benevolence as Social Control: A Critique of an Interpretation." *Journal of American History,* LX (1973), 23–41.

Blanks, W. D. "Corrective Church Discipline in the Presbyterian Churches of the Nineteenth Century South." *Journal of Presbyterian History,* XLIV (1966), 89–105.

Brewer, William H. "Henry H. Garnet." *Journal of Negro History,* XIII (1928), 36–52.

———. "John B. Russwurm." *Journal of Negro History,* XIII (1928), 413–22.

Cooper, Frederick. "Elevating the Race: The Social Thought of Black Leaders, 1827–50." *American Quarterly,* XXIV (1972), 604–25.

Cutler, William W., III. "Status, Values and the Education of the Poor: The Trustees of the New York Public School Society, 1805–1853." *American Quarterly,* XXIV (1972), 69–85.

Egerton, Douglas R. "'Its Origin Not a Little Curious': A New Look at the American Colonization Society." *Journal of the Early Republic,* V (1985), 463–80.

Fox, Dixon Ryan. "The Negro Vote in Old New York." *Political Science Quarterly,* XXXII (1917), 252–75.

Goin, Edward F. "One Hundred Years of Negro Congregationalism in New Haven, Conn." *Crisis,* XIX (1920), 177–81.

Gravely, Will B. "The Rise of African Churches in America (1786–1822): Re-examining the Contexts." *Journal of Religious Thought,* XLI (1984), 58–73.

Grimsted, David. "Rioting in Its Jacksonian Setting." *American Historical Review,* LXXVII (1972), 361–97.

Gross, Bella. "*Freedom's Journal* and *The Rights of All.*" *Journal of Negro History,* XVII (1932), 241–86.

———. "Life and Times of Theodore S. Wright, 1797–1847." *Negro History Bulletin,* III (1939–40), 133–38, 144.

Heale, M. J. "From City Fathers to Social Critics: Humanitarianism and Government in New York, 1790–1860." *Journal of American History,* LXIII (1976), 21–41.

Hershberg, Theodore. "Free Blacks in Antebellum Philadelphia: A Study of Ex-slaves, Freeborn, and Socioeconomic Decline." *Journal of Social History,* V (1971–72), 183–209.

Hirsch, Leo, Jr. "New York and the Negro from 1783 to 1865." *Journal of Negro History,* XVI (1931), 382–473.

Jacobs, Donald M. "David Walker: Boston Race Leader, 1825–1830." *Essex Institute Historical Collections,* CVII (1971), 94–107.

Lapsansky, Emma J. "'Since They Got Those Separate Churches': Afro-Americans and Racism in Jacksonian Philadelphia." *American Quarterly,* XXXII (1980), 54–78.

Levesque, George. "Interpreting Black Ideology: A Reappraisal of Historical Consensus." *Journal of the Early Republic,* I (1981), 269–87.

Litwack, Leon F. "The Abolitionist Dilemma: The Antislavery Movement and the Northern Negro." *New England Quarterly*, XXXIV (1961), 50–73.

Luker, Ralph E. "Bushnell in Black and White: Evidences on the 'Racism' of Horace Bushnell." *New England Quarterly*, XLV (1972), 408–16.

———. "The Social Gospel and the Failure of Racial Reform, 1877–1898." *Church History*, XLVI (1977), 80–99.

MacMaster, Richard. "Henry Highland Garnet and the African Civilization Society." *Journal of Presbyterian History*, XLVIII (1970), 91–112.

Mathews, Donald G. "The Second Great Awakening as an Organizing Process, 1780–1830: An Hypothesis." *American Quarterly*, XXI (1969), 23–43.

Pease, Jane H., and William H. Pease. "Antislavery Ambivalence: Immediatism, Expediency, Race." *American Quarterly*, XVII (1965), 682–95.

———. "Black Power—The Debate in 1840." *Phylon*, IX (1968), 19–26.

———. "Negro Conventions and the Problems of Black Leadership." *Journal of Black Studies*, II (1971), 29–43.

Porter, Dorothy. "David Ruggles, an Apostle of Human Rights." *Journal of Negro History*, XXVIII (1943), 23–50.

Quarles, Benjamin. "Black History's Antebellum Origins." *Proceedings of the American Antiquarian Society*, LXXXIX (1979), 89–122.

Quarles, Benjamin, ed. "Letters from Negro Leaders to Gerrit Smith." *Journal of Negro History*, XXVII (1942), 432–53.

Schor, Joel. "The Rivalry Between Frederick Douglass and Henry Highland Garnet." *Journal of Negro History*, LXIV (1979), 30–36.

Sernett, Milton. "First Honor: Oneida Institute's Role in the Fight Against American Racism and Slavery." *New York History*, LXVI (1985), 101–22.

Sherwood, Henry N. "Paul Cuffee." *Journal of Negro History*, VII (1923), 153–229.

Shiffrin, Steven H. "The Rhetoric of Black Violence in the Antebellum Period: Henry Highland Garnet." *Journal of Black Studies*, II (1971), 45–56.

Stanley, John L. "Majority Tyranny in Tocqueville's America: The Failure of Negro Suffrage in 1846." *Political Science Quarterly*, LXXXIV (1969), 412–35.

Stone, Lawrence. "Prosopography." *Daedalus*, C (1971), 46–79.

Swift, David E. "Black Presbyterian Attacks on Racism: *Journal of Presbyterian History*, LI (1973), 433–70.

———. "'O' This Heartless Prejudice.'" *Wesleyan*, LXVII (1984), 13–17.

———. "Samuel Hopkins: Calvinist Social Concern in Eighteenth Century New England." *Journal of Presbyterian History,* XLVII (1969), 31–54.

Thurston, Eve. "Ethiopia Unshackled: A Brief History of the Education of Negro Children in New York City." *Bulletin of the New York Public Library,* XXXII (1947), 143–68.

Walker, Clarence. "The American Negro as Historical Outsider, 1836–1935." *Canadian Review of American Studies,* XVII (1986), 137–54.

Warner, Robert A. "Amos Gerry Beman (1812–1874): A Memoir on a Forgotten Leader." *Journal of Negro History,* XXII (1937), 200–21.

Wesley, Charles H. "The Negroes of New York in the Emancipation Movement." *Journal of Negro History,* XXIV (1939), 65–103.

———. "Negro Suffrage in the Period of Constitution-Making, 1787–1865." *Journal of Negro History,* XXXII (1947), 143–68.

———. "Participation of Negroes in Anti-Slavery Political Parties." *Journal of Negro History,* XXIX (1944), 32–74.

White, David O. "The Fugitive Blacksmith of Hartford: James W. C. Pennington." *Connecticut Historical Society Bulletin,* XLIX (1984), 5–29.

———. "Hartford's African Schools." *Connecticut Historical Society Bulletin,* XXXIX (1974), 47–53.

Work, Monroe N. "The Life of Charles B. Ray." *Journal of Negro History,* IV (1919), 361–71.

Wright, Marion Thompson. "Negro Suffrage in New Jersey, 1776–1875." *Journal of Negro History,* XXXIII (1948), 168–224.

Theses and Dissertations

Bruser, Lawrence. "Political Antislavery in Connecticut, 1844–1858." Ph.D. dissertation, Columbia University, 1974.

Burke, Ronald K. "Samuel Ringgold Ward, Christian Abolitionist." Ph.D. dissertation, Syracuse University, 1975.

Carter, Ralph D. "Black American or African: The Response of New York City Blacks to African Colonization, 1817–1841." Ph.D. dissertation, Clark University, 1964.

Christian, Howard N. "Samuel Cornish, Pioneer Negro Journalist." M.A. thesis, Howard University, 1931.

DeBoer, Clara M. "The Role of Afro-Americans in the Work of the American Missionary Association." 2 vols. Ph.D. dissertation, Rutgers University, 1973.

Freeman, Rhoda G. "The Free Negro in New York City in the Era Before the Civil War." Ph.D. dissertation, Columbia University, 1966.

Howard, Victor B. "The Anti-Slavery Movement in the Presbyterian Church." Ph.D. dissertation, Ohio State University, 1961.

Jacobs, Donald. "A History of the Boston Negro from the Revolution to the Civil War." Ph.D. dissertation, Boston University, 1958.

Johnson, Clifton H. "The American Missionary Association, 1846–1861: A Study of Christian Abolitionism." Ph.D. dissertation, University of North Carolina, 1958.

Lapsansky, Emma Jones. "South Street Philadelphia, 1762–1854: 'A Haven for Those Low in the World.'" Ph.D. dissertation, University of Pennsylvania, 1975.

Pasternak, Martin B. "Rise Now and Fly to Arms: The Life of Henry Highland Garnet." Ph.D. dissertation, University of Massachusetts, 1981.

Senior, Robert C. "New England Congregationalists and the Anti-Slavery Movement, 1830–1860." Ph.D. dissertation, Yale University, 1954.

Simmons, Adam D. "Ideologies and Programs of the Negro Anti-Slavery Movement, 1830–1861." Ph.D. dissertation, Northwestern University, 1983.

Thomas, Herman E. "An Analysis of the Life and Work of James W. C. Pennington, A Black Churchman and Abolitionist." Ph.D. dissertation, Hartford Seminary Foundation, 1978.

Ulle, Robert. "Black Churches in Pre–Civil War Philadelphia: A Study of Four Congregations." Ph.D. dissertation, University of Pennsylvania, 1986.

Walker, George E. "The Afro-American in New York City." Ph.D. dissertation, Columbia University, 1975.

Winch, Julie P. "The Leaders of Philadelphia's Black Community, 1787–1848." Ph.D. dissertation, Bryn Mawr College, 1982.

INDEX